How to Do *Everything* with Your

eBay Business

About the Author

For much of his adult life, Greg Holden has been hunting down and reselling collectibles, oddball items, and antiques of all sorts. In his younger days, he assembled an old sports car from pieces of three different sports cars. He bought and restored a century-old townhouse. Now, he hunts down fountain pens, watches, and other items online. Greg has written nearly 20 books on computers and the Internet, including *Internet Auctions for Dummies* and *Cliff's Notes Guide to Buying and Selling on eBay*, both published by Hungry Minds. His lifelong interests in literature and writing and the history of Chicago recently culminated in the book *Literary Chicago: A Book Lover's Tour of the Windy City*, published by Lake Claremont Press. He lives in Chicago in the house he restored along with his two daughters and an assortment of pets.

How to Do *Everything* with Your

eBay® Business

Greg Holden

McGraw-Hill/Osborne

New York Chicago San Francisco
Lisbon London Madrid Mexico City
Milan New Delhi San Juan
Seoul Singapore Sydney Toronto

The McGraw·Hill Companies

McGraw-Hill/Osborne
2100 Powell Street, 10th Floor
Emeryville, California 94608
U.S.A.

To arrange bulk purchase discounts for sales promotions, premiums, or fund-raisers, please
contact **McGraw-Hill**/Osborne at the above address. For information on translations or
book distributors outside the U.S.A., please see the International Contact Information page
immediately following the index of this book.

How to Do Everything with Your eBay® Business

67890 FGR FGR 01987654

ISBN 0-07-222948-9

Publisher	Brandon A. Nordin
Vice President	
& Associate Publisher	Scott Rogers
Acquisitions Editor	Marjorie McAneny
Project Editor	Julie M. Smith
Acquisitions Coordinator	Tana Allen
Technical Editor	Amy Hoy
Copy Editor	Brian MacDonald
Proofreaders	Linda Medoff, Pat Mannion
Indexer	Valerie Perry
Computer Designers	Tabitha M. Cagan, Tara A. Davis
Illustrators	Kathleen Fay Edwards, Lyssa Wald
Series Design	Mickey Galicia
Cover Series Design	Dodie Shoemaker
Cover Illustration	Tom Willis

This book was composed with Corel VENTURA™ Publisher.

Dedication

To my mother and father, and to the fun we've had finding, restoring,
and selling treasures of all sorts

Contents at a Glance

Contents

PART III	**Business Practices for eBay**	

Acknowledgments

Whether you are writing books for a living or selling on eBay either part-time or full-time, much of your work seems to be done alone. But the truth is that you're never really alone. There are plenty of people sitting at *their* computers who are depending on you, who are waiting for you, who are rooting for you to be a success.

Any successful sale on eBay depends on help and cooperation from lots of people, from the individual who provided you with the item to the sell to the companion who helped you carry it home to the shippers who made sure it reached its destination. Trust and cooperation make online auctions work. I've often been struck by the fact that the most successful auction sellers are also the most generous with their time and experience. They have taught me that the more helpful you are, the more successful you'll be in return.

In the same way, writing a book about selling on eBay depends a community of individuals you might never meet face to face. First, I want to thank the eBay sellers who took the time to talk to me either on the phone or by e-mail and share their knowledge. Thanks go to Chad Gibbons, Jo Stavig, Buddhachick, Bob Kopczynski, Don Colclough, Jon and Steve Brothers, decoray, Shiela Schneider, and Andy Noise.

I also want to acknowledge my own colleagues who helped me with research and editing, and who are important members of my own professional community: Ann Lindner, Madonna Gauding, and Pam Parrish.

I have been impressed with the enthusiasm and encouragement I have received from all the folks at Osborne-McGraw Hill, starting with Margie McAneny, who got the ball rolling (and kept it rolling smoothly); Julie Smith, who served as project editor; technical editor Amy Hoy; copyeditor Brian MacDonald; and publicity manager Bettina Faltermeier.

Thanks also to my agent Neil Salkind and everyone at Studio B Productions. Last but not least, thanks to my mother and father, who instilled the love of giving new life to someone else's castoffs-a practice that carries over perfectly to the new electronic flea market, eBay. Bargain hunting is an art I'm now passing down to my two daughters, Zosia and Lucy, as their sharp eyes are becoming ever more skilled at finding just what they're looking for at thrift shops and garage sales. Sharing so many adventures with them puts fun in my life, especially when they allow me to share their ever-widening circle of loving friends and pets.

Introduction

Just a few years ago, it seemed like everyone (including yours truly) was describing the Web as the new Wild, Wild, West for businesspeople—a place where they could strike out on their own, stake a claim, open up their own storefront, and start to do business for the first time. Well, the bloom is off the rose, as far as e-commerce on the Web is concerned, but eBay remains a thriving destination for anyone who wants to make a few extra bucks or even start a new career as an auction seller.

eBay has quickly become a part of everyday life rather than a novelty enjoyed by a few. Now that eBay has been around for several years, it has become more reliable and easier to use. It has also inherited both the good and bad aspects of the free market—the people who are trustworthy and community minded, as well as those who don't follow through with transactions and actively try to swindle other people. Luckily, the first group of eBay users far outnumbers the second. eBay's network of trust still makes it great place to realize the highest possible profits on online sales and start up your own online business. It's also giving a new lease on life to antique dealers and small business owners who have suddenly found a worldwide market of eager bidders rather than local people who drove or walked to their stores.

This book is for especially for people who want to sell regularly on eBay—those who want to run a business selling on eBay. "Running an eBay business" can mean a variety of things. It might mean you sell full-time on eBay, as some experienced and successful sellers do. It might mean you make small but regular part-time income selling after work or on the weekends. Or it might mean you sell a handful of items on eBay each month. This book assumes, though, that you want to sell regularly on eBay, and that you want to be a successful seller. It assumes that you're already familiar with eBay, at least as a buyer. Part I, "Get Started With eBay" starts at the beginning—deciding what you want to sell, how you want to sell it, and who you want to sell it to. You also get suggestions for how to do the kind of strategic buying that will keep your business flowing smoothly rather than having fits and starts simply because you've run out of merchandise to sell.

Part II, "Improve Your Competitive Edge," seeks to take you beyond being a casual eBay seller who completes transactions once in a while, to someone who sets up a system for selling on a regular basis. In Chapter 5, You learn the importance of building an initial positive feedback rating to build your credibility as a seller. You learn how to make your auctions stand out from the crowd and build goodwill with potential bidders by providing complete, honest descriptions of your sales merchandise. In Chapter 6, you learn how auction management software and online services can streamline the process of getting sales online and storing images, and provide you with records that are sure to come in handy at tax time. In Chapter 7, you learn about different options for promoting your eBay sales through creating Web pages, such as eBay's About Me page and eBay Stores, as well as your own Web site. In Chapter 8, you explore the ins and outs of one of the most important ways to attract bids: providing good images of your merchandise.

Part III, "Business Practices for eBay Auctioneers," takes a look at the "back end," indispensable business operations that can take your eBay sales business to a new level. Chapter 9 focuses on different ways to serve your customers, including answering questions, sending out e-mail responses promptly, and accepting payments. Chapter 10 focuses on two essential operations that you might overlook otherwise— packing your merchandise and shipping them out safely. Chapter 11 explores ways to be a participating member of the eBay community, by leaving feedback, using e-mail effectively, and making use of eBay's extensive selection of discussion forums.

Part IV, "Sell Specialty Items on eBay," examines the wide variety of auction venues that make up eBay's auction world, and that you might overlook in your zeal to get conventional auction sales online. These chapters examine how to sell vehicles ranging from motorcycles to airplanes and yachts on eBay Motors; how to trade business goods and services; how to sell books and other fixed-price items on Half.com; and how to use the high-end, traditional auction house that's affiliated with eBay, Sothebys.com.

Part V, "Keep your eBay Business Running Smoothly," covers strategies for streamlining your eBay business once you've gotten it off the ground. In Chapter 16, you learn how to protect yourself and your customers' security. In Chapter 17, you get advice on how to fulfill your accounting and tax requirements. In Chapter 18, you are introduced to legal considerations that can keep you from getting in trouble. In Chapter 19, you learn how to deal with the common sorts of difficulties that eBay sellers occasionally confront. Some of these are common-sense approaches, while others take advantage of various problem-solving mechanisms that eBay has put in place for individuals just like you.

I didn't write this book with the intention that you would read it from beginning to end like a story. Like the Web itself, you should be able to skip around from chapter to chapter to find the information you need to know immediately. Plus, you'll find special elements to help you get the most out of the book:

- ■ **How to...**   These special boxes explain, in a nutshell, how to accomplish key tasks. Read them to discover key points covered in each chapter.

- ■ **Notes**   These provide information that's often very important to gain understanding of a particular topic.

- ■ **Tips**   These tell you how to do something smarter or faster.

- ■ **Cautions**   These point out potential pitfalls that you need to steer around so you can keep operating smoothly.

- ■ **Sidebars**   Here I address topics that are related to the subject at hand and that illuminate it in a new way.

Within the text, you also find words in special formatting. New terms are in italics, while specific commands you need to choose or type yourself are in boldface.

Along the way, you'll read comments and tips by individuals who sell on eBay on a daily basis, and who are generous enough to share their expertise with you. The information isn't all just coming from me, but I've compiled it with the help of these online experts. Don't get upset if a Web page or a piece of software isn't exactly where it's described in the book. eBay's site changes all the time, as does the rest of the Web. That's part of the fun of doing business online. If a web page isn't where the book says it should be, try entering only site name (such as www.ebay.com) or use a search engine to search for the topic you're looking for.

I wish you happy selling on eBay. Relax, have fun, and enjoy being an online merchant; tell me your own experiences and whether this book has helped you by dropping me a line at greg@gregholden.com

Part I

Get Started with eBay

Chapter 1

Become an eBay Auction Expert

How to...

■ Establish your goals for selling on eBay

■ Decide whether to be a full- or part-time eBay seller

■ Get the big picture of how eBay works

■ Understand your hardware and software requirements

■ Follow the eight steps to selling on eBay

■ Calculate and pay your eBay sales fees

The phrase "working at home" used to be a contradiction in terms. Way back in the twentieth century, when you worked at home, you wore different clothing than you did in the office. You had more relaxed mannerisms and habits. But these two scenarios have changed. Offices have casual dress days, and working at home means much more padding around the kitchen in your bathrobe and slippers and talking on the phone.

Working at home can mean that you run a full- or part-time business in which you conduct transactions with customers from around the world, thanks to the Internet. One of the most exciting and potentially lucrative ways to work from home is to sell merchandise online with the biggest and most successful online auction site, eBay. eBay is known as a place where you can sell or buy at auction: you put an item up for sale by publishing a description and (usually) a photo of it on eBay's Web site. Prospective buyers find your item for sale and submit bids by filling out a form right on the auction page. The person who has the highest bid when the auction ends is the winner. In addition, eBay allows you to sell items for a fixed price, and has special areas for selling vehicles, business services, and high-end antiques, each of which is described in this book.

Whether you want to sell on eBay full- or part-time depends on your needs and the amount of time you have available. If you've been laid off and need some extra income to fill up the time between jobs, you have lots of time to devote. If you already have a full-time job and are trying to make some extra money, you're limited to off-hours such as evenings and weekends. An eBay business is flexible enough to handle each of these situations. First, you need to decide what you want to accomplish.

Set Goals for Your eBay Business

The first step in starting up any business, whether it's on eBay, on your own Web site, or in the offline, brick-and-mortar world, is to set your goals and objectives and then develop strategies for attaining them. In the traditional business world, it's called coming up with a business plan. A business plan requires you to ask yourself some basic questions of the sort that can apply to your eBay business, too:

- Why do you want to sell on eBay?

- What do you want to sell?

- Are there enough buyers for what you want to sell?

- How do you define "success"?

The first question is deceptively simple. It forces you to focus on your goals for your eBay business. Do you want to sell full-time? Do you want to find new customers for a sales business that you already operate, either on the Web or through a storefront? Do you need to expand an e-commerce business that's flagging? Or do you just want to make some extra money each month to help with expenses? The second question is also important: Since you're going to be spending many hours per week on your business, you need to make sure you're working with merchandise you know and hopefully enjoy buying and selling.

The third question involves market research: make sure there aren't a thousand people already selling what you want to sell on eBay. If the market is already flooded, you'll have a hard time breaking in. Switching merchandise or sales categories can help you find more bidders (see "Decide What to Sell" later in this chapter). The final question is essential: envision how you want your eBay business to function ideally once it's up and running. What will make you happy—being able to leave the office and work at home? Being able to help your spouse out with some extra money while taking care of the kids? Or just being able to pay the bills at the end of the month? Defining success will help you design your business and encourage you to feel satisfied when you reach your goals, too.

Jump Start a Brand-New Business

Selling on eBay is a terrific way to start up your first business. That's because eBay provides you with a well-established framework in which to operate. There are rules that sellers and buyers alike have to follow, and an elaborate system of feedback that helps keep people honest. Once you get used to buying and selling on eBay, the move to running an online business is not that dramatic. It's probably easiest to start out selling a limited number of items each month before you consider trying to handle the 50, 100, or even 200 items a week that some busy sellers put online.

Selling on eBay Part-Time

You don't have to sell on eBay as your full-time "day job" in order to generate a steady income. Far from it: one of the busiest sellers I know, Bob Kopczynski (eBay User ID: maxwellstreetmarket) has a full-time job. His wife and various relatives and neighbors help him put 20 to 30 items up for sale each day. Chad Gibbons (eBay User ID: boomer1967) works on eBay about ten hours a week. Despite ongoing health problems, he manages to put 100 to 200 sales online each week for himself and several individuals whose items he sells on consignment.

Selling on eBay Full-Time

Few things are as rewarding—and as exhausting—as working on your own full-time from home. I know whereof I speak. I worked in an office for many years and dreamed of being able to stay at home and raise my children while writing. When I was able to make the move to being a full-time freelancer, that's when the hard work really began. The moment you make the decision to support yourself full-time, you've got to be prepared for long hours. It's the same with selling on eBay. When it becomes a full-time business, you've got to develop a schedule; the things that were simply an enjoyable hobby before, like scouring garage sales and flea markets, become work. You might develop a schedule like the one in Table 1-1. (It starts on Thursday because that's when most garage and estate sales start.)

At the same time, it's hardly all work and no play. You've also got to be prepared for freedom—for being able to run your own schedule, work when you want, and spend time with your family or friends when you want. You can sleep until 10 A.M. and work from 1 P.M. to 9 P.M. if you want. You can accompany your kids on field trips or hit the golf course in the morning and work on getting your sales online in the afternoon.

Find Customers Worldwide

A number of the sellers I interviewed while writing this book used to operate, or still operate, storefronts where they sell antiques or other merchandise. eBay has revolutionized life for such sellers. On one hand, they had to start selling online

Day of the Week	Morning Tasks	Afternoon/Evening Tasks
Thursday	Estate sales	Unpack, schedule more sales for weekend; post office at 3 P.M.
Friday	Estate sales	Unpack, research items, prepare descriptions
Saturday	Flea market	Personal time
Sunday	Personal time	Check sales that are ending today; send out end-of-sale notifications
Monday	Send out more end-of-sale e-mails	Take photos for new sales; ship and pack; post office at 3 P.M.
Tuesday	Take photos, prepare descriptions	Get sales online; ship and pack last week's sales; post office at 3 P.M.
Wednesday	Get more sales online	Look through classifieds and find estate sales; answer e-mail inquiries; ship and pack last week's sales; post office at 3 P.M.

TABLE 1-1   Sample Schedule for Full-Time eBay Sellers

just to keep up with the competition. On the other hand, once they did start to sell at auction, they found a new and dramatically wider audience for what they have to sell.

Many auction enthusiasts are savvy shoppers who need to save money on things they purchase either for personal or business use, and the time spent searching for them in conventional sales outlets. They're actively seeking rare items to add to their collections. They don't have time to schlep around the country for months or years visiting antique stores, flea markets, and sales to find them. They're happy to find something they want on eBay and have the chance to obtain it from the comfort of their own homes. If you're a seller, your adrenaline starts to rush when you anticipate having two bidders who will offer you far more than you ever expected for what you have to sell.

Give Yourself a Financial Cushion

One reason for selling on eBay is to get a source of extra income that you can put aside for a rainy day. Some eBay sellers use their auction revenue for their children's tuition. Others use it for vacations. The fact is, once you have a system set up that enables you to sell, you can adjust how active you are based on your needs. You're not required to sell the same number of items every week. I know at least one eBay seller who sold full-time for several years, then decided to take a full-time office job. She still sells on eBay, but not nearly as often as she did before. The important thing is that it's nice to have that extra income to call on when you need it.

Uncover Collectors and Specialty Buyers

One seller I interviewed, Don Colclaugh (eBay User ID: mrmodern) found an artificial leg at an estate sale. He had no idea whether anyone would want such a thing on eBay, but he put it online anyway. He ended up selling it for more than $100. eBay attracts collectors from all walks of life, many of whom are passionate about what they want and will pay anything to get it, provided you have the right item. eBay's Community Chatter newsletter reports about the 1941 beer can that sold for $19,000 (see Figure 1-1), and the fishing lure (Item number 2708468802; search for it on eBay's Completed Auctions) that sold for an astonishing $31,857.50.

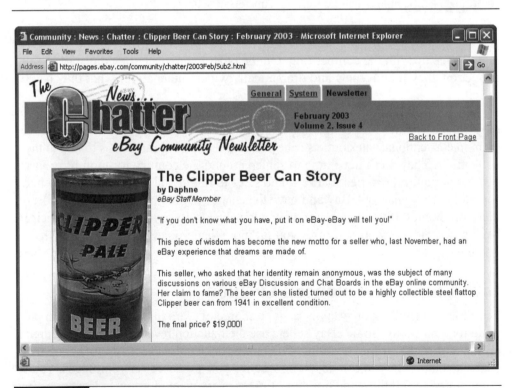

FIGURE 1-1   This beer can's seller never dreamed someone would bid $19,000 for it.

eBay Bestsellers
eBay Gave Him a "Reason to Get Up in the Morning"

It's often said that eBay has the potential to change your life. I've met many sellers whose careers have been changed by eBay. But I don't think I've met anyone to whom eBay is more important than Chad Gibbons.

Chad, 25, lives in Windsor, Ontario, and goes by the User ID boomer1967 on eBay. Like many young men, he has collected sports cards since childhood. He first started using eBay in 1999, in fact, to trade cards. "I started selling cards because there were many that I didn't really want, so I sold them off to buy more."

In 1999, Chad was diagnosed with kidney failure. He had to take a medical leave from his regular job. The three years while he was waiting for a kidney transplant were difficult.

"When I was sick for those three years eBay helped me by making me get up in the morning. I *had* to get up: I had to mail stuff out and do e-mails and get next week's auctions ready to go, then to the bank to cash checks. All those things that needed to be done were keeping me preoccupied and not thinking about how sick I was."

To supplement his income, Chad started selling on consignment for other people. He now has up to four consignment customers, and he conducts as many as 100 to 300 auctions per week using eBay's Turbo Lister software, which is described in Chapter 6. Amazingly, he estimates that he is able to conduct that many auctions while only spending ten hours a week on eBay-related activities. "I have met lots of people and made a few friends from eBay. The people on eBay are the best people imaginable."

In August, 2002, Chad received a kidney transplant. Everything went smoothly, except that being in the hospital for two weeks made it difficult for him to keep up with his mailings and auctions. Just a few months out of the hospital, Chad had his best sales month to date, selling 477 out of 530 items and grossing $2,656. He's now sold about 5,000 items and has been highlighted as one of eBay's Power Sellers of the Month.

Chad suggests that when you are planning your own eBay business, sell items about which you know something. Also sell items for which there is a proven demand on eBay. "Always be there for the customer to answer questions and concerns."

Know How eBay Auctions Work

eBay's auction site is complex, and has its own tricks and quirks. On top of that, many of the individuals who buy and sell regularly on eBay have been doing so for years and are well acquainted with how the system works. Don't start placing items up for sale without knowing what's involved first. Be sure you read eBay's User Agreement (**http://pages.ebay.com/help/policies/user-agreement.html**) so you know what you can and can't do. The following sections provide you with some more rules of thumb.

Set a Time Limit

Time plays an important role in eBay sales. First of all, eBay is located in California, so the advertised time when auctions begin and end is in Pacific Standard Time. eBay calls this "eBay Time," and you can check the current eBay time at **http://cgi3.ebay.com/aw-cgi/eBayISAPI.dll?TimeShow** (see Figure 1-2).

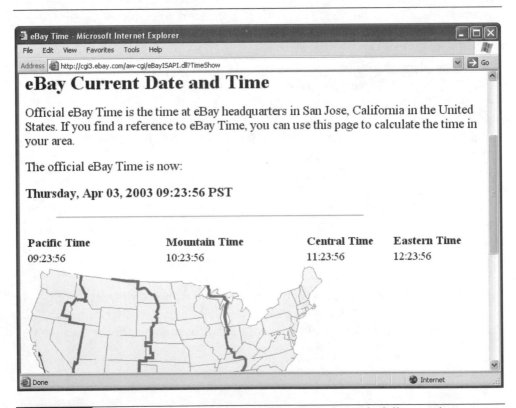

FIGURE 1-2   eBay time is an important consideration when scheduling auctions.

In most cases, you get auction descriptions online by filling out the Sell Your Item form (see Figure 1-3). You access this form by clicking Sell in the eBay navigation toolbar that appears on virtually all eBay pages. Page 3 of the Sell Your Item form allows you to schedule your auction and select how long the sale will last.

As you can see from Figure 1-3, auctions can begin at one of two times:

■ On the exact moment they appear online, which is the moment the auction description is posted on one of eBay's servers.

■ On a time you schedule, if you are willing to pay 10 cents to schedule this auction.

The reason why you need to pay attention to when a sale starts is because the starting time controls the ending time. For instance, if you start an auction at 6:05 P.M. on a Thursday and you specify that the auction should last three days, the auction will end at 6:05 P.M. the following Sunday. Most sellers believe that it's best to have

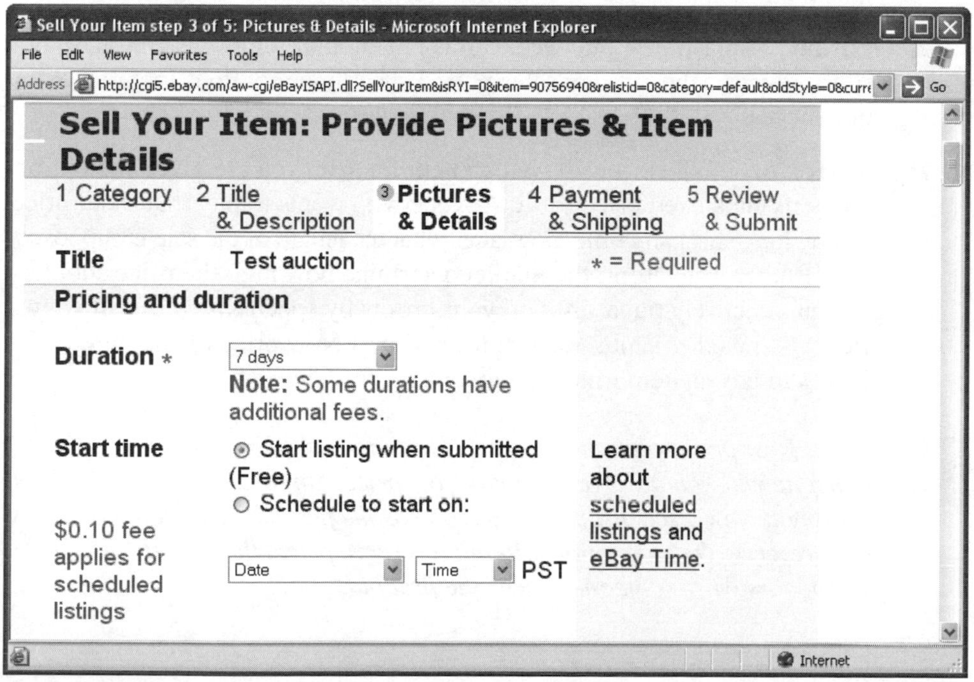

FIGURE 1-3   The Sell Your Item form is the basic way to get sales descriptions and photos online.

sales end on a weekend, when the largest number of bidders has time to shop and bid online. Page 3 of the Sell Your Item form asks you to choose the length of your auction. You have the following options:

- **Three-day**   Three-day auctions work best for things that bidders are wild about because they're the newest got-to-have-'em item. Three-day sales also work well around holiday time when shoppers are in a hurry to have items shipped to them.

- **Five-day**   Five day auctions are also useful at holiday times when people are in too much of a hurry to buy at a seven-day or ten-day auction. They might also work well over holiday weekends such as Labor Day or Memorial Day. The only real advantage to a five-day auction is that it gives you a little more time to gather bids than the three-day variety.

- **Seven-day**   Seven-day auctions are the "classic" and most popular variety on eBay. By letting a sale go on for seven rather than three or five days, you give yourself time to get more bids and hopefully a higher price. Seven days gives buyers the opportunity to track a sale during the week and then place their final bids over the weekend, if you schedule it to end then.

- **Ten-day**   Sometimes, one weekend is not enough for a sale. Many eBay sellers advocate the ten-day sales period even though it does incur an extra ten-cent fee.

- **Buy It Now**   Whenever you list an item for sale, you are given the option of specifying a fixed price for it. Anyone who wants to pay that fixed price can buy the item at any time, no matter what the length of the sale is supposed to be. Rather than letting the market determine how high the price should go, you effectively put a limit on your profits by specifying a Buy It Now price. On the other hand, you can use a Buy It Now price to encourage bidders to buy an item immediately at a profit to you.

NOTE   *Buy It Now prices and auction bids don't mix, so there's no chance that someone will "outbid" your Buy It Now price. On a reserve price auction, the Buy It Now price disappears as soon as the first bid is placed that meets your reserve. On an auction without a reserve price, the Buy It Now price disappears when someone places the first bid.*

NOTE *If you sell multiple items, you can streamline your work significantly with special auction software and online auction services, some of which enable you to schedule sales so they all go online at specified times. See Chapter 6 for more.*

Build Customer Trust

In any kind of e-commerce, the seller needs to build trust and confidence in buyers who never meet them in person. The one-on-one contact that the Internet provides can do a lot toward building such confidence: quick e-mail responses, speedy shipping, and honest descriptions all encourage buyers to check out your sales in future and keep bidding.

When it comes to encouraging bids initially, the single best way you can develop trust is to develop a good feedback rating. That can only be done over time, by making a commitment to follow through quickly and honestly on all of your transactions, whether you are purchasing or selling. Any buyer can check your feedback rating by clicking on the feedback number that eBay lists next to your name. Your eBay ID card appears. Your goal is to have the sort of feedback as boomer1967, who is profiled earlier in this chapter.

When it comes to gaining good feedback through selling, the two most important things you can do are things you might overlook at first: packing your merchandise carefully and shipping it out quickly. Because these two tasks are so important, I've devoted extra attention to them in Chapter 10.

Provide Clear Images

The online equivalent of placing your auction merchandise on a table so prospective customers can preview it before bidding is to open a digital version of the image in your Web browser window. The clarity of the image you see depends on the clarity of your computer monitor and the quality of your computer's video card. (I discuss these and other hardware requirements for participating in Internet auctions in Chapter 2.)

Because the image is broken down into tiny segments of digital information called *pixels,* and the visual details have been compressed into special graphics formats used on the Web in order to get them online, you don't get a perfect representation of the image when you see it online. If you can provide more than one image, so much the better. There's really no excuse not to present multiple views of an item, since digital cameras make photography so easy. decoray, an eBay seller profiled in Chapter 10, took five separate images of the head vase shown in Figure 1-4. Each image was sharp and well-lit and taken from a slightly different angle. The last image was of the label at the bottom of the vase.

Write Clear Descriptions

No matter how clear the images are, there's no substitute for your own knowledge, much of which is provided by or augmented by research. Part of the fun of creating auction listings, in my opinion, is taking the time to find out something about what you want to sell—how old it is, how rare it is, and what makes it special. You can do your research at one of the many Web sites that describe antiques and collectibles, for instance. One of the best and easiest places to do research, though, is on eBay itself. Just go to the Search page (http://pages.ebay.com/search/items/search_adv.html), check the box next to Completed Items only, enter your search terms, and click the Search button (see Figure 1-5). You can search through past auctions for similar items.

The main thing about auction descriptions is that they need to be complete and honest about any flaws or shortcomings in what you're selling. You don't want to get in a dispute with a buyer about a chip or crack in something that the buyer

eBay item 2626166288 (Ends Apr-08-03 18:45:00 PDT) - Relco 7.5" Head Vase Girl with Hand - Microsoft In...

File   Edit   View   Favorites   Tools   Help

Address   http://cgi.ebay.com/ws/eBayISAPI.dll?ViewItem&category=1233&item=2626166288   Go

Done   Internet

FIGURE 1-4   eBay sales depend on good descriptions and digital images displayed online, supplemented by research.

doesn't discover until the package is unwrapped. Be honest up front, and you'll avoid such surprises while building trust among your customers. (Besides, if a buyer really wants what you have to sell, chances are a few minor flaws won't discourage them from bidding anyway.)

TIP   *Read what other auction sellers have said about their items. You might be able to benefit from their research. Many sellers reuse parts of other sellers' descriptions in their own auction listings. Is it a violation of copyright? It may be, technically, but sellers don't seem to mind because so many of them copy or rewrite one another's descriptions.*

```
http://pages.ebay.com/search/items/search_adv.html - Microsoft Internet Explorer
File    Edit    View    Favorites    Tools    Help
Address    http://pages.ebay.com/search/items/search_adv.html                    Go

Search          Advanced        By Seller       By Bidder       Search
                Search                                          Stores

Search (required)
Enter words or item number
Head Vase              All of these words  ▼   Search   tips


Refine your search (optional)
Price range                             Words
($)         from     to                 to
Category    All Categories       ▼      exclude
Expand      ☐ Title and description
            ☑ Completed Items
Type        only
            ☐ Buy It Now Items
            only
                                                        Internet
```

| FIGURE 1-5 | Research past sales on eBay to find out more about the items you want to sell. |

Decide How You Want to Be Paid

Watching bids come in on your item, exchanging chatty messages with other sellers in the eBay Café or the other eBay message boards, and researching your sales items can be so much fun that you forget about the real purpose of why you're starting an eBay business. Why, you're in this to make money, of course. Remember?

The simplest and most effective way to accept payments from your customers is through credit cards. Your high bidder or buyer (for a Buy It Now item) submits a credit card number, either to you or to a payment service, the funds are transferred in a matter of minutes, and you can ship the item out immediately. When it comes to accepting credit cards, you have two general options. Most eBay sellers sign up for an account with eBay's own payment service, PayPal. PayPal streamlines the process of accepting credit card payments: Buyers tell PayPal to debit their credit card accounts, and PayPal receives the payments, subtracts its transaction fees, and forwards the money on to you. If you accept PayPal transactions, you get to add a standard logo to your auction listings, like the one shown in the following image.

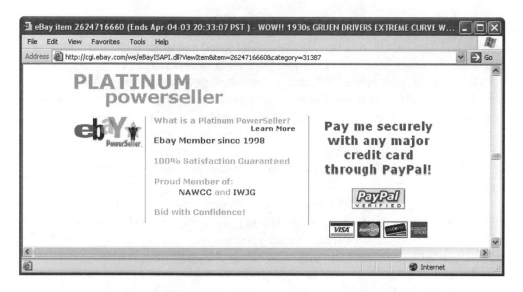

On the other hand, some sellers don't like PayPal because of the fees that it charges. They limit their payment options to accepting checks or money orders from their customers. This process takes longer because you depend on the mail to get you the money. If a personal check is involved, you're safest if you delay shipping until the check actually clears the bank.

Otherwise, if you're planning to be in business for the long haul, you can establish a credit card merchant account, either with your own bank or with a company that specializes in providing such accounts.

Get the Hardware and Software You Need

Before you can step up to the auction block, you need to connect to the Internet, and in order to do that, you need some basic computer hardware and software. Buying and selling through auctions, like other types of electronic commerce, don't require a super-fast connection to the Internet. Nor do you have to spend thousands for a computer with the latest multimedia bells and whistles. A detailed description of hardware and software you *do* need is presented in Chapter 2, but here is an overview of the kinds of things you need to get started.

Buy the Right Computer and Monitor

The good news is that buying and selling on eBay don't require much computing overhead. In other words, if you can get on the Internet and surf Web sites, and if you have enough memory to run an image editing program as well, you should be able to sell successfully on eBay. However, the speed and quality of your computer, monitor, and other hardware *can* affect your auction experience.

Hard disk storage space isn't an issue for most new computers, which come with hard disk drives that store one or more *gigabytes* (GB) of data. (A gigabyte is a thousand megabytes (MB).) Any hard disk capable of storing a gigabyte or more should be fine for your needs. (Many new computers come with hard disks of 10, 20, or more gigabytes these days.) If you're buying a used computer, beware: Don't come home with less than a gigabyte of storage space, or you'll run out of room before you know it.

Going online, using a Web browser, and shopping for auction treasures doesn't require huge amounts of memory, but if you plan to put up goodies for sale, you need some additional software, and each program requires RAM. For example, you may want to do one of the following (all of which require RAM):

- **Create a Web page**   A Web page or Web site can help advertise you or your business, if you have one (see Chapter 9).

- **Capture digital images**   You're likely to get more bids if you provide a clear computerized image of your items by scanning them or using a digital camera (see Chapter 8). Saving the images on your hard disk can quickly consume storage space unless you delete the image files as soon as the sale ends. Running a good image editing program like Adobe Photoshop or Photoshop Elements does require a lot of RAM, however.

The cost of RAM keeps going down, so you should load your computer with as much as you can in order to streamline the process of creating auction listings, not to mention listening to Internet radio, downloading video clips, and the many other multimedia events that increasingly popular parts of the online user experience.

Pick a Scanner or Digital Camera

Hardware requirements for auction sellers are a bit more extensive than those for buyers. You need a way to take images of the merchandise you want to sell and capture those images as digitized computer files. Including a clear, sharp image on your Web site greatly increases your chances of selling your product or service. You have several choices for digitizing:

- Taking photos with a digital camera and saving the image files on your computer.

- Taking photos with a conventional camera and then scanning them into your computer.

- Taking conventional prints or slides and having a photo lab send them back to you on CD-ROM or posting them online so you can copy or reuse them.

After you have an image in the form of a computer document, you can transfer it to a Web site to let potential buyers take a look (see Chapter 8).

Install Web Page and Auction Software

For the most part, the software you use to conduct transactions on eBay is the same as the software you use to view sales, bid on items, surf Web sites, and exchange e-mail with others. You don't need special software to get your sales online, to format auction listings or Web pages that describe you or your business, or edit photos—but they can help, especially when your sales activity increases.

In addition, software that enables you to keep track of your financial activity so you can prepare your taxes more efficiently, apply for loans or merchant accounts, or perform other tasks can make your business life much easier as well. You'll find out about Web page software in Chapter 7, digital image editors in Chapter 8, auction listing software in Chapter 6, and accounting programs in Chapter 17.

Become a Power E-Mail User

Aside from the Web browser that you use to create auction listings, e-mail is probably the single most important tool you have as a seller. E-mail is what you use to answer questions, notify bidders that they have won, tell bidders that their item has shipped, and remind buyers when they are slow to follow through on their commitments. When you sell at auction, it's important to use all aspects of e-mail fully. These include:

- **Signature files**   A signature file is a bit of text that you can append automatically to each of your outgoing e-mails. Such a file tells others your User ID, the name of your Web site if you have one, and any other contact information you want to provide. It's a great way to get free marketing for your auction business.

- **Attachments**   Sometimes prospective bidders who are particularly interested in an item will ask you for more information and possibly more detailed photos. Although you should post such additional images on the auction listing itself, you might also want to attach them to e-mails you send to interested buyers.

- **Checking your e-mail**   Get an e-mail account that you can access from the Web; also consider getting a wireless device that you can use to check your e-mail, such as a Web-enabled cell phone or a handheld device, so you can get those messages as soon as they arrive.

- **Vacation notices**   If you're going to be out of town, make sure your sales don't end while you are gone. If you are going to be away, be sure to put a vacation notice on each of your auction listings that tells bidders when you'll be back.

TIP   *For more about using e-mail, see Chapter 11.*

Follow the Eight-Step eBay Sales Plan

As long as you're at least 18 years old, you can be a student, the CEO of eBay (yes, Meg Whitman is reported to have sold her college textbooks on Half.com), or a trash collector—you can still sell on eBay. You don't need any experience in business. You just need to follow the rules, gather good feedback by being honest and responsive, and sell items that people want—the kinds of things that merchants have depended on throughout the ages.

First, you need to start by registering as an auction seller. eBay makes you register as a seller even if you are already a registered eBay buyer. You can use the same username and password; the main purpose is to put your credit card on file so eBay can charge it if necessary. (See Chapter 2 for more.) The following steps give you a miniature version of the process described in detail in subsequent chapters so you can begin the process of selling on eBay.

Decide What to Sell

Sometimes, it seems like you can sell anything on eBay. Some people certainly *try* to sell oddball, weird, tasteless, or even illegal materials. eBay quickly removes the most offensive things. (See Chapter 8 for descriptions of items that eBay considers offensive or illegal.) But if you are trying, as this book assumes, to develop an ongoing eBay sales effort, you need to identify materials that eBay customers are actually going to bid on and buy on a consistent basis. Based on what I've learned and been told by longtime sellers, you need to choose items that:

- **You like to sell**   Choose things that you know and love, and that you know well enough that you can come up with reasonable reserve and Buy It Now prices. You'll be working with these items for years at a time; don't sell clothing if you are really interested in sports equipment and collectibles, for instance.

- **People actually want**   Shop around on eBay and see which items get bids and which don't. Don't waste your time buying, and then reselling, merchandise that just isn't desirable to begin with.

- **Are easy to ship**   Keep in mind that you'll not only be buying merchandise and hauling it home, but that you'll need to photograph it, pack it up, and probably haul it to a shipper (unless you pay extra for pickup; see Chapter 10).

- **You have room to store**   Sellers who deal on eBay on a regular basis soon need to buy merchandise on a regular basis, too. The question of where and how to store that stuff can become a problem. Sellers have given up their basements, garages, and eventually rented warehouse space just to store the merchandise they're planning to sell in the future.

In my experience, the items that sell best on eBay are ones that are offbeat and that appeal to specialists or collectors. Items also are more likely to sell if you include more than one good-quality photo and if you write honest descriptions.

Choose One or More Categories

What you sell also involves decisions about where to sell—which one of eBay's hundreds of auction categories is right for your particular item. If you decide to specialize in a particular type of item, you might find that certain categories become places that you frequent on a regular basis. Getting to know the category in which you're going to deal is a good idea—get to know who the big players are in a category, and study what they sell and how they describe what they have. Don't try to copy what they do—rather, pick items that are slightly different and put your own personal spin on your descriptions so you can attract your own customers.

Enlist the Help of Friends and Relatives

What to sell, and how many items to sell, also depends on whether you are going to do the work yourself or whether you're going to develop a team of assistants. Selling on eBay is ideal for two or more people—two spouses, two domestic partners, two friends, or two relatives. You're sure to have some nieces, nephews, or cousins around who can help you with packing and shipping—or photographing or doing other computer work with which you're uncomfortable.

Collecting and then selling dolls, action figures, cards, or other goodies can be a great family activity. Your kids can keep you company and help you shop for the most desirable collectibles and keep you informed about the latest trends. They can help look up addresses, affix labels, and relieve some of the burden of shipping things out.

Set the Price

You don't always need to worry about setting a price at all on eBay. It depends on how you decide to sell. I go into more detail on starting bids and reserve prices in Chapter 3, but here's a quick rundown of the kinds of prices you might need to consider:

- **Starting Bid**   This is the price at which bidding starts.

- **Reserve Price**   This is the lowest price at which you will commit to sell something. If bids don't reach the reserve price, you don't have to sell. Usually, the reserve price is secret, but some sellers do reveal the reserve price of an item right in its description.

- **Buy It Now Price**   If you want to sell something at a fixed price, you can specify it, either in addition to placing the item at auction, or as an alternative to an auction.

- **eBay Stores price**   If you have enough positive feedback, you can set up an eBay store: a page where you list items on eBay for a reduced, fixed price for 30 days. It's a great place to unload items that didn't sell the first time or to find another way to sell stock from your store if you have one (see Figure 1-6). Find out more at **http://www.stores.ebay.com**.

NOTE   *Setting a minimum bid as the least amount you are willing to accept often discourages buyers who need to feel they are getting a bargain for something. Many such sales end with no one placing any bids.*

Many auction sellers don't worry about reserve prices at all. They simply put a starting bid of $1 or so on an item and let the marketplace determine the price. The risk, of course, if that you might lose money on what you sell without a reserve— you could conceivably pay $10 for a lamp and sell it on eBay for a high bid of $6 if you don't put a reserve of, say, $15 on the item. On the other hand, items that are advertised as having no reserve price do tend to attract more attention than those with a reserve, because bidders are attracted by the certainty that the item will sell

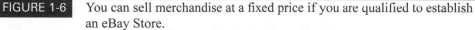

FIGURE 1-6   You can sell merchandise at a fixed price if you are qualified to establish an eBay Store.

and the possibility that it will sell at a bargain price. If the seller loses a few dollars on one particular item, he or she will probably make it up on others that are sold without reserve and that attract lots of bids.

> **TIP**   *The pricing strategy you choose is up to you, and it doesn't have to be applied to every item you sell, either. You can put a set of items up for auction with no reserve and see how they sell, while putting others up for sale with a reserve.*

Provide Good Online Photos

As much as I would like to think that words are the most persuasive medium around, I have to admit that photos are probably the most important sales feature you can include with your merchandise. Items that are put online without any photos just aren't going to get as many bids as they could. There's no excuse not to include photos, either, because the range of options for capturing digital images is growing all the time. Digital cameras and scanners are growing more affordable, too.

Don't be stingy with creating and posting photos of your sales items. Often, bidders will ask you for more photos if you haven't included enough to begin with. You'll get to know how many you should include. There's no rule about how many photos you should include of a particular object; as a general rule, however, two to six photos taken from different angles is a good range. Often, wristwatches need multiple photos in order to show all the different features (see Figure 1-7). See Chapter 8 for more about capturing digital images of your sales items and putting them online.

Pile On the Information

If you run a brick-and-mortar business, you'll probably be surprised by the important role descriptions play in making sales on eBay. After all, in a store, you place your items in the window or on a shelf and put a tag on them. Perhaps the tag identifies the item and provides some basic information about it, perhaps not.

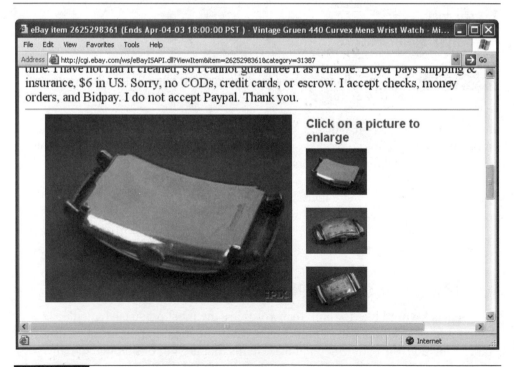

FIGURE 1-7   Include multiple images of an item, especially if it is detailed or intricate.

On the Internet, shoppers decide whether or not to buy something based in large measure on how much information you provide about it. Yes, the price matters, and yes, the experience and level of trust the seller inspires is also important. But when several similar items are available on eBay, many placed up for auction by reputable sellers, the ones with more information are more likely to get the most bids. A good description is:

- ■ **Concise**   Good descriptions don't have to be long. They describe sizes, dates, colors, and other characteristics.

- ■ **Upbeat**   Selling means telling prospective buyers why an item is exceptional and desirable and why they need to have it.

- ■ **Complete**   Along with the good points, be up-front about any cracks or flaws the item has. Also be sure to include model numbers and serial numbers for collectors who are very knowledgeable and are looking for specific items to fill out their collections.

The best descriptions engage a bidder's imagination and get him or her to envision how the merchandise might be used, or (if it's a used item) how others used it in the past. See Chapters 3 and 4 for more about creating good descriptions.

Give Good Customer Service

Customer service on eBay is a little different than customer service in either a retail store or an e-commerce Web site. On eBay, a substantial amount of customer contact takes place before a sale is made, and it mostly takes the form of answering questions by people who have either bid on your items or are considering placing a bid. In addition, you might be answering questions from individuals who don't turn out to be your actual customers. After all, a single item can have only one high bidder or buyer, but you might receive six, ten, or even (if you're lucky to get this much interest) twenty questions from bidders before the sale ends. Customer service on eBay, to a large extent, is a matter of checking your e-mail and responding to it in a professional and prompt manner.

After a sale, customer service means making sure the merchandise is sent out quickly and that it arrives in good shape, as described in the next section.

Process Those Sales

Once a sale is completed, you need to communicate to your high bidders or buyers that you are competent and in charge. Send them an e-mail message to notify them that they are the winner and congratulate them on making such a good purchase.

Provide them with shipping information, and ask them to respond as soon as possible. Once you receive payment, you need to pack your items carefully. Many sellers include notes or extra gifts with their items; you don't have to do this, of course, but it helps build goodwill. It's more important to include bubble wrap or other materials in the package to protect what you're sending, and to get it out to the post office or shipper in good time. See Chapter 10 for more on this important aspect of building an eBay business.

Pay Your eBay Fees

Everyone's got to pay the piper for the services they receive, and eBay is no exception. After you sell something on eBay, it's time to pay the fees charged not only for selling items but for listing them. eBay calls its listing fees *insertion fees*, and the fee charged when you actually sell something a *final value fee*. You have to pay your insertion fee whether you sell your item or not. The fee is based on the higher of two amounts: your starting bid or your reserve price. For instance, if you sell something with a starting bid of $1 and a reserve price of $40, your insertion fee is $1.10; if you have no reserve price and your starting bid is $1, the insertion fee is $0.30.

If your item sells, you then have to pay a final value fee; for reserve price and no reserve auctions, the "final value" is the final bid. On a reserve price auction, the final value fee is only charged if the reserve is met. If the final value is, for example, $100, the final value fee is about $3.38.

eBay makes it quite easy to pay your fees. You can configure your seller's account so you pay by check, money order, credit card, or by debiting a checking account. Find out more about configuring your seller's account at **http://pages .ebay.com/help/sell/payfees.html**.

Deliver the Goods

The final step in becoming an eBay auction expert is shipping out your merchandise quickly and safely. You've got to find good shipping boxes, pack your items safely with plenty of packing material if necessary, and get the package to the mailer quickly. You've got to provide your customers with different shipping options. You'll get to know your local postal employees and mailing services well. The professionalism with which you ship has a direct impact on the amount of positive feedback you receive. Shipping is sometimes overlooked by eBay sellers when they start out, and that's why I've devoted a whole chapter to the subject: see Chapter 10 for more detailed information.

Where to Find It

- **eBay User Agreement**
  http://pages.ebay.com/help/policies/ user-agreement.html
  Rules of what you can and can't do on eBay's site as far as listing auctions
  for sale and bidding on them.

- **Current eBay Time**
  http://cgi3.ebay.com/aw-cgi/ eBayISAPI.dll?TimeShow
  A page that verifies the current time in eBay's home location (in other
  words, Pacific Standard Time) and other time zones in the U.S.

- **eBay's Help page on Seller's Fees**
  http://pages.ebay.com/help/ sell/fees.html
  An overview of the fees eBay charges sellers, including tables to help
  you calculate them.

- **eBay Stores**
  http://www.stores.ebay.com
  Home page of a section of eBay's site where merchants can sell items
  at a fixed price for 30 days.

Chapter 2

Start Selling with eBay

How to...

■ Learn the ins and outs of selling on eBay

■ Decide how you want to sell on eBay

■ Pick the categories on which you'll sell

■ Build positive feedback by bidding and buying

■ Set up a seller's account

Before you start selling on eBay, you need to know the secrets and the tried-and-true approaches that can make your auction business a success from the start. You're joining a well-established business community, and one that is proving to be popular and resilient despite (or perhaps, because of) the ups and downs of the economy. To stand out from the crowd and make sales, you have to know how to compete on an equal footing with individuals who have auctioned off hundreds, even thousands, of items over a period of years.

You've also got to gain the attention, as well as the trust, of bidders from all walks of life and all levels of computer experience. Some are wary of purchasing at auction because they've heard stories about sellers who take bidders' money and never ship what they've sold. To build trust, you need to present your sales items—and yourself—in a professional, businesslike manner and give the impression that you are an expert seller even though you're just starting out. That's what this chapter will do: give you a head start so you can jump right in and sell like a pro.

Learn the Culture of eBay

When you're only a bidder, eBay is all fun. You can shop, find bargains, compete with other bidders, and enjoy the thrill of being the high bidder when the auction ends. When you make the move to being a seller, you have to change your perspective. Selling on eBay can still be fun, of course. In fact, it adds a new dimension to your interactions with the other members of the eBay community. And it can certainly be fun to have extra money around at the end of the month to pay bills or treat yourself to some presents.

By changing your perspective, I mean that you need to regard your selling activities as a business, and treat them as such. You're going to have to do a lot of hard work, whether it means getting up early on a rainy Friday morning to hit the local estate sales, hauling your wares into and out of the house, packing your merchandise carefully and taking stacks of boxes to the post office, or waiting in line to ship everything out to your customers. You need to be dedicated and keep your ultimate goal in sight: generating a regular source of income through selling on eBay. The following sections help prepare you for what's in store so you can hit the ground running and start selling (a process described in Chapter 3).

eBay's Own Educational Programs

When it comes to learning how things work, I'm a big proponent of reading books, but as a book author, I'm not exactly an unbiased authority on the subject. One good way to learn all about eBay quickly is to read a book like this one and supplement your learning with some live events and tutorials provided by eBay itself. That way, you'll get the very latest information about changes in eBay's procedures for sellers, and you'll get to meet some other sellers in person.

TIP   *eBay's Education area includes links to tutorials for sellers, seller workshops held on the message boards, and instructions on how eBay works in general. You'll find it at **http://pages.ebay.com/education/index.html**.*

eBay University

You can pick up advanced tips and meet some experienced sellers and eBay staff people alike by attending one of the live workshops eBay sends around the country. The cost to attend is nominal, and you can learn a huge amount in a short period of time (see Figure 2-1). eBay's education events are organized into different tracks, and each city has a different selection of classes:

- **One Track Seminars**   If you're just starting out, and you can find a One Track Seminar in your area, you can learn all about eBay in a single day. In the morning, courses are held for beginners, while advanced topics are covered in the afternoon.

- **Two Track Seminars**   If you're already an experienced eBay user, look for a Two Track Seminar, which lets you take a full day of classes in either the Beginner or Advanced Track.

- **Road Shows**   If you don't have a lot of time to spend, look for a Road Show, a series of four hour-long courses held in an area.

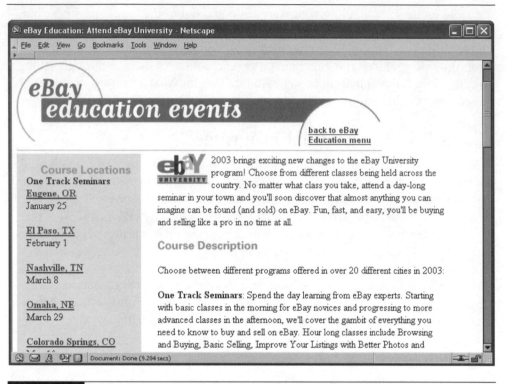

FIGURE 2-1   When a live eBay workshop comes to your area, strongly
consider attending.

TIP   *eBay's upcoming schedule of education programs, including
the community event held once a year, can be found at
http://pages.ebay.com/university/index.html.*

Power Sellers and Workshops

If you can't attend a live event in your area, you always have access to one of
the best ways to learn about eBay—online workshops held by experienced sellers.
When I checked, the titles of upcoming seminars all seemed useful for sellers:

- How to Ship Large and Delicate Items

- Listing Designer (how to make your descriptions more professional,
  add character, and have fun)

- Outlet Malls—Catalog Returns and Overstock

These, too, are held on specific days. If you're present, you can ask the hosts questions by posting them on a message board, and having the host respond to you with an answer while the workshop is going on.

However, you don't have to be present at a workshop to benefit from it. The workshops are archived so you can review past discussions any time. Just scan the list of previous workshops in the right column of the Workshop Events Page (see Figure 2-2).

> **TIP** *You'll find a list of eBay's upcoming online seller workshops at* ***http://members.ebay.com/aboutme/workshopevents/****, along with a list of archived workshops. You can also reach past workshops at* ***http://forums.ebay.com/forum.jsp?forum=93****.*

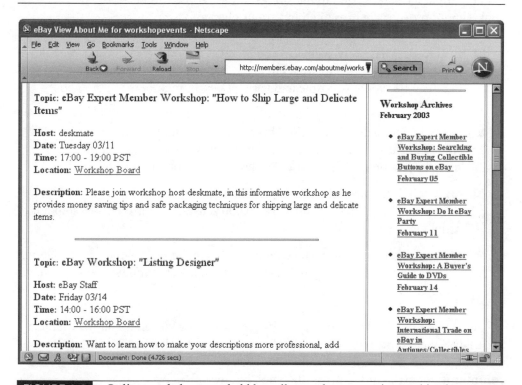

FIGURE 2-2   Online workshops are held by sellers and you can view archived events any time you wish.

Be Encouraged by Success Stories

As I write this, eBay is one of the few parts of the world e-commerce that are not only doing well but continuing to grow with leaps and bounds. More and more individuals are taking to selling on eBay part-time, to get a little extra money, or have even moved to making eBay their sole source of income. The amazing thing to me is that people figured out on their own that they could make a living selling solely on eBay, or supplementing other sales with eBay auctions. eBay didn't market itself as a place where you could create your own eBay business; eBay sellers figured that out by experience. They realized that no matter how offbeat or unusual the item, they could find a buyer for it somewhere around the world. They also discovered that, with a worldwide pool of buyers available, they were likely to get a far higher price online than they could selling through an antique store, flea market, or garage sale. Listen to the stories of the people I interviewed for this book, whose profiles are presented in various chapters:

- Bob Kopczynski sells as many as 600 items a month and doesn't even do it full-time. He works part-time buying at estate sales and selling on eBay, but his wife works full-time and various family members and neighbors help out.

- Don Colclough decided to close his antique store and sell full-time on eBay when he realized he could make his own hours, save on travel time, and get more buyers online than ever came through the front door of his store.

- eBay seller decoray sold an antique photo of a tavern for more than $700; he estimates that he's sold as many as 10,000 separate items on eBay, shipping as far away as Africa.

- Sheila Schneider has had a hard time finding regular employment as an interior designer in Portland, Oregon, but she's been supplementing her income nicely through eBay.

Need more inspiration? eBay regularly features its own sellers on the Member Spotlight page, **http://pages.ebay.com/community/people/spotlight.html**. You'll also find member profiles in the eBay newsletter, the Chatter, **http://pages.ebay.com/community/chatter/index.html**, shown in Figure 2-3.

FIGURE 2-3   eBay's own newsletter can inspire you with profiles of successful sellers.

Beware of eBay Scams and Shams

This book doesn't present a glowing picture indicating that selling on eBay always goes smoothly, and that problems never occur. On the contrary, eBay's very popularity attracts an assortment of swindlers, cheats, and outright crooks who seek to victimize buyers and sellers alike. If you're aware of the potential pitfalls and know how to avoid them, chances are you'll run into very few problems during your career as a seller.

When you hear about eBay in the news, you usually hear about the weird, often illegal, things that people put up for sale on the auction site. The more notorious things are quickly removed by eBay itself. You should avoid breaking the law or eBay's own rules for sellers by reviewing the lists of questionable and prohibited items described in Chapter 16.

That's not to say you can't put odd, quirky, or downright weird things up for auction on eBay. A check of the odder eBay categories, such as Slightly Unusual, Really Weird, Totally Bizarre (which are under the Weird Stuff category, which is under the Everything Else category), or the Other subcategory under the Metaphysical category will cure you of that notion right away. The important thing is that you should watch out for typical scams that plague eBay buyers and sellers alike, such as:

- **Deadbeat bidders**   These are individuals who refuse to pay for what they have bought. You run into these folks far less often than you might think, however.

- **Scam artists**   eBay members regularly get junk e-mail from individuals who claim to be representatives of eBay or the payment service PayPal, and who try to trick members into giving them their passwords or other confidential information. The perpetrators can then "hijack" the user's eBay account.

- **Shill or fake bidders**   Some of the bidding activity on your merchandise may be fishy. An article on the Auction Bytes Web site (**http://www.auctionbytes .com/pages/abn/y02/m04/i05/s01**) reported on programs that reward customers for clicking through to the eBay Web site, registering, and bidding on auctions. *Shill bidding* is a prohibited and dreaded practice conducted by some disreputable eBay sellers who agree to run the price up on auction items so high bidders have to pay more than they would otherwise.

You'll find more detailed descriptions of the kinds of problems you can run into as an eBay seller, and some suggestions for overcoming them, in Chapter 19.

eBay Bestsellers
Making the Move from Bidder to Auctioneer

Like many eBay sellers, Jo Stavig (eBay User ID: vintagevisionjo) is no stranger to antiques and collectibles, or even to putting her wares up for sale. She rented space in an antique mall in Chicago for several years, but she wasn't happy with the 10 percent commission the mall charged on each sale, and things just weren't selling fast enough. When she cleaned out her mall space, her home became

2

filled with boxes full of twentieth-century memorabilia. With the holidays coming, she became convinced that it was time to make the move from being a buyer on eBay to starting to sell.

"I had some silver, crystal and glass items that I was nervous about taking to the mall because I didn't have a locked cabinet there (you had to pay extra for that)," says Jo. "I had some inventory left over when I moved out of there, and now I had the problem of where to put it all. It seemed that eBay would be a more cost-effective way to sell and reduce my collection."

Even though she had sold merchandise, and was used to buying on eBay, Jo still found the process of becoming a seller "somewhat intimidating." She had to make a series of decisions about how to ship, whether she would ship overseas, how to accept payments, and whether she would accept returns. Next came the issue of how to take photos, and where to store them online. Then the technical preparation—where to load your photos from, how to take photos. Her husband Steve helped by taking photos with his mini DV (digital video) camera, then touching the images up using the sophisticated graphics program Adobe Photoshop. "I put together a couple of backdrop fabrics on a drawing table, and I have a couple of clip-on lights that I can manipulate."

She signed up for PayPal, one of several payment methods that enabled her to sell overseas. She decided to take personal checks. Finally, she was ready to go online with her first sales. "It was exciting. I found it more exciting as a seller than as a buyer. At the end of an auction, watching a new bid suddenly come up was really something. My first really exciting sale was a set of six nineteenth-century silver-plated forks that I bought at a rummage sale for 10 cents each. They went for $78. I knew they were that good, but I didn't think they were that good!"

"I have not come up with a bad check policy. I haven't gotten a bad check yet." Jo uses the U.S. Postal Service's (USPS's) Priority Mail for most of her shipping, and orders boxes through the USPS Web site. She emphasizes the importance of packing and shipping with care. "You can never use too much packing material. I thought I knew packing really well, because I worked in an art gallery, but found out I did not. There was a breakage on something that arrived in two pieces. I refunded part of the sales price. The buyer didn't send it back. If something gets broken, filing a claim with the post office is really difficult."

In Jo's first four months as a seller, she has sold about 100 lots, including "bunches and bunches of Christmas ornaments. I've been spending quite a lot of time doing it. I've been doing freelance interior design, and other types of consulting, so it definitely helps with bills."

Jo's main piece of advice: "It's worth spending some time as a browser and a buyer first before you sell. I purposely tried to accumulate some feedback as a buyer and got a feedback rating of 30 before I went out there as a seller."

The biggest benefit, she concludes, "is being able to get rid of all that stuff all around the house! Also, being able to sell things in a more timely manner, things that would have been sitting around in the mall for months without a buyer. I've enjoyed the contacts with buyers, which can seem amazingly personal. In mall space, other people were selling for me, and I had no contact with my customers. Now, on eBay, people will write me back, saying things like 'I love the way this looks, this is better than it could possibly be.' That's been an unanticipated benefit of it for me."

Do Your Research

Before you start selling on eBay, do your homework. Know which kinds of sales attract lots of bids and which turn out to be duds. Scan the message boards to get an idea of the kinds of problems sellers tend to confront, so you can watch out for them yourself. In order to succeed, any business needs to come up with a business plan, and online businesses are no different. A business plan doesn't have to be an elaborate production. The most important things are to make sure what you want to sell, determine where you want to sell it, and verify that there's a market of buyers for the kinds of merchandise you want to put up for auction. The sections that follow provide you with some other tips for planning your eBay business.

Learn by Bidding

Few, if any, people start out selling on eBay without having bid on some items first. You *can* open an account and start selling without any other experience on the auction site, but I don't recommend it. The best way to get a feel for how transactions proceed and are completed is to bid on and purchase something yourself from a reputable seller.

Perhaps the biggest benefit of bidding and buying before you start selling is the fact that you are able to accumulate positive feedback simply by following through with payment in a timely manner. You get some stuff you need or want, hopefully at a bargain price, and you get the feedback that you can then use to help you attract bidders when you start to sell. When you get to a feedback level of 20 or 30, people can tell you've used eBay for a while and are likely to be a reputable seller. At that point, you can start putting your own items up for auction.

Pick Items that People Want

It doesn't do any good to put items up for sale that no one wants, that don't get any bids, and that only consume the time and energy required to photograph and list them. Rather than trying to sell new dolls that were distributed at fast-food restaurants a few months ago and that aren't hard to find, try to sell older, limited edition dolls, preferably in their original packaging. Take a few minutes to look through the categories in which you have chosen to list your merchandise to see not only what's desirable, but what items turn out to be dogs on the market. You might be better off giving the undesirables away to charity or on eBay's Giving Board (**http://chatboards.ebay.com/chat.jsp?forum=1&thread=59**).

> TIP *eBay puts out a number of publications for buyers and sellers in especially popular areas, and they contain tips on what constitutes a good sales item. This newsletter has tips for people who sell antiques:* **http://www.ebay.com/antiquesnewsletter/Vol1Issue6.html**.

Pick the Category In Which You Want to Sell

eBay started out with only a handful of categories in which to sell items. It's since grown to about 8,000 different categories. Yes, it's true, bidders often find what they're looking for through keyword searches that bypass the category system altogether, but it still matters where you sell your merchandise. Do a search of eBay's current or completed auctions to find items that resemble what you have to offer, and see what categories they were listed in.

Because there are so many possible categories, it's quite possible that what you want to sell could fit in one or more categories. If that's the case, you only have to spend a few dollars more for the extra listing fee that enables you to list something in more than one category.

"If you're not sure which category is best, or if an item has two groups of collectors, try to sell it in two categories," suggests eBay seller decoray, who says he's sold more than 6,000 items on the auction site. Although the fee for listing an item in two categories is $5.00 instead of the $2.50 for one category, the extra investment is worth it. It pays to think the way your prospective customers think, he says.

Get Registered

Just as you had to register with eBay when you started to buy, you have to register to become a seller as well. Even if you already have an eBay User ID and password and have accumulated feedback as a buyer, you still need to create a Seller's Account. That way, eBay is able to maintain a record of your contact information if they need to contact you. eBay also requires you to put your credit card name on file so they can deduct Final Value Fees, listing fees, and the other fees that go along with getting your auctions online.

To start the process, click the Sell button in the toolbar that appears near the top of virtually any eBay page. Click the **seller's account** in the phrase "Create a seller's account." Follow the steps shown on subsequent pages to set up your account. You'll be asked, early in the process, to enter your credit card information and your billing address. This might seem a bit off-putting, but don't worry. eBay only uses this information to charge you when it comes time to pay your seller's fees—not when you register.

Pick a Good User ID

Perhaps you already have a User ID that you use for bidding on eBay. Even if you do, when you start an eBay business you might want to consider changing it. Why? Your name is part of your identity, and therefore, it's part of your business identity as well. Names that are frivolous, silly, or potentially offensive might turn away bidders. Whether you are creating your first User ID or thinking about changing, consider the following:

- Make your ID reflect your business. If you sell buttons, for example, try to work the word "button" into your name.

- Don't use your e-mail address. For one thing, you don't need to, as buyers and sellers can find you by clicking **Ask seller a question** from one of your auction listings. I made the mistake of using my e-mail address as my User ID, and I was flooded with junk e-mail.

- Don't use the @ or & symbol—other letters, numbers, and symbols are okay.

- Don't use blank spaces; if you need to separate two words, use a single underscore character (SHIFT-HYPHEN).

- Don't use a URL as your User ID.

- You aren't allowed to use the word "eBay" in your User ID.

When you create a new User ID you get an icon that looks like a miniature pair of sunglasses next to your name. The icon tells other eBay users that you changed your User ID or obtained a new User ID sometime within the past 30 days. Remember that, if you ever have second thoughts about a User ID, you are allowed to change it 30 days after you create it.

NOTE   *Changing your User ID doesn't mean you lose your accumulated feedback. eBay carries your feedback from your previous ID to your new one.*

Create a Secure Password

Passwords are the most basic level of security on the Internet, and, when used by themselves and not protected by encryption or other means, one of the least secure. You can improve the inherent security of the eBay password you create by following a few simple principles:

- Don't use a word in the dictionary. Some hackers use password-cracking software that looks up all of the words in a dictionary to try to uncover just this sort of password.

- Don't make it too short. Hackers also try to crack passwords using "brute force" attacks that generates a vast quantity of random characters and submits them to the computer at very high speed. Keep your password between six and nine characters.

- Don't make it too long and complicated. You won't be able to remember it, or you'll easily mistype it.

- Use a recognizable phrase, like My eBay Auction Business, and use the initials MEAB. Mix the characters into upper- and lowercase: mEAb. Add a number that is meaningful, such as your street address: mEAB1553.

TIP   *Some easy-to-use software programs are available to help you manage not only your eBay password but the many other passwords you probably use to get online, read your e-mail, and register to use other Web sites. Look into Whisper 32 (**http://www.ivory.org/whisper.html**), and PassKeeper (**http://www.passkeeper.com**).*

Get the Computer Equipment You Need

Making the move from only buying on eBay to selling on a regular basis is like moving from being a backup player on a sports team to a starting player. You become a full participant. Accordingly, you need to make sure your Internet connection and your computer equipment are up to snuff. This section provides some tips on what you need to put your sales listings together.

Remember, when you shop for memory or other computer hardware, save your receipts. You may be able to record and deduct all these purchases as business expenses on your tax return if you make money selling through auctions (and you will!).

NOTE   *If you're satisfied with your Internet connection and equipment or if you sell on consignment, you can skip this section. This section is for those of you who are eager to start wheeling and dealing but aren't sure what equipment you need. Keep in mind that I'm examining the ins and outs of running an eBay business. I'm not talking about selling something once a month or a few times a year. For occasional selling, you can use any computer equipment that gets you on the Internet. For regular sales that generate part or all of your income, though, it pays to get the best equipment and Internet connection you can afford.*

Internet Connection

In theory, you can create and upload auction listings from a computer at your public library or at a relative's house, but when you start selling, you're going to need to check your e-mail regularly for inquiries from prospective bidders. You'll also want to experience the end-of-auction excitement as bids go up on your items. You really need your own Internet connection so you can get on eBay any time of the day or night.

Chances are your computer has a modem built into it that you can use to connect to the Internet. A *modem* is a hardware device that translates your computer's digital data to signals carried over other types of electronic cables. A conventional analog modem translates the digital computer information into analog data that can be sent over ordinary phone lines. People who make a phone call to their Internet Service Provider (ISP) to connect to the Internet are said to have a *dial-up modem connection*. These days, most analog modems operate at a speed of 56 kilobits per second (Kbps), which is a minimal speed for using the Internet.

You can do better than a conventional modem these days. I highly recommend that you look into a Digital Subscriber Line (DSL) or cable modem connection, if one is available in your area. These are *direct lines,* which keep you connected at all times, rather than just for the length of your modem's phone call. Besides freeing up a phone line, a direct connection is typically light years faster than a dial-up modem connection. Cable modems receive data from the Internet through a cable TV company's existing underground fiber optic cable and may be available from one of your local cable providers. DSL is a cost-effective "starter" type of direct connection to the Net that uses conventional telephone lines to transfer data at very high speeds. You may be able to get a DSL connection from your local phone provider or an ISP such as Earthlink (**http://www.earthlink.com**).

If you do use a phone line to get online, probably the most important telephone- or connection-related decision you can make is to install a second phone line for your online buying and selling. Having a second line is pretty much a necessity if you plan to do business online regularly—or if your children or significant other uses your existing phone line even on a semi-regular basis.

CAUTION *If you have a "day job" in addition to your eBay sales, don't get in the habit of putting merchandise up for sale or checking your auction listings from your office computer. You can easily get in trouble for misusing company resources. To stay out of the doghouse, set up your own system at home.*

Computer

Buying and selling on eBay, like other types of electronic commerce, doesn't require a machine with the latest super-fast processor and multimedia bells and whistles. Nevertheless, the speed and quality of your computer, monitor, and other hardware can affect your auction experience. If your machine is slow and your modem a crawler, it could take an inordinate amount of time to get multiple sales items online. If you can't inspect a detailed screen image of your image as it appears on eBay, you might not be able to correct or retake it if you need to. Make sure you have, at the very least:

- A reasonably fast computer—in other words, one with at least a 300 or 400 MHz processor. The speed at which a processor operates is measured in megahertz (MHz).

- Lots of Random Access Memory (RAM). Along with browsing the Web and checking e-mail, you're likely to be operating scanning and image editing software, which can be memory-intensive. Get a minimum of 128MB of RAM, and more if you can afford it.

FIGURE 2-4   Improve your auction experience by shopping for computer equipment on eBay itself.

Where better to buy computer equipment, if you need it, than eBay's own Electronics & Computers category? You might find a bargain, and if you pay up quickly, you'll get another positive feedback mark as well (see Figure 2-4).

> **TIP**   *If you need to find out more about computer hardware terms and descriptions of what to buy, check out* How to Do Everything with Your PC *by Robert Cowart, published by Osborne McGraw-Hill.*

Monitor

Your monitor is the window through which all the action on eBay occurs. A clear, sharp monitor can help you verify that your images are of good quality. A monitor that's especially spacious (say, 17 or 19 inches or more) enables you to open to several browser windows at a time, so you can monitor multiple sales as they come down to the wire.

When it comes to buying online, a good monitor and a video card are two of the most important investments you can make. In order to know whether an item is exactly what you want, you have to be able to see it clearly. Sometimes, too, the only reference you have for an item's quality is an onscreen image.

It's tempting to scrimp on computer monitors, especially if you're a bargain hunter like me. You can find cheap monitors for $100, or even less if you buy a used one. Because monitors are so important to your auction experience, though, don't scrimp on this important component. If you can afford it, purchase a 17-inch or bigger monitor instead of the smaller 14-inch variety. Even an extra inch makes a huge difference whether you're looking at word-processing documents or Web pages.

Computer monitors display graphic information that consists of little units called *pixels*. Each pixel appears in a computer image as a small dot. The pixels are so small that they're hard to see with the naked eye unless you magnify an image to look at details close up. The higher the resolution, the better the image appears. A monitor *resolution* of 1280 x 1024, for example, refers to the number of pixels that the monitor displays. Another important point to consider when shopping for monitors is the maximum refresh rate at the monitor's resolution. Anything less than 75Hz produces visible flashing in the image that is guaranteed to be annoying.

NOTE   *Features like refresh rates don't apply to LCD monitors. LCD stands for Liquid Crystal Display, a way of displaying images on a monitor in which back light shines through liquid crystals on the screen. LCD enables the use of flat-panel displays by laptops and other computers.*

Software You'll Need

For the most part, you can sell on eBay using the same software you use to buy: your Web browser and your e-mail software. However, when you start to sell, you'll probably start to use those tried-and-true programs in some new ways. Plus, you might want to install some auction-specific software.

E-Mail Software

Although a Web browser provides you with a port of entry for getting involved with auctions, e-mail often seals the deal. E-mail communication is essential for exchanging both pre-sale and post-sale information between buyers and sellers. You can, and should, ask sellers for background information about items in which you're interested.

As far as obtaining e-mail software, this isn't usually something you have to worry about. You'll probably use the e-mail software that comes with your Web browser: Outlook Express for Internet Explorer or Netscape Messenger for Netscape Communicator, or America Online's e-mail client. All of these programs handle the features mentioned below.

After the sale, you need to provide shipping information and answer bidders' questions through e-mail. It pays to be proficient with some of the finer points of e-mail communication, such as the following:

■ **Quoting**   Almost all e-mail programs let you quote from a message to which you're replying so you can respond easily to a series of questions and remind the sender what he or she said earlier.

■ **Attaching**   Attaching a file to an e-mail message is a quick and convenient way to transmit information from one person to another. For instance, it's common to e-mail a photo of an item that isn't displayed on the Web. If you do this, be sure to send the image in a common graphics format your recipient can view, like GIF, JPEG, TIFF, or PCX.

You might also want to attach a signature file to the end of your e-mail messages that describes who you are and provides the name of your eBay business (if it has a name), your User ID, and other contact information, as described in Chapter 11.

Web Browser

When it comes to using Internet auction services, your tried-and-true Web browser will see you through. However, when you sell, you have to run this familiar software through a few more paces than usual. You need your browser to:

■ Display sale items you want to buy or sell after you put them online, so you can make sure the listings and images look the way you want.

■ Preview any personal Web pages you create, such as an About Me page or an eBay Store (see Chapter 7).

■ Support some level of Internet security, such as encryption or secure transactions, so you can register, place bids, or change your seller's account information if you need to.

In addition to having an up-to-date browser with the latest features, having more than one kind of browser installed on your computer is often a good idea so you can test the way your auction sales look, if you use HTML formatting like colors or headings. For example, if you use Microsoft Internet Explorer because that's what came with your operating system, be sure to download the latest copy of Netscape Communicator as well.

Image Editing Software

You need a graphics editing program either to create original artwork for your Web pages, or to crop and adjust your scanned or digitally photographed images. The software you need to adjust or crop photographic image files almost always comes bundled with the scanner or digital camera, so you don't need to buy separate software. I discuss auction images in Chapter 8, but the two image editing programs I use the most are Paint Shop Pro by Jasc Software (**http://www.jasc.com**) and Adobe Photoshop Elements (**http://www.adobe.com**).

Auction Software

If you plan to present lots of auction items for sale on the Web and envision a full-fledged online business that includes customer service options and online purchases, you may want to look into software specially designed to help you present items for sale, track bids, or even set up your own auction service. One of the most popular programs is eBay's own Seller's Assistant (**http://pages.ebay.com/sellers_assistant/index.html**). Virtual Auction Ad Pro by Virtual Notions also gives you a user-friendly way to create auction listings (**http://www.virtualnotions.com**) and is a program that I've personally found easy to use.

Other software that helps you manage multiple sales at once is described in Chapter 6.

Image Capture Device

A good photo is pretty much a must-have for attracting bids on your merchandise. A picture is worth a thousand megabytes of information, in online terms. The photos that appear on eBay auctions need to be digitized—in other words, they need to be in the form of computer files rather than the paper photos you normally get back from your photo processor. You have a variety of options for obtaining digital images of your sales items:

- Take photos of your merchandise with a conventional camera and have your photo processor return them to you on CD or store them online so you can retrieve them.

- Take photos with a digital camera and save the image files on your computer.

■ Get conventional photos back from your photo processor and scan them into your computer using a device called a *scanner*. The most common type of scanner is a flatbed scanner, which resembles a miniature photocopier. It is primarily used for scanning paper items, but can be used for some small three-dimensional objects, with varying degrees of quality.

Scanning is the process of turning the colors and shapes contained in an image such as a photographic print or slide into digital information (that is, bytes of data) that a computer can understand. You place the image in a position where the scanner's camera can pass over it, and the scanner turns the image into a computer document that consists of tiny bits of information called *pixels*.

Scanners have been around for a while, which, in the world of computing, means that prices are going down at the same time that quality is on the rise. The bargain models are well under $135, and I've even seen a couple priced on eBay for under $50 or less.

Unless you already have a scanner at home and know how to use it, chances are you're better off with one of the first two options. Buying your own digital camera and learning how to use it is ideal and cost-effective because it saves you photo processing costs. The advantage of using a digital camera is that it's portable and convenient. A digital camera connects directly to your computer, so you can save images right to disk. You can get photos online in a matter of minutes without spending money or time having them processed and printed conventionally. Not so long ago, digital cameras cost thousands of dollars. These days, you can find good digital cameras that provide a resolution of 1.0 megapixels or above and made by reputable manufacturers like Nikon, Fuji, Canon, Olympus, and Kodak in the $50 to $100 range on eBay. You have to make an investment up front, but this particular tool can pay off for you in the long run. Not only can you use the camera for your auction offerings, but with the addition of a color printer, you can even print your own photos, which can save you a pile in photo lab costs.

However, if you're a techno-phobe and are most comfortable with your conventional camera, let your photo processor save the photos in digital format for you.

Handheld Device

This is a pretty high-tech option, but it's worth noting that, if you use cell phones or handheld computing devices that can browse the Web, you can use them to check out your eBay auctions while you're on the road. Find out more on the eBay Anywhere Wireless page (**http://pages.ebay.com/anywhere/**), as shown in Figure 2-5.

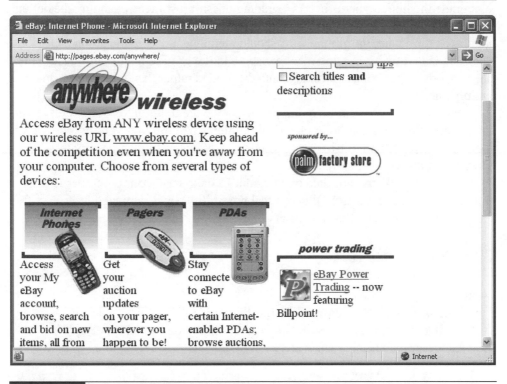

FIGURE 2-5   Use your Web-enabled cell phone or handheld device to check on your auctions while you're away.

Protect Your Investment

Remember, when you run an eBay business, your computer isn't just a toy for playing games or a tool your kids use to do their homework. It's business equipment. Be sure to protect your investment by taking steps to guard against damage or data loss.

Be sure your computer has anti-virus software installed that is configured to automatically scan your incoming e-mail for virus attachments as you download your messages.

Protect your equipment against electrical problems that can result in a loss of data or substantial repair bills. A *power surge* or *spike* (a sudden increase in voltage) can damage your equipment. Electrical storms can damage ungrounded equipment, and blackouts can put you offline and prevent you from getting work done, which can hit you in your pocketbook.

At the very least, make sure that your home office has grounded three-prong outlets. (Even if the rest of your house has old-fashioned outlets, pay an electrician to upgrade the line to your office.) Upgrading doesn't just mean changing the outlets themselves, however; it means using a three-wire cable to bring electricity to the outlet. The third wire, the ground wire, should literally connect to the ground. Usually, electricians do this by burying a copper spike in the ground near your house. This causes shorts or lightning strikes to go into the ground rather than into your computer equipment.

Another must-have is a *surge suppressor,* a device that guards your equipment against power surges and other electrical problems. A common variety is a five- or six-outlet strip with a built-in protection device. You can find surge suppressers at hardware and computer stores.

Be sure to back up your data on a regular basis in case your computer is lost or stolen (if you use a laptop, this is a real possibility) or is damaged by fire, coffee spills, floods, or other natural disasters.

Where to Find It

- **eBay Education**
  http://pages.ebay.com/education/index.html
  Links to tutorials for sellers and workshops conducted on eBay's message boards.

- **eBay University**
  http://pages.ebay.com/university/index.html
  A list of upcoming road shows and workshops held around the country.

- **eBay Workshop events**
  http://members.ebay.com/aboutme/workshopevents
  Links to excellent tutorials and workshops for sellers held on eBay's message boards and archived online.

- **eBay Member Spotlight**
  http://pages.ebay.com/community/people/spotlight.html
  Profiles of eBay users presented by eBay itself in brief question-and-answer format.

- **The Chatter**
  http://pages.ebay.com/community/chatter/index.html
  eBay's own community newsletter.

- **eBay Anywhere Wireless**
  http://pages.ebay.com/anywhere
  Instructions on how to retrieve auction data on your cell phone or PDA.

Chapter 3

Become an eBay Auctioneer

How to…

- Get your eBay business up and running, step by step

- Decide how you want to sell on eBay

- Choose the right types of auctions for your needs

- Add highlighting to gain extra attention

- Use eBay's Listing Designer to boost graphic interest

- Get sales online with the Sell Your Item form

- Know how to manage sales while bidding is still open

- Procure inventory so you can keep your business running smoothly

It's time to get down to business—e-business, eBay style, that is. Any business endeavor requires some planning beforehand. Happily, setting up a sales operation on eBay is far simpler than starting a brick-and-mortar operation. You don't have to purchase or rent a store or office space, and you don't have to install lots of furnishings or equipment. You don't have to hire employees (at least not yet).

In fact, if you are already online and bidding on eBay, you've got most of what you need to get started. At this point, you just need a little bit of confidence, and you need to make a few choices. In fact, you can break down the process of starting an eBay business into a series of decisions:

- What kind of eBay business do you want to run?

- What are you going to sell?

- How are you going to take photos?

- How are you going to accept payments?

- How are you going to ship?

Each of those questions will be covered, in varying levels of detail, later in this chapter.

Decision 1: Custom-Design Your eBay Business

There are any number of different ways in which you can sell on eBay. Just because you settle on one option to begin with doesn't mean you have to stay with it all the time, either. Some sellers start by selling part-time, and then quit their day jobs and sell on eBay full-time. Others fall into selling on eBay as their sole source of income after they lose their job; they sell full-time for a while to make ends meet, then move to selling part-time when another job shows up. The beauty of eBay is that you can tailor the type of selling to fit your needs. The various options are described in the sections that follow.

Sell Part-Time on eBay

You can easily fit eBay auction sales activities around your full-time work schedule. Plenty of people do so, from those who sell only a handful of items a month to people who put twenty items online each day. Bob Kopczynksi, who has an active eBay auction business profiled in Chapter 4, works full-time at another job, but his wife devotes all of her working hours to eBay, and they have several other staff people on call as well.

You should, in fact, set a moderate goal for your initial sales on eBay. Starting out by selling perhaps five or six items will help you to ease into the system and get used to how it works. It depends on the amount of time you have available, the number of items you have to sell, and your level of ambition.

Become a Full-Time Auctioneer

When you sell on eBay full-time, you make all of your income through eBay. It's not clear how many people actually do this, but the fact is that individuals all across the country and around the world are selling regularly through the auction site. You get an idea just how many full-time sellers there are by doing a search for Trading Assistants in your state (see the sidebar for this URL on the following page). You're likely to find lots of individuals with very high feedback, many of whom are probably selling either full-time or on what might be called a "most-of-the-time" basis.

When you sell full-time, you have to make a substantial commitment. You'll be checking your e-mail regularly, and putting up auction descriptions, packing, and taking photos on a regular basis. You'll probably benefit by coming up with a regular schedule that calls for you to visit the post office or shipping store at certain times of the week, answer e-mail queries at certain times, take photos at certain times, and so on. You'll also need to come up with a way to accumulate items to sell, because you'll be running out of them eventually and you'll need to replenish your inventory.

Sell on Consignment

One of the easiest ways to get started with selling on eBay, especially if you aren't sure whether you want to sell online at all, is to have someone do the selling for you and see if you like the process. It can be exciting to watch your items sell. My friend Pam does this, in fact; she has been placing her silver dinner sets and other treasures with her friend, an experienced eBay seller named Jo Stavig. Pam expressed great excitement at being able to clean out some the clutter in her house while not actually having to do the work of taking photos and creating auction descriptions.

If you're interested in having some experienced eBay sellers, called *Trading Assistants,* sell your items for you, go to the Trading Assistants home page (**http://pages.ebay.com/tradingassistants.html**) shown below.

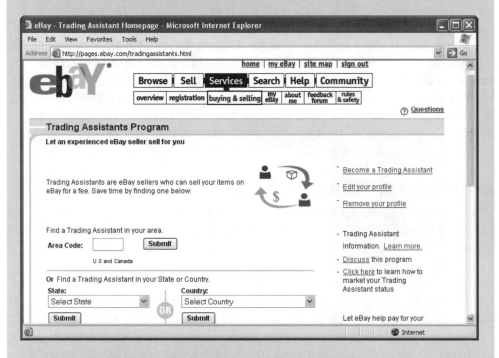

Expect to pay a fee of about 10 percent of the sale. Look for someone in your local area so you can bring your items to the seller, who can then photograph them for you and ship them out when bidding ends. In the process, you'll learn a lot about what it takes to sell on eBay. You may just get bitten by the eBay sales bug and decide to start selling on your own.

When you set up an eBay business, there are also tax and accounting implications, which are addressed in Chapter 17. You can do it all alone, but you'll benefit greatly if you have someone to help you divide the labor. Chances are this will be a spouse, relative, or significant other.

eBay Bestsellers
When Selling Online Is Fun

A friend of mine whom I'll call Buddhachick (not her real User ID) sold full-time on eBay for several years, selling as many as 20 to 50 items each week. When she recently took a full-time job, she had to cut back considerably on her sales activities, and now sells only a handful of items at a time. Nevertheless, she still regards selling on eBay as an enjoyable and even creative activity, one that has enabled her to meet plenty of nice individuals from all over the world.

"I sell only vintage and antique stuff," she says. "I basically spend a lot of time combing the newspapers for estate sales and antique auctions, sometimes in my local area and sometimes not so local; every Thursday night, I'm checking Internet newspaper sites for garage sales. Sometimes, I have to get there at 6:30 or 7 A.M. to wait in line so I can find some treasures. My mother was an antique dealer, and my boyfriend's Dad was in the business. For me, the fun of it is selling stuff I really love.

"It's a little like gambling for me, in that if you find something really valuable, it can be really exciting. One time there was a 1970s belt buckle I bought for $1. It had the words 'Jesus Christ Superstar' on it. It looked like it was from the original 1970s musical. I sold it for $40. Another time, I helped a woman who bought estates empty the house. She said I could have anything that was left. I laughed because it seemed there was nothing left. I stood on a chair and looked up near the ceiling in the basement. I pulled out all this junk. Way in the back there was a cigar box full of fishing lures. I sold one really rare one for $1,000. It was my biggest sale."

Buddhachick had some suggestions about how to handle problems that might arise during and after the sale, though she emphasized that such problems don't occur often. "I do watch my auctions while they are going on. Sometimes people ask me to end the auction early. I never do. A new seller has to do what they think is right. Only once has the offer been higher than the eventual sale price. I just say, "Thank you for your offer" and try to be as courteous as I can, even when I know they are trying to rip me off.

"When an auction ends, I also have a standard end of auction e-mail that I send out. I also have one that says, 'I haven't gotten your payment yet.

Thank you for bidding. Here are the details of how you can pay, and the shipping costs, and the price.' About five percent of my high bidders have turned out to be deadbeats. It hasn't been a huge problem."

Buddhachick has been able to put her skills to good use when writing descriptions. "One thing I learned is that I have marketing skills I didn't think I had. I got a degree in creative writing in college, and I put it to work. I think the art of writing the description is important. I have a lot of friends who watch my auctions because they like the way I write my descriptions, and it really makes a difference."

What makes a good description? She says she learned a lot from reading the descriptions created by other sellers. "Someone wrote, 'I have no doubt the bidders would be thrilled with the condition of this item,' and I thought, that's a really good way of saying that the condition is really good. So I try to say things like that, too. If something has a stain on it, I use the word 'mark' or 'spot.' I don't say 'stain.' If it's a tablecloth, I say, there are a few spots where someone must have dribbled coffee. That way the stain is part of the interesting history of the item. I don't go over the top. I try to be honest but creative.

"Another time I had this old Barbie doll in a really tight dress. It was one of the first Barbies. It looked like a 1950s nightclub singer. I said, 'You'll have your Barbie sing "Happy Birthday, Mister President," in an outfit that's great for serving mint juleps.' Writing creative descriptions keeps me interested, too. If you're doing 20 or 30 descriptions in a day, you've got to keep yourself interested."

Taking photos is not a big production: she tapes a one-color piece of cloth against the wall, and photographs the item on a table. If the item is light, she uses a dark background, and vice-versa. Buyers who refuse to follow through with payment aren't a big deal, either. "If you have any kind of business, you'll run into those kinds of things. I don't hold it against people. I've never had a check bounce, and I have more than 1,000 feedback."

As far as shipping, she uses the U.S. Postal Service. "I like going to the post office; people there know me, and it's convenient. I myself hate to pay high shipping costs when I buy, so I keep the shipping cost down. I offer Priority Mail or Parcel Post. I don't charge a handling fee.

"I have a lot of friends on eBay, and we'll swap information from time to time about what sells and what doesn't," she concludes. "I don't do this full-time now, but I think I spend more than 40 hours a week on it. Still, it doesn't seem to take that much time when you are having fun."

Supplement Web Site Sales

Lots of online businesses supplement their Web site sales with eBay auction sales.
They use their Web sites to advertise their businesses and give their customers a
way to contact them. They put some of their merchandise up for sale there, but
they also use eBay to get top dollar for especially desirable items. The Bruce
Hershenson site shown in Figure 3-1 claims to have sold more than 80,000 items
on eBay.

Boost Brick-and-Mortar Sales

Companies that do business traditionally sometimes sell on eBay in order to empty
out excess inventory or simply make some extra profit. In the "excess inventory"
category, no less an entity than the U.S. Postal Service has used eBay to sell off

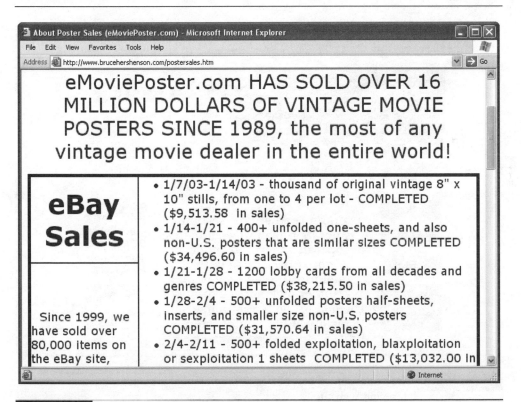

FIGURE 3-1   eBay can supplement the sales on your Web site, if you have one.

unclaimed items, according to a story on the AuctionBytes Web site (**http://www .auctionbytes.com/pages/abu/y202/m05/abu0070/s02**). I've seen plenty of antique dealers who have brick-and-mortar storefronts sitting at their computer terminals behind their cash registers, checking on their eBay sales. Arena Leather Shop of Cookeville, Tennessee regularly sells on eBay (User ID: idoleather) as well as through its brick-and-mortar outlet and its Web site (see Figure 3-2).

Decision 2: Pick the Auction that's Right for You

eBay resembles a virtual ice cream store for auction buyers and sellers. Sales come in many different varieties—flavors, you might say. You can add additional interest to the flavor of sales you pick by featuring them so they stand out from other sales— you can make the listings bold or highlight them in a color, or you can feature them

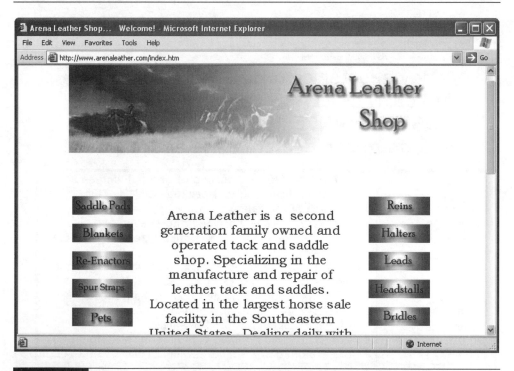

FIGURE 3-2   eBay sales can be part of a sales program that includes a brick-and-mortar store and Web site.

in a special category. Which one is the right one for your needs? Here are some quick points to consider based on my experience:

- Keep your starting bid low. Set it to the least amount you're willing to take. Don't use your starting bid as your reserve bid. I often see valuable items that have a starting bid of, say, $100. This basically tells bidders that the seller has set a reserve price of $100. Once in a while, you'll see a bid on such an item, but most times, you'll see a big 0 in the Bids category. Large starting bids turn people away, because bidders don't feel they'll be getting a bargain.

- Do some research by going to the local library and looking up value in a price guide; or search eBay's Completed Auctions to see what similar items have sold for on the auction site.

- Consider going with No Reserve for some items—not necessarily the ones you have paid a lot for, but ones that weren't expensive to begin with. No Reserve sales tend to get more bids than others (though this isn't a hard-and-fast rule).

- If you have a number of items to sell that are exactly the same and that don't constitute a set, such as a set of six jazz albums you uncovered in the bargain bin at a music store, consider a Dutch Auction format.

In general, a good item will sell no matter what reserve price, starting bid, or Buy It Now price you put on it. Over and over, you find people who were astonished to find that they had a beer can from the 1940s and sold it for more than $16,000, for example. (See Uncle Griff's Web site, **http://www.unclegriff .com**, for this and other success stories.) Don't agonize too much over these details; just put your items out there and give them a chance to sell through a good description and clear images.

Review Your Auction Options

Real estate sellers have always known that location counts for a great deal. Locating your sale in the right part of the eBay auction world can make the difference between making your sale a hot item or a dud. Whether you're a full-time or a sometime trader, one of the first steps to mastering eBay is simply understanding the different kinds of auctions that are available to you. The following sections give you an overview of the various auction categories on eBay.

Regular Online Auction

The classic type of eBay auction, the one you see most of the time, enables sellers to sell to the highest bidder after a fixed length of time. Auctions can list 3, 5, 7, or 10 days (real estate auctions can run for 30 days). eBay simply calls this a "regular" auction.

NOTE   *Ten-day auctions will cost you an extra ten-cent listing fee. This fee does not apply to three-, five-, or seven-day auctions.*

Reserve Price Auction   A reserve price auction is the same as a regular auction in that it lasts for a fixed amount of time, and the sale goes to the high bidder—but the difference is that the high bidder only wins if his or her bid meets or exceeds an amount the seller has designated as a *reserve price*. A reserve price protects a seller against selling something for less than what it's worth. If a seller simply won't part with something for less than $50 because that's what it cost in the first place, the seller puts a reserve of $50 on the item. Bidders only know that there is a reserve price; the auction listing makes it clear whether or not the reserve price has been met or not. The actual reserve price is kept secret. See "When to Use Reserve Auctions" later in this chapter for more.

Online Auction with Buy It Now Price   You can also sell an item for a fixed price called a Buy It Now price. However, if you choose the Online Auction format, the Buy It Now price disappears when the reserve price is met. For instance, if you have an item you paid $10 for and you think (and hope) it's worth $20, you can put a reserve price on it of $10, and an initial bid of $1. Additionally, you can put a Buy It Now price on the item of $20 in the hope that someone will purchase it immediately at the price you consider ideal.

CAUTION   *The problem with Buy It Now is that it depends on you making an accurate estimate of how much an item is really worth in a worldwide marketplace full of collectors whose tastes and pocketbooks you can't really predict. You never know if the item you sell at a Buy It Now price of $20 might really have sold for $200 to someone who was looking for an item to fill out his or her collection.*

Fixed Price

A fixed price sale isn't really an auction: you offer something for sale at a fixed Buy It Now price, and you don't allow people to bid on the item. People can buy it at any time during the sale for a fixed price.

NOTE *You can also sell at a fixed price through an eBay Store—a Web site you can set up on eBay after you have accumulated a feedback rating of 60 or more. Things can be for sale for 30, 60, 90, or 120 days at a time. See Chapter 7 for more about setting up an eBay Store.*

Dutch Auction

A *Dutch auction* is one in which the seller puts two or more identical items up for sale. The seller then specifies the minimum successful price for each of those items, as well as the number of items available. Potential buyers can buy at or above the minimum for the number of items in which they are interested. At the close of the auction, the highest bidders purchase the items at the lowest successful price (that is, the lowest bid that is still above the minimum price).

An example should make this easier to grasp. Suppose you uncover a box full of ten Chuckles the Cat Bean Bag Babies at a garage sale. You put all ten up for sale at the same time in a single Dutch auction. You specify a minimum bid of $20 for each cat. Eighteen separate bidders place bids: One bids $30, two bid $25, three bid $24, two bid $22, two bid $21, and the rest bid $20. The ten highest bidders win: these are the individuals who bid $30, $25, $22, and $21, respectively. However— and this is the confusing part—in a Dutch auction, they all purchase at the *lowest* successful price, which is $21. Those who bid $20 lose out because there are no more than ten cats available.

Fixed-Price (on Half.com)

If you have surplus items for sale, such as books or electronics equipment, and you are at all anxious about auction sales, Half.com provides an attractive and straightforward alternative. Sellers put up items for a fixed price; there is no bidding. There's also little or no chance for fraud; buyers pay Half.com, which then turns around and pays the seller. See Chapter 14 for more about selling on this unique alternative to eBay.

Real Estate Auctions

You would be amazed at how many individuals put up real estate for sale through eBay. The system works particularly well if you have property for sale that might appeal to a wide variety of bidders throughout the world—such as a time share in the Bahamas, for instance. Your ad can appear for 30 days or 90 days in eBay's Real Estate section (see Figure 3-3).

FIGURE 3-3 Real estate can sell well when it appeals to a worldwide audience.

Business Services

Most of eBay's categories allow you to auction off tangible items, whether they are as tiny as beads or as sizeable as yachts. But one category, eLance, gives professionals a place to auction off their services to other businesses. If you have talents as a graphic designer, a writer, or other professional, you can register and bid on projects. eLance brings businesses and service providers together like the want ads or employment agencies; find out more about this innovative auction service in Chapter 13.

> TIP *The information contained in this section changes all the time. You can get the latest list of eBay's auction options at* ***http://pages.ebay.com/help/sell/formats.html***.

Club99 Auctions

A group of eBay users have created their own auction category within the eBay auction universe. The home-grown auction, called Club99, takes place the second

Saturday of every month. Merchandise is offered at an opening price of 99 cents with no reserve price. The auctions last a week. You won't find exotic Italian sports cars or Babe Ruth autographed baseballs here. The typical Club99 auction is a single object such as a book, CD, alarm clock, shirt, or another household or personal item. Find out more about this special Saturday event at **http://members.ebay .com/aboutme/club99**.

How to Use Reserve Auctions

Most of the auctions you find on eBay are reserve price auctions. A reserve price is a way you can protect your investment: it's a price you set that represents the lowest price at which you are willing to sell an item. Usually, your reserve price isn't disclosed to bidders, so they are encouraged to bid as high as they wish. If someone's bid goes above the reserve price you have specified, you are required by eBay to sell it to that high bidder. On the other hand, if the bids that have been placed fail to meet your reserve price, you aren't required to sell to anyone.

NOTE   *Just because no one meets your reserve price, that doesn't mean you can't sell. You and the high bidder can negotiate a sales price. You can send an e-mail saying, "My reserve price was $____ and I'll sell it to you for that much," for instance. Or, if you think you'll have better luck trying again, you can relist your item in a couple of weeks.*

Here's an example. Suppose you find a doll from the 1960s at an estate sale for $20. Naturally, you want to sell the doll for at least $20 plus your listing fees and any expenses you have incurred in obtaining the item (gas, time, effort, and the time involved in creating the auction listing. You put a reserve price of $25 on the doll when you create the auction listing. You also set an initial bid—a bid at which you want the auction to start—of as low as one cent, but more commonly, about $1. You do this in the Sell Your Item form (see Figure 3-4).

NOTE   *You have an additional option to consider—whether you want to give bidders the option to stop the sale and simply sell the item for a fixed price that you consider reasonable. Suppose, for the doll in question, you've done some research through doll catalogs and completed eBay auctions and you have determined that it must be worth $100. You put a Buy It Now price of $100 on the doll, which gives bidders the opportunity to buy it immediately. You save some time and trouble, and you sell to someone you can be reasonably sure is going to follow through with payment.*

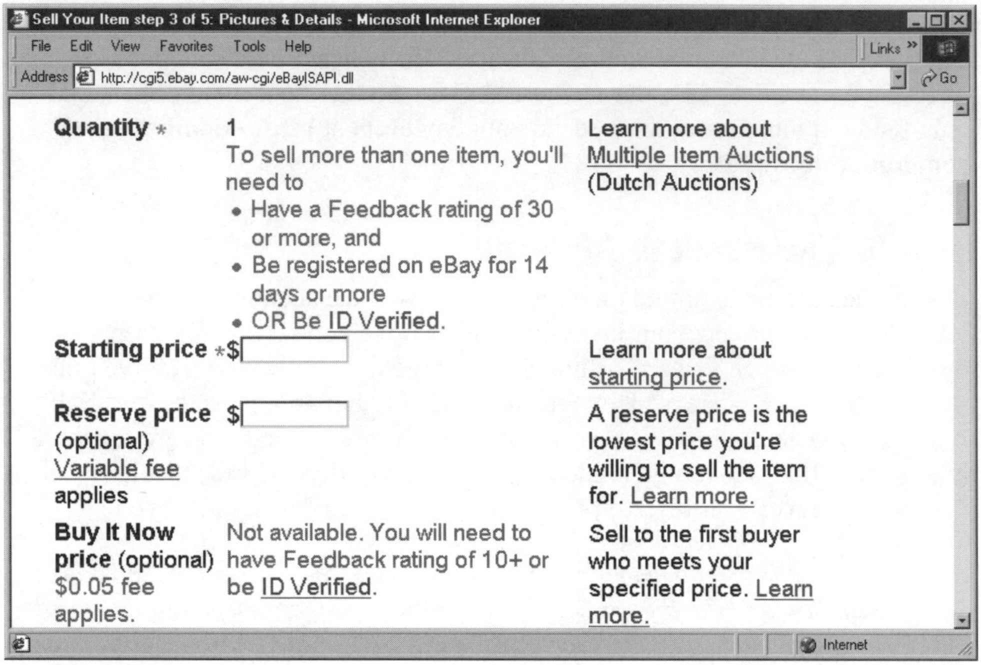

```
Sell Your Item step 3 of 5: Pictures & Details - Microsoft Internet Explorer        _ □ ×
File   Edit   View   Favorites   Tools   Help                              Links »
Address  http://cgi5.ebay.com/aw-cgi/eBayISAPI.dll                           ⟋ Go
```

Quantity *   1
                 To sell more than one item, you'll
                 need to
                 • Have a Feedback rating of 30
                   or more, and
                 • Be registered on eBay for 14
                   days or more
                 • OR Be ID Verified.

Starting price *$ [   ]

Reserve price $ [   ]
(optional)
Variable fee
applies

Buy It Now   Not available. You will need to
price (optional) have Feedback rating of 10+ or
$0.05 fee   be ID Verified.
applies.

Learn more about
Multiple Item Auctions
(Dutch Auctions)

Learn more about
starting price.

A reserve price is the
lowest price you're
willing to sell the item
for. Learn more.

Sell to the first buyer
who meets your
specified price. Learn
more.

```
                                                              Internet
```

FIGURE 3-4   A reserve price protects your investment, but remains concealed from
             bidders while the sale is going on.

The prevailing wisdom about starting bids is that, the lower the starting bid, the more likely you are to attract any bids at all. Higher starting bids scare off bidders who are afraid that the bidding will go too high and they'll never win.

There's another consideration about setting the starting bid, however: The lower the starting bid, the more bids are required to meet your reserve price. This can work to your advantage, however: a sale that attracts 30 bids or more is designated as a "hot item" and eBay adds a matchstick icon to its listing. This tells bidders that the item is especially desirable and is likely to attract more attention.

When to Use Featured Auctions

Chances are you've spent a considerable amount of time finding, hauling, photographing, and describing your merchandise. You can go a step further and make your sale items appear exceptional by placing them in special categories. Featuring an item in these specialized categories costs extra, and items offered for sale in those categories tend to cost more, too. But the merchandise in these featured categories generally is unique and hard to find.

Featured Auctions

Featured Auction listings appear at the top of the main Listings page, which is accessible from the menu bar at the top of every page on eBay. Additionally, some Featured Auction listings are randomly selected to appear on the eBay home page. However, there's no guarantee when or whether a certain item will appear in this well-traveled, highly popular location.

To create a Featured Auction, you need to meet certain requirements. You must have ten or more positive feedback comments, and the merchandise listed can't include adult items or things that eBay judges to be "illegal, illicit, or immoral." Find out about Featured Auctions and Category Featured Auctions (more information on these in the next section) at **http://cgi3.ebay.com/aw-cgi/eBayISAPI.dll?Featured**.

Featured Plus! Auctions

Sellers must have a feedback rating of at least ten to list items as Featured Plus! Auctions, but they aren't subject to the other restrictions that apply to Featured Auctions (see the previous section). Featured Plus! Auctions appear at the top of the first Web page for the eBay category in which they fall.

Paying the extra $19.95 listing fee is a good way to get attention for an exceptional item, particularly if the listings in its category run to 30, 40, or even more Web pages. As with Featured Auctions, the seller decides whether an item is special enough to fall into this category.

> NOTE *Featured Auctions or Featured Plus! Auctions don't have to be more unique or notable than other auction listings. In fact, they might be items that need a little extra attention in order to attract bidders.*

The Gallery

Another way to gain extra attention for your merchandise is to include a photo of it in the category in which it is listed. Such photo-enabled descriptions are called Gallery Listings. They carry an additional 25-cent listing fee. The eBay Gallery used to be a separate photo album of its own; now, the Gallery appears right in the category. When people see your listings in the in the category, they appear with a photo next to them (see Figure 3-5) and can stand out from other listings that have no Gallery photos.

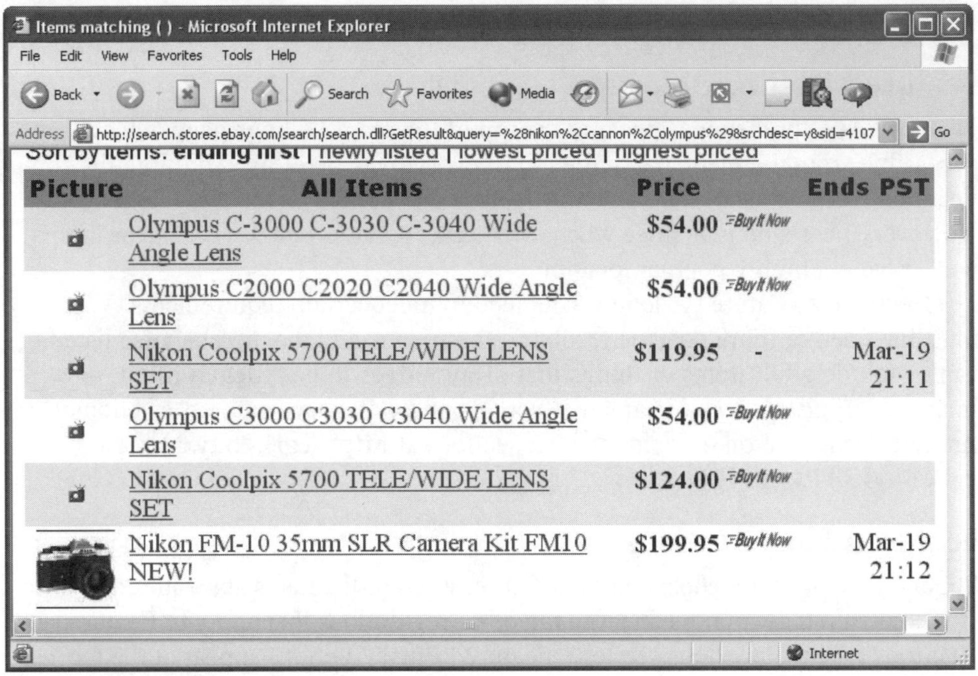

File   Edit   View   Favorites   Tools   Help

Back   Search   Favorites   Media

Address http://search.stores.ebay.com/search/search.dll?GetResult&query=%28nikon%2Ccannon%2Colympus%29&srchdesc=y&sid=4107   Go

Sort by items: ending first | newly listed | lowest priced | highest priced

Picture	All Items	Price	Ends PST
	Olympus C-3000 C-3030 C-3040 Wide Angle Lens	$54.00 =Buy It Now	
	Olympus C2000 C2020 C2040 Wide Angle Lens	$54.00 =Buy It Now	
	Nikon Coolpix 5700 TELE/WIDE LENS SET	$119.95 -	Mar-19 21:11
	Olympus C3000 C3030 C3040 Wide Angle Lens	$54.00 =Buy It Now	
	Nikon Coolpix 5700 TELE/WIDE LENS SET	$124.00 =Buy It Now	
	Nikon FM-10 35mm SLR Camera Kit FM10 NEW!	$199.95 =Buy It Now	Mar-19 21:12

Internet

FIGURE 3-5   Gallery listings use photos to make your merchandise stand out from the crowd.

They can also click on the Gallery View link in the View box on the left of a listing page to see only Gallery items in that category (see Figure 3-6).

To add your image to the gallery, simply save your image in JPEG format and check a box when you list your item. If you want something to really stand out, you can pay an additional fee of $19.95 to sell it in the Gallery Featured format. Such items appear in a special Featured section above the gallery; Gallery Featured photos are twice as big as other photos.

TIP   *Find out more about JPEG, GIF, and other image-related alphabet soup in Chapter 8.*

Other Featured Categories

Imagine that you've shown up at the local flea market at the crack of dawn, hoping to get the best place for your table full of sales merchandise. How do you get the most attention? You place yourself near the entrance, or near a frequently-visited

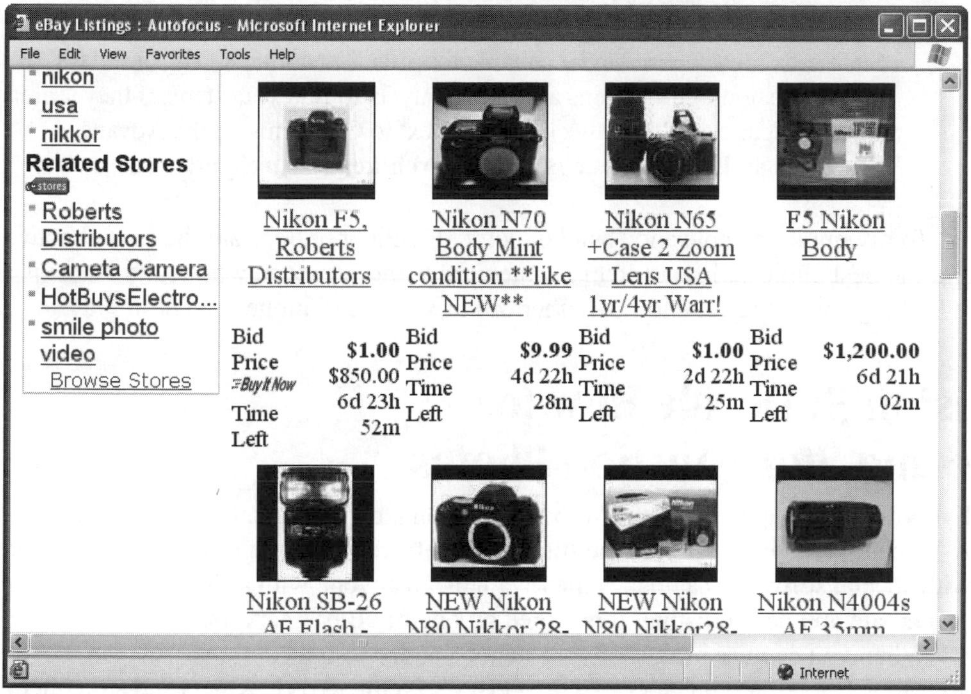

3

FIGURE 3-6   Gallery listings also appear on this page for viewers who like to shop by catalog.

facility such as the refreshment stand. You arrange your space with eye-catching merchandise.

Similarly, eBay provides you with a variety of other ways to get more attention for your merchandise in a long page full of listings. Examples include:

- You can make a listing bold for an additional fee of $1.00.

- You can highlight the auction listing with a band of color for $5.00.

- Featured In Search, which costs $19.95 per item, is used only with Buy It Now items; it places such items at the top of a search results page.

- Home Page Featured. Such items "have a chance" that they will appear in a list of items that appear on eBay's home page. eBay doesn't guarantee that they will actually appear there, however. Just to have the opportunity costs $99.95. (The Home Page Featured items are also listed on a special page full of featured items.)

■ Gift Auctions. Sellers pay an extra dollar to have a gift icon included along with their listing title and to have the items included in a special gift category. Such gifts are supposed to be suitable for gifts for Mother's Day, birthdays, or other occasions. Gift autions also allow buyers to find your items if they search on a gifts page or if they check the box next to Gift Items on the Advanced Search page (**http://pages.ebay.com/search/items/search_adv.html**).

To my mind, the bold and "band of color" highlight options are the cost-effective and the best choices. If your item is noteworthy and someone who really wants it is looking for it, they'll find it whether or not you spend money to feature it.

Decision 3: Decide How to Take and Store Auction Photos

Everything that appears on the Web is stored on a computer called a Web server. A Web server is connected to the Internet twenty-four hours a day, and is equipped with special software that makes files available to anyone with a Web browser. When you create an auction listing, it is stored on one of eBay's servers.

When you capture images of your items, you have some options. You can move your files from your computer to one of eBay's Picture Services sites and store them there. eBay lets you store one image per sale for free; the rest are subject to charges. Because of the cost (and image quality considerations, which I explain in more detail in Chapter 8), you might want to find another home for your image. You may, for instance, choose one of the auction management services mentioned in Chapter 7. These services come with their own storage space for auction images. Or you can use the storage space that comes with your Internet access account.

Before you can find a home at all, you have to have some images to put there. Are you going to have a friend or relative take photos for you? Or are you going to buy a digital camera and do it yourself? In any case, you need to decide how you're going to take good-quality digitized (in other words, computerized) images, because good photos are critical to sales. See Chapter 8 for a run-down of the options.

TIP *You might hear the techy sounding term* upload *in connection with storing images and creating Web pages. When you download a file, you copy it from a Web server to your computer. When you upload, you move a file in the opposite direction, from your computer to a server online.*

3

Decision 4: Figure Out Your Payment Options

Transferring payment for something that's purchased online, whether it's through an auction or through an e-commerce Web site like Amazon.com or Landsend.com, is one of the most nerve-racking things you can do with your computer. The big danger, from a seller's standpoint, is that you'll run into a high bidder who changes his or her mind or backs out of the deal for some other reason—you'll never get paid, and you'll be forced to re-list what you sell. Buyers, for their part, have the great fear that they'll hand over payment to a seller who will take the money and run without ever bothering to ship what's been purchased.

These things do happen, unfortunately, but my experience indicates that they occur less often than you might think. A number of options for getting payment from buyer to seller have been used with success by thousands of eBay users, and while they're described in some detail in Chapter 9, here is a brief summary of the kinds of choices you need to make now, before you start putting up items for sale.

Should You Use an Payment Service?

Brief answer: Yes. An *payment service* is a company that serves as an intermediary between someone who provides goods or services and someone who pays money in exchange for those goods and services. Instead of sending a check or money order to a seller directly, the buyer pays the service, which transfers it to the seller. Depending on the service, both the seller and buyer have to have accounts with the same payment service.

One payment service, PayPal, is widely used on eBay, and in fact was purchased by eBay not long ago. But PayPal charges fees that make some sellers unhappy, and other services such as BidPay (**http://www.bidpay.com**) are also popular. The point is that payment services make buyers feel more secure about bidding, and you need to use at least one service in order to sell on eBay. Keep in mind that PayPal and BidPay only offer minimal protection for buyers or sellers. Although PayPal does verify the IDs of charge card users in the United States, credit card fraud still occurs. And BidPay offers no protection at all.

TIP   *The Escrow service Escrow.com offers a more secure environment for buyers and sellers than BidPay or PayPal. Escrow.com withholds payment to sellers until after the buyer has received the merchandise and approved it. The service also verifies payments by credit card so sellers are protected against fraud.*

Should You Accept Checks?

Short answer: Yes, with qualifications. Many sellers accept checks for years without encountering any that turn out to have rubbery qualities (in other words, that are returned for lack of funds). Even if you do run into bad checks, that doesn't mean you should penalize all of your buyers by refusing to accept checks altogether. Just put a note on your auction listings that puts buyers on notice that, if they send you a check, you will wait ten days to two weeks for the check to clear before you send shipment. The veteran seller decoray, who is profiled elsewhere in this chapter, includes an extensive note about checks with each of his auction listings (see Figure 3-7).

Should You Accept Credit Card Payments?

Quick answer: Not yet, unless you already accept credit cards through a brick-and-mortar store or an e-commerce Web site. Enabling yourself to accept credit cards is typically an involved process, as is the matter of verifying credit card information

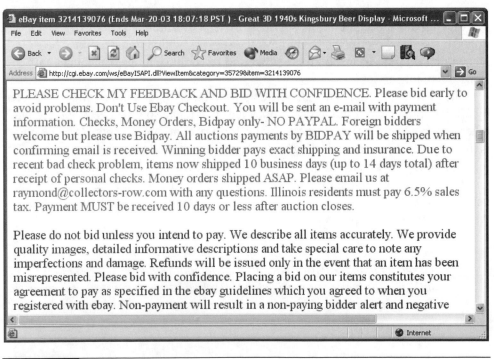

FIGURE 3-7   Tell buyers up front that you'll accept checks but won't ship until they clear.

and dealing with chargebacks—the cost of purchases removed from someone's account if their credit card was used fraudulently. You need some sort of hardware or software to process the credit card data your buyers send; you need to pay fees to the banks or merchant account companies that actually process the payments. Get yourself well-established as an eBay seller before you tackle this one.

Decision 5: Pick Your Shipping Options

Getting your merchandise where it's supposed to go, quickly and safely, is one of the things that buyers note when they leave feedback for sellers. And at this early stage, accumulating positive feedback should be one of your big goals (along with generating income, of course). Therefore, you need to determine—now, before you start making sales—how you're going to pack and ship your merchandise.

First, you need to pick a shipper. Most eBay sellers choose between the United States Postal Service (USPS), United Parcel Service (UPS), or Federal Express. The USPS's Priority Mail is especially popular because of delivery times as low as two days and the free, high-quality boxes, labels, and other shipping materials sellers get to use. But FedEx's Ground and Home Delivery options are competitively priced, especially for heavy items. In any case, you'll need to start accumulating large quantities of boxes, bubble wrap and other packing material, packing tape, labels, and other goodies. See Chapter 10 for more details.

Conduct Your First Auction

Let's say you've made the decisions you need to get started. You've got your ducks in a row and you're ready to start selling. To make sure, go through the following checklist:

- You've signed up for a seller's account with eBay and submitted your credit card information.

- You have accumulated some positive feedback through bidding and buying at auction.

- You've determined the general type of eBay business you're going to run.

- You've accumulated the merchandise you're going to sell.

- You've purchased a digital camera or figured out another way you're going to capture digital photos of your merchandise.

- You've picked some categories in which you're going to sell your merchandise.

■ You've signed up with a payment service and decided on other methods of accepting payment.

■ You've gotten together your shipping materials and picked a shipping method.

At last, you're ready to get some sales online and start getting bids. The following sections describe how to get started.

Gather Your Materials

Pull together the items you plan to sell first. Don't start with too many items at once; for starters, just try a handful so you can get used to the process gradually. Get a good quality digital camera, or consider assembling a "photo studio" including auxiliary lights and solid-colored backdrops you can use for photos.

Come up with a *boilerplate* text that you can use with all of your auction listings—standard text that you include with each of your descriptions and that applies to all of your items. Buddhachick, the seller profiled earlier in this chapter, has a particularly friendly boilerplate:

I take personal check, PayPal, and money orders.

SORRY MICHIGAN BUYERS, PLEASE ADD 6% SALES TAX!

Please do not be alarmed if it takes me a day or two to send you your total. I have several jobs and with the new USPS policies, calculating totals is a bit time consuming!

It is my goal that all buyers will have a pleasant experience doing business with me. I am reasonable, honest, and I make every effort to describe each item accurately. If shipping is not quoted in description, I will charge actual shipping only. Clothing and textiles are sold as is, directly out of estates unless otherwise noted. I do not take responsibility for uninsured items. I will contact you sending you an "eBay Checkout Invoice." Thanks for looking and HAVE FUN!!

You might say something about your payment options and about your policies as a seller. Save this document as a text file that you can paste into the Sell Your Item form whenever you create an auction listing.

Do Your Product Research

Look on your sales as a pleasant, creative experience. You are creating miniature sales campaigns, one for each item. Telling the story of how you found an item and describing how it looks can be fun (at least, it is for someone like me, who enjoys writing and describing things anyway).

At the very least, take a few minutes to look around at search engines and collectors' Web sites, as well as some price guides in the library, to find out exactly what you've got and what you might be able to get for it. You just might discover that you have a real treasure once you do a little research with a respected resource such as the popular Kovels price guide. The Kovels Web site (**http://www.kovels .com**) shown in Figure 3-8 contains more than 340,000 items in its database.

FIGURE 3-8   Do some research so you can create compelling descriptions of your merchandise.

Pick the Right Auction Category

Once you prepare to sell items on eBay, you take a different perspective to categories than you do as a buyer. Your goal is to find the category (or categories) in which you're most likely to find people who are interested in bidding or buying what you've put online. You want to find those ideal buyers who not only like what you're offering but who've simply got to have it to complete their collection. These are people who probably know more than you do about your item, who collect similar items as well. Do a search for items that seem similar to yours and see in what categories they appear.

You aren't limited to listing your item in one category. In fact, if you think your item could fit well in two different categories, you'll find it cost-effective to list in two places. You pay two listing fees as well as any upgrade fees such as Bold or Gallery. (You can't list real estate in two categories, however.)

If you are at all apprehensive about putting something up for sale, do a test. you'll notice that one of the categories in the list is simply called Test. This enables you to put your sale online without having other users bid on it. It's a place where you can make sure your images appear the way you want and that you have used the Sell Your Item form correctly.

TIP *You'll find a complete list of categories, plus the number of items currently up for sale in each one, at* **http://listings.ebay.com/pool1/listings/list/ overview.html**.

Create Your Descriptions

Once you've gathered details about what you're selling and taken some photos (see Chapter 8), you can begin filling out the Sell Your Item form and actually creating auction listings. You only need to click the Sell button in the toolbar that appears on nearly all eBay pages to access the form. (You may be prompted to sign in with your User ID or password first, unless you're already logged in.) The form itself contains tips on how to provide good information. But just for good measure, here are a few more tips.

Your Auction Title

The title of your auction listing is critical. When shoppers conduct searches on eBay and come up with lists of auction items, they'll come up with your title as well as others. Make your title no longer than five or six words. Be sure to pack as much relevant information in those five or six words as possible. The more

3

information you can put in, the better your chances of selling. Don't waste valuable space using tired terms such as L@@K or !!Wow!! which are overused and have no effect on buyers. Try to put in dates and brand names if you can: rather than saying "Beautiful Pottery Vase," say "Pink Roseville Pottery Vase 1934."

Also, remember to be honest: if something is a reproduction rather than an antique, don't bury that fact at the bottom of a description. Lack of forthrightness will turn buyers off; they may never look at your auctions again.

Category

As I mentioned, eBay presents you with hundreds of different categories. Look for items that are similar to yours. Also, try to imagine the kind of person who might want what you have to sell, and try to envision how it might be used. This might suggest the category where such an individual might look for it.

Picture URL

URL stands for Uniform Resource Locator, a standard address that enables anyone with a Web browser to locate an object or Web site that's on the Internet. You get the URL for your image from the site where you have stored your image. This can be eBay's own Picture Services or another photo hosting service. See Chapter 9 for more details about adding images.

Minimum Bid

A minimum bid is a starting point. It's like the auctioneer in an auction saying, "Bidding will start at one dollar. Do I hear two dollars?" It's generally a good idea to pick a small minimum bid, such as $1, for the starting point. Many bidders pick an amount that represents the very least they're willing to accept for an item as the minimum bid. It's not at all uncommon to see items that start at $100. But you'll often notice that such auctions attract no bidders at all. Sellers are likely to turn bidders off by setting a sizeable minimum. Let the bidders feel they're getting a bargain when they start out; you set a reserve price to ensure that an item won't sell for less than a certain price.

The Description

On the Internet, unlike other media, information sells. The more you can say about a sales item, the more likely you'll generate interest in it. The most experienced sellers try to create descriptions that engage the viewer's imagination—that induce viewers to imagine what that pair of gloves might feel like, or how they might use that automatic juicer, or how that old Ford Thunderbird would look in their driveway.

TIP *Don't be reluctant to point out any flaws in what you are selling. You don't want bidders to discover flaws when they unpack the item. You want them to know exactly what they're getting—and to know that you're an honest seller whom they can trust.*

Use Listing Designer

A feature that appeared as I was writing this book, Listing Designer, is accessed from page 3 of the Sell Your Item form. It's an interactive utility that lets you pick a theme and a layout for your item (see Figure 3-9). There is an extra charge of ten cents for each item for which you use Listing Designer. However, many sellers will find this a bargain because Listing Designer has one big plus: it shields sellers from having to know HyperText Markup Language (HTML). HTML is the set of markup instructions that lets you create Web pages. Without using Listing Designer, the only way to format auction listings is to write the HTML by hand and paste it into the Sell Your Item form.

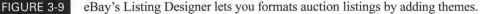
FIGURE 3-9   eBay's Listing Designer lets you formats auction listings by adding themes.

TIP *You can find out more about Listing Designer at **http://pages.ebay.com/ sell/designer-landingpage**.*

Monitor Your Sales Activity

Once your sale goes online, you'll probably want to keep an eye on it just to see when the bids come in, and to check out exactly who bids on it. This is when all your hard work pays off. You'll need to check your e-mail in order to field questions from interested customers. If you receive several questions that are in a similar vein, you may want to edit your description to include the answer as additional information. Even while your sale is ongoing, you can change the item's category or add additional text or photos any time you want.

If you want to add photos or details to your auction descriptions (for instance, in response to questions posed by your bidders), use the to Adding to Your Item Description page shown in Figure 3-10 (**http://pages.ebay.com/services/buyandsell/ add-to-item.html**) and filling out the form.

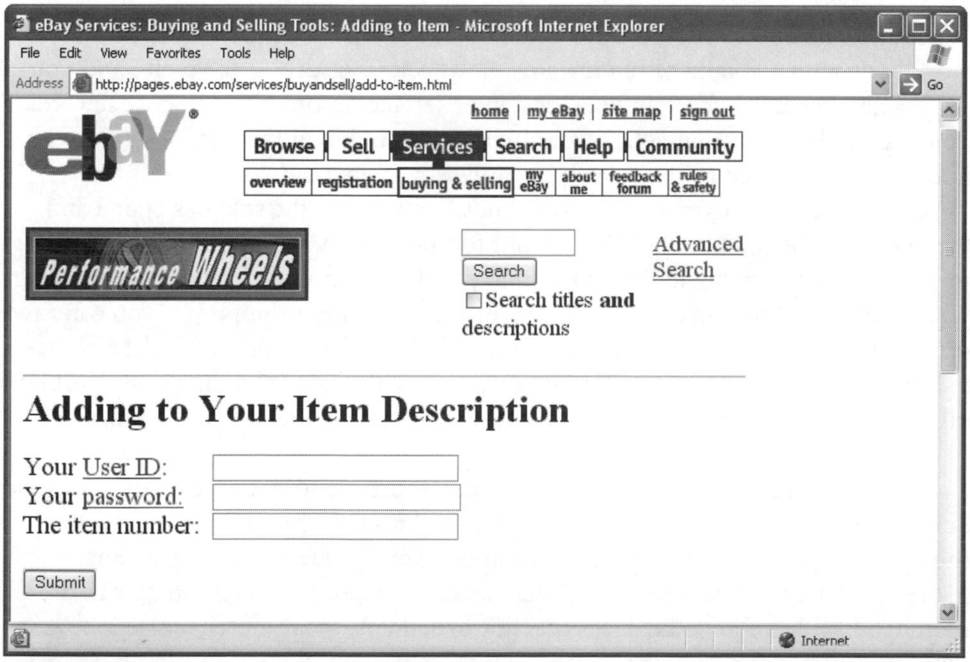

FIGURE 3-10   You can add photos after your sale has started.

Can You Edit Your Description?

It's a good idea to read your description closely and make sure it's accurate before you post the listing online. That's because changing your description isn't a straightforward matter—at least, not after bids have been received on that item. After all, the people who place bids might take offense if the description changes and other bidders can act based on new information they didn't have originally.

The Adding to Your Item Description page mentioned earlier only lets you add to a description. If you want to actually edit an auction listing, click the **revise** link on that auction page. This lets you change *everything* about the auction. However, if bids have been placed on that item, clicking "revise" will not let you edit the actual auction listing unless you cancel all the bids. If you don't want to cancel any bids, you can only add to the description, not change the original.

Close the Deal

When the sale ends, in some ways a new round of work begins. In this case the work ends with a couple of big rewards, however: you receive payment, and you get positive feedback for your good customer service. In order to get those rewards, you need to begin by contacting your high bidder or buyer promptly—within the hour after the sale ends, if you can, but at least within a day.

eBay sends the buyer a stock e-mail notification that the sale has ended and the person is the high bidder. You should follow quickly with your own e-mail, in which you congratulate the winner and provide them with directions for paying you. You'll need to find out how the buyer wants the item shipped (if you offer two different shipping options, such as Priority Mail and Parcel Post). You'll also need to know where the buyer lives so you can calculate the exact shipping cost—virtually all shippers charge based on weight, the size of the package, and the distance to be shipped.

After payment comes in, before you celebrate, send out an e-mail acknowledgement to your bidder to let them know that you have received the check, money order, PayPal account transfer, or credit card payment. More importantly, you need to tell the customer when you're shipping out the merchandise. It's a good business practice to send out your merchandise the same day that the payment arrives, or the day the payment clears your bank. (Most banks will let you know if a check is cleared either by phone or in person.) Try not to wait more than a week until after the payment clears, or you risk having your buyer leave you negative feedback.

3

Resell an Item

Hopefully, most of the items you put up for sale on eBay will actually go to a bidder or Buy It Now buyer. However, you'll probably put up some items that don't attract any bids at all. That doesn't mean you need to give up selling the item. You attract more (or higher) bids at a later date by providing better images, changing the title or description, or going with No Reserve—removing the reserve price altogether. You can relist your item if the following applies:

- You didn't receive any bids on a regular auction and you did not hold a Dutch auction.

- Fewer than thirty days have passed since the closing date of the first auction.

- You didn't receive any bids that met your reserve price if you originally held a reserve price auction.

eBay does charge you a second insertion fee if you relist your item, but if your item sells the second time you put it up for sale, eBay will refund you the second insertion fee. (But if it doesn't sell the second time, you still need to pay the second insertion fee.)

Paying eBay's Seller Fees

How does eBay make the money that made it one of the most successful e-commerce operations in recent years? It makes money from people like you who sell items on its site and who are charged fees. You need to pay a fee before the sale, called an *insertion fee*, just to list an item for auction. You must pay the insertion fee whether or not the transaction is successfully completed. The insertion fees in place as this was written are listed in Table 3-1.

After your item sells, you pay eBay a commission called a *Final Value Fee*. The final value fee isn't a flat fee, but is calculated based on the final sale price or the type of item sold. Table 3-2 indicates how to calculate final value fees.

Opening Value/Reserve Price/ Buy It Now/Minimum Bid	Insertion Fee
$0.01-$9.99	$0.30
$10-$24.99	$0.55
$25-$49.99	$1.10
$50 and up	$2.20

TABLE 3-1   eBay Insertion Fees

Sale Price	How to Calculate Final Value Fee	Example Final Bid	Final Value Fee
$25 or less	Multiply sale price by .0525. Round the number to the nearest penny.	$23	$23 x .0525 = $1.2075 Final Value Fee = $1.21
$25.01 to $1,000	Take $25 of the sale price and multiply it by .0525. Multiply the sale price minus $25 by .0275. Add the two calculations.	$800	$25 x .0525 = $1.31 $775 x .0275 = $21.31 $1.31 + $21.31 = $22.62
$1,000.01	Follow steps for a sale less than $1,000 but take the amount over $1,000, multiply it by .015, and add that to remaining amounts.	$2,500	$25 x .0525 = $1.31 $2,475 x .0275 = $68.06 $1,500 x .015 = $22.50 $1.31 + $68.06 + $22.50 = $91.87

TABLE 3-2 Calculating Final Value Fees

How do you actually pay eBay's insertion fees and final value fees? You have a couple of options. You can use eBay Direct Pay, in which eBay automatically deducts your bank account each month if fees apply. You can have eBay charge a credit card, or you can have eBay invoice you and pay by check or money order. If you sell only occasionally, it makes sense to pay invoices as they arrive.

TIP   *eBay's current selling fees are listed at **http://pages.ebay.com/help/ sellerguide/selling-fees.html**.*

Keep Your Store Well-Stocked

When you're selling on eBay occasionally, you can sell whenever you find something at a yard sale or secondhand shop. If you want to create an eBay business that provides you with a steady source of part-time or full-time income, acquiring inventory you can then sell on eBay becomes a major part of your operation. You'll do better if you can do strategic buying: buying good items at an economical price that you can then auction off at a profit on eBay. How, exactly, do you do strategic buying? The following sections provide some suggestions.

Know Your Field

There's a store not far from me that specializes in clothing and memorabilia from the 1960s and 70s. The owners, a husband and wife, head over to the local resale shop every morning when the store opens at 11 A.M. They are among the first customers, and they find plenty of inventory over there. I know because I often go there myself. The difference is that, while I'm not looking for anything in particular, they know exactly what they want and what their customers are looking for: cool "retro" clothing and bric-a-brac that they can wear to parties or add to their collection of nostalgia.

You can learn a lesson from these folks, and from the many eBay sellers who deal in American memorabilia of the second half of the twentieth century. You don't have to pick a particular type of item, necessarily; you only have to pick a period and study it well. When you go out shopping at garage or estate sales, know what you're looking for. The better you know what's valuable, the better your chances of uncovering a hidden treasure.

Know Where the Good Stuff Is

When you're shopping for inventory, it pays to look where you are likely to find quality merchandise. The Chicago area where I live is known as a particularly good source of secondhand collectibles. But some areas within the area, such as the suburbs north of Chicago where many high-income people live, yield better results than others. Look for garage and estate sales in such neighborhoods in your own area. Often, local newspapers that cover individual towns or groups of towns contain more listings for estate sales and garage sales than major metropolitan newspapers. The area I mentioned is covered by a chain of newspapers that lets you browse through its garage and estate sale listings online, as soon as they come out. You can scour the classifieds (see Figure 3-11) and plan your Friday or Saturday shopping activities accordingly.

Once you have an area in mind and a general sense of what you're looking for, you can shop through the typical venues where collectibles and valuables are sometimes found:

- Garage sales

- Secondhand stores

- Auction sales

In addition, you might find inventory by buying at local retail or wholesale outlets that are having closeouts or that sell merchandise at reduced prices.

- Discount club stores

- Dollar stores

- Going-Out-of-Business sales

Look through classified ads online to plan shopping trips.

No matter where you shop, another tried-and-true tip for finding bargains is "Buy off-season." You'll find the best prices on Christmas decorations in July, not in November. Similarly, winter is a great time to stock up on sports equipment, croquet sets, badminton sets, barbecue equipment, and other outdoor merchandise.

Many of the people who scour eBay looking for auction bargains aren't collectors at all, but dealers in antiques and collectibles who are looking for inventory. While it's unlikely (though not impossible) that you'll find someone buying a bargain item on eBay that he or she will later attempt to sell for a profit on eBay, you do find people who buy on eBay to stock their antique stores or to provide stock they can sell at a flea market or a show.

Where to Find It

- **Trading Assistants Homepage**
  http://pages.ebay.com/ tradingassistants.html
  Search page where you can locate eBay sellers who will sell on consignment.

- **Sell Your Item form**
  Click the **Sell** button in the eBay toolbar (no URL)
  A form you fill out to get your auction sales online.

- **Selling Formats page**
  http://pages.ebay.com/help/sell/formats.html
  List of current eBay sales formats, with fees if applicable.

- **Category Overview page**
  http://listings.ebay.com/pool1/listings/list/ overview.html
  Long list of eBay sales categories and subcategories, plus the number of items currently being offered in each one.

- **Adding to Your Item Description page**
  http://pages.ebay.com/services/ buyandsell/add-to-item.html
  Form you can fill out to add more details to the description of an item you currently have up for sale.

- **Selling fees page**
  http://pages.ebay.com/help/sellerguide/selling- fees.html
  List of eBay's current fees for listing and selling items.

3

Part II

Improve Your Competitive Edge

Chapter 4

Tips and Strategies for Online Sellers

How to…

- Turn your hobby into a business by setting long-term goals
- Build confidence among bidders by gaining credibility as an expert in your field
- Create honest and complete product descriptions that encourage bids
- Solve problems and get inside tips by networking with other sellers
- Attract bids by selling without a reserve
- Handle problems in a businesslike manner
- Obtain merchandise at a bargain so you can resell it
- Gain attention for your auctions by linking and advertising

You've learned the basics of buying and selling on eBay. You've even put that old cuckoo clock that used to clutter your attic or that old Mickey Mantle baseball card up for sale. You've started to accumulate some positive feedback. You're thinking to yourself: "I can do this. This auction sales thing is actually fun!" In other words, you've been bitten by the eBay selling bug—the eBug, you might call it.

Now it's time to take your auction sales to the next level. You need to turn what's currently an occasional thrill into a regular routine. Once you come up with a system for selling on eBay, you can begin to boost your sales income to new levels. The mechanics of buying and selling individual items on eBay are relatively simple. Turning your eBay sales hobby into an eBay business is more involved. In many ways, it's a matter of changing your perspective—of making the eBug work for you.

In this chapter, you'll get some insider tips—tips I've gleaned from my own experience, and from talking to eBay sellers about how to change your sales perspective. You'll learn that you need to keep the long-term establishment of a successful business as your ultimate goal, which might mean writing off quick profits or occasional problems. You'll learn how to work with the eBay community rather than operating as a "lone wolf." You'll learn to boost sales by selling with no reserve and by letting the market determine the final price. Finally, you'll learn how to find inventory, implement some marketing tricks, and drum up free advertising so you can stand out from the competition.

Work for the Long Term

People are what make eBay run well, but when it comes to making sales, you need to look to the numbers. Various numbers can induce shoppers to place bids: the number of items you have for sale at one time, which tell bidders that you're likely to be a professional and not a "fly by night" seller; the reserve price and opening bid prices you set; and the most important kind of number that directly affects your sales— your feedback rating. The eBay sellers who are able to earn a steady supplemental income or who sell on eBay full-time tend to be the ones with high feedback.

Go Retail

What, exactly, constitutes "high feedback" these days? As eBay grows and becomes more established, the amount of feedback displayed by the Power Sellers goes up as well. Right now, according to the sellers I interviewed for this book, there's a threshold in the 1,000 to 1,200 feedback range. If you have feedback in the range of 200 to 1,000, you are certainly doing well, and customers are certain to know you are an experienced eBay merchant. But when you reach 1,000, something happens.

"I call it 'going retail,'" comments Bob Kopczynski, a longtime eBay seller who is profiled later in this chapter. "When my feedback rating went over 1,000, I started getting more bids and higher prices for what I was selling. It was like people recognized me as a retail businessperson, not just a part-time seller. It's the difference between someone who has been running a brick-and-mortar store for ten years and someone who just opens a store down the street. The store that's been established is going to get the most business."

I'm not suggesting that you need to shoot for a feedback rating of 1,000 specifically before you can be a successful eBay businessperson. Not at all; however, this is a book about running an eBay *business*, not just selling on eBay once or twice a year. A feedback rating of 100 or 200 is great in its own way. If, however, you want to make all or part of your regular income through selling on eBay, you need to set your sights higher—the higher, the wider your perspective will be, and the better your chances of success.

Build That Feedback

How do you build your feedback ratings? It takes time, effort, commitment—and a systematic way of completing transactions and shipping out merchandise. Do everything you can to build your feedback by putting up lots of no-reserve sales and shipping them out promptly to your high bidders or buyers.

The eBay feedback ratings at the time I was writing this book are shown here:

As you can see, a rating of 1,000 isn't that high, relatively speaking. Suppose you sell 20 items a week—you'll get to 1,000 in a year, provided all your responses are positive—and provided all of your customers actually leave feedback, which doesn't always happen. Come up with a plan for how you can get to 20 sales per week: you need to obtain merchandise by scouring flea markets, auctions, or garage sales; consider enlisting the help of friends and relatives who can assist you with packing and shipping; come up with a weekly schedule and stick to it. Such a schedule would call for you to get your sales online, say, on Monday morning; end your sales on the following Monday; get a new batch of sales online late Monday; respond to bidders Monday night or Tuesday morning; ship out on Thursdays and Fridays; and so on. Also remember to remind your customers, after they have received the goods, to leave a feedback comment. Otherwise, they might well forget to do so. In fact, you should expect to have to remind your buyers to leave feedback—a large proportion don't bother to do so on their own.

4

Go By the Numbers

You need to establish a long-term "numbers goal" for your eBay sales. The moment you declare to yourself, "I'm going to have an 800 feedback rating by the end of the year," or "I want to be making $1,000 a month on eBay by the end of the year," your perspective changes. Individual sales become less important than your cumulative sales figures. Turning sales around quickly and keeping your customers satisfied becomes the top priority. Rather than focusing on this or that individual sale, you start thinking of coming up with a system, and building volume, with the ultimate goal of building profits.

Build Your Credibility

Most consumers have needs that are pretty straightforward. They want a reason to buy from you as opposed to all of those other sellers that populate eBay's auction listings. They want to feel they can trust you; they want to get what they pay for quickly. Above all, they are looking for a bargain. To some extent, you can't control whether they get a bargain or not. You put an item up for no reserve, or you set a modest reserve, and the market takes care of the rest.

You can, however, control how much trust your bidders can place in you. In many professions, service providers go to school to add some significant letters to their names, such as Ph.D., M.D., J.D., or C.P.A. You can do the same in auction sales. Bob Kopczynski, who's profiled later in this chapter, went to school and became a licensed auctioneer. You don't have to do that, yourself, but you can demonstrate that you know something about what you're selling. You can

■ Operate a Web site or online store devoted to your area of interest. Bob Kopczynski, who goes by the User ID maxwellstreetmarket on eBay, also has a Maxwell Street Market Web site (**http://www.maxwellstreet.market.com**), shown next.

■ Moderate a discussion group (popularly called a newsgroup) devoted to what you buy or sell. It's relatively easy to set up a newsgroup in the Alt category, though groups in other areas are difficult to establish and maintain. The Web page editor Microsoft FrontPage helps you set up a discussion group on your own Web site.

■ Answer questions on eBay's message boards.

■ Answer questions in Internet newsgroups about your area of interest.

4

If you have written any essays or books about the type of merchandise you typically sell, so much the better. Even if you don't do any of the foregoing, you can still create an About Me Web page that tells visitors something about you and what you do, and your commitment to customer service as well. Here, too, Bob Kopczynski provides a good example. His About Me page (see Figure 4-1) is as extensive as they come; it includes a history of his eBay business, a link to his Web site, a list of employees, a phone number, and terms of sales.

FIGURE 4-1   An About Me page can be used to build your credibility as an eBay businessperson.

Prove You Are a Professional

You can boost your sales if you are able to show people that you are professional in your manners and your behavior. Being professional doesn't mean you need to sell on eBay full-time, or that you need to run your own online business. Rather, it has to do with how you communicate—how quickly and completely you respond to questions from bidders, how well you deal with problems, and how promptly and carefully you pack and ship what you sell.

Be Honest, Be Thorough

The more information you provide about your auction item, the better your chances of getting bids.

Honesty is certainly the best policy when it comes to selling online in any venue, including eBay. At the very least, it lets buyers know about any defects or flaws your merchandise has before they even bid, so they won't be surprised when they actually receive what they've purchased. Accuracy shows your customers that you are making every effort to be honest and up-front with them. Some sellers go into a lengthy bit of detail about defects in their sales items, especially for items that they know are desirable in and of themselves. Once again, you can look to Bob Kopczynski's listings. The description shown in Figure 1-2 is honest about defects, but plays up the parts of the package that are in exceptionally good condition, too.

CAUTION   *Keep in mind that many of the individuals who buy your eBay items are professionals themselves. Often, they're longtime collectors or antique dealers who hope to resell your wares in their own stores. You can't fool people who are "in the trade," nor should you try to.*

Attract Bids with Information

The more information you include with your auction descriptions, the more likely you are to make a sale. That doesn't mean you have to spend acres of valuable computer screen real estate getting around to the point. You need to state, in the very first sentence, what it is you are selling and what qualities make this item stand out from the crowd. Be sure to mention that it is a one-of-a-kind piece, in perfect condition, or in a rare color. Try to get a one- or two-word mention of the item's most desirable quality in the auction title, if you can.

Auction bidders are in a hurry. They might only stop in at your sale for a short period of time before moving on to your competitors' wares. Suppose you're trying to sell something that might not seem desirable at first, like a pair of used

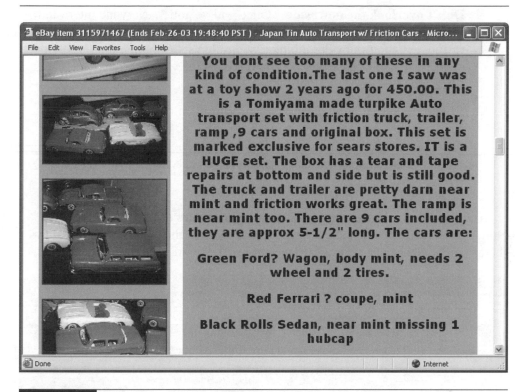

You dont see too many of these in any kind of condition.The last one I saw was at a toy show 2 years ago for 450.00. This is a Tomiyama made turpike Auto transport set with friction truck, trailer, ramp ,9 cars and original box. This set is marked exclusive for sears stores. IT is a HUGE set. The box has a tear and tape repairs at bottom and side but is still good. The truck and trailer are pretty darn near mint and friction works great. The ramp is near mint too. There are 9 cars included, they are approx 5-1/2" long. The cars are:

Green Ford? Wagon, body mint, needs 2 wheel and 2 tires.

Red Ferrari ? coupe, mint

Black Rolls Sedan, near mint missing 1 hubcap

FIGURE 4-2   Don't be reluctant to describe any defects, so purchasers won't be surprised.

sneakers. How, you ask, could you make sneakers seem attractive? Here are a few suggestions:

- **Lead with a hook**   Hook your bidders' attention with some quick statements that show why your item is exceptional, such as "Rare 1967 Chuck Taylor Converse All-Stars, Size 12."

- **Be a historian**   Describe your item's provenance—which, in auction-speak, means the history or origin of an item. Tell where you got the object, how old it is, who used it, and so on: "These classic high-top Chuck Taylors, in the hard-to-find red color, had only one owner—the seller's cousin. They show very little wear and even come in the original box."

- **Don't overlook the downside** Once you've gotten everyone interested by gushing about the item's good points, be sure to avoid surprises or misunderstandings by describing any problems: "Although thoroughly dry cleaned, a subtle basketball odor remains. Some wear on right heel; laces have been replaced."

- **Finish on a high note** Don't end on a problem note; provide a closing sentence that reminds people why they should be buying this wonderful item. You might even provide a note about payment options or shipping costs, or restrictions (you don't take personal checks, or you won't ship overseas, for instance).

You'll find some of these approaches in the brief sales description shown next. Notice how the description starts with a good mention, then describes some flaws ("brassing" means the gold overlay has worn off), then finishes on a positive note.

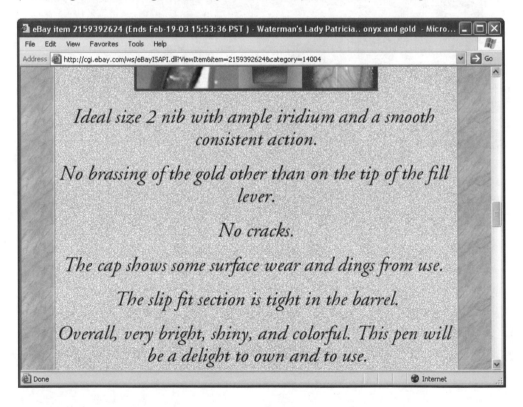

Throw in a Lagniappe

When I was in New Orleans, I went to some garage sales in the French Quarter and became acquainted with the wonderful local custom of the *lagniappe* (pronounced "lan-yap")—something extra that's thrown in along with the sale. Nothing builds goodwill with your customers like an extra touch you can add to your item(s) when you ship them out.

At least one of the sellers I interviewed, Don Colclough (who appears in Chapter 5), occasionally adds an extra item if one is available. "Sometimes we will sell a set of six glasses," he told me. "You can only sell them in groups of six. Even if you have seven of them, people just won't bid if you try to sell them all. If we sell a set of six, we will throw the seventh one in for free." If you sell dozens or even hundreds of items at a time, it might be impractical to throw in an extra gift with every sale. But if you can, consider doing so. You'll go a long way toward keeping your customers happy—not to mention getting some glowing feedback.

CAUTION *Attempts to get attention for auction listings by using the @@@ or !!!! keys multiple times are overused. I don't think they grab anyone's "eye space" because so many others use them. Let your description speak for itself.*

Build Your Volume

What does it mean to build a lot of sales? How do people build the volume that enables them to earn a steady income on eBay? You can find indications on eBay itself. Just find a seller you regard highly who has a high feedback rating, and look up the sales that have been conducted recently by that seller. For instance, to look up the completed sales by Bob Kopczynski, do the following:

1. Go to the eBay Basic Search page (**http://pages.ebay.com/search/items/ basicsearch.html**).

2. Click **By Seller**.

3. Enter the seller's User ID (maxwellstreetmarket) in the Single Seller box.

4. Next to "Include completed items," click the button next to the option that describes the number of auction sales you want to retrieve: Last Day, Last 2 Days, Last Week, Last 2 Weeks, or All.

5. Click the Search button. You are presented with a list of auctions recently completed by this busy seller, as shown here:

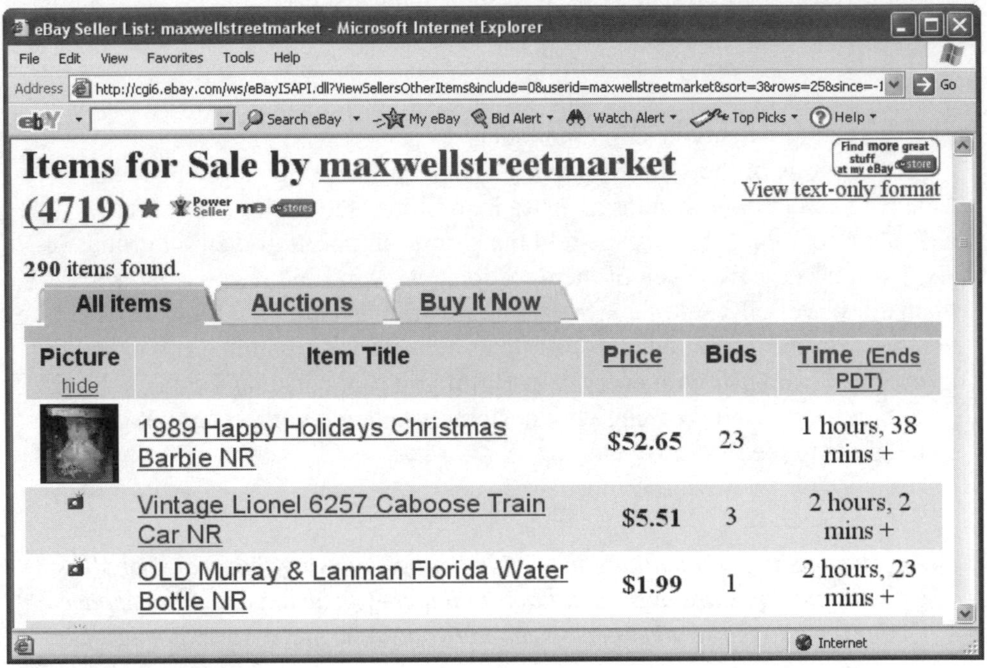

For instance, when I checked Bob's sales, I found that he completed anywhere from 20 to more than 50 sales per day. Most of these sales attracted bids; a few ended without attracting any bids, as indicated in Table 4-1.

Get Help from Family and Friends

Very few of the auction sellers I know who sell on eBay frequently do the work all themselves. Often, two people divide up the tasks: the buying, the carrying, the photography, the publishing, the shipping, and the bookkeeping.

Date	Sales Completed That Day	Sales with No Bids
2/14/03	26	3
2/15/03	21	1
2/16/03	34	11
2/17/03	52	7

TABLE 4-1   Bob Kopczynski's Sales Record

The moment you start to think in terms of selling hundreds or even thousands of items each year, you've got to think about getting assistance. Look first to your family: enlist your kids, your brothers and sisters, anyone who has time and is willing to help. Many sellers employ neighbors or college students who are home for summer vacation. Don't try to do it all yourself. Distributing your work load will keep you able to ship purchased items out quickly and enable you to remain courteous with your customers.

4

Use an Auction Manager

When you're trying to sell multiple items at once, it can be invaluable to enlist the help of an auction service: a business that assumes the responsibilities of managing your auctions for you. A program like Auction Helper (**http://www.auctionhelper .com**) sends notices and invoices to high bidders and maintains records of your sales so you can add up totals at tax time. You can find out more about using such services in Chapter 6.

TIP   *The eBay Services: Buying and Selling Tools page (**http://pages.ebay.com/ services/buyandsell/index.html**) contains links to services that can help manage your sales, such as Selling Manager. UK Auction Help (**http://www.ukauctionhelp.co.uk/sitemap.php**) provides a Web page full of tips for auction buyers and sellers alike, including suggestions on how to manage auctions and build volume.*

Schedule Your Sales

Experienced sellers know that, if you have an especially desirable item, it's likely to sell no matter when the auction ends. However, they also know that auctions that end when the majority of bidders are available are more likely to gain the highest prices. Here are some suggestions for when to schedule your auctions:

- Sales that end on weekends are more likely to get bids because many more bidders have the time to shop.

- Sales that end on Sundays—particularly, Sunday nights—tend to get more attention at the end of the sale.

- Some sellers start sales on Thursdays and schedule them to last for ten days: that way, they'll end on a Sunday, and bidders will have two weekends to shop and place bids.

Beware of any holidays like Memorial Day and Labor Day that might take place near the end of your sale: people who are traveling won't be able to bid, and you might not get as much attention for what you're selling.

CAUTION   *Be sure not to end the sale at a time when eBay is down for maintenance. Frequently, eBay goes offline around 3 A.M. PST on Friday mornings. (You'll find announcements of such system shutdowns at **http://www2.ebay.com/aw/ announce.shtml**.) If you attempt to end your sale then (this is more likely for overseas users than those in the United States), you should get a notice from eBay advising you to pick another time. Instead, you should be aware of the occasional maintenance and avoid Friday morning endings.*

eBay Bestsellers
Recapturing the Spirit of the Chicago Entrepreneur

Chicago, which is my home town, has a rich history as a center for manufacturing and commerce. Those of us who love to buy and sell treasures of all sorts benefit from that history. We fondly remember a place called the Maxwell Street Market, a huge open-air flea market where you could find virtually anything for sale, and which lives on in a smaller (not to mention cleaner) form every Sunday morning.

As a child, Bob Kopczynski used to visit Maxwell Street with his father. Today, he and his wife Katy keep a little bit of Chicago history alive with his eBay business, which goes by the User ID of maxwellstreetmarket. Bob, who works full-time as a construction manager and runs his eBay business in his off-hours, first became interested in eBay when he was looking for computer equipment and souvenirs related to the rock group Van Halen. Then, on a whim, he decided to sell a pair of tickets he had to the original Woodstock music festival held in 1969. "I said to myself, I'll put 'em for sale up there on eBay, and we'll just see what happens." Bob was immediately clued in to the promise of selling eBay when the tickets, which normally would have sold for $30 or $40, fetched a whopping $150 online. He convinced his wife Katy to start selling on eBay, put up $250 to get started, and the rest is history.

"When Don (Don Colclough, who is profiled in Chapter 5) and I started out, we were ridiculed," laughs Bob. "People thought we were crazy." Today, maxwellstreetmarket is very much an eBay business. Katy left her job as a schoolteacher three years ago. Now she works full-time at the business, handling bookkeeping and answering questions from buyers. Bob handles purchasing by scouring estate sales and flea markets and does photography. A neighbor, Nancy Armstrong, makes sure the sales go online. At least five Kopczynski family members help with crating, packing, cleaning, and the many other duties that are required to sell anywhere from 20 to 50 items per day on eBay.

The business has expanded along with the Kopczynskis' suburban Chicago home. First, Bob and Katy worked out of their basement. They made enough on eBay to build a pool and a deck. Then they had to build a garage just so they could store their eBay inventory (Bob calls it "the garage that eBay built"). Now, they rent warehouse space in several locations.

The Kopczynskis put a premium on credibility and customer service. They have built a steady income by putting customers first. "I have a goal to make people feel comfortable," Bob explains. "Eighty percent of people are still not comfortable with buying online, even though they love auctions. The big hurdle is, why would I send someone I don't know money? I set a goal to become a licensed state auctioneer; I have to take classes and pay $500 every year to keep my license. I sometimes do auction off high-end items like cars or boats on site, but 99 percent of my auction business is on eBay. I mention that I am a licensed auctioneer in my eBay listings, and I think that tells people they can rely on me. It's well worth the expense because it tells people I am well established."

The family's eBay operation is a business in many other ways. For one thing, it's part of KMK Management Co., Inc., Auctioneers and Estate Liquidators, a company of which Bob is President and CEO. Bob says one reason he decided to incorporate was liability; the corporation has limited liability if a customer decides to sue for some reason. "I pay a CPA to do our taxes, we do collect sales tax charged to Illinois residents. Besides that, we pay our employees' payroll taxes, too."

The businesslike emphasis pays off in customer relations. Bob and Katy don't run into too many deadbeat bidders. They estimate that only two to three percent of their customers fail to follow through with sales. More than 99 percent of the feedback they receive is positive. When they do run into problems with customers, they don't make a big deal about it. "We're not going to chase you if you don't pay us. We'll send you a couple of reminders, and then we tell eBay to pursue you. Then, we just wait 10 or 14 days and relist it."

The matter-of-fact approach to the business applies to sales, too. Bob has a policy of selling everything on a no-reserve basis—even highly desirable items for which he may have paid $100 or more. "I'll put up a Tiffany lamp at a starting bid of $1.99 with no reserve. Almost all of our auctions are conducted that way. The no-reserve policy quickly eliminates competition that sets an opening bid. My items tend to sell higher than ones with a reserve. Personally, when I'm shopping on eBay, I pass up any auction that has a reserve. You don't always get your cost back. You don't always make money on everything you sell. But it's a matter of volume and turnover—that's what counts. If you pay $200 for something and if it sits on a shelf for six or eight months, it's no good. Volume is the magic—better to get the money quickly and build up lots of sales."

Bob doesn't specialize in one particular type of item, although he personally collects vintage toys, radios, and musical instruments. He says he is "continually surprised by how much some things will bring. We even sell empty toy boxes—people who know what they are and who collect toys will pay for them."

Bob estimates, in fact, that a high percentage of his own customers are antique and collectible dealers who buy on eBay and resell items in their own brick-and-mortar stores. "I would like to have 90 percent collectors and dealers as my customers because they will pay a higher price, and they're not likely to turn out to be deadbeats."

In order to turn around 600 to 700 items a month, Bob uses an auction management service called Auction Helper (**http://www.auctionhelper.com**). "The auction management service does the shipping. They send an e-mail to the high bidder that says, "Click here to get your invoice and your seller's address." The buyer has a printable invoice with all of the details printed right on it."

Bob's number one tip to would-be eBay businesspeople? "Don't get hung up on making a ton of money on every single item," he says. "You have to let it go. Not everybody makes money on every investment. If you had brick and mortar store stuff, you'd run into losses too—something might get damaged, or your employees might take stuff. It's the same on eBay. You just have to let it go and move on to other sales."

Be Community-Minded

Why has eBay continued to grow and prosper while other online auction sites (not to mention a host of e-commerce retailers) have gone to that great Recycle Bin in the sky? It's not the ups and downs of the economy, which are always present. It's because of the strength of eBay's user community, and eBay's ability to build that community.

The eBay Community isn't simply a place where you can submit feedback and view feedback of other users. It's the best way (along with books like this) to get inside information from other experienced sellers—tips you'd need weeks or months to learn otherwise. You can also find out who your competition is by talking to other users and searching the message boards—and devise ways to stand out from the crowd—by being a group participant.

Share Information

You learn a lot about selling on eBay by talking to the entrepreneurs who already sell there. That might sound obvious, but working at a computer tends to be a solitary operation. (I'm speaking from experience.) After a few successful sales, you think you can do it all yourself, without anyone else's help.

You are likely to be cured of this notion the moment you scan the current messages on the eBay Café or on the product-specific message boards. You'll regularly find such seller-specific questions as "What do I do about this deadbeat bidder who…," "My bidder showed up and refused to pay for the ___ when he saw it," or "How do you handle 40 or 50 sales per week?"

In many ways, the best source of information about specific problems or situations you encounter on eBay is by consulting your fellow eBay users. You might also encounter eBay sellers while waiting in line at an estate sale, or in a crowd at an auction.

TIP   *Consider creating a name tag that says "eBay User" instead of your "real" name. Wear it to sales events such as auctions or flea markets. You just might meet some fellow eBayers with whom you can share tips and experiences.*

Know Your Competition

Why is it that when a gas station appears on one corner of a busy intersection, another one appears right across the street? They don't necessarily take business away from each other. In fact, they tend to draw people to the same area, and both outlets get more business than they otherwise would.

It's the same with auctions. Sure, you'll see others selling the same things you are in the same categories. Be happy for the crowded activity. If you were all alone in a category, would you get as many bids? Probably not.

How many times have you seen pages full of the same kinds of sales items, often with nearly identical descriptions? It can be instructive to look at how the sales are presented and to analyze which get the most bids—or any bids at all. For example, many vintage gloves go up for auction without getting any bids. Which of the listings in Figure 1-3 would you investigate if you were a buyer?

```
eBay Listings : Gloves - Microsoft Internet Explorer
File   Edit   View   Favorites   Tools   Help
Address  http://listings.ebay.com/pool3/plistings/list/all/category14075/page3.html?from=R11
```

	Vintage 24" Black leather gloves MINT *SEXY*	$21.50	3	3d 11h 02m
	GLOVES LADIES VINTAGE ACCESS*	$4.99	-	5d 10h 26m
	16 pair of Vintage gloves	$5.00	-	5d 09h 24m
	Lot of ladies' vintage leather, suede gloves	$5.00	-	5d 05h 28m
	RED~~~~HOT~~~ 3/4 length ~~~~RED GLOVES	$15.99	1	5d 03h 09m
	Burgundy Leather Gloves from France	$9.99 $18.00 [Ad]	-	5d 02h 59m

FIGURE 4-3   Study other sales and try to learn sellers' "trade secrets."

This isn't a scientific analysis by any means, but the gloves up for auction like those shown in Figure 4-3 seem to get bids if they have a good thumbnail photo next to them, and if descriptive words are included in the brief auction title such as "Sexy" or "Red Hot."

Another benefit of visiting the message boards on a daily basis is getting to know other sellers. It also pays to scout around the other sales in your area of interest after your sales go online, not only to make sure your sales are presented correctly and all of your images appear clearly, but to know if anyone is selling the same things you sell—and doing a better job of it than you are.

Relax, It's Only a Sale

When you begin to think in terms of making hundreds of sales rather than individual sales, and of selling on eBay for years to come rather than on a week-to-week basis, you don't take each sale so seriously. You'll benefit in the long run by not getting bogged down in problems and details, as described in the sections that follow.

Shed Your Reserve (Price, That Is)

You probably know from your own eBay buying that "no reserve" (usually designated NR) auctions get more attention than those with a reserve. Does that mean you should sell everything without a reserve? Different sellers take different approaches. When you're starting out, your impulse is to protect your investment with a reserve price on all your sales. Many sellers go no reserve for all sales except their most expensive. When my mother asked me to sell some of her antiques at auction, she insisted that I put a reserve price on them so she could be sure to recover what she had originally paid for the goodies.

However, when you're dealing in volume and turning your eBay sales activities into a business, it only makes sense to go with no reserve as often as possible—that is, for all sales except those items for which you originally paid a substantial amount.

Time and time again, auction sellers have told me that they get the most interest and the highest prices for items that they offered for little or no reserve. I once wrote about a woman who found a depression glass coaster at the bottom of an auction box full of other items. In other words, it cost her almost nothing. She put a reserve of $10 on it and an initial bid of $1. She ended up with more than 20 bids and the glass sold for more than $200.

Control When Your Auction Ends

Suppose that valuable porcelain lamp you just put up for sale takes a tumble off the shelf and shatters in bits on the concrete floor of your basement? Suppose your aunt, who gave you that painting to sell, suddenly decides to donate it to an art museum instead? In such cases you can cancel your sale. eBay provides you with a form that allows you to explain the reason for ending the sale early. The form lets you choose between canceling all bids or selling to the high bidder and canceling all other bids. After you fill out the form, an e-mail message is automatically sent to any bidders explaining that the sale was ended early.

On the other hand, you can also extend the end of your auction—if your item has not yet received any bids. Sometimes, when sellers conduct a three-day auction and their item does not receive any bids during those three days, they extend the auction one day. The moment a bid comes in, the auction must either end at the currently advertised time, or you must cancel it. Some sellers will list for 3 days, and if they get no bidders will extend the duration one increment at a time until they reach 10 days (this is done via the item revision link on the description page).

Control Your Emotions

You're bound to run into problems during your time as an eBay businessperson. Someone will e-mail you and leave negative feedback because they're not happy with what they purchased. Or the item you sent got lost or delayed in transit and your customer is understandably displeased. What's the best way to respond to such problems? Longtime sellers know it's best not to get emotionally involved. Even though you are involved in a person-to-person sale, this is a business transaction. Keep cordial at all times when you're communicating with someone who is unhappy. File a complaint in the Rules & Safety Support area (**http://pages.ebay.com/help/basics/select-RS.html**) and let eBay pursue those bidders who turn out to be deadbeats. Other than that, try to resolve disputes yourself in an effort to avoid negative feedback. Consider coming up with a stock response when you run into an unhappy camper. That way, bidders will get some money back, you keep your positive feedback, and you dodge a dispute:

> My Auction Company, Inc., puts costumer service first and is committed to keeping you happy. If you are unhappy with what you have purchased, we will refund your purchase, less a shipping fee.

> You can't give a refund to everyone who complains, of course—nor should you. I'm only saying that sometimes, it's better to resolve disputes yourself and write off a moderate financial loss once in a while.

NOTE *You can cancel someone's bid if you notice that they have received substantial amounts of negative feedback and have not followed through with other sales. If a bidder contacts you and asks to be taken out of the sale, or if he or she is located overseas and your description clearly states you will not ship overseas, you can also cancel a bid. When you do so, you should e-mail the individual to explain the reason for the cancellation. The bid cancellation form is located at **http://pages.ebay.com/services/buyandsell/seller-cancel-bid.html**.*

Resell Items When You Need To

If something doesn't attract any bids, or you had to cancel your auction early, or the bidders didn't meet your reserve price, simply wait a week or so and then relist the item. You can relist by returning to the completed auction page and clicking the link **Relist item**. You get a small bonus the first time you relist: If your item sells the second time around, eBay refunds you the Insertion Fee. If it doesn't sell the second time, however, you will have to pay the Insertion Fee.

> TIP
>
> *Don't simply repeat the original auction description when you relist something. Look around at other eBay sales descriptions of similar items and try to identify some adjectives that might generate excitement, or add some phrases that suggest how people might be able to use what you are trying to sell. Consider going no reserve, or lowering the opening bid price when you relist.*

4

Buy Strategically So You Can Resell

Once you've got the routine of selling down to a regular system, the big challenge isn't actually making sales on eBay. Rather, the challenge is finding merchandise you can resell. Many of the sellers I spoke to spend a considerable amount of time each week gathering merchandise at garage sales, flea markets, estate sales, auctions— wherever they can find it. As anyone who has tried to make a purchase at a conducted sale (a sale of someone's possessions that is conducted by a professional dealer rather than the homeowner) knows, such sales are likely to have great bargains, but the competition for them is fierce. Often, you have to stand in line for hours before the sale opens just so you can have a chance at finding treasures. If a sale opens at 9 A.M., for instance, you might have to get in line at 6 A.M., 5 A.M. . . . who knows?

There aren't many tricks to obtaining inventory you can resell online. It requires a lot of commitment and "sweat equity." Here are a few suggestions I've discovered in my own bargain hunting over the years and from talking to eBay sellers:

- **Don't do it alone**   If you work as a team, you can find more merchandise than you could alone. You'll also have help hauling away what you buy. Some sellers hire college students to go to sales before the sun is up and wait in line for them; they show up at a more reasonable hour, ready for the hunt.

- **Buy off-season**   Often, resale shops have plenty of winter clothes in spring and fall, and summer clothes in winter, for the simple reason that most people don't need them at that time. Buy off-season and store your inventory so you can sell it at a time when most of your customers will actually want it.

- **Become a dealer yourself**   If you become a licensed auction seller or if you are an antique dealer, put out advertisements suggesting that people who are retiring or moving out have you conduct their house sale. You never know—you might be able to find a bargain or two for yourself.

- **Try dollar stores**   One of the most interesting trends in the world of bargain hunting is the proliferation of stores that sell all, or most, of their wares for a dollar of less. All too often, the shelves are full of junk, but once in a while, you can find pop culture memorabilia or good books you can pick up for a bargain.

- **Join a warehouse club**   Costco, Sam's Club, and other warehouse stores deal in volume; sometimes you can find DVDs or computer games at two-for-one promotions at these brick-and-mortar discount warehouses.

- **Look for bargains online**   Some discount outlets hold their own online auctions, and you should definitely check them out. The Sam's Club auction page shown in Figure 4-4 (**http://auctions.samsclub.com**) is a great place to find bargains you can resell on eBay. You can shop online at Costco (**http://www.costco.com**) and at other bargain outlets like the 99¢ Only stores Web site (**http://www.99only.com**).

> **TIP**   *Know when the garbage pickup days are for your own neighborhood and any neighborhoods where people who are well-off live. Be sure you start scouring alleys either the night before or early in the morning on garbage day. I, personally, am not above "garbage picking" or "dumpster diving" in order to uncover bargains that others are discarding. For a primer on this popular activity, read the online diary "Dumpster diving: an Introduction" at* **http://www.kuro5hin.org/story/2003/1/29/215523/088**.

Drum Up Some Free Advertising

Everyone who sells online needs to drum up business by doing some form of marketing and advertising. By choosing to sell on eBay, you take a big step toward getting lots of attention for you and your merchandise. You can go even further by marketing your eBay sales.

For example, you might include links to your eBay Store, your About Me page, or to a specific sale in a posting you leave in an Internet newsgroup that's related to what you are selling. That's how I first found out eBay ever existed, back in the mid-1990s. I subscribed to a newsgroup for individuals who collect and sell antique

FIGURE 4-4   Shop online at warehouse clubs to find bargains you can resell.

fountain pens. In the course of reading postings, I frequently saw listings by dealers that contained links to pens they had up for auction on eBay. I clicked one of the links, and instantly became an eBay junkie.

Link to Your Web Site, and Vice Versa

If you have a Web site, whether it catalogs the members of your family or the items your business has for sale, use it to promote your eBay auction listings. Selling on eBay is a remarkably personal activity. Buyers remember sellers, and if they have a good experience with you, they are quite likely to check you and your sales out once in a while to see what you have to offer. Many eBay sellers include links to their eBay auctions on their Web sites, and their auction listings or eBay Stores/About Me pages include links back to their Web sites.

If you have a business card, include it with the items you ship out, and make sure it includes your Web site URL as well as your e-mail address and other contact information.

Where to Find It

■ **eBay Services: Buying and Selling Tools**
http://pages.ebay.com/services/buyandsell/index.html
Links to services such as Selling Manger, and to pages where you can revise
your item description, cancel an auction, cancel a bid, or relist an item.

■ **UK Auction Help**
http://www.ukauctionhelp.co.uk/sitemap.php
A Web page full of tips for auction buyers and sellers alike.

■ **eBay System Announcements board**
http://www2.ebay.com/aw/announce.shtml
Announcements of times when eBay will be offline for maintenance.

Chapter 5

Spruce Up Your Auction Presentation

How to…

- Create a sales template so you can produce multiple auctions quickly
- Attract bids with descriptions that engage shoppers' imaginations
- Research your merchandise so you can describe it accurately
- Check your spelling so you don't look unprofessional
- Take time with your presentation to build bidders' interest
- Format auction listings with HTML to grab more attention
- Add a counter to your auction listing
- Choose design templates with eBay Seller's Assistant

Unlike personal or family Web pages, auction listing pages aren't primarily about you. They don't need to be graphically eye-catching. You don't need to impress anyone with your design sense or even your sense of coolness. Your primary goal is to induce people to bid—as often as possible—and to eventually make a sale. Yet, a few well-chosen words and some good images can make the difference between zero bids and a "Hot Match" icon, which signifies a sale that's received avid attention.

Auction listings are a little like personal ads in their presentation. You want to stand out from a crowd through good photos, quick descriptions, and a few choice words. You're trying to get viewers to explore a little further by engaging their imaginations, by giving them just enough information to get them to discover a little more about what's being advertised.

You can also use your auction presentations to create an identity for your eBay business. Just as you try to build credibility through a good feedback rating and professional handling of sales, you can do it through your choice of colors, the name of your business, and a consistent presentation. This chapter examines ways to give your eBay auction pages some "razzamatazz" while streamlining the process of getting your auctions online.

Create a Sales Template

When you use eBay's Sell Your Item form, you are essentially filling in the blanks. You're putting standard information into a standard format so you can get the basic information online.

There's nothing wrong with using the Sell Your Item form to create an auction listing, but a successful eBay business is built on volume and efficiency. Suppose you get to the point where—like many of the sellers I profile in this book—you need to get 20, 30, or even more items online every day. If that's the case, you need to come up with a system—or rather, a *template*.

A template is commonly used to prepare a publication that appears periodically, such as a newspaper or a magazine. It's a preformatted set of items that appears the same from issue to issue. A template saves time, and it lets readers know what to expect. After a while, they use the standard elements in the template to process information more quickly.

Many eBay sellers create an auction template in the form of a HyperText Markup Language (HTML) Web page. The template contains the name of their business (if they have one), their shipping and payment policies, and any other phrases that apply to all of their auctions. I've taken the liberty of altering one of the auction listings of eBay seller mrmodern, who is profiled in this chapter, and showing it in Figure 5-1.

The beauty of a template is that your auction listing is actually half-complete before you even start. After you've taken your photos (see Chapter 8) and researched your item (see "Do Your Research" later in this chapter), simply paste the material that is unique to each sales item (the name, the description, and the links to images) into the template. You simply upload the pages, reopen their original template file, and paste in the descriptions that apply to the next sales item.

> **NOTE**   *eBay has a service called Seller's Assistant that streamlines the process of creating templates. See "Use eBay Seller's Assistant" later in this chapter for more information.*

In Figure 5-1, I've drawn a big X to mark the spot where the unique description and photos should appear in the template. mrmodern's template has another formatting trick: it's been formatted as an HTML table, a container that allows Web page contents to be arranged in the form of rows and columns. In this case, the table serves two functions. First, it keeps the auction listing at a fixed width so it's easier to read; it takes up a single column in the middle of the page. Second, the table has been divided into two rows. The first row sets the MrModern logo apart from the text beneath it. Tables are useful ways to organize the contents of Web pages and gain some control over how they turn out.

> **TIP**   *One of the first tutorials on HTML is still one of the best. Beginner's Guide to HTML (**http://archive.ncsa.uiuc.edu/General/Internet/WWW/ HTMLPrimerAll.html**) includes information on tables and how to use them to design Web pages.*

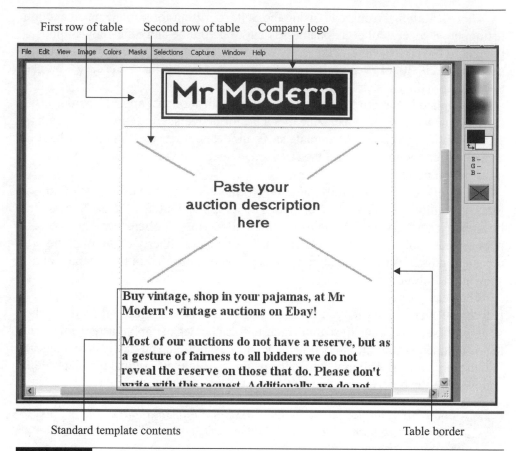

First row of table   Second row of table   Company logo

Standard template contents   Table border

FIGURE 5-1   A template lets you create auctions quickly in "cookie cutter" fashion.

Consider Getting Some Design Help

The Web was made for do-it-yourselfers. You can publish your own photos, text, and Web pages in no time. But just because you *can* do something on your own doesn't mean that it's a good idea. When you're just starting out with an eBay business, it pays to spend a little time (and possibly a little money) designing a template.

Since you're going to be online for years, and you're probably going to sell hundreds or perhaps even thousands of items, a few hundred dollars paid to a designer at the beginning will pay off in the long run. The single best investment you can make is the few hundred dollars it will probably cost to create a logo for your business. You can use it not only on your auction pages but on business cards and stationery you have made.

It's worth securing the services of a professional designer for this purpose. The designer can create a consistent look for your business that includes the look of your auction listings. The look of your logo and your use of color and other design elements can complement what you sell and tell people that you are committed not only to customer service, but to obtaining quality items. The Silk Road Trading Concern's auction listings, one of which is shown in Figure 5-2, are a perfect example.

The business name shown in Figure 5-2 is a textual logo. It's difficult to create such a logo without the help of sophisticated graphics software like Adobe Photoshop (**http://www.adobe.com**). It might be difficult to tell from Figure 5-2, but each Silk Road auction listing has a background image that seems to "float" behind the text and images. Such background images are another feature of HTML that you can use in your eBay auction listings. This particular auction listing uses an HTML table that the page designer has configured to have invisible borders for the layout, but it does include nice designs in each corner that are derived from the Tibetan "endless knot" design and that complement what's being sold. A consistent, professional appearance like this has a direct bearing on how many bids you get.

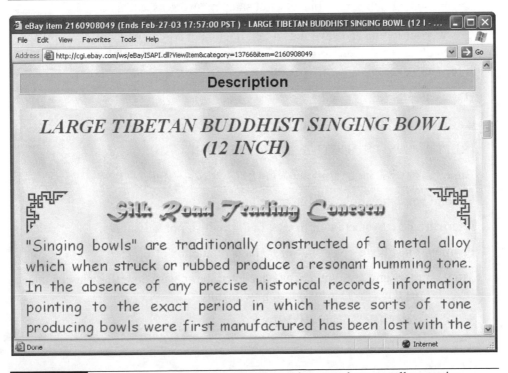

FIGURE 5-2   Your use of color and type can complement what you sell at auction.

TIP *Many of the graphic designers who advertise their services on the eBay-affiliated site eLance (**http://www.elance.com**) specialize in creating logos and developing graphic designs for businesses.*

Pick Standard Items

Once you have come up with a "look and feel" for your auction listings—one that might include a background, colors, graphics, and a logo—you need to add the parts of the template that you want to be the same from listing to listing. In the world of publishing, this sort of content is called *boilerplate*. This text might include

- The name of your business

- Your shipping options

- Your payment options

- Your contact information

- Any additional statements about your policies, such as money-back guarantees, not selling to first-time bidders, not shipping overseas, and so on.

Create your listing and save it as a text document so you can simply copy and paste the contents from auction to auction. Your auction boilerplate might look like the following:

Higher Grounds

Coffee Collectibles for Cost-Conscious Collectors

[REPLACE WITH AUCTION DESCRIPTION]

Buyer to pay $7.50 for shipping via USPS Priority Mail.

Ground shipping also available on request

International customers will pay extra air mail shipping charges.

Payment must be received within 10 days of auction closing.

Money orders and personal checks accepted, but please note that checks take seven to ten days to clear before item will ship.

We also accept BidPay and PayPal.

Illinois residents will be responsible for an additional 8.75% sales tax.

Feel free to e-mail us with questions. We will be happy to provide additional information as needed.

If you decide to use HTML formatting to present your auction, include the necessary HTML commands (which are called *tags*) right in the body of the listing. (See "Using HTML to Dress Up Items" later in this chapter.) You can also use a program that gives you the option of editing the visible contents of Web pages as well as the HTML code, such as Macromedia Dreamweaver or Microsoft FrontPage.

5

Add the Description

Once you have a template and boilerplate, you need to come up with what you might call the "silverplate" part of your listing: the actual description that applies to the merchandise itself. You do this by opening the Sell Your Item form:

1. From just about any part of the eBay site, click the **Sell** button in the navigation bar at the top of the page.

2. Sign in as a seller and create a seller account if you need to (see Chapter 3).

3. When the Sell Your Item form appears, fill it out. Paste your template into the Description box in the form (shown in Figure 5-3). Then add the details specific to the item you are listing, and put your sale online. You can use some tricks when you're creating the contents of your description to make your sale more attractive to bidders, such as imaginative words and good images, as described in the sections that follow.

TIP   *Auction listings don't have to be completely unique. Although it's not a good idea to completely copy someone else's description and paste it into your own listing, you can use good descriptions as a "starting point" for creating your own if you are tired or in a hurry. Auction descriptions, like other Web publications, are protected by copyright, as described in Chapter 18. However, the truth is that plenty of eBay sellers "reuse" one another's descriptions as a shortcut even though it's not technically correct. You can at least shop around other descriptions to get inspirations and tips for their own listings.*

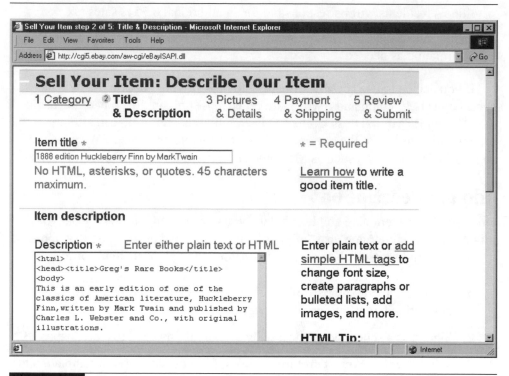

FIGURE 5-3   Paste your auction template into the Description box in the Sell Your Item form.

Fine-Tune Your Descriptions

A picture may be worth a thousand words, and good images are perhaps the most important elements you can use to grab someone's attention and get them to click that all-important Place Bid button. The way you describe your sales item is important, too. You can take a lesson here from the big, traditional auction houses such as Sotheby's (whose online version, Sothebys.com, is described in detail in Chapter 15). Staff people at such institutions (or sellers who register as Sales Associates) often painstakingly research the history of what they're selling and present detailed descriptions both in their sales catalogs and in their live auctions. An example is shown in Figure 5-4.

The example in Figure 5-4 shows that descriptions don't have to be long to be effective. Rather, a little background about what you're selling and a few telling details count for a lot. Some ways to spice up your own descriptions are presented

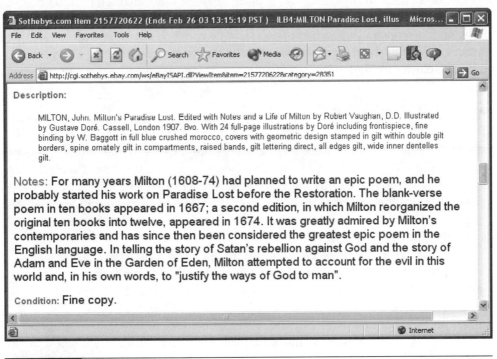

FIGURE 5-4   Some history and background on what you're selling can attract bidders' interest.

in the sections that follow. All it takes is some research, some imagination, and some attention to detail.

Do Your Research

Occasionally, you'll run into bidders who know far more about what you're selling than you do. The merchandise practically sells itself because this is what your customers have been looking for. You might be able to sell an empty toy box for hundreds of dollars if it's the box to a toy that someone needs to fill out his or her collection.

Most often, though, your sales need a little "push" from you in the form of information. Information sells on eBay. Before you put something up for sale, do some research online and find out everything you can about what you're selling. Tell people when the item was made, whether or not it is considered rare, and anything else you can uncover.

The eBay seller mrmodern, who is profiled later in this chapter, told me he keeps one computer screen open to prepare his auction listings, and another open to the search service Google (**http://www.google.com**). While he creates his auction listings, he can find out details about what he's selling and pass them along, as indicated earlier in Figure 5-4.

Generate Excitement

If you can generate some excitement among shoppers and get them to visualize how they might use or enjoy something, you're more likely to gain bids. This isn't just something that's well known on eBay. Some online catalog sites (in particular, Lands End, **http://www.landsend.com**) let customers virtually "try on" clothing on a 3-D model they make of their own bodies. Put yourself in your bidders' shoes (or gloves, as you'll see in a moment), and encourage them to want to wear, use, or simply enjoy what you have to sell.

Your goal as an auction seller is to capture, in a few sentences, what makes your object unique or interesting. I admit, you can't do this for every single item you try to sell. (How exciting can you make a matched set of drawer handles, for instance?) But if you can pick a few choice descriptive words for some of your sales, you'll do better overall. Suppose you turn up a set of old bathroom lights that you want to sell. How can you make them seem interesting? Here's how mrmodern described them:

> Here is a great pair of Streamline Art Deco chrome and milk glass bathroom wall sconces. The lights are made to mount on either side of a mirror and each have an outlet on the bottom. The chrome backplates are 15" long by 2.5" wide. The milk glass tubes are 12" long by 2" in diameter. Both tubes have the chrome ring cap. Good chrome throughout…One tube is perfect, but the other has a chip and crack 1" up from the end. Turned to the back, the chip cannot be seen. Best bet is to have them shortened 1" so the chip and crack will be gone. The shades will still extend ¼" beyond the top edge of the backplate…Either way they are a great pair or original 1930s wall lights.

The thing I notice about this description is that some effort has been put into suggesting how the lights can be used, what can be done with them, and where they might go in a house. It's not just a straight description of what the items are and how big they are. When I last looked, the lights had attracted a bid of $101.

Use Your Dictionary

Buyers on eBay are often wary of sellers to begin with. Unless they know you and trust you, they might doubt that they can rely on you to follow through on your end of the deal. Anything you can do to make yourself look more professional helps your chances of getting more bids. For that reason, you should spell check your auction descriptions before you put your sale online. You might even have a Web browser window open to the dictionary Web site, Dictionary.com (shown in Figure 5-5), so you can look up troublesome words while you are doing the work. Check your spelling.

There's another, more obvious reason for checking your spelling before your sale goes online: you don't want to get facts and figures wrong. You don't want to turn $250 into $2500 or 25$0, for instance. A spell-checker won't catch a numerical

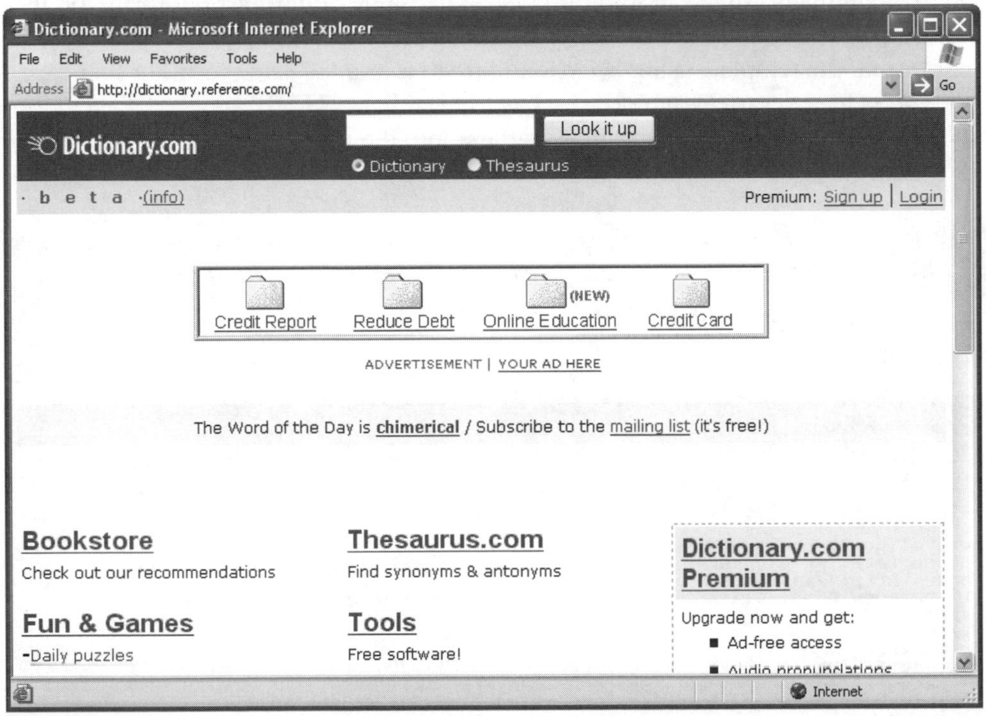

FIGURE 5-5   If you don't check your spelling, you might appear unprofessional or careless.

error like this, so there's no substitute for proofreading your description carefully before it goes online. Read it out loud so you can slow down and catch errors more easily.

Using HTML to Dress Up Items

Part of calling attention to your auction items is the ability to direct the eyes of busy, hurried shoppers toward the most important parts of your sales descriptions. That's where HTML comes in. HTML is the set of commands that's used to format all of the pages you enjoy not only on eBay but on the rest of the World Wide Web. By using HTML to format headings in bold or large type, you can call attention to the name of an item or an especially important feature, such as its age or condition.

To get HTML formatting in your auction descriptions, you simply type the HTML commands in the Description box in the same Sell Your Item form you use to create your auction. If you use a template to present lots of auction listings, you can format the template using HTML and paste it into the same form. In that case, it's a good idea to save the template as a text file with the HTML commands' includes, so you can copy the contents and paste them into the form. An example is shown in Figure 5-6.

TIP *eBay's Help page that describes how to use HTML in auction listings is located at **http://pages.ebay.com/help/sell/html_tips.html**.*

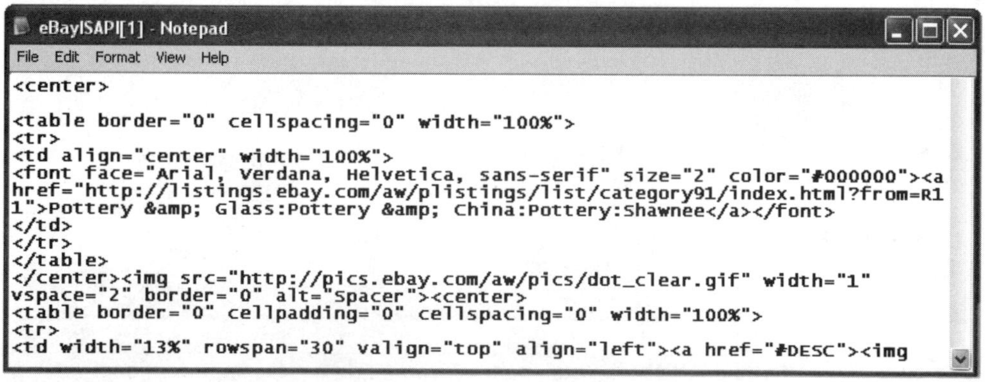


```
<center>

<table border="0" cellspacing="0" width="100%">
<tr>
<td align="center" width="100%">
<font face="Arial, Verdana, Helvetica, sans-serif" size="2" color="#000000"><a
href="http://listings.ebay.com/aw/plistings/list/category91/index.html?from=R1
1">Pottery &amp; Glass:Pottery &amp; China:Pottery:Shawnee</a></font>
</td>
</tr>
</table>
</center><img src="http://pics.ebay.com/aw/pics/dot_clear.gif" width="1"
vspace="2" border="0" alt="Spacer"><center>
<table border="0" cellpadding="0" cellspacing="0" width="100%">
<tr>
<td width="13%" rowspan="30" valign="top" align="left"><a href="#DESC"><img
```

FIGURE 5-6 Save your template in text format so you can copy and paste the contents.

HTML: The One-Minute Version

This isn't a book about HTML and formatting Web pages—there are many other books on those subjects, not to mention Web sites, tutorials, classes, and videotapes—so I'm not going to go into great detail on what HTML is or how to format a Web page using HTML. I will, however, give you a one-minute overview so you know what I'm talking about in this chapter.

> **TIP** *If you want to learn more about HTML, consult the Osborne-McGraw Hill books* HTML: A Beginner's Guide, *by Wendy Willard,* How to Do Everything with HTML, *by James Pence, or* HTML: The Complete Reference, *by Thomas Powell.*

HyperText Markup Language (HTML) is the set of commands (called tags) that are used to *mark up* text or images so they can be displayed on the Web. Using HTML commands, a Web browser will be able to display the following text as bold:

```
<B>This text is bold.</B>
```

The following text will be displayed in Heading 1 format:

```
<h1>This is a Web page heading</H1>
```

You can make a reference to a JPEG image using the following HTML so a Web browser can display it on your page:

```
<IMG SRC="image.jpg">
```

How, exactly, do you create all these nifty HTML tags? You have two options: the hard way and the easy way. The hard way is to enter all the tags by typing them manually into a text document. This requires you to actually learn HTML, or at least, to copy the tags from a book or Web site and apply them to your own purposes.

The easy way is to use a software program called a Web page editor. Such a program shields from having to create or actually see the HTML commands you create. Rather, you click buttons, choose menu options, and make use of other graphically friendly elements to format Web pages. Two of the best programs are Dreamweaver by Macromedia Inc. (http://www.macromedia.com) and Microsoft FrontPage (http://www.microsoft.com/frontpage).

The problem with using such Web page editors, from the standpoint of eBay, is that you eventually have to look at the raw HTML commands when you paste them into the Sell Your Item form. Even if you create and format a nice template using one of these programs, you'll need to choose a command such as View Source or View Code to view the HTML commands, copy them, and paste them into the auction description form.

Of course, you don't have to use HTML at all to format your auction listings. But if you want to create a business identity and stand out from the crowd, a little formatting is all you need.

TIP   *An easy-to-use and reliable program called Virtual Auction Ad Pro by Virtual Notions (**http://www.virtualnotions.com**) will also help you generate formatted auction ads without having to learn HTML.*

Making Your Auction Count with a Counter

One of the most popular features that eBay sellers add to their auction listings (besides images and text, that is) is a *counter*—a utility that records the number of visits that are made to that auction listing. A counter sits on an auction page (or on any Web page) and records the number of times the page has been viewed. It doesn't tell you who is viewing those pages, or whether each of the visits recorded is by a unique viewer. A counter that records 10 visits, for example, might only record visits by two individuals—one who has seen the page nine times and one who has visited just once.

A counter that indicates to visitors that a page has been visited a high number of times indicates to people that there must be a lot of interest in the item, and suggests that they may want to place a bid themselves. On the other hand, if a counter has a low number, it may turn people away. If it has a high number of visits but just a handful of bids, it might even suggest that there's something wrong with the item being sold— or that bidders are biding their time and preparing to bid at the very last minute.

To my mind, counters only have limited value, whether on an auction page or a regular Web page. They're more of a curiosity than a marketing tool. A type of counter that makes sense to me is a *private counter*—one that doesn't actually appear on the auction listing itself but is only visible to the auction seller. The easiest way to get either a private counter or a visible one is to choose an option from the counter options at the bottom of page 3 of the eBay Sell Your Item Form. Other private counters are available from a number of different sources, and many of them are free. Of course, you have to sign up with the auction service that provides you the counter, and that includes the one provided by ManageAuctions.com and shown in Figure 5-7.

You can go a step further and install a counter provided by Andale.com that provides detailed information about when your auctions were viewed each day and how many times they were viewed . During the process of registering to use the counters, you can uncheck a box so you won't receive unsolicited e-mail from Andale.com. You can go to **http://www.andale.com/corp/products/track.jsp** to find out more about installing Andale.com's counters.

5

Auction Site: eBay.com;   Seller ID: charles927;   Item #: 220694467

Day\Hour	00	01	02	03	04	05	06	07	08	09	10	11	12	13	14	15	16	17	18	19	20	21	22	23
12/14/1999																								1
12/15/1999	2				1	1			1		1	2			1	1	3	2	4	3		2	2	1
12/16/1999					1	1				1				1			1		1	4	2			
12/17/1999						4			2					2				2	1			2		
12/18/1999	1	1							1			1		1	1	2	2		1		1			1
12/19/1999						1				1	2			1				1			2	1		
12/20/1999						1		3	2				2			7	5	1		2	2		3	2
12/21/1999				3	2	2	3	1	1	4	3	1	1	1	1		1	2		2				
12/22/1999						1			1	1	2	1					1	3		7	1			2
12/23/1999	1			3	2		3	4	2	4	4	12	2	11	5	7	11	14	13	6	12	14	10	9
12/24/1999	6	1			2	7	8	5	10	6	5		8	10	10	7	8	11	21	22	20	27		4
Totals	10	2	0	3	6	8	18	18	11	20	19	24	7	22	20	27	30	29	35	40	47	41	44	20

We offer a variety of counter styles, including a confidential type (with hidden number but visible icon), as illustrated below:

0123456789   0123456789

0123456789   0 1 2 3 4 5 6 7 8 9

FIGURE 5-7   A private counter is only visible to the seller who installs it.

TIP

*CQ Counter, which comes in both a free version that requires banner ads to be displayed on your site or an ad-free version that costs $19.95 per year, goes a step beyond simply recording the number of times your page has been viewed. It reports on the sites that your visitors come from before they view your pages, how many times your pages have been reloaded, and the IP addresses (an identifying series of four numbers that is assigned to every computer connected to the Internet) of your visitors' computers. Find out about it at **http://cqcounter.com**.*

eBay Bestsellers
Making a Good Presentation

Image is important to Don Colclough (eBay User Id: mrmodern). For one thing, he wants his eBay customers to know that he will solve any problems that arise, and that customer service is paramount to him. Don Colclaugh and Lisa Polito have gained control of their own lives through selling on eBay. They are able to set their own schedules thanks to their eBay business. They don't have to commute to work; they can work on their own schedule; they run their own work space, too.

"I've been selling on eBay since April 1999," says Don. "By September of that year we had sold our antique store and moved out. It was beating a dead horse." He and Lisa found a 3,000 square foot space in a former bank building in Oak Park, just west of Chicago, where they set up their full-time eBay business. That's where the Don and Lisa store their inventory and work on their three-computer network, keeping a regular business routine even though they don't work the conventional 9 A.M. to 5 P.M. schedule.

"We go to work five days a week, from 1 P.M. to 9 P.M.," says Don. "Every day at 4 P.M. UPS picks up our outgoing shipments. At 4:30 I make a run to the post office. We mostly ship UPS because it's simpler for the delivery guy to simply load everything on the truck. But for smaller items we use the post office. Then we take a break to eat. After that we work from 5:30 to 9 P.M., putting items up for sale on eBay. Lisa writes all the sales tickets and does all the paperwork. During the summer, we have young men in college who work for us and help us writing auctions."

Besides the time spent in their office-warehouse space, Don and Lisa, like many other eBay sellers, spent countless hours waiting outside estate sales and hauling home the treasures they've gathered. You have to run your eBay sales like a business in order to build volume, Don advises. "We closed 200 auctions this past month, and we have six months worth of inventory stored up at any one time. There are times when we buy an item at 7 o'clock in the morning and we have it up for sale that same afternoon."

The businesslike system applies to the way sales are presented online. Initially, Don developed a basic auction format with a standard choice of type fonts and colors, and standard statements about payment and shipping. Once the basic format was set, he and his coworkers only had to type up individual descriptions and paste them into the preset format.

"When I write an auction, I am pretty cut and dried about it. I just give the size, general condition, rarity. If it is something special, I will do a little research to find out some of the history of the item, and tell bidders something about it. When Lisa writes an auction, she caters to the Martha Stewart crowd, and she tends to be a bit more decorative and descriptive; she tells people how they might use a particular item. It stimulates the brain of the reader, and encourages them to make a bid."

Photos are an essential part of any auction description. "I'm not averse to putting 15 pictures online," he says. "We keep photos pretty small, perhaps a quarter of the size of the average computer screen. We try to include a range of photos, showing every aspect of an item, from every angle."

Don and Lisa specialize in twentieth-century furnishings, household items, and collectibles of all sorts. He fondly recalls the unusual items he has sold—such as a prosthetic leg for $430—but the most unusual sale was that of a complete pharmacy. The pharmacy, which was located at Elston and California Avenues in Chicago, was sold by Don and his friend Bob Kopczynski (who is profiled in Chapter 4). "We sold the complete pharmacy for $13,000 to a man who was opening a gift store in Jackson Hole, Wyoming," says Don. "It wasn't a bad deal for him, considering that it might cost as much as $200,000 to outfit a complete store from scratch. We had to work back and forth a bit with the buyer to arrange the shipping; it cost $3500."

Don's biggest tip to new eBay sellers is the importance of following through quickly when sales are completed. "Don't delay the shipping. There's no need to delay, especially when you use PayPal. Try to get the merchandise out the next day. People are often flabbergasted at how fast our shipping is. If someone sends us a personal check and we see that they have 500 feedbacks and they are all positive, we won't wait until the check clears to ship, either."

It's a strategy that's kept the amount of negative feedback to a minimum (at this writing he and Lisa had 3,269 positive feedback comments and 26 negatives).

5

In general, Don reports, all his dealings with eBay users tend to be positive—only two or three percent of his sales turn up deadbeat bidders.

"First, give us the opportunity to resolve the problem. We will resolve it. We made a form that we include with every completed auction. It says, 'We hope you are happy with your item. If you are not happy, here is our toll-free number—give us a call.' We give them a money-back guarantee, too."

The high level of service has a direct result in repeat business "I know people check us every day to see what we put online," he says happily.

Use eBay Seller's Assistant

Many of the approaches to making your auctions stand out from the crowd that I've already described in this chapter are included in two utilities provided by eBay itself. These utilities, Seller's Assistant Basic and Seller's Assistant Pro, are designed to help you get your photos online and give your auction descriptions graphic interest.

From the standpoint of graphic presentation, Seller's Assistant Basic and Pro both provide you with a variety of templates you can use to present your sales items. Each template has its own graphic design. Unfortunately, you can't get a look at these designs without subscribing to the monthly service. You can try out either the Basic or Pro versions free for 30 days, but after that eBay begins charging you ($4.99 per month for Basic and $15.99 for Pro) unless you cancel. Just follow these steps:

1. Go to the eBay Seller's Assistant page (**http://pages.ebay.com/sellers_assistant/index.html**) and click **Subscribe Now**.

2. When the Seller's Assistant Subscription page appears, fill in your User ID (if necessary; it may already be filled in) and password, and click **Sign In**.

3. When the eBay Seller's Assistant Subscription page appears, click **Subscribe** next to the version of Seller's Assistant that you want.

4. Read the User Agreement, and then click *I Accept*.

5. Click **Download Seller's Assistant Basic** (or Seller's Assistant Pro, depending on the version you have chosen).

6. When the File Download box appears, click **Open**. The file downloads to your hard disk.

7. When download is complete, the InstallShield Wizard opens automatically. Follow the steps shown in the wizard to install Seller's Assistant.

8. Start up Seller's Assistant by clicking Start | Programs (All Programs on Windows XP) | eBay | Seller's Assistant Basic.

9. When the License Agreement window appears, read the License Agreement, then click **I Agree.** You may have to insert your original Microsoft Office CD-ROM in order to update the software.

10. The Seller's Assistant program leads you through a series of initial setup tasks. When you're done, the program window opens (see Figure 5-8).

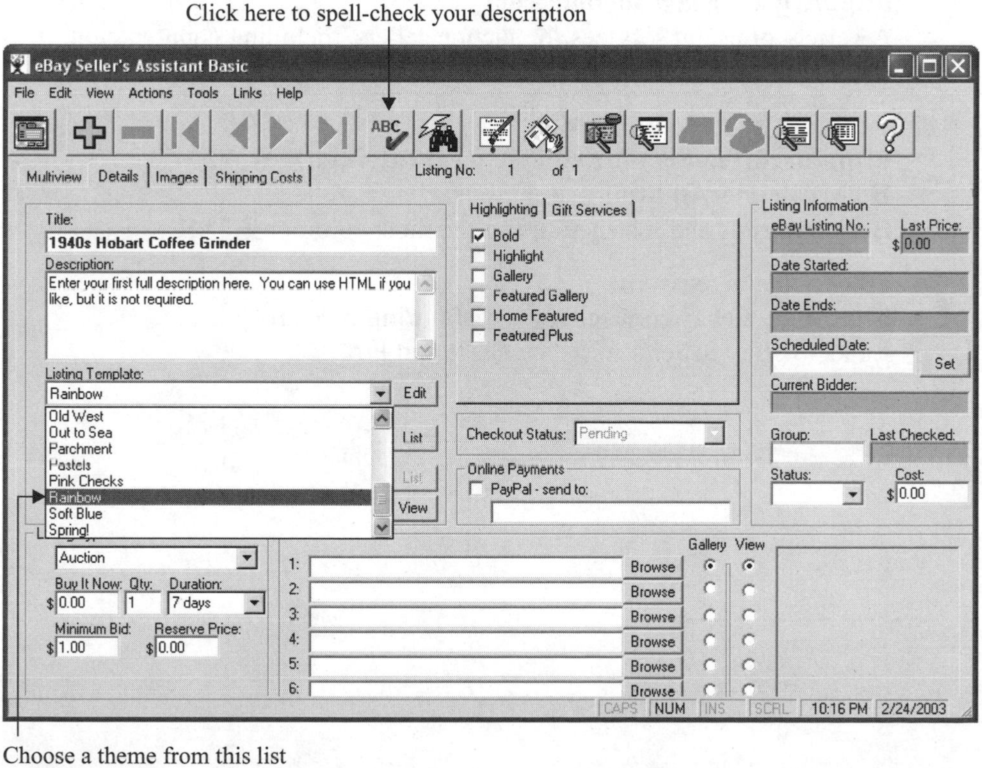

Click here to spell-check your description

Choose a theme from this list

FIGURE 5-8 Seller's Assistant lets you choose a graphic theme and spell check your listings.

Seller's Assistant comes with a set of 20 built-in themes; you preview them by clicking the Edit button next to the drop-down list of themes in the Seller's Assistant window.

NOTE *Seller's Assistant Pro does carry a higher monthly fee than Seller's Assistant Basic (which is deducted from your eBay seller's account), but it provides you with some useful features that will make managing multiple auctions a lot easier, including the ability to track your inventory, print shipping labels, and create sales reports. These features are discussed in Chapter 6 along with other software that helps you manage multiple auctions.*

Where to Find It

- **ManageAuctions.com**
  http://www.manageauctions.com
  A variety of useful services for auction sellers, including counters you can add to your sales pages.

- **Beginner's Guide to HTML**
  http://archive.ncsa.uiuc.edu/General/Internet/WWW/
  HTMLPrimerAll.html
  Basic tutorials and instructions on the most common HTML tags.

- **eBay Seller's Assistant**
  http://pages.ebay.com/sellers_assistant/index.html
  Links to eBay Seller's Assistant Basic and Pro.

Chapter 6

Manage Multiple Auctions

How to…

- Use eBay's own software for managing and scheduling multiple auction listings

- Automate eBay auction listings with third-party software you install yourself quickly

- Use an auction service for better management

- Track your eBay sales with eBay's browser toolbar

- Manage your eBay activities with a My eBay page

- Use Seller's Assistant to create multiple auction listings quickly

Henry Ford knew the value of automation. So does the McDonald's restaurant mega-chain. Once you get the hang of selling at auction, you're likely to jump in the game with both feet and start to sell lots of items at once. As your eBay business grows and you can prepare sales more quickly, the more you'll want to automate tasks that are repetitious. Why? The more time you save, the more sales you'll be able to list, and the greater the revenue those sales can generate. At the same time, you'll be able to focus on the parts of your eBay business that really interest you: creating and describing merchandise, finding merchandise you can sell, completing transactions, and other good things.

This chapter discusses ways you can speed up your business and run it more efficiently so as to reduce stress at the same time you boost your productivity. You can automate the process of publishing photos online, keeping records of your sales income, and maintaining data about your sales. These are ambitious goals, but they are ones you need to shoot for if you want to make a steady living on eBay.

Start with eBay's Management Tools

The logical place to start is with the tools eBay provides its own sellers, which are described in the following sections. If you need help or have questions, you can access the message boards for any of these software tools and get help from other users and eBay staff people who monitor discussions.

eBay provides a variety of software options for creating groups of sales listings, formatting them with user-friendly design elements, tracking sales while they're online, and even sending automated e-mail responses and printing out labels in order to complete transactions in a more streamlined fashion. In fact, it can be somewhat confusing when it comes time to choose between the eBay sales tools because their functions overlap in some respects. Table 6-1 indicates what each of the tools discussed in this section does and why you might choose it.

Tool	Main Features	Cost	Pros and Cons
Turbo Lister	Lets you create multiple listings and format them without using HTML; you can schedule listings to go online at specific times; you can track your remaining inventory.	Free	You are required to have 20MB of disk space and at least 64MB of RAM to run the Windows-based software; you either have to download it or obtain a CD-ROM version.
Selling Manager	Enables you to relist items but not to create or upload new listings. Lets you track sales online, print labels, and send preformatted e-mails.	Free for first 30 days; $4.99 per month thereafter	You don't have to download and install software; you access the service from eBay's Web site. It's similar to Seller's Assistant Basic, but includes relisting and label-printing features that Seller's Assistant doesn't have.
Seller's Assistant Basic	Provides you with 20 templates for designing sales listings; allows you to upload listings in bulk.	Free for 30 days; $4.99 per month thereafter	Very similar to Selling Manager, but you need to download and install the Windows-based software, and you have the ability to upload sales auctions based on other sales. It will eventually be replaced by Selling Manager.
Seller's Assistant Pro	Enables you to create your own macros so you can repeat a sequence of steps; leave automated feedback in bulk; use multiple User IDs.	Free for 30 days, then $15.99 per month thereafter	Many of its features are provided more cheaply (or for free) by Turbo Lister or Selling Manager.
My eBay	A Selling tab gives up-to-date information on sales that are pending, sales that are completed, and unsold items.	Free	A convenient place to track all of your sales in one location, though you can't perform any management functions.

TABLE 6-1   eBay Tools for Auction Sellers

NOTE *Another bulk listing tool that's been around on eBay for several years, Mister Lister, is being phased out at this writing. Mister Lister users are encouraged to use Turbo Lister instead.*

Speed Things Up with Turbo Lister

Turbo Lister (**http://pages.ebay.com/turbo_lister**) is software that you download and install, and that eBay provides to sellers for free. It enables sellers to sell lots of items at the same time, and to design those sales by means of templates that enable them to format descriptions without having to know HTML. Finally, you can manage the items you create with Turbo Lister—scheduling them to all start and end at a specified time, or duplicate sales details so you can use them over if needed.

Turbo Lister presents you with a wizard-like interface. A wizard is a set of screens or Web pages that leads you through a particular set of procedures. The Turbo Lister wizard should be familiar to anyone who has used the Sell Your Item form.

How to ... Install and Use Turbo Lister

1. Start up Internet Explorer and go to the Turbo Lister Download page (**http://pages.ebay.com/turbo_lister/download.html**).

2. Click Web Setup. If a Security Warning dialog box appears, click Yes to proceed with the download.

3. After the Turbo Lister Setup application downloads, the InstallShield Wizard application opens. Follow the steps presented by the wizard to download the full set of Turbo Lister software.

4. Once installation is complete, The Turbo Lister application should open automatically, and the Welcome to Turbo Lister screen should appear, with the heading "What would you like to do?"

5. You could choose Open a sample Turbo Lister file to see how a finished file might look. For this example, choose "Set up a new Turbo Lister file," then click Next.

6. In the next screen, enter your eBay User ID and password, then click Next.

7. In the next screen, click Connect Now and Turbo Lister will connect eBay to retrieve your account information. Once your account information has been retrieved, click File | New | Item from the Turbo Lister menu bar to open Create a New Item wizard.

8. Choose the country you want to sell in, and choose a format for your sale—an auction, a store, or a real estate advertisement. Click Next.

9. Enter a title for your item in the Item Title drop-down list.

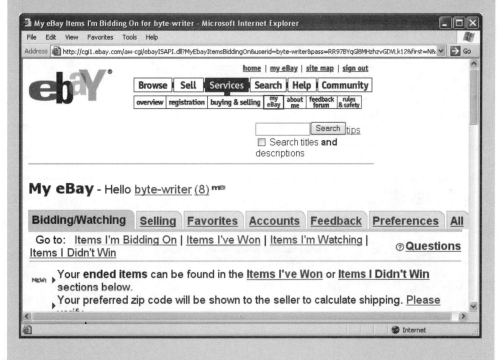

10. Either enter the category number, if you know it, in the Category box, or click Find Category.

11. Click the plus signs next to the categories in the Select a Category box to pick the category where you want to sell the item.

Turbo Lister ☒

Helpful Tips

Be sure to include words in the title that will attract buyers to click on your listing. You might also include abbreviations such as "NR" or "NIB" for "No Reserve" or "New in Box."

→ Learn more.

Create a New Item

Enter an Item title
The title is what buyers will see first, so make sure it's clear and compelling.

Item Title | Maxfield Parrish print The Lone Wolf 1931   ▼ |

Select a category for your item

If you know the category number, enter it below or click the Find Category button.

Category | 20143 --> Art\Prints\Modern (1900-49)\Limited Editions   ▼ | Find Category

2nd Category | ▼ | Find Category
(optional)   Note: if you choose a second category, your Insertion Fee and some Listing Upgrade Fees will double.

Enter Item Specifics
Help buyers find your item more quickly by specifying the information below.

Type	Medium	Age
Not specified	**Not specified**	**Not specified**
Subject	Dominant Color	Largest Dimension
Not specified	**Not specified**	**Not specified**

Other Tasks

Search on eBay

Help for this page

Add / Change

< Previous   Cancel   Next >

12. Click the Add/Change button in the Specifics section to enter item specifics if you want to. Then click OK.

Select a Category ☒

Art\Prints\Modern (1900-49)

⊞ Antiques
⊟ Art
  Digital Art
  ⊞ Drawings
  Folk Art
  ⊞ Mixed Media
  Other Art
  ⊞ Paintings
  ⊞ Photographic Images
  Posters
  ⊟ Prints
    ⊞ Antique (Pre-1900)
    ⊞ Contemporary (1950-Now)
    ⊟ Modern (1900-49)
      Limited Editions
      Open Editions
  ⊞ Sculpture, Carvings
  Self-Representing Artists
⊞ Books
⊞ Business & Industrial
⊞ Clothing & Accessories
⊞ Coins
⊞ Collectibles
⊞ Computers & Office Products
⊞ Consumer Electronics

OK   Cancel

13. Click Next. The next screen of the wizard, which is entitled "Step 2 of 3 – Design Your Listing," gives you something the Sell Your Item form doesn't: a user-friendly HTML editor that enables you to choose a design template for your auction listing. Even if you don't use Turbo Lister for bulk auction listings, it's worth installing the software just to get this feature. In the Themes box on the left side of the screen, choose a design from the Themes list. In the Layout section, choose a layout for your item's photos. You can specify that they appear to the left of the description, to the right, at the top, at the bottom, or as a series of images called a Slide Show.

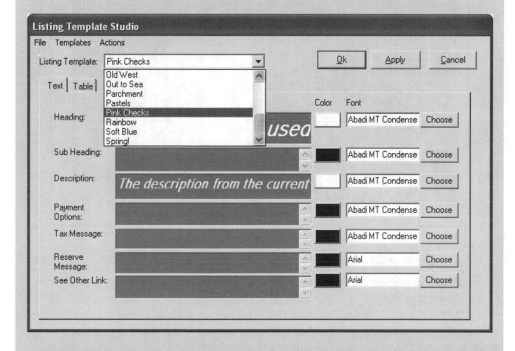

14. Insert a photo by clicking the box labeled "Click Here to Insert a Picture." In the Insert Picture – eBay Picture Services section, click the Look In drop-down menu to locate a photo on your hard disk that you want to include with the description. Click Insert to add the image. Then click in the text box (the box enclosed by dashed lines) to position the text cursor so you can type your item description or paste it from a text file. Click Preview to make sure your layout looks the way you want. Then click Next.

15. Click Next to open the "Step 3 of 3 – Format Specifics" page, where you add specific details about your listing such as the duration of the sale, the starting bid, and the reserve price. When you're done, click Save. You return to the Turbo Lister main screen, where this auction and any others you have created are listed.

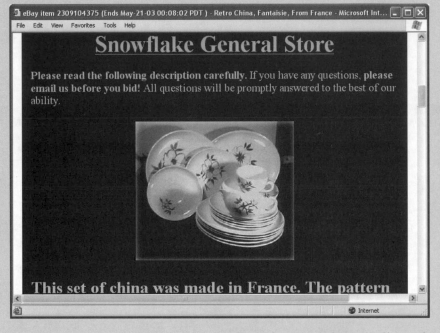

16. When you're ready to start your sales, select them from the list and click Add to Upload. If you want to schedule your sales to go online automatically, select them, then click Schedule to start on, and enter a date or time.

NOTE *Turbo Lister is free to download and use. It's the successor to a utility called Mister Lister that enabled eBay sellers to put dozens of auctions online at once. You can download the software directly from **http://pages.ebay.com/turbo_lister/download.html** and find a full set of system requirements as well. The software does not work on Macintosh systems, however; it's supported by Windows 98, ME, NT, 2000, and XP. You need 20MB of hard disk space to use the software. If you'd rather use a CD-ROM to install the software rather than downloading the 18MB worth of files (perhaps you have a slow connection), you can obtain it for a $2.99 handling fee from eBay-o-rama, eBay's online store (**http://www.ebayorama.com**).*

> **TIP** *If you have questions about Turbo Lister or have problems using the software, check the Turbo Lister Discussion Board (**http://forums.ebay.com/ forum.jsp?forum=34**). You can see if someone else has encountered the same problem, or ask a question if you need help.*

Use eBay's Selling Manager

Turbo Lister is a terrific selling tool, but it does require some overhead—after all, you have to download and install the program so you can run it on your computer. Another sales management tool that eBay provides, Selling Manager, is one that you don't download at all. Rather, you access it at **http://pages.ebay.com/selling_ manager**. You sign up to use the service free for 30 days; if you decide to keep using the service, eBay charges you $4.99 per month.

Selling Manager, like Turbo Lister, provides you with sales templates that you can use to design your auction listings. It also lets you schedule auctions and manage ones that are already online. You can even use it to print shipping labels or relist groups of items that you didn't sell the first time around. eBay provides Turbo Lister so you can create groups of auction listings and get them online; it gives you Selling Manager so you can manage your sales once they're online, and complete transactions in a more automated fashion.

> **NOTE** *You can use Selling Manager to keep track of your sales on all areas of eBay except the fixed-price sales you list on Half.com (see Chapter 14). You need Internet Explorer 4.0 or later, Netscape Navigator 3.0 or later, or AOL Web browser 3.0 or later to use Selling Manager. However, because it's a tool you access online rather than run on your own computer, you don't need to worry about special memory and processing requirements.*

Selling Manager is built into another eBay feature that is normally of interest primarily to auction buyers—a starting page called My eBay that lets you track items you've bid on and items you've purchased. When you subscribe to Selling Manager, your My eBay page is given an additional section in which your pending auction listings are listed. Selling Manager also gives you seven preformatted e-mail messages that you can use to answer questions from prospective bidders and complete transactions after an auction ends.

One thing to keep in mind is that the original My eBay page (which is free) already has a Selling tab that lets you track sales. I suggest that you try the free version of My eBay before you move up to Selling Manager, which is really useful only if you begin to sell dozens of items a month.

Create a My eBay Page

My eBay is a useful tool that you can use whenever you're buying or selling on the auction site. It's a Web page that eBay provides to keep track of things you have bid on. There's also a Selling tab that you can use to keep track of your current sales.

My eBay isn't something you have to set up or subscribe to use. Any time you want to access My eBay, click the **my eBay** link at the top of the eBay navigation bar that appears on just about every eBay page. A page like the one shown in Figure 6-1 appears.

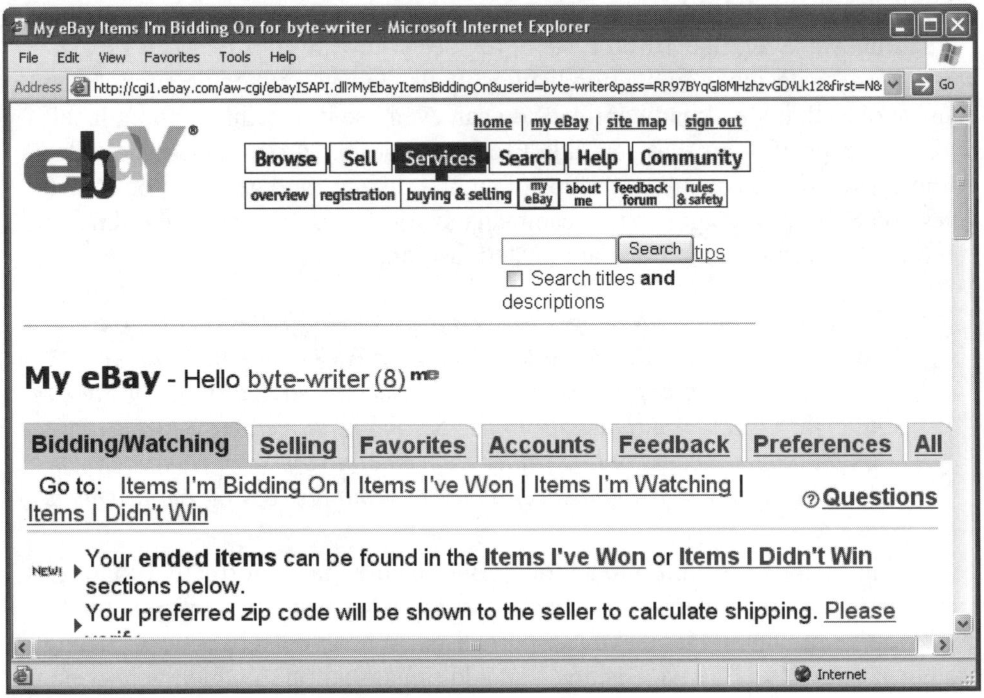

FIGURE 6-1   My eBay lets you track your sales and other auction activities online.

Did you know?

Tabs and Links

My eBay contains a variety of useful links to Web pages and utilities that can help you buy or sell more efficiently on eBay. The page is divided into six separate tabs, each with its own contents and options: Bidding/Watching; Selling; Favorites; Accounts; Feedback; and Preferences. A seventh tab, simply labeled All, presents all of your My eBay information on a single, information-packed page.

The Selling tab gives you a place to track sales. It's broken into three sections: Items I've Sold, Unsold Items, and Pending Items. You can change the number displayed in the "Show Items for Past ___ Days" box to have the page present as few as two days' worth of sales up to a maximum of 30 days. But My eBay only enables you to see what's been sold, how many bids have been received, and so on. You can't use the page to upload sales, schedule sales, or relist items. You need to use Turbo Lister or Seller's Assistant to create and upload sales and Selling Manager or Seller's Assistant to perform management functions.

6

TIP   *Many sellers make their My eBay page their home page—the page that appears when they first open their Web browser, and that appears when they click the Home button in the Internet Explorer toolbar. Open My eBay, select the URL in the Address box of your browser, and press CTRL-C to copy the URL to your clipboard. Choose Tools | Internet Options, make sure the General tab is selected, click in the Address box in the Home Page section, and press CTRL-V to paste the URL. (If you use Internet Explorer 6, you can simply click Use Current to make the currently displayed Web page your home page.) Click OK to make the page your home page.*

eBay Toolbar

As I was writing this chapter, eBay was testing a trial version of eBay toolbar, a nice utility you can add to your browser toolbar. The toolbar's features mostly help you search and track items you're bidding on, not items you're selling. However, you can click Watch Alert to alert you to the progress of any sale on eBay, including one of your own. Since, as a seller, you may very well shop on eBay, the toolbar can be useful for obtaining inventory, too. Once you download and install the toolbar by clicking on the Install Toolbar button on the eBay Toolbar page, a search box and set of options appear.

```
Item Specifics                                          _  □  ✕

Item Specifics
Please enter the Item Specifics below.

            Type  [ Print-Ltd Edition          ▼ ]
          Medium  [ Lithograph                 ▼ ]
             Age  [ 1900-1949                  ▼ ]
         Subject  [ Landscape                  ▼ ]
   Dominant Color [                            ▼ ]
 Largest Dimension[ 24" - 40"                  ▼ ]
   Country/Region [ North America              ▼ ]

                      [    OK    ]      [  Cancel  ]
```

> **TIP** *You can find out more about the toolbar and download it at **http://pages.ebay.com/ebay_toolbar**. The eBay Toolbar only works with Windows 95 or later systems, not the Mac OS. It also requires you to have Microsoft Internet Explorer 4.0 or later or Netscape Navigator 4.08 or later installed.*

Use Seller's Assistant

Seller's Assistant is software that enables you to create and manage your sales. At this writing, it comes in two versions, Basic and Pro.

Seller's Assistant Basic

The Basic version's features are mainly covered by a newer product, Selling Manager, which will eventually replace it. If you haven't yet chosen any sales tool, I advise you to pick Turbo Lister and Selling Manager, which let you create and manage sales items with just about all of the functionality of Seller's Assistant Basic. Frankly, I find the eBay's selling software somewhat confusing, and because Selling Manager is now available, I think you should skip using Seller's Assistant Basic because it's going to be phased out anyway.

Seller's Assistant Pro

Seller's Assistant Pro is a souped-up version of Seller's Assistant that is designed for eBay sellers who sell all the time and need to automate tasks such as leaving feedback for many customers at once, or printing sales reports for tax purposes. These are two features the program performs that aren't covered by the other eBay software mentioned earlier in this chapter. Here are some others:

- You can create *macros* (a recorded series of steps that you perform on an application) so you can repeat just about any task you perform on eBay with your Web browser.

- You can generate invoices for your customers.

- You can automatically fill in feedback for your customers—not very personal, but a real time-saver.

The question you need to ask yourself is this: do these advanced features make Seller's Assistant Pro worth $15.99 a month? Is it also worth downloading the 20MB file and installing the program on your computer?

One advantage of using Seller's Assistant Pro (or Basic, for that matter) is the number of templates from which you can choose. Turbo Lister, the free software tool described earlier in this chapter, only provides you with about ten templates. The Seller's Assistant packages come with 20 different designs (see Figure 6-2). Another advantage is the fact that both versions of Seller's Assistant include a spell-checker so you can make sure your auction descriptions don't contain any obvious typos.

6

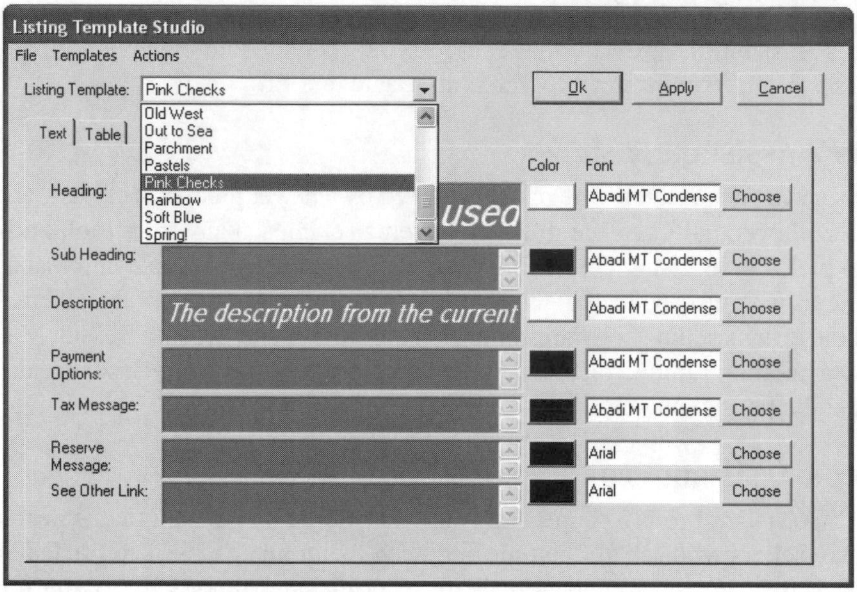

FIGURE 6-2   Seller's Assistant gives you great flexibility in designing auction listings.

If you don't like a particular typeface or color that's included with one of the Seller's Assistant templates, you can always click the Edit button and customize a template so it looks just the way you want.

> TIP   *You can find out more about both Seller's Assistant Basic and Pro at **http://pages.ebay.com/sellers_assistant/index.html**.*

Find a Third-Party Auction Manager

Not so long ago, you had to hire an outside auction management service to perform slick sales-type functions like sending out automated e-mail announcements to each of your high bidders after a sale ends, or scheduling your sales to go online while you're not even at your computer. eBay has since come up with Turbo Lister and Selling Manager so advanced sellers can accomplish such automated tasks.

Nevertheless, you still might want to install third-party software (software that's made for managing eBay sales, but provided by a company other than eBay). Or you might want to secure the services of a company that will manage your eBay sales for you so you can concentrate on answering e-mail, finding new inventory, or shipping out items you've sold. Both options are described in the sections that follow.

Auction Software: Auction Wizard 2000

Auction Wizard was created by Standing Wave Software, Inc. in 1999 to handle the estate sale of a pair of Hollywood memorabilia collectors whose estate was being liquidated on eBay. A more full-featured version of that product, Auction Wizard 2000, was subsequently developed to help especially active eBay sellers manage their sales activities. In addition to giving you the ability to format auctions, send automated feedback, and upload multiple sales, the program is especially strong in its ability to handle "back end" functions of an eBay operation, including:

- **Managing your inventory**   If you take the time to record each of the items in your warehouse or storage area, Auction Wizard will keep track of remaining inventory as items are sold.

- **Keeping tabs on income and expenses**   If you record your expenses and income in Auction Wizard's interface, you enable the program to perform basic accounting functions that can prove helpful at tax time.

- **Printing invoices and reports**   Auction Wizard performs these tasks for a more affordable fee than eBay's own Seller's Assistant Pro.

Auction Wizard 2000 also gives you the ability to import images from a variety of image formats and convert them to the standard Web image formats, GIF and JPEG. A built-in image editor lets you rotate, crop, and otherwise manipulate images so they appear in a compact format that doesn't interfere with your description. You can even use Auction Wizard as a full-fledged Web page creation tool to create your own Web sites.

Some Auction Wizard 2000 users are so satisfied with the program that they have started their own discussion boards to share tips about it and answer one another's questions. It's a great place to go if you want to learn about the pros and cons of the software from people who actually use it. One board, created by user Jacki Espino (eBay User ID katiebird), is located at **http://pub83.ezboard.com/ bauctionwizarddiscussionboard**. Jacki's sales give you an idea of how Auction Wizard can be used to format listings on eBay (see Figure 6-3).

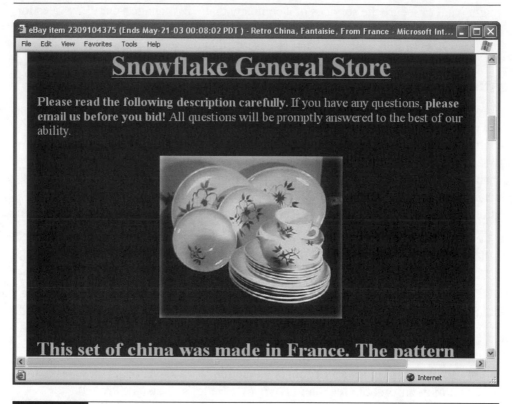

FIGURE 6-3   Third-party auction software can help you format descriptions without having to learn HTML.

Of course, Auction Wizard 2000 isn't the only auction software in town. Other popular programs include:

- AuctionSubmit (**http://www.auctionsubmit.com**)

- AuctionTamer (**http://www.auctiontamer.com**)

- eLister (**http://www.blackmagik.com/elister.html**), which is notable because it is designed to work specifically with the Macintosh operating system (version 8.5 or later)

TIP   *Find out more about Auction Wizard 2000 at* ***http://www.auctionwizard2000.com***. *You can try the program out free for 60 days. After that, you must purchase a one-year license for $75. The license must be renewed each year for $50.*

Auction Services

A managed service is functionality that is provided online, and that you usually access by connecting to the service with a Web browser. Rather than having to download and install software that needs to be updated on a regular basis, you subscribe to the service for a monthly or yearly fee. It's up to the service provider to update the software and make sure it works correctly.

Managed auction services—companies that provide services online that you can use to create auction listings, get your sales on eBay, upload and store images, and manage sales—are even more plentiful than software programs. Such services give you a number of advantages:

- **Image hosting**   After you post one item image online, eBay charges you for each subsequent image per item. By paying a flat monthly fee to a managed auction service, you can access its other auction features, including image hosting. In the long run, you can save money by using the outside service.

- **Auction statistics**   Some auction services report on statistics such as the number of visits your auctions have received in a particular day or even a specified hour in the day. They can tell you how much money your auctions have generated over the past several weeks.

Auction services also perform the functions covered earlier in the discussion on Selling Manager, Turbo Lister, and Seller's Assistant Pro, such as automated feedback, printing mailing labels for each sale, and leaving feedback automatically.

The best-known auction management services are described in Table 6-2.

Service	URL	Fees
AuctionHelper	**http://www.auctionhelper.com**	1.95% of gross sales ($0.15–$1.25 per item) plus a $0.02 eBay fee per each sold item
Auctionworks	**http://www.auctionworks.com**	2% of each sale ($0.10 minimum, no maximum) or hosting fees of $14.95 to $99.95 per month
ManageAuctions.com	**http://www.manageauctions.com**	$0.06 per listing plus other charges ranging from $4.95 to $24.95 per month

TABLE 6-2   Auction Management Services

TIP   *You'll find an extensive (though not comprehensive) list of managed auction services on the AuctionBytes web site (**http://www.auctionbytes.com/cab/pages/ams**). You don't need to hire an auction service if you have the time and energy to do the work yourself, of course. But I think it makes sense to use a managed auction service if you offer a substantial number of sales each month (perhaps 50 or more, though this is not a hard-and-fast rule) and you don't have family or friends to help you create listings, send e-mails, and keep your accounting records.*

Where to Find It

- **Turbo Lister page**
  http://pages.ebay.com/turbo_lister
  A page full of links that explain eBay's Turbo Lister feature and provide the software for download.

- **eBay Selling Manager**
  http://pages.ebay.com/selling_manager
  A page where you can learn about, and sign up for, a service that lets you automate relisting, e-mailing bidders, and completing transactions.

- **eBay Toolbar**
  http://pages.ebay.com/ebay_toolbar/
  A toolbar you can use to track sales and send alert notices at the end of a sale (including your own)

- **eBay Seller's Assistant**
  http://pages.ebay.com/sellers_assistant/index.html
  More eBay software tools for creating and managing auction listings.

Chapter 7

Create Your Own Web Pages

How to...

- Tell buyers about yourself with an About Me page

- Gather all of your sales in one place with an eBay Store

- Create your own Web site with a free Web host

- Rent Web space for free with your Internet Service Provider

- Shoot the works with a full-featured Web hosting service account

- Include the must-have features on your Web site

One nice thing about eBay is that it allows you to start your own e-commerce business immediately, without having to build or stock a real brick-and-mortar store. But your eBay sales can be helped by the presence of a *virtual* store—a digital, text-and-image store on the World Wide Web.

Chances are you've already got a Web page out there somewhere in cyberspace. Maybe you use it to talk about yourself and your hobbies, or to show off photos of your family or your pets. Well, you can also use the Web to talk about your business. You can create a simple Web page called an *eBay Store* that links to your current auctions. The eBay Store page, in turn, can list the URL of a full-fledged e-commerce site that enables shoppers to make purchases. The synergy that results from linking eBay auctions to an eBay Store or Web site can build credibility for your business and boost your sales, too.

If you've already created auction listings and completed transactions with satisfied customers, you've done much of the work involved in creating a business Web site. You only need to take one more step: creating a set of Web pages devoted to your commercial activities. You've got plenty of options for creating pages: You can create a simple About Me page on eBay; create an eBay store; or launch your own full-fledged Web site. As an entrepreneur, you owe it to yourself to take the next step and create Web pages that boost your eBay sales even further.

It's not necessary to set up an eBay Web page or a full-fledged e-commerce Web site to back up your auction sales, of course. Plenty of successful sellers never set up a Web site at all; they let their sales descriptions and customer service do the talking. Starting up an e-commerce Web site makes sense if you already have a business operation and your eBay sales are intended to supplement it. It's also a natural step forward if you are finding enough success on eBay that you want to sell through a Web site as well. Whether you want to set up another sales venue through an eBay Store, or set up your own Web-based catalog and shopping cart, you can use your eBay auction experience as a starting point for further development.

MeBay: Create an About Me Page

If you sell on eBay, there's really no excuse not to create an About Me page. It only takes a matter of minutes—in fact, it's about as easy as creating your first auction listing. About Me is a feature that eBay offers to all of its participants and that promotes the community atmosphere that eBay is continually touting. eBay really does work by people getting to know and trust one another.

By taking a little time to create a simple page that tells people a little about you, you increase the chances that people will bid on your merchandise. Not only that, but you get another cool icon placed to your User ID as it appears on your auctions. If shoppers click your "me" icon (see Figure 7-1) they'll be taken directly to your About Me page.

As you can see in Figure 7-1, the seller known as silkroad—the Silk Road Trading Concern—has two links to Web pages: an About Me page and an eBay Stores page. Not only that, Silk Road has all the bases covered by running a Web site (**http://www.silkroads.com**). Each of these options is discussed in this chapter.

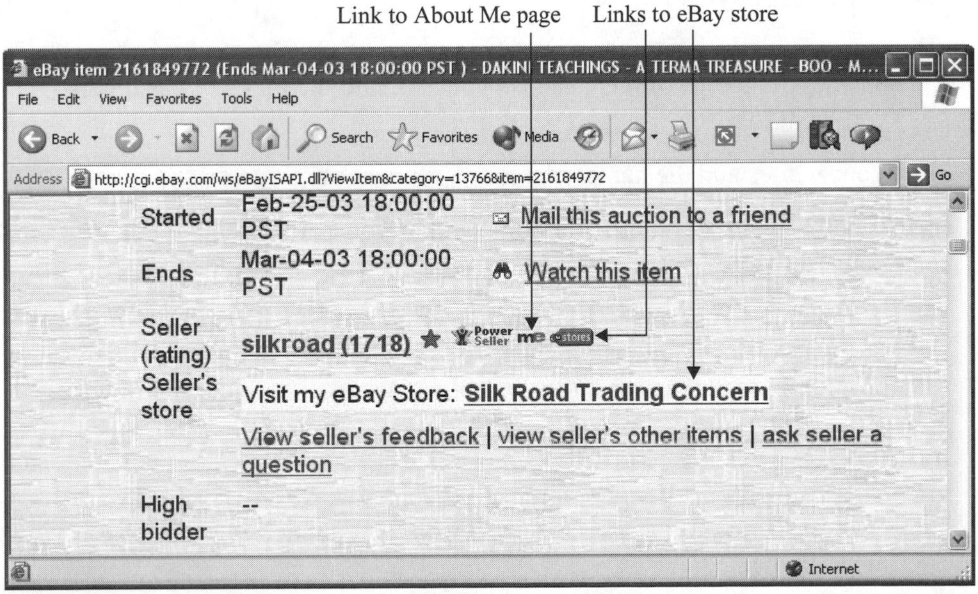

FIGURE 7-1   Advertising your About Me page

Gather Your 411

The name *About Me* says it all: it's a place where you talk all about you personally—why you use eBay, what you sell, what you're interested in, or where you live. You can use an eBay Store or a Web site to focus on your business rather than your personal side. Of course, these aren't firm dividing lines: You can use About Me to promote your business, and your eBay Store to promote yourself and your business. No matter how you make use of these resources, however, they are sure to help drive people to your auction listings and the all-important Submit Bid button.

Before you start to create your About Me page, you just need to gather a little information. The amount of detail you provide depends on how active a seller you are, how many different kinds of items you sell or collect, and whether your page is about you personally or just about your auction activities. The best way to find out what to say on your About Me page is to search the About Me pages of other sellers. Unfortunately, there's no eBay page that gathers all the About Me pages in one set of links (you'd probably have tens of thousands of links in one place, which wouldn't necessarily be helpful). Rather, you find a seller who's reputable and presents sales items in a professional manner, and click that seller's About Me link. You'll discover that typically, eBay sellers tend to include information such as:

- The name of your business.

- A mission statement: a few sentences that describe the purpose of your business, the type of merchandise you sell, and the kinds of customers you want to reach.

- Your names and the names of your partners or employees.

- Whether you sell on eBay full time and, if you don't, what you do for your "day job."

- What makes your business distinctive or noteworthy. Don't be bashful; promote yourself enthusiastically. Tell people that you are committed to providing quality merchandise, excellent customer service, and the like.

- Your most recent feedback.

- Your background. If you're fortunate enough to have any honors, awards, or professional affiliations associated with your auction sales, by all means mention them.

■ A set of links to your current auctions. You might also include links to any other Web pages or Web sites you have created.

■ Contact information. Your Web site needs to list all the ways in which buyers or prospective customers can reach you if they have a question or need some information. You don't need to publish your actual street address, of course; some eBay sellers prefer to use a post office box for extra security. But you should certainly include an e-mail address and possibly a phone number as well.

That's quite a list. Frankly, if you have any more to say, you should create an eBay Store or a Web site for yourself or your business. For now, just take a few minutes to think about and write down what you're going to say. Jot down some biographical notes and have a friend look them over, or suggest additional tidbits you can convey to the world.

7

TIP   *If you have more to tell the world about your hobbies, your family, your business history, or your thoughts about society in general, place a link on your About Me page that leads visitors to a Web page that contains more information. You'll learn how to create such pages later in this chapter.*

Create Your Page

When you've got your content in order, follow these steps to get your About Me page online:

1. Make sure you're connected to the Internet, start up your Web browser of choice, and enter the URL **http://members.ebay.com/aw-cgi/eBayISAPI .dll?AboutMeLogin** to go to the About Me login page.

2. Read the instructions, then click **Create** and edit your page.

3. When the "About Me – Step 1" page appears, review the Web page layouts that are available to you. Then click the button next to the arrangement you want: Two column layout, Newspaper layout, or Centered Layout. The first two options are shown in Figure 7-2.

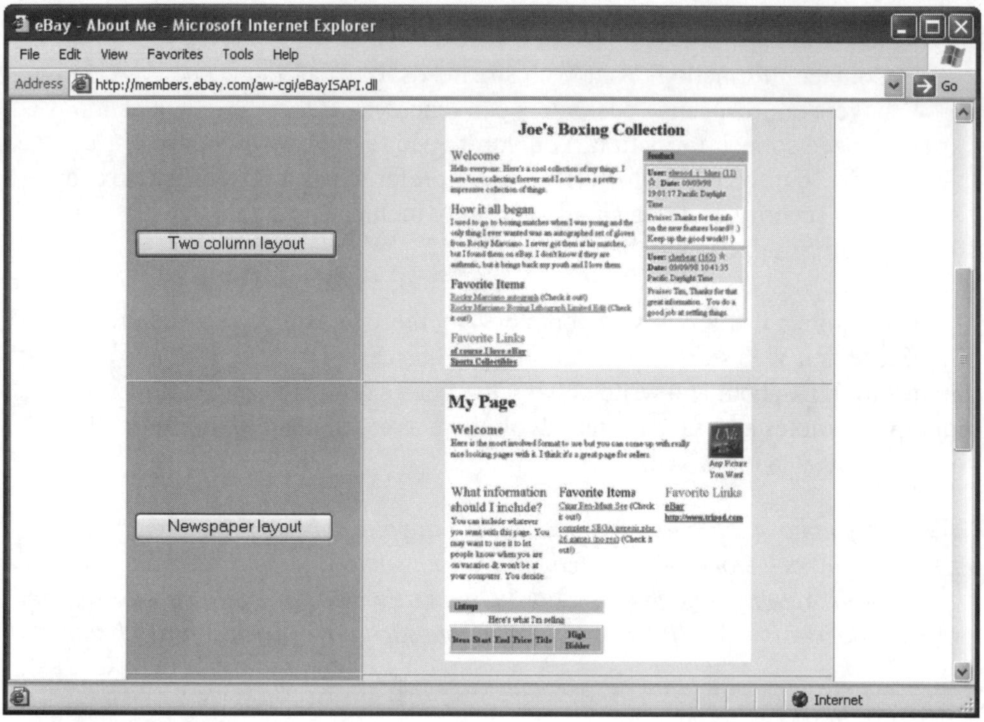

FIGURE 7-2   Pick the About Me layout option that matches your range of subjects.

TIP   *You might choose the two column layout if you want to address a variety of different subjects, such as you, your family, your hobbies, and your business. The newspaper layout works well if you want to present various bits of information about the same topic (the different items you sell online, for instance). The centered arrangement is a good choice if your content—such as a brief description of your store—is short and sweet.*

4. When the "About Me – Step 2" page appears, you fill out a form that helps create the contents for your page. Choose a title for your page and add some information in each of the boxes. Also select the option that indicates how many eBay feedback comments you want the page to contain. When you're ready, click Preview Your Page to see your page and make sure it looks the way you want.

5. If you don't like your page's layout, click **Start Over** to try one of the other two options. You'll be asked to confirm that you want to delete by clicking Delete, and then you'll return to the "About Me – Step 1" page, where you can pick a different layout. Otherwise, if you're happy with your work, you can click **Edit Some More**, **Save My Page**, **Edit Using HTML**, or **Start Over**.

Once you click **Save My Page**, your page goes on the Web where everyone can see it. The Silk Road Trading Concern's About Me page is shown in Figure 7-3.

Silk Road Trading Concern created an About Me page at the same time it created its eBay Stores page (see "Set Up Shop" later in this chapter). That's why it has the Stores logo at the top. Most About Me pages don't contain the Stores

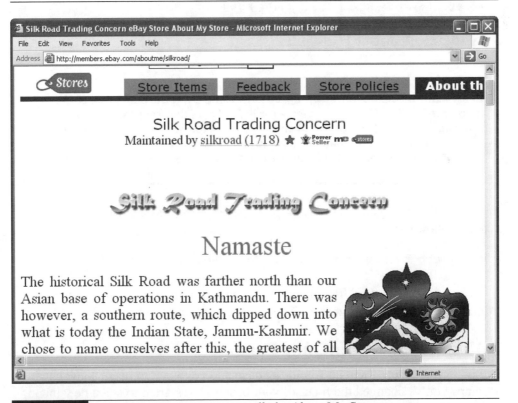

FIGURE 7-3   An About Me page can actually be About My Store.

logo. More typically, About Me gives an individual seller a place to talk about him or herself. Chad Gibbons' About Me page is more typical.

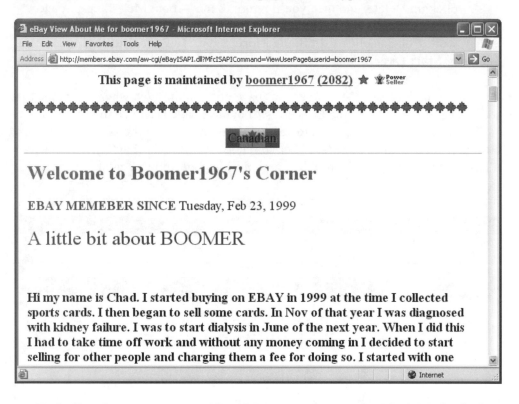

Typically, when you create an About Me page, you are assigned a URL that looks like the following:

```
http://members.ebay.com/aboutme/[Your User ID].
```

You can refer to this URL in your Web pages or e-mail messages. Consider adding it to your e-mail signature file so people can find it more easily.

Edit and Spruce Up Your Page

Suppose you have created an About Me page and you want to make some changes. Perhaps you've changed the focus of your business or started to sell a new line of merchandise. Editing an About Me page used to be easy: you went to the About Me Login page and clicked **Create and edit my page** to retrieve your current page and edit it. Not any more. Now, you only have two options:

■ Create a new About Me page from scratch

■ Edit the raw HTML for your current About Me page

If you want to edit your About Me page, you'll have to be subjected to looking at HTML code, which can be intimidating if you haven't worked with it before. (I don't understand why eBay doesn't make this process easier for its members.) You go to the About Me Login page, click **Create and edit your page** and, when the page appears, click **Edit** some more. The HTML version of your page appears (see Figure 4).

The nice thing about working with HTML is that you can do some spiffy formatting, such as adding images, creating headings and subheadings, and the like—provided you know what you're doing. The bad thing about working with HTML is that, well, you have to work with it at all. You might just prefer to re-create your page from scratch; save the contents as a text file beforehand so you can cut and paste when you want to remake it.

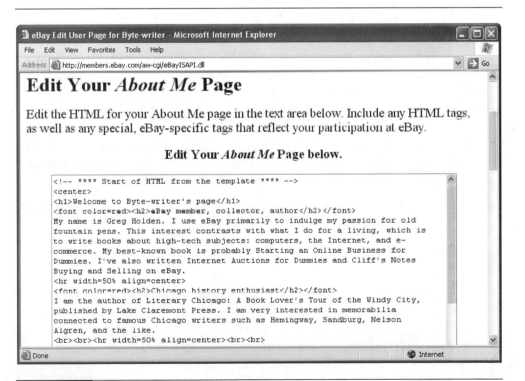

FIGURE 7-4   To edit an existing About Me page, you have to work with HTML code.

Create an eBay Store

Big-time retailers know that to maximize your income and reach the greatest number of customers, you need to sell in more than one way, using more than one type of sales technique. Auto dealers have known this for years. Look at all the ways you can purchase a new car: you can buy it outright; you can put down a down payment and finance the rest; you can lease it for a fixed period of time. You can go to an auto dealership, shop online, or visit a place where a number of auto dealers are gathered under one roof, called an auto mall. By marketing your products in a variety of ways, you attract the widest range of customers.

In much the same way, you can supplement your eBay auctions with items you put up for sale for a fixed price in an eBay Store. Setting up an eBay Store is much the same as renting space in a shopping mall, but with two big advantages: eBay is likely to be cheaper, and likely to attract more shoppers than most other malls due to its sheer popularity.

Shopping malls have never proved very successful on the Web. Early attempts at gathering shops under a single Web site umbrella so people can find them more easily just didn't work. The Web makes it easy to find Web-based retailers through user-friendly search engines and easy-to-remember URLs like **http://www.walmart.com**. Only a few Web-based malls remain, such as MSN Marketplace (**http://marketplace .msn.com**, and Yahoo!Store (**http://store.yahoo.com**).

Why, then, would you consider setting up an eBay Store in addition to your eBay auctions? I'll give you three reasons:

- eBay attracts more than 13 million visitors per month, according to Neilsen/Netratings' weekly Top 25 Parent Companies list (**http://pm.netratings.com/ nnpm/owa/NRpublicreports.toppropertiesweekly**).

- You can drive regular buyers to your store with the Stores logo that appears next to your User ID.

- The cost is only $9.95 per month for a basic subscription plus nominal listing fees.

- If you really want to sell some items at a fixed price, and you find that Buy It Now doesn't attract buyers, you might have better luck with an eBay Store.

NOTE   *You need a minimum feedback of 20 and an ID Verify listing to open an eBay Store. See Chapter 16 for more on eBay's ID Verify program.*

The following sections discuss each of these points in more detail.

Save a Few Bucks

To set up your own Web site with a hosting service might cost $50 a month or more. Even if you rent space in an online mall that gains a large number of visitors, you'll have to pay a monthly fee as well as listing fees or fees charged for each item you sell. eBay Stores compare favorably to other malls as indicated, as far as the basic monthly hosting fee. But keep in mind that an eBay Store, unlike the other hosting options, doesn't give you any ability to collect credit card payments from your customers. Table 7-1 gives a comparison of the fees for Yahoo!, Amazon, and eBay.

Gain Eyeball Space

The idea behind shopping malls, whether they are down the street or on the Web, is that they attract a higher number of visitors just because they gather multiple sales outlets under one roof. If you pick a marketplace that is particularly "sticky" (in other words, that has enough resources and services that visitors tend to stay around for a while) you're more likely to get shoppers.

Attract Your Own Customers

One advantage of setting up an eBay Store, to my mind, is that you do the marketing in many ways. If you build up a steady clientele through your regular auction sales, you stand a good chance of having those regular customers visit your eBay Store. The more bidders you attract to your auctions, the better your chances that someone will stop by your store.

Do Buy It Now One Better

Buy It Now has its pros and cons. On the plus side, it's not a hidden price like a reserve price. You know exactly what the seller wants to charge for an item, and you can buy it immediately. Buy it Now is also highly popular and a good way to

Store Host	Monthly Rent	Listing Fee	Final Value Fee
Yahoo!Store	$49.95	$0.10 per item per month	5% (plus 3.5% for transactions that originate on Yahoo!)
Amazon zShops	$39.95	N/A	$0.99 plus 15% of sales price (or 10% for electronics items)
eBay Store (Basic Subscription)	$9.95	$0.05 per item	5.25% (for items priced at $25 or less)

TABLE 7-1   Comparison of Online Store Options

make sales. On the other hand, offering a Buy It Now price on something as well as the option to bid on that same item at auction is a contradiction, in my opinion: it contradicts the original purpose of the sale. People shop for auction items in the hope of getting a good deal. They want to save a few bucks, and they hope to find something unusual or rare at a good price. Buy It Now takes away the feeling that bidders are somehow "beating the system" by making them pay a set price that's not necessarily as much of a bargain as an auction would be.

At an eBay Store, people are shopping with a different set of criteria. Sure, they still want bargains, and they'll never buy something if they feel like you're overcharging them. But they're primarily there because they are already familiar with you or your business, and they want to see what else you're offering. If they are loyal to you and they feel they can trust you, they won't mind paying a fixed price if they find something that's really desirable.

If you already sell at auction and have your auction sales gathered on your About Me page, there's no reason why you can't sell through an eBay Store as well. Silk Road Trading Concern has a number of items for sale through its store (see Figure 7-5).

Of course, eBay Stores can help you reach new customers, not just people who have already purchased from you at auction. They might find your store on the eBay Stores home page (**http://www.stores.ebay.com**)—provided you pay $49.95 per month to get yourself placed in that prime real estate.

What, you ask, is the downside to the rosy picture I'm painting? It's the same as with any store: there's no guarantee you'll get enough business to make the store worthwhile, and it takes work, time, and commitment. If you're already spending 30, 40, or 50 hours a week on your auctions, expect to add several hours more for your store. You can't just put your merchandise up for sale and then let it sit there for weeks at a time. People will assume that the selections never change and they'll stop coming altogether. You've got to put new items up for sale regularly and ship items out quickly, just as you do with auctions. You can close your store if you go on vacation, but you'll have to wait 30 days before you can reopen it once again.

NOTE
There's another downside to selling via eBay Stores: the items you sell aren't retrieved by users who use eBay's popular Search page. They only appear in response to a Seller search.

Set Up Shop

Once you have convinced yourself that an eBay Store is right for you, it's easy enough to get started. If you don't already have a business name, you should decide

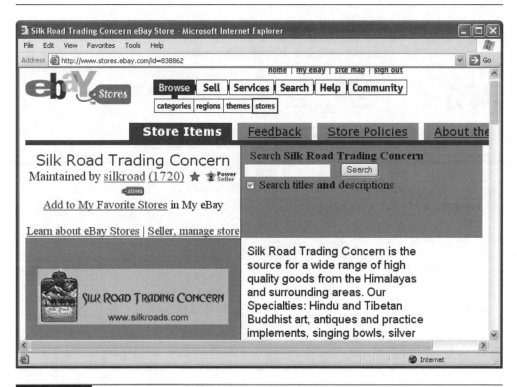

FIGURE 7-5 An eBay Store gives you another way to reach existing customers.

on a name for your store; it needn't match your User ID. Identify a group of items you want to put up for sale, and settle on the prices you want.

> **TIP** *You should, in fact, use the same business name and graphics for all of your sales, including your auctions, your About Me page, your eBay Store, or your Web site if you create one. A consistent presentation helps you establish an identity and builds trust among your customers, who will be able to recognize you that much more quickly.*

Once you've got the preliminaries covered, go to the eBay Seller Landing page (shown in Figure 7-6), and click the conspicuous **OPEN STORE NOW!** button.

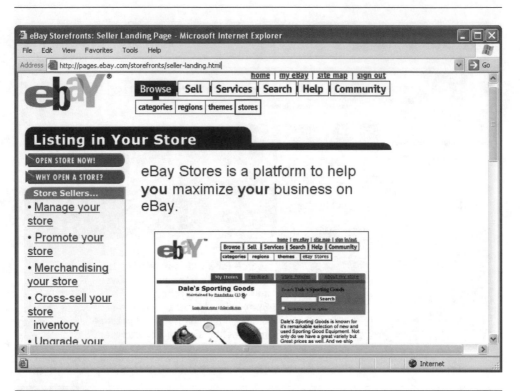

FIGURE 7-6   Come to this page to start creating your eBay Store.

How to ... Create Your Store

Log in with your password, if you aren't logged in already, and click **Sign In**. Read the statement that says you are subject to the same user Agreement that governs your auction sales. Then click **Continue** to connect to the Store Content page, where you begin to create your store.

The Store Content page presents you with a form that you fill out to locate your store and describe it to potential customers.

1. First, you select one of 14 main categories for your store. Pick the category you use most for your auctions—or choose Everything Else.

2. Enter your store's "brand name" in the Store name box

3. Type your address in the Seller's payment information section.

4. Write an agonizingly short (250 characters or less) description of your store in the Store description area. (You add more information in Step 9 if you run out of space.)

CAUTION *You don't get much room to sell your store—each field in the Store Content page is limited to a small number of characters. If you really want as many words as you need to create your own store, opt for your own Web site instead. Otherwise, type your content in any text editor and count the number of characters using the program's Word Count feature (it's under the Tools menu).*

5. Fill out some additional information about what makes your store unique in the Store specialties box (you only get 200 words this time).

6. In the Custom store categories area, enter the types of sales categories under which your merchandise will be sold. Supposedly, these choices are optional. However, when you want to sell an item, you have to list it under one of the categories you have already defined here. Do yourself a favor and come up with some categories under which your merchandise will be listed.

7. Specify your payment methods and ship-to locations, and your sales tax specifications (see Chapter 17).

8. In the "Store customer service & return policy" box, type in any money-back guarantee, customer service numbers, return policies, or Square Trade memberships you can boast. You have to enter 90 characters or less here; the field is required.

9. Be sure to take advantage of the opportunity to sell yourself and your store even more in the "Additional store information" box. You get 200 more characters to tell people how long you've been selling on eBay, how long you've been in business, and so on.

10. Optionally, if you haven't created an About Me page, you get the chance to do so after the "Additional store information" box. The advantage of creating an About Me store here is that, when users click on your About

7

Me logo, they'll be taken to your eBay Store, just as they would if they clicked on your Stores logo.

11. Next, you get to choose colors for your eBay Store. Be sure to pick an accent color of some sort—black and white just looks too stark and uninviting for an online store.

12. Finally, you choose graphics for your store. If you already have an About Me page or a Web page, you can simply choose one of your existing image files for your store. Otherwise, you have two choices: create a logo for your store, or use a predesigned eBay graphic. The predesigned images are overused and don't distinguish your store in any way. I strongly suggest that you create a logo as described later in this chapter.

Give yourself a pat on the back: you've created your store and now you can start selling on it.

TIP   *You can always change your store's category or description by clicking the **Seller, manage store link** on your store's home page.*

List Your Sales Items

Once you've made the decisions needed to create your eBay Store, you'll probably find listing items for sale a breeze, especially if you are already adept at putting up items for auction on eBay. The principles described in Chapter 3 for creating auction listings and Chapter 8 for creating good images apply. But there's one big difference: you don't have to worry about setting reserve prices or starting bids. You also don't have to worry about monitoring bids as they are placed. There aren't any bids at all; rather, you set a fixed price and the item is listed at that price for 30 days.

eBay Bestsellers
Auction Sales from the Top of the World

Selling on eBay and other online venues gives you freedom. You can work where your interest—or your merchandise—lies. That's true for Steve Brothers and his father Jon, who collect and sell South Asian art and ethnographic items from Kathmandu, Nepal, high in the Himalayan mountains. Most of their items are spiritual or religious in nature, with the emphasis on Tibetan Buddhist and Hindu art and jewelry. eBay is only one of several sales venues for Jon and Steve. They sell new items through Silk Road Trading Concern (**http://www.silkroads.com**) and old and ethnographic items through Himalayan Mercantile (**http://www.himalayan-mercantile.com**). They also sell to wholesale clients around the United States and around the world—all without a conventional brick-and-mortar storefront.

The Brothers family has sold more than 3,500 items on eBay since 1998, and in that time, they've met some wonderful people who have become their close friends, as well as other sellers who've caused problems.

"eBay is indeed a community, and like all communities it has its saints and its miscreants," says Steve. "Competition is stiff in our genre, but generally speaking, our competitors seem to be very decent folks. I would not describe it as cutthroat, but I would not characterize it as a particularly altruistic, either. In the early days of eBay we used to have a lot of trouble with people 'stealing' text from our auction descriptions, and in several instances our photos as well. If imitation is the most sincere form of flattery than we were being paid very high compliments, but frankly it was more annoying than anything else. We work hard to present an informative and attractive presentation in the auction context, so it was always a bit disheartening to have someone take what we had gone to considerable effort to create, and use it to compete against us."

All of the Silk Road images that appear on eBay include an identifying logo that serves as a "branding logo," which makes it more difficult for other sellers to reuse.

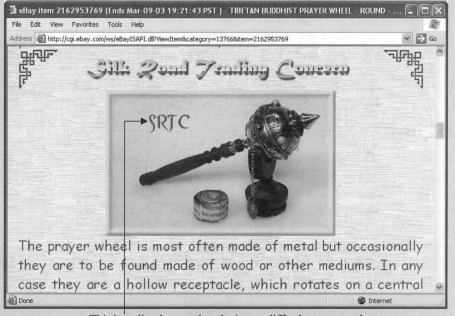

This branding logo makes the image difficult to copy and reuse

Silk Road Trading Concern, the eBay sales using the User ID silkroad, and Himalayan Mercantile are all family operations. Steve and his wife, who is a native of Nepal, travel throughout the region, collecting sale items and researching the traditions behind them. Steve writes the text and creates and manages most of the auctions using eBay Seller's Assistant, while Jon Brothers handles transaction fulfillment and shipping.

Even from the mountains of Nepal, Steve can monitor auctions on eBay with immediacy. "There have been innumerable items that have exceeded our expectations in terms of the type of price they might fetch. On the other hand there have also been great offerings that have flopped from a sales perspective. It's always exciting to watch bidders "fight it out" in the last minutes of an auction, but the frequency of that has fallen off in the past year and a half or two—partly due to the economy, perhaps, but also due to 'sniping software.'"

Steve advises eBay sellers not to follow his example in selling specialty items, however. "My advice for anyone who really wants to make a living on eBay is to sell some mainstream items—something that a good percentage of the general population wants or, better yet, needs. Fringe items that appeal to a subculture like Tibetan Buddhist practitioners are not all that lucrative. There are a lot of sellers but a relatively finite number of buyers. For prospective eBay sellers, I'd say choose some categories of items you are interested in. Research the market and try to gauge demand. If there is a demand, try to determine if the market in question needs or can support another seller of that type of item. If so, try to determine what ways you can set yourself apart from the pack, whether with attractive pricing, customer service, etc. Essentially, try to determine what will make you as a seller into a desirable source for a given item."

Publish Your Own Web Site

About Me and eBay Stores are easy ways to promote your business. But the really effective way to promote trust is to create your own set of interconnected Web pages—in other words, a Web site. On your site, you can talk about yourself and your qualifications in as much detail as you wish. You can also promote your business if you have one. An eBay Store or About Me page can be the glue that links an online business and an auction listing.

You don't *have* to provide a Web site if you plan to sell at auction. For the most part, it makes sense to take this additional step if one of the following applies to you:

- You're in a business related to the items you're selling.
- You plan to make auction sales a significant part of your income.

■ You plan to sell not only through eBay but through a catalog you present on your Web site, so all the income from the sale (less sales tax) comes to you and not to your Web host.

The first step in creating your auction Web page is to decide where your page is going to live online. Your site needs to be hosted on a Web server (a computer that is connected to the Internet all the time, and whose primary purpose is to make Web pages available to anyone with a Web browser) so others can view it. In other words, you need to find a hosting service—a company that functions like a virtual landlord, giving you space on a computer where you can set up shop. This is only the first step of a three-step process:

1. You pick your Web host.

2. You create your Web pages. You either use a user-friendly online tool such as a form you fill out to create a page, much the same as eBay's About Me or Stores features, or, you purchase and install Web page creation software and design your pages on your own computer.

3. You get your pages online. If you create your site using your host's online tool, you'll use another tool provided by that same host to move your files to the Web server where they can be seen by everyone. If you create your Web pages yourself, you need to move the files from your computer to the Web server. Sophisticated Web page tools like Dreamweaver and FrontPage can do the file transfer for you. Otherwise, you have to use a special File Transfer Protocol (FTP) program to do the moving.

It's worth taking some time to pick the right host because where your page is located can affect how you create it and how it looks. When it comes to finding a home for your Web pages, you have several options:

■ **A free hosting service**   There aren't too many free Web hosts left, but you can use Yahoo! GeoCities.

■ **Your own ISP**   If you have an account with a company such as America Online (AOL) or Earthlink, they'll usually give you space to create a simple Web site as part of your monthly Internet access fee.

■ **A company that doesn't function as an ISP, but only hosts Web sites** This is a business that hosts Web sites, and that provides lots of handy tools and help for creating sites.

Your choice of host also has an impact on how you create your Web pages. If you aren't technically minded and have no interest in the technical aspects of designing Web sites, you'll enjoy using the simple forms-based Web site creators provided by AOL, Yahoo! GeoCities, and Tripod: You fill out a form, and your Web pages are created and automatically placed online. If you want to be in control and make everything look just the way you want, you'll probably prefer using a Web page creation tool like Dreamweaver or Microsoft FrontPage and publishing your page yourself with your ISP or a Web hosting service. These basic options are described in the following sections.

Use a Free Web Hosting Service

If you want to create your own full-fledged Web site (and possibly get a second e-mail address if you need one), sign up with one of the organizations that give anyone space on a Web server where they can publish their own set of interconnected Web pages. One advantage of signing up for an account with one of these organizations is that they are targeted at users who have little or no experience setting up Web pages. You'll find Help pages and other instructions to lead you through the steps in becoming a Web publisher. Another advantage is that you become part of another community of Web surfers. You can join clubs and interact with other users who also publish their pages on the site, just as you can with eBay community members. On the downside, you usually have to display ads on your site. Here are some sites to consider.

Yahoo! GeoCities

Yahoo! GeoCities (**http://geocities.yahoo.com/home**) is one of the oldest and most successful of the free online services. It not only provides users with a place on the Web for their personal home pages, but also supplies easy-to-use Web page forms that format the Web pages for you (see Figure 7-7), as well as programs that transfer (or, in technospeak, *upload*) the files from your home computer to GeoCities. Like eBay, GeoCities tends to be a world unto itself. Members identify themselves as being part of a "neighborhood" of individuals with similar interests.

You can sign up for a free account with GeoCities, but you'll have to show ads on your Web pages. Plus, your URL (your Web address) will have to take the form **http://geocities.yahoo.com/[*your Yahoo! userid*]**. To move up to an easy-to-remember URL like **http://www.mysiteorbusiness.com**, you'd have to pay $8.95 per month for the GeoCities Pro hosting package. (GeoCities also offers a $4.95 per month hosting option.)

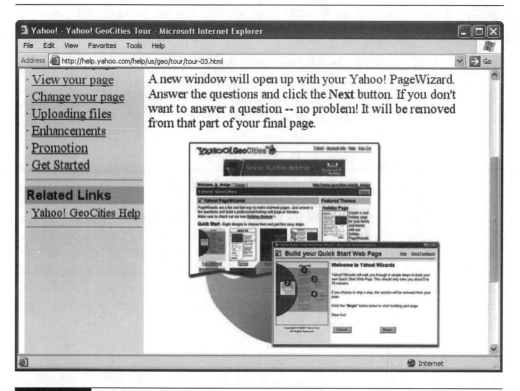

FIGURE 7-7   If you use GeoCities, you can create Web pages using Yahoo!'s Page Wizard utility.

Tripod

Tripod (**http://www.tripod.com**), which is owned by the Internet search service Lycos, also has an active site that hosts lots of individual Web surfer home pages. Members can chat and post messages on message boards. Like Yahoo! GeoCities, Tripod offers users a free Web site hosting service that is ad-supported. Other ad-free hosting options are available, ranging from $49.5 to $19.95 per month.

Tripod is distinguished from Yahoo! GeoCities in that its free service includes 20MB of space (compared with 12MB for GeoCities), and its monthly fee packages include software that lets you create those popular running diaries called Weblogs. Users of all packages (including the free one) also gain access to a library of clip art images they can use to spice up their Web pages.

TIP *If you're looking for Web space for nothing and you don't mind displaying ads on your Web pages, consider free hosting packages offered by companies such as Netfirms (**http://www.netfirms.com**), which gives you a whopping 25MB of server space plus the ability to create Web page forms that are backed up by CGI (Common Gateway Interface) scripts. Freeservers (**http://www.freeservers.com**) gives you 12MB of space and a choice of Web page creation tools as well.*

Host With Your Own ISP

An Internet Service Provider (ISP) is a company that gives individuals or businesses access to the Internet. For the most part, ISPs give customers dialup accounts or cable modem or DSL lines that let them connect to the Internet. Along with Internet access, most ISPs also let users create personal home pages and publish them on a Web server. The advantage of using an ISP as your host is that it's convenient and free, and you get the service anyway. Most ISP Web servers are fast and reliable. On the downside, you're pretty much on your own when it comes to obtaining software to create your Web pages, and with publishing those pages by moving them from your computer to the ISP's Web server.

America Online

America Online (AOL) is a wildly popular site for Internet access and, if you already have an account with AOL, you should certainly consider setting up a Web page with them. If you have an account with AOL, you automatically gain 2MB of Web server space where you can store your own Web pages. This might seem like only a small amount of room, but it's more than enough for a moderately-sized Web site, given that the typical Web page only consumes 5K to 30K of disk space, not including images. Not only that, but each of the seven separate usernames you can create on AOL is entitled to 2MB of space, giving you a total of 14MB to work with.

- **My FTP Space**   This is AOL's catch-all term for a number of Web page resources. One of those resources, 1-2-3 Publish, works like Yahoo!'s Page Wizard and eBay's own About Me feature: you create a Web page by filling out a form with your Web browser. You can use another Web page design if you want to. You can only reach My FTP Space from within AOL's software, using the keyword My FTP Space.

■ **AOL Hometown (http://hometown.aol.com)**   This is America Online's site on the Web where individuals can create Web pages. You create the page using 1-2-3 Publish, and you locate it on AOL Hometown so anyone on the Web can find it, not just AOL users. One difference between this and the preceding services is an orientation toward business-oriented Web sites. If you sell antiques on eBay, for instance, you might want to create a Web site in the "neighborhood" called Furniture & Antiques, which is shown in Figure 7-8.

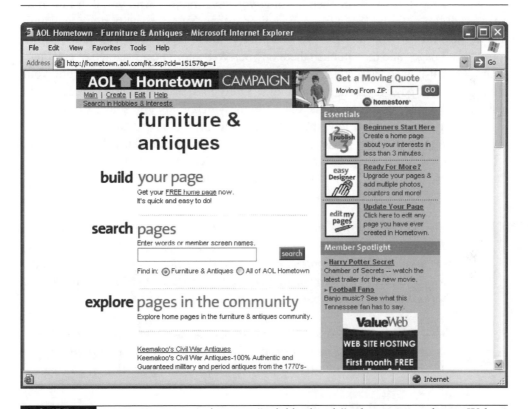

FIGURE 7-8   AOL Hometown gives you "neighborhoods" where you can locate Web pages with others who share similar interests.

Other ISPs

America Online isn't the only ISP in town, of course. Virtually all ISPs give their customers some Web hosting space along with Internet access. I have some friends who have set up their Web sites with Earthlink (**http://www.earthlink.com**), and I have created a couple of Web sites with my own ISP, XO Communications (**http://www.xo.com**), as well. Earthlink gives you a pretty good deal: at this writing, they offer unlimited dialup access for $10.97 for the first six months and $21.95 per month thereafter. Users get 10MB of free Web space and a Web page creation tool called Click-n-Build, too.

When you use an ISP for Web hosting, you save money. And you don't need to necessarily go with the ISP's free Web editor, either. You can easily download and install the editor of your choice. By *Web page editor,* I mean software that lets you format Web pages and then publish them on your Web site. The advantage of creating your own ISP-hosted Web site is control: you can design your page by selecting your own colors and page layouts, and adding as many images as you want. In contrast, a simple Web page feature such as that offered by eBay lets you select a basic page layout that may or may not look the way you want. On the other hand, creating your own Web page and hosting it with an ISP is complex: you're pretty much on your own when it comes to selecting Web page software and learning how to publish your documents with the ISP. It's not all that difficult to learn some HTML, of course, as you can see in the examples in Chapter 5.

NOTE   *Some ISPs discourage individual users setting up commercial Web sites with the Web space that comes with a personal account. If you want to set up a business site to supplement your auction sales, they want you to pay extra for a business Web site account. Check with your own ISP to see what options are available.*

TIP   *It's not hard to find ISPs. You can also peruse some lengthy and detailed lists of ISPs such as The List (**http://thelist.internet.com**) or Providers of Commercial Internet Access (**http://celestin.com/pocia**).*

Use a Dedicated Web Host

If you are planning on running a full-fledged online business, I recommend that you pay a monthly fee and sign up for a full-featured account with a company that is primarily concerned with making Web sites like yours available online. A dedicated

Web hosting service (one that does only hosting, and not Internet access) gives you more disk storage space, more services (such as statistics that report on the number of visits to all of the pages in your site, where your visitors are coming from, and so on), and customer service that is (or at least, should be) a cut above that provided by ISPs or free Web hosts.

Typically, your account with a Web host should enable you to get a "vanity" domain name (in the form **http://www.mysite.com**), anywhere from 50MB to multiple gigabytes of Web space (depending on how much you want to spend each month), as well as multiple e-mail addresses. You may want to look for a hosting package that gives you the ability to process Web page forms by means of computer programs called CGI scripts. You might even get shopping cart software that enables you to set up an online sales catalog from which people can make selections. Your Web host may be able to help you obtain a credit card merchant account as well (see Chapter 9). Each of these types of e-commerce features is a significant step up from a simple Web hosting account, and each carries with it an additional degree of technical complexity. If you are interested in creating an e-commerce Web site, be sure to find a hosting service that will lead you through the process in a user-friendly way without making you set up CGI scripts or other technical features completely on your own.

The following table sums up the Web site alternatives covered in this chapter:

If you want to…	Set up this Web site alternative
Let your eBay customers get to know you better	An About Me page
Sell items for a fixed price	An eBay Store
Have total control over your store and sales	An e-commerce Web site

Find the Right Web Site Creation Software

What software should you use to create your Web pages? If you're on a shoestring and you don't want the trouble of choosing, purchasing, and installing software, consider using Netscape Composer, the Web page tool that is built in with the Web browser package Netscape Communicator. Composer is absolutely free, and it contains plenty of features for creating tables, forms, and other sophisticated Web page elements (see Figure 7-9).

If you don't use Netscape's browser or if you would rather use a more powerful tool, consider Macromedia Dreamweaver (**http://www.macromedia.com**) or

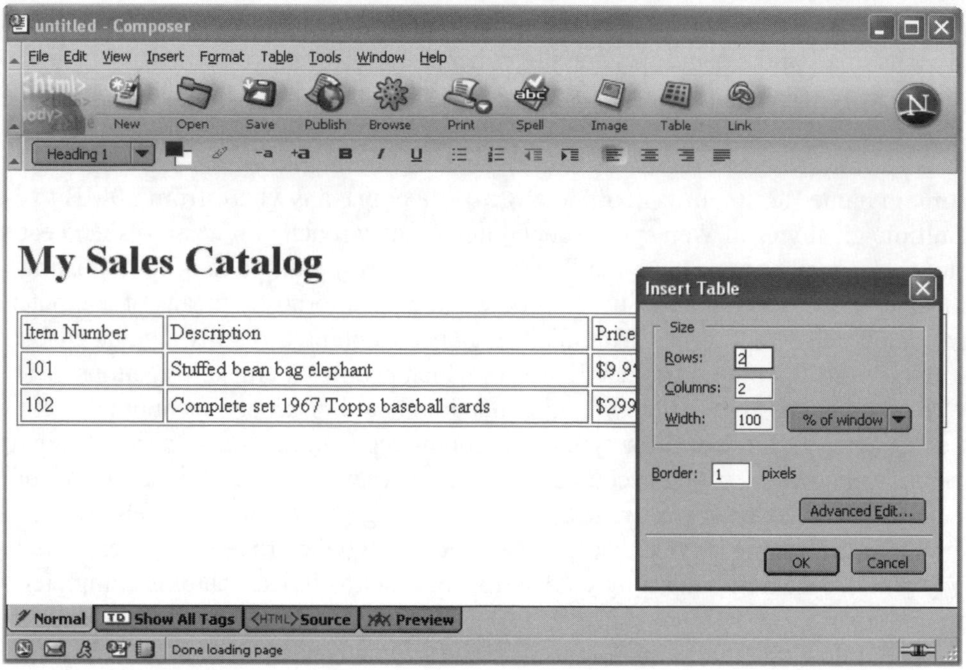

FIGURE 7-9   Netscape Composer is available for free with Netscape's Web browser.

Microsoft FrontPage (**http://www.microsoft.com/frontpage**). These two high-powered programs give you all the tools you need to create Web sites, and they have the ability to move your Web pages from your own computer to your host's site as well. Dreamweaver is shown in Figure 7-10.

Regular Maintenance and Upkeep

On the Web, it's clear what's hot and what's not. One of the worst insults you can get in cyberspace is to be called the keeper of a *cobWeb* page. Make sure your page is always fresh by updating it often. Add new features and remove dated material. Don't put up a page and leave it unattended for long periods of time. Don't include links to your current auctions on your regular Web site; you'll have to update them constantly. Leave such links for an About Me page, where they'll be updated automatically by eBay.

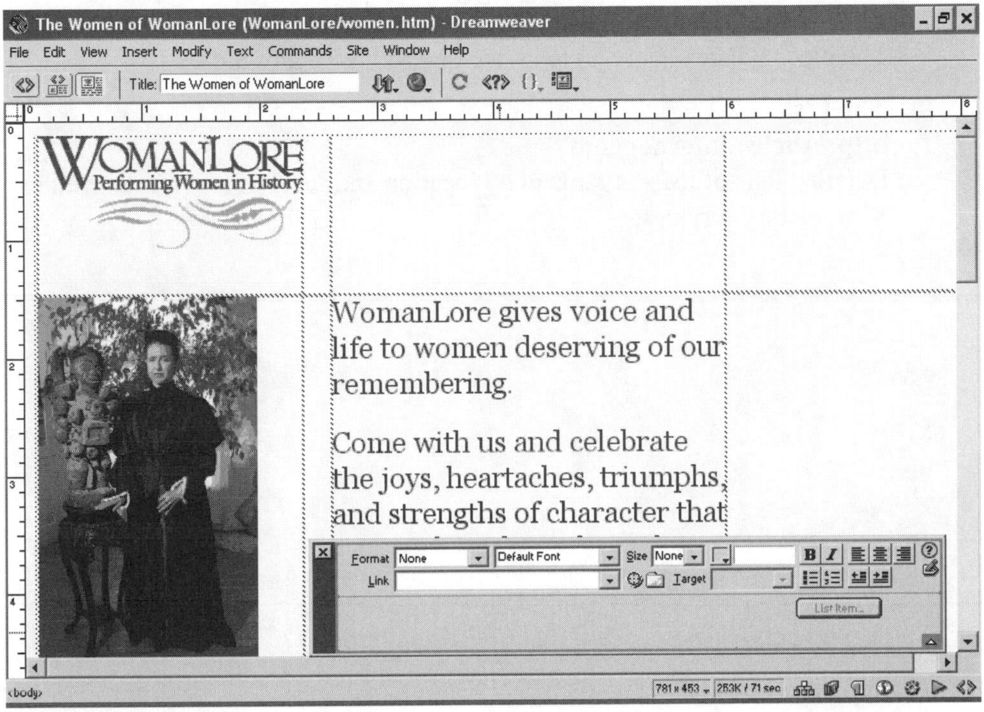

The Women of WomanLore (WomanLore/women.htm) - Dreamweaver

File   Edit   View   Insert   Modify   Text   Commands   Site   Window   Help

Title: The Women of WomanLore

WomanLore gives voice and life to women deserving of our remembering.

Come with us and celebrate the joys, heartaches, triumphs, and strengths of character that

Format None   Default Font   Size None
Link   Target
List Item...

781 x 453   253K / 71 sec

FIGURE 7-10   Macromedia lets you monitor and organize entire Web sites and publish them online.

An even better reason to update your Web site is that you get the chance to rework and improve it. Don't be afraid to consider your site as being continually under construction and something you can always upgrade.

Where to Find It

■ **eBay About Me login page**
http://members.ebay.com/aw-cgi/eBayISAPI.dll?AboutMeLogin
A form you can fill out to begin the process of creating an About Me page on eBay.

■ **eBay Stores home page**
http://www.stores.ebay.com
The welcome page for eBay Stores—the place where customers go to shop.

■ **eBay Storefronts: Seller Landing page**
http://pages.ebay.com/storefronts/seller-landing.html
The place where sellers go to create or edit their eBay Stores.

■ **The List**
http://thelist.internet.com
Detailed lists of ISPs organized by location and level of service, as well as Web hosting services.

Chapter 8

Create Digital Images that Sell

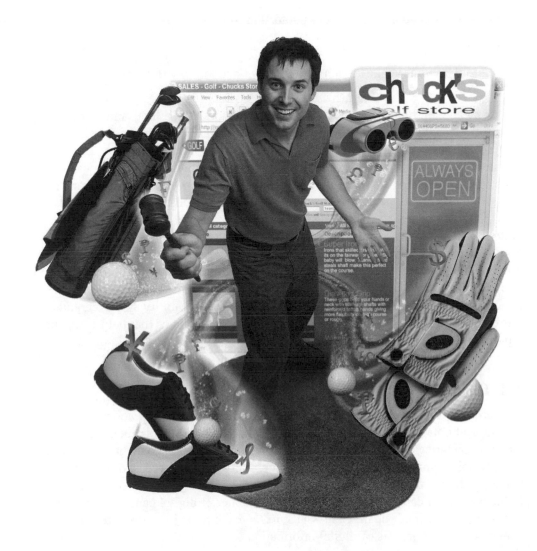

How to...

- Learn to capture digital images of your sales merchandise
- Scan flat (or nearly flat) objects with a flatbed scanner
- Work with common Web graphics formats
- Edit images to optimize their on-screen presentation
- Assemble your own amateur photo studio
- Store your images online
- Link to your images to appear with your auction description

For many auction bidders, a good image is worth more than a thousand words of description. Many of the eBay denizens who scour auction categories searching for unusual, rare, or simply oddball items already know what they want. They scan the description primarily to determine about an item's condition. They pay close attention to the images that accompany the auction listing, however. The more images you have and the clearer they are, the better your chances of getting bids.

Unless you're selling something that's rare and eagerly sought-after, you've pretty much got to have one or more images to go along with its sales listing on eBay. There's really no excuse for not creating those images, even if you're the proverbial techno-phobe. Digital cameras are becoming more affordable and easy to use. You can also call on friends and photo labs to provide you with computer images if you need to. Digital imaging is well within your ability, however, and this chapter will show you how to create good-quality graphics that help you gain top dollar for what you want to sell.

Capture Those Images

The term *capture* probably makes it sound like you need to go out and rope a wild animal. But obtaining images that you can publish on the Web is much easier than that. By "capturing" an image so you can use it online, I mean that you have to create, save, or obtain images in the form of computer files—in other words, digital images. Once you have a digital image in your computer, you can get it on your Web page. In the process of capturing a digital image, a scanner or digital camera turns the image into very small squares, known as *pixels*. Each pixel in a computer image contains one or more bits of digital information.

Digital images that consist of pixels are called *bitmaps*. Bitmaps are images that have been saved in a format that makes them easy to display and transmit online. Scanned photos on Web pages should be clear, small in size, tightly cropped, and compressed so they appear quickly in a browser window.

NOTE   *TIFF (Tagged Image File Format), PNG (Portable Network Graphics), GIF (Graphics Interchange Format), and JPEG (Joint Experts Photographic Group) are all bitmapped image formats used in computer graphics. JPEG and PNG are used to present photos on the Web, so you need to save your digital photos in one of these two formats. eBay Picture Services only supports JPEG, however.*

Are you keeping all of these technical details straight? You won't be quizzed on them. The least you need to know is this: you need to get images of your sales items into your computer in JPEG or PNG format. How do you obtain (or "capture") digital images of your auction merchandise? You've got four basic options:

8

- ■ **Take a digital photo**   The most practical and affordable option is to use a digital camera to take a photo of what you want to sell. The camera saves the image directly to computer disk. Digital cameras like the one shown in Figure 8-1 are becoming more affordable all the time; you can take as many photos as your camera's memory will hold and transfer them to your computer in a matter of seconds.

- ■ **Scan the image**   Scanners like the flatbed model shown in Figure 8-2 are less expensive than digital cameras—you can find them at Buy It Now prices of $40 to $60. You can also rent time on a scanner at a branch of Kinko's Copies. Or you can borrow a friend's scanning device. Simply take a conventional photo of an object with a camera and scan the image to convert it to the computer file.

- ■ **Use a photo lab**   You can take a conventional print or slide photo and have the photo lab return the images to you on computer disk instead of as prints or slides.

- ■ **Capture a digital video image of the object**   Digital video cameras like the one shown in Figure 8-3 take still images that you can save directly to disk. Plus, you can take high-quality video of your family, too.

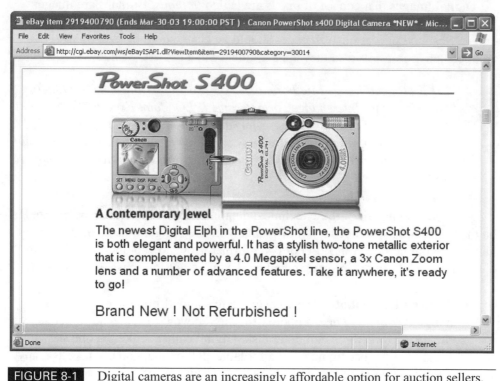

FIGURE 8-1   Digital cameras are an increasingly affordable option for auction sellers.

The option you choose depends on how many auctions you plan to conduct, on your budget, and your level of comfort with technology. If you only plan to put a few auctions online once in a while, you can take photos with a conventional camera and have a photo lab convert your images to digital files, but this can quickly get expensive. You can use a scanner, but these work best with flat objects such as magazines, and their size is limited by the size of the device's scanning area. Your most economical option is probably to use a digital camera, as described in the following section.

Use a Digital Camera

Digital cameras bring a new level of convenience to capturing images that can be viewed and edited on a computer. My own experience tells me that this is how

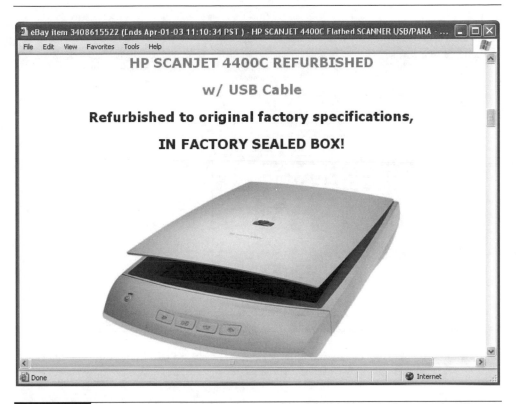

FIGURE 8-2 Flatbed scanners are inexpensive but designed mostly for scanning flat objects.

the majority of eBay sellers take their auction images. There are so many digital cameras on the market that this chapter isn't going to attempt recommendations at which model is best for you to buy. Rather, it assumes that you already have a digital camera and you're looking for some tips on how to use it to capture auction images.

Most digital cameras give you two ways of composing images. You can look either through the viewfinder (the little window on the back of the camera) or the Liquid Crystal Display (LCD), the miniature screen that lets you preview images. To my mind, the LCD is preferable because it's more precise. But don't depend on the little framing square that's supposed to indicate what's going to be in the final

FIGURE 8-3   You can use digital video cameras to capture still images of your auction items.

image to be perfect. Leave some extra room around the edges when you frame your images (see Figure 8-4).

Digital cameras give you the ability to preview images and simply throw them out and redo them if they aren't the way you want. Virtually all digital cameras allow you to zoom in on your subject as well. As a general rule, the closer you are the sharper your image. You should try to get as close as possible to your subject before taking the photo.

Purchase a Scanner

If you consistently sell printed material such as postcards, stamps, or historical documents, you should use a device that's specially designed to capture those images in the form of computer files—a flatbed scanner. A scanner is computer hardware that digitizes a single object by moving an optical device much like a camera across it. There are different types of scanners around, but the most practical and easiest to use is a flatbed; its name reflects the fact that the bed on which the photo or other image is placed is flat.

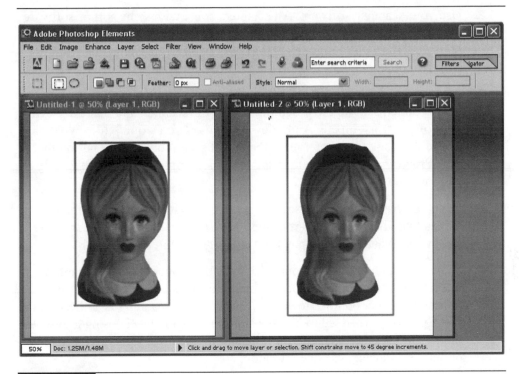

FIGURE 8-4   The image on the left is too tight; the other is just right.

TIP   *Scanners are sometimes advertised as having very fine resolutions. While this is important if you intend to scan images for printed booklets, if you're scanning for eBay or the Web you only need a resolution of 72 dpi (dots per inch), and any scanner can scan at that relatively coarse setting. But it's a good idea to scan at 144 or 300 dpi and then reduce the resolution using an image editing program in order to get better detail.*

Scanning, Step by Step

After you buy a scanner and set it up, you won't find it that difficult to use. However, some rules of thumb can ensure that your objects turn out clear and sharp:

1. Pick a good image. Remember that your images won't appear in print; they'll be seen on a computer screen. You have to account for those shoppers who have old, murky monitors. Select high contrast images—images that have a clear difference between light and dark areas.

2. Use your scanning software. All scanners come with some sort of software that lets you scan the images and save them in various formats. Sometimes, scanners come with programs that act as *plug-ins* (programs that work within another graphics program like Adobe Photoshop).

3. After you install the software, following the instructions that come with your scanner, start up the program, turn on the scanner, and make a preview scan of your first image. A preview scan gives you a quick idea what an image will look like after you do the actual scan. Look for the button that says Preview, such as the one in the lower-left corner of the DeskScan II window, shown in Figure 8-5.

4. Once you have the preview scan on screen, crop it. *Cropping* an image means that you select the part of the image that you want to appear in the final version and leave out parts of the image that aren't essential.

5. Select an input mode. An input mode tells the scanner how you want the information in the image to be captured. For most auction images, you'll choose the Color option. However, if what you're scanning is a black and white photo, you can reduce the file size dramatically by choosing grayscale mode. On the other hand, if you're scanning line art, a signature, a cartoon, or another drawing, use line art mode.

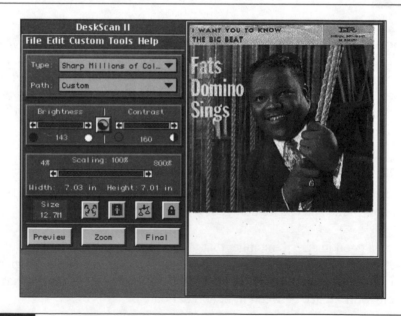

 FIGURE 8-5   A preview scan lets you crop or reduce an image before you make the final scan.

6. Set the resolution. Since you're scanning auction images for the Web, choose 150 or 300 dots per inch (dpi). Since computer monitors can display no more than approximately 72 dpi, reduce the resolution to 72 dpi in a graphics program.

7. Make adjustments. All scanning software comes with brightness and contrast controls that you can move to see if the image improves. You can do this later using image editing software, but why not save yourself the work by making improvements at the scanning stage?

When you're done with all the preparation work, you can press the Scan button and finally scan your image.

> TIP
>
> *It's a good idea to calibrate your scanner before you start making scans. Calibrating means that you match the scanner to your monitor so that your image previews are accurate. the exact procedure differs from scanner to scanner. But in general, you make a test scan of an image. Next, you use your scanning software's calibration controls. The exact menu options vary depending on the software used.*

8

You Can Scan More than Just Paper

A scanner can be great for scanning flat objects for the Web, but you can also scan some three-dimensional items, like watches or almost-flat toys. Just drape some black cloth or clothing over the object so it covers the glass and you'll have a clean background behind what you're scanning. If a scanner is all you have, you can use it to scan items that are bigger than the scanning surface (such as LP-record albums) in pieces and then reassemble them using an image editing program (see "Choose a Graphics Editor" later in this chapter).

You can also find scanners that do more than just scan—they function as color copiers and fax machines as well. They, too, are becoming more affordable all the time and they regularly show up on eBay for Buy It Now prices under $200.

Set Up Your Photo Studio

Most eBay sellers who take their own digital photos (in other words, most eBay sellers) set up a miniature photo studio in their home. It's easy enough to set one up, and not that expensive, either. Here's a shopping list for what you'll need:

■ **A table**   I'm talking about a moderately-sized table on which you can place and light your sales items. Things that are too large to fit atop the table can go in front of it.

- **Lights**   Make an effort to obtain professional studio lights. I say more about this in the section on lighting that follows.

- **Tripod**   A tripod like the one show below is a stand with extendable legs on which you can place your camera. A tripod isn't just to hold the camera still while you snap the shutter. In a photo studio, a tripod enables you to position the merchandise and the camera just right and adjust the lighting as well. Once you point your camera at your table, you can leave it there from photo to photo.

- **Power supply**   Instead of having to replace batteries every few days, purchase the rechargeable variety.

- **Display stands**   If you're selling jewelry and other items that consist of multiple pieces, you'll do well to purchase a display stand that includes a riser—something that makes the items stand up so you can photograph them better.

- **Fabric**   A solid, seamless background is a must-have for good photos of auction merchandise. Go to the local fabric store and get several lengths of four- or six-foot wide fabric in several solid colors. Black is pretty much required for light items; also get a light neutral color such as white, gray, or beige so you can choose the color that makes the item look the best.

Give Your Piece a Chance

All the lighting, backgrounds, and even the best digital camera in the world can't make up for forgetting to do some basic things when you actually take your photo. For instance:

- **Whip out the Windex**   Be sure to take a towel and wipe off what you're selling. Brush the cat hairs off those clothes, polish that silver, and wipe the dirt smudges and fingerprints off those plastic slim-line phones. But remember to take care not to wipe too hard or use too strong a cleaner or you'll damage what you're trying to sell.

- **Move in for a close-up**   Most good digital cameras have powerful zoom lenses; use them to get nice and close on your item before you actually take the photo. If you're too far away, you'll lose detail and your item might even look out of focus.

- **Clean up the area**   A smudge on a wall or a stray toy on the floor can distract attention from what you want people to look at.

- **Clean your lens**   If you've been using your camera outdoors or if you have forgotten to put on the lens cap recently, wipe off the lens (with a clean, photo-quality lens cloth rather than a shirtsleeve or paper towel) so you don't obscure your image.

- **Check your focus**   The autofocus feature on many digital cameras doesn't work perfectly all of the time. Take a good look through the viewfinder or LCD and adjust the focus manually, if necessary, before you click.

8

One of the many nice things about digital cameras is that you can take as many photos as you want, erase the ones you don't like, and save only the best. Don't be reluctant to photograph an image from many different angles and with many different levels of zoom. You can publish as many photos as you want with your auctions— though I never seem to see more than six or eight at any one time. Don't limit yourself to one or two.

Studio Lights

If you need to take lots of images, and you've been plagued by dim and deeply shadowed images, you might consider a drastic upgrade and buying studio lights for your eBay images. The problem is that the built-in flash on a digital camera comes from only one direction and is apt to leave shadows around the edges of what you're photographing. Two or three good studio lights with umbrellas to diffuse the light, like the ones shown in Figure 8-6, will do the trick.

Let the Sun Shine

You may want to take your photos outdoors in order to avoid the problems caused by homemade backgrounds and shadows caused by indoor spot lighting. (As an alternative, you can place your item by a window that catches the sun and put a white cotton cloth or bed sheet over the window to diffuse the light.) It can be tricky to take photos outdoors, because the sun can produce shadows that actually make merchandise more difficult to see rather than easier. But on a bright cloudy day, the lighting outdoors is even and very good. Steve Brothers of Silk Road

FIGURE 8-6   Professional studio lights will pay off in the long run.

Trading Concern (User ID: silkroad) shoots all of his merchandise outdoors—
in Nepal. He says:

> "We use a digital camera to photograph our items. I prefer to shoot outdoors in
> indirect light. Taking product photos is something one gets better at over time.
> The clients will guide you in terms of the necessity for auxiliary detail photos.
> We only ran one front view in the early days, and people would e-mail us asking
> for extra shots. We eventually realized that some items such as statues or paintings
> often require multiple shots—side views, back views, or close-ups."

Choose an Image Format

Whether you use a digital camera or scanner to save your images to disk, you need
to choose a file format in which to save them. The file formats that are especially
designed to process photos on the Web, JPEG and PNG, process digital information
in an image and compress files to make them consume less disk space. All Web
browsers can open and display files in these formats. Of these two, eBay recommends
that you save your image in JPEG format.

NOTE *Both GIF and JPEG images display correctly on eBay auction pages.
JPEG, however, is generally a better format for photographic images
with lots of colors, while GIF generally works better for line drawings.*

If you pay extra for a photo lab to create digital images for you, you can
tell the service to save the files as JPEGs. Otherwise, you can do so yourself by
using the software that comes with your scanner, digital camera, or other hardware
device. Usually, you save in JPEG format by choosing File | Save from the program's
menu bar and then choosing JPEG from the list of formats that are available. You
also need to save the file with the file name extension JPG (or, on a Macintosh, JPEG).

NOTE *JPEG compresses image files, but it provides you with several different levels
of compression from which to choose. The higher the level of compression,
the smaller the image file. At maximum compression, however, you lose
some information in the image, and the image doesn't appear as sharp
as it can if you use a lower level of compression. If you're not sure which
level to choose, try High or Maximum compression to keep the file size as
small as possible.*

Create Images that Sell

You've got a snazzy new digital camera, you've read the instruction booklet, and you've even taken a few test images. You probably think all you need to do now is point, click, and upload to get your photos on the Web along with your auction descriptions. You *can* do that, and it's even possible that some of your photos will come out perfectly the first time. Remember, though, that I'm trying to provide you with instructions for running a successful eBay business. An important part of consistently selling at auction is coming up with a system for creating good images that attract attention and help people decide whether what you're offering is a good match for what they need.

The fact is, most of the time, the images you take of your auction items are going to need some adjustments before you put them online. If you devote a few minutes to brightening your images, cropping them, they'll show your objects in their best light (and I mean that literally). You'll separate your images from the ones I see on all too many eBay auctions that are too large, take too long to appear, and are dark and fuzzy to boot. You'll have another way to show your prospective customers that you are a professional and serious about selling on eBay.

Choose a Graphics Editor

Often, images aren't good if you capture them straight from your scanner, digital camera, or other input device. Instead, after you save your image in JPEG or PNG format, you can then edit (or, in photographic terms, *retouch*) the image in a graphics program to improve its appearance.

Personally, I like a program called Adobe Photoshop Elements which, you'll be happy to know, comes bundled with many digital cameras. If you get this software along with your camera, you've got a great deal. Here are the kinds of things you should adjust with Photoshop Elements or another graphics program:

- **Adjust contrast and brightness**   The *contrast* of an image is the degree of difference between its light and dark tones. *Brightness* refers to the vibrancy or energy of the colors or shades of color in the image. Images displaying adequate levels of contrast and brightness are easier to view on a monitor. Photoshop Elements' controls are shown in Figure 8-7.

- **Resize images**   Resize images so that they're smaller than originally scanned and fit well on the eBay auction Web page. (Look through your graphics program's menus to find a resize option.)

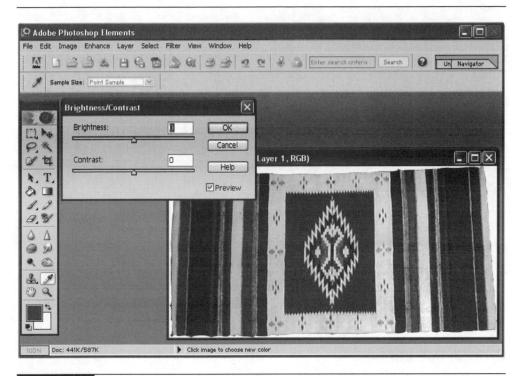

FIGURE 8-7   Graphics editors give you great control over an image's appearance.

TIP *Generally speaking, an image that's two or three inches wide and perhaps four to five inches tall is a good size. File sizes of 20 to 30K or less are also desirable.*

■ **Zoom in on what's important**   *Cropping* refers to the practice of cutting out unnecessary details and keeping a certain area of the image on which you want to focus. It makes the image size smaller so that the photo fits better in a Web browser window. By making the image smaller, you also make the file size smaller. An image that's, say, 12K in size appears on-screen much faster than does one that's 100K in size.

Keep File Size Small

You can't depend on your bidders to have relatively fast cable modem, DSL, or other fast connections. You don't know whether they're viewing your images on

Other Graphics Editors

Photoshop Elements (and its "big brother" program, the professional graphics editor simply called Photoshop) are terrific programs, but they consume lots of memory and disk space. (Photoshop Elements 2 requires 128MB of RAM and from 150 to 350MB of hard disk space.) I also like the simpler Windows program Paint Shop Pro, by Jasc, Inc. (**http://www.jasc.com/pspdl.html**).

If you are a Macintosh user, and you don't want to invest in a complex program like Adobe Photoshop Elements, Thorsten Lemke's GraphicConverter is a great shareware ($35) graphics program. You can download or purchase it from **http://www.lemkesoft.de/us_index.html**. iPhoto is a free program that runs on any Mac that uses OS X: find out more at **http://www.apple.com/iphoto**.

an old, slow computer or a speedy new one. Your goal is to make your images consume as little memory as possible, so they appear in the browser window right away. These are simple tasks that you can perform in virtually any graphics editor to optimize your images for quick viewing.

Crop Those Photos

Simply scanning an entire photo from edge to edge and putting the entire photo on your Web page usually results in an image that takes up more space than it should—in terms of physical size (height and width) as well as disk space. Cropping a photo does two things:

- It concentrates the viewer's eye on the most important area
- Makes the file size and the image size smaller

Cropping an image is important and you should do it whenever possible. The smaller an image file is, the quicker it will appear on your bidders' computer screens. You do this by clicking the cropping button, positioning your mouse pointer just above and to one side of the image, clicking and holding down your mouse button, and dragging your mouse down and to the opposite side of the image. Release your mouse when the subject of your photo is outlined with the marquee box.

Cropping photos whenever possible literally reduces the number of bits of information in the photo. A 196×232-pixel photo might contain 13K (13,000 bits) of information; reducing it to 120×142 pixels reduces the size dramatically. It's important to keep photos small in size to ensure that they fit within the smallest computer screens. Remember that although a minority of Web surfers have 21-inch flat-screen monitors; many others have 17-inch monitors that are actually only about 12-inches in width. Within that space, a user may configure a Web browser window to be only 7 to 10 inches in width. Smaller photos aren't that hard to see clearly on Web pages because people typically sit very close to their computer screen. Keeping your images 3 to 6 inches in width is a safe measurement that most people will be able to see in their entirety.

Set the Resolution

Earlier in this chapter, I mentioned that scanned images are made up of little bits of information called pixels. Those dots are small, but they aren't always the same size. When you scan an image, you have the option of making the dots *really* small so that the image appears extra smooth. This is called setting the *resolution* of an image. The size of the dots is expressed in dots per inch (dpi). The higher the number of dots per inch, the smaller the dots are, and the finer the image will be.

Setting the resolution is a simple matter when you are preparing images for eBay. Scan at 300 dpi resolution, then reduce the resolution to 72 dpi when you edit the image in a graphics program.

8

TIP   *If the image seems dark or "muddy," adjust the brightness and contrast. In most scanning programs, the brightness and contrast controls are sliders that you can move either to the left or right. Try them out and see if the image improves. If you're happy with the image as is, leave the brightness and contrast set to zero.*

Create Thumbnail Images

You can use a graphics program to create a *thumbnail* or miniature version of an image to a larger, more memory intensive version. The smaller version (which takes up only a small amount of memory, and appears on screen quickly) gives the viewer a glimpse of what the full image will look like, and the chance to decide whether to view the full image in greater detail. Clicking on the link brings a larger, more detailed version of the image to screen (which is larger in size, and takes longer to appear on screen).

Take Time With Your Presentation

The way you present your merchandise has a big effect on whether people will pass them by or make a bid. If you have clothing to sell, or if you regularly sell watches or jewelry, by all means invest in some mannequins on which to mount them (see Figure 8-8). They'll look much better if people can visualize how they look on a human body, rather than laying flat on a table. Where better to find mannequins than on eBay itself?

Don't be reluctant to include lots of clear photos with an item, no matter how "unpicturesque" it might appear. For instance, how many photos can you take of an old hat? mrmodern included so many good close-ups in this listing that, if the hat would have fit me, I would have bid on it myself.

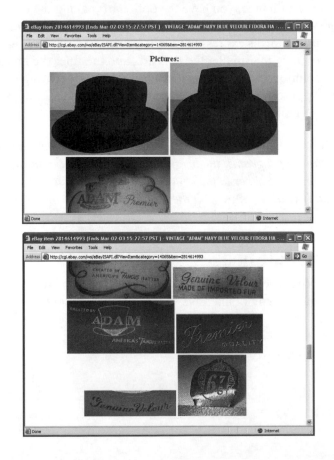

FIGURE 8-8   Be sure to display clothing or jewelry on mannequins.

Find a Home for Your Images

In order for images to appear on auction listings or other Web pages, they need to find a home—a virtual home, that is, in the form of space on a computer that's connected to the Internet all the time, called a Web server. You've got plenty of options for finding that home. Your ISP may provide you with storage space; you can send your photos to eBay's Picture Services; or you can sign up with a full-time photo hosting service. The options are described in the sections that follow.

eBay Picture Services

eBay's own photo hosting services, eBay Picture Services, has undergone some changes in the past few years. For one thing, it used to be called eBay iPIX. For another, it used to be the object of much criticism. eBay iPIX was accused of problems with image quality and limitations of size. eBay Picture Services is easier to use, and the quality is better as well—especially if you use the full-featured version

How to ... Upload an Image

1. From any eBay page, click the **Sell** button in the toolbar.

2. Choose the category in which you want to sell you item.

3. Log in with your eBay User ID and password and click **Continue**.

4. Fill out the Sell Your Item form. The Basic Version of Picture Services appears by default (see Figure 8-9). Click **Browse** to locate the image file (or files) you want to add. Locate the file on your computer, click **Open**, and the image is added to the list of files to upload when you create your auction listing at the end of the form.

5. However, if you use a Windows computer, click the link **Try our full featured version** just to the right of the Basic Picture Services. If a dialog box appears asking if you want to download an ActiveX Control or Java Applet, click Yes. (You need these mini-programs to use the other version of Picture Services.) The Full-Featured Picture Services appears.

6. You can upload an image using Full-Featured Picture Services in one of two ways. Click on a box to select a photo file on your computer. Or, you can click on a photo file stored on your computer and drag the file to one of the picture boxes in the Add Pictures page.

NOTE   *Full-Featured Picture Services works only with Windows computers; Basic Picture Services works with Macintosh or Windows.*

that lets Windows users drag image files from their computer to the Sell Your Item form to get them online.

eBay Picture Services seems to be shaping up as far as image quality, but if you sell large quantities of merchandise on a regular basis, you still might want to shop around. The service lets you include one image per item for no charge. You are charged a nominal fee (at this writing, 15 cents) for subsequent images of the same item. Suppose you sell 100 items per month, and you post an average of two

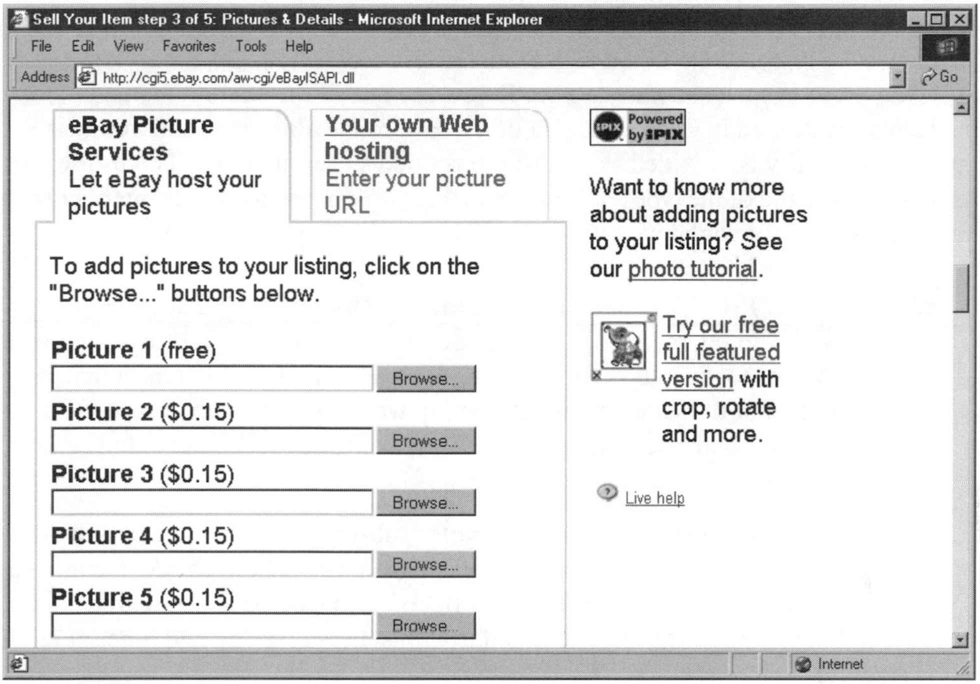

FIGURE 8-9   eBay Basic Picture Services

images of each item. You could easily end up paying an extra $15 per month just for image hosting. It pays to at least know your options when it comes to finding a Web server that can host your digital image file (that is, one that enables you to place the file in a directory on the server so that someone with a Web browser can access it).

> **TIP**   *eBay University includes an online tutorial that explains how to take digital photos and add them to your auction listings at **http://pages .ebay.com/education/tutorial/course2/photo_1.html**.*

Other Photo Hosts

It pays to shop around when looking for a Web server that your auction images can call home. After all, if your images don't appear reliably and quickly, your bidders might well leave your sale and bid on someone else's items. Another consideration is the software you use to get your images from your computer to the Web storage space. You may have to use a special program that does the transfer by using a special set of instructions called File Transfer Protocol (FTP). Other services (such as AOL) provide such software to you. If you use one of the auction management packages mentioned in Chapter 6, you don't have to install special software, either; the transfer utility is provided as part of the service's user interface. The following list describes some of the types of Web hosts that you can use to make your auction image files available online:

■ **Your own ISP**   The first place to turn is to the company that gives you access to the Internet: your Internet Service Provider (ISP). Providing users with access to the Internet and hosting Web sites are two different functions, certainly, but the same organization may well perform them. Many ISPs provide you with use of at least 10MB of Web site space at no additional cost to you.

■ **America Online (AOL)**   AOL enables subscribers to create and publish their own Web pages or to place simple image files on the Web. (As mentioned in Chapter 7, you get as much as 14MB of Web storage space with a basic AOL account.) AOL is quite popular with sellers on eBay and other auction services.

■ **A Web hosting service**   The same Web hosting services that publish your Web sites give you space that can be used for posting images and Web pages alike. See Chapter 7 for suggestions.

■ **An auction management service**   Most services that help you manage your auction sales, such as ManageAuctions.com (**http:// www.manageauctions.com**) and AuctionHelper.com (**http://www .auctionhelper.com**) make it easy to upload your image files.

■ **A photo hosting service**   A few Web sites specialize in providing space where eBay and other auction users can publish auction images to accompany sales listings. PixHost (at **http://www.pixhost.com**), for example, enables you to host two images on its site for free; after that trial usage, hosting images costs 50 cents each for 30 days, which is far more expensive than eBay's own Picture Services. However, you can upload files using your Web browser, as described in the site's online tutorial (see Figure 8-10).

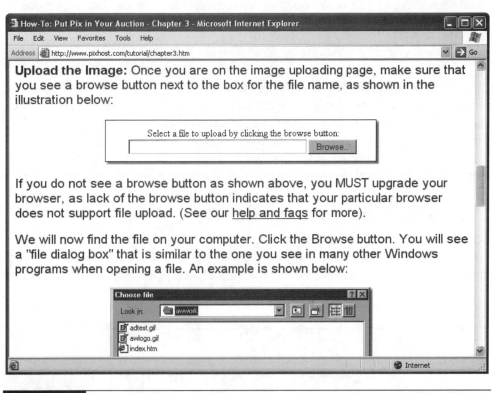

FIGURE 8-10   An image hosting service gives you a way to upload image files with your browser.

TIP   *If you use Adobe Photoshop Elements 2, you have the ability to move files from your computer to storage space with the online photo service Shutterfly (**http://www.shutterfly.com**). You can even upload the files after you edit them in Photoshop Elements, without having to use a special file transfer program. Mac users can get 100MB of storage space through Apple's .Mac subscription service, which costs $99 per year after a free 60-day trial period.*

Linking to Your Image

After you create a digital image and add it to your host site, you add that image to your sales description by specifying the URL for the image on the eBay Sell Your Item form. All ISPs provide customers with instructions on how to figure out their Web page URLs. Call the Customer Service section of your ISP, or check the company's FAQ. A common convention is to assign a URL that looks like this (this example is for a JPEG image, which has the filename extension .jpg)

```
http://www.yourISP.com/~yourusername/filename.jpg
```

After posting an image online, verify that it actually appears on your page. The most common cause of a broken image or question mark icon appearing with your description instead of the image itself is an incorrect URL. If you're typing the URL from scratch, you must get it right exactly: A single blank space, capital letter, or typo in an URL can prevent a Web browser from locating the image and displaying it on-screen.

Upload Your Image to the Gallery

You can also specify whether to place any images that accompany your listing in the eBay Gallery as well as displaying them on the auction Web page itself. If you put a number of your images in the Gallery (at 25 cents per image), you can create

FIGURE 8-11   For an extra 25 cents, you can create your own photo Gallery.

your own photo gallery. If someone searches for your items and clicks Gallery View, they can see them all at once (see Figure 8-11).

The Gallery is a collection of images that auction sellers submit of items they're currently offering for sale. Buyers can browse through the images and click one in which they're interested; clicking the image takes them to the auction sales page where they can read a description and place a bid if they so choose. The Gallery doesn't display all the images that accompany auction listings—only the ones for which sellers pay the extra 25-cent fee for extra exposure in the Gallery. (You can splurge and pay $19.95 to place your image in a featured area of the Gallery as well.)

TIP   *You can create a link to your own Gallery page that you can include on your own Web site or your About Me page. Be sure to replace the eBayUserID string with your own user ID:*

```
<a href=http://search-desc.ebay.com/search/search.dll?MfcISAPICommand=
GetResult&query=eBayUserID&srchdesc=y&ebaytag1=ebayreg&ebaytag1code=0&ht=
1&SortProperty=MetaEndSort&sc=1&st=2> Click here to view my Gallery auctions
</a>
```

8

Where to Find It

■ **eBay University photo tutorial**
http://pages.ebay.com/education/tutorial/ course2/photo_1.html
An online tutorial that briefly explains how to capture and save images and get them online.

■ **eBay Picture Services**
http://pages.ebay.com/help/basics/ pictureservices.html
An overview of eBay's photo hosting service, plus links to a FAQ and an online tutorial on how to add a photo to your auction listing.

■ **Photos/HTML Discussion Board**
http://forums.ebay.com/db1/forum .jsp?forum=99
Discussions about how to post photos on eBay and edit auction listings with HTML.

Part III

Business Practices for eBay

Chapter 9

Accept Payments and Serve Your Customers

How to…

- Use e-mail to answer prospective bidders' questions
- Send out end-of-auction notices and reminders
- Respond to complaints and problems after the sale
- Accept checks and money orders safely
- Take advantage of payment services that streamline transactions
- Accept credit card payments
- Verify credit card purchasers' information

Putting your first sale online is exciting. Watching the bids come in is a thrill. Watching the action as the sale closes can make your pulse pound. But the real rewarding part—the real satisfaction—comes when you are paid for what you sold. All of your hard work pays off when you get a check in the mail or you have a notice that funds have been transferred to your account.

Before you get to the payment stage, you need to interact with your customers at several critical stages. How you respond to bidders who make inquiries as well as your auction winners has a direct bearing on the level of trust and professionalism you present online. Providing good customer service not only makes transactions go more smoothly, it also builds goodwill on eBay as a whole and has a tangible benefit in terms of the positive feedback you receive.

Sellers on eBay have an advantage when it comes to the end of the sale. They have lots of alternatives for receiving payment. The main problem is the deadbeat seller—the one who never sends payment in the first place. Once people respond to your e-mails and send payment, it's likely that things will go smoothly. Yes, checks bounce once in a while. Yes, there is credit card fraud. But the overwhelming majority of transactions go smoothly, and most buyers are courteous and fun to deal with. That's why sellers keep coming back to put items up for sale. This is when eBay is really fun. This chapter spells out your options for receiving payment.

Customer Service

eBay grew to become so popular because people who use it are, for the most part, trustworthy. Encounters tend to be positive rather than negative. If transactions on eBay went badly more often than not, the service would not be so popular. As a seller, you need to know how to handle your customers with care in order to preserve that atmosphere of goodwill.

Even if you don't own a brick-and-mortar store and don't manage a big corporate retail outlet, you need to provide good service to the people who buy from you, just like the big guys. In fact, because you're a lone seller, you can add a personal touch that big e-commerce retailers can't match. A pack of coffee included with a coffee maker, a few bags of tea included with a teapot, and a quick and courteous answer to a question can build a good reputation as well as a dependable customer base.

Become an E-Mail Expert

The best advice I can give to you as far as dealing with prospective bidders and buyers on eBay is to keep in constant e-mail contact, and keep your communications courteous and friendly whenever possible. Respond to inquires quickly, and send out end-of-sale notices as soon as you can after the auction ends.

Answer Questions

Responding to e-mail inquiries is one of the most practical and important ways in which you can build good customer relations. Try your best to answer questions posed by bidders as quickly as you can—within one day or less if possible. In your auction listings, be sure to include whether you plan to be out of town for a length of time so customers will know that there might be a delay in your responses to their inquiries.

Also make an effort to be professional in your communications with customers. What does that mean, exactly? It means spelling correctly, using correct grammar, and using salutations like Hello, Thanks, Best Wishes, or Sincerely. These little details are the substitute for the nuances of tone of voice, gestures and facial expression that you can't express online. You'll get even more points if you thank people for writing:

> Thank you for your inquiry regarding the Sheaffer Scrip Ink container. This is a display container that was probably used in pen shops. However, it does contain ink, and the ink appears to be liquid and useable (I haven't used it myself, however; I can't guarantee that you could actually write with it.) There are a couple of minor tears in the box and an ink stain on the bottom; otherwise the box is in excellent condition.

Don't forget to check my other auctions for fountain pens and other writing accessories that you might also enjoy.

Best wishes,
Greg Holden

> **TIP** *Some of the best tips for dealing with eBay buyers and sellers in a courteous manner—even when they get mad at you for some reason—can be found on the Web site of eBay's longtime seller and instructor Uncle Griff (**http://www.unclegriff.com**).*

Send the End-of-Sale Notification

Many big-time eBay sellers sell multiple items every single day, and they need to use auction software of the sort described in Chapter 6 to send out e-mails in bulk to their winning bidders. If you don't sell quite so often and you have the time, however, you should take the time to send out personal notifications to your high bidders once they have won what you're offering. The notification letter can still start out as a template with fields that you customize. You don't have to re-create it from scratch for every sale. You might create a letter like the following that covers all the main points: the item sold, the shipping costs, the payment method, your address, and a time frame for payment.

I am happy to announce that you are the winning bidder for eBay item #122334455, the Shaeffer Scrip ink container. I look forward to a smooth transaction ending in positive feedback for both of us.

I accept payment by PayPal, a personal check, cashier's check, or money order. Please send the following within the next 7 days:

Winning bid amount: $29.95

Shipping (Priority Mail): $6.00

TOTAL Amount Due: $35.95

If you want me to ship by Express Mail, tell me and I will calculate a new amount for you. Please include either a copy of this e-mail address with your payment, or write the eBay item number on your check. Send to:

Greg Holden
1234 Anywhere Street
Chicago, IL 60611

If you pay by personal check, your order will ship after a 14-day clearing period.

Thank you for your winning bid. I am happy to be working with you toward a smooth transaction.

Best wishes,
Greg Holden

If you want to make some extra points marketing your other sales, you can include a link to your About Me or eBay Stores page or to another Web site. But most buyers just want the facts, and if they're happy with the merchandise and the speed of the transaction, they'll search out your other sales eventually.

Use eBay's Checkout Option

Rather than having to calculate your shipping and handling totals in your end of the auction e-mail message, you can expedite the transaction by entering the details in the Sell Your Item form when you prepare to put your sale online. That way, your customers can use eBay's Checkout feature to calculate the charges themselves when the sale ends (see Figure 9-1).

Send a Payment Reminder

Correspondence with customers gets less pleasant when you have to send a payment reminder to someone who hasn't yet paid for your auction items. However, that doesn't mean you need to lose your courteous, professional approach. Being nice when things aren't going perfectly is a sure-fire way to get positive feedback from grateful customers, in fact. Be businesslike and firm when you send your reminder; keep in mind that payment may have been lost in the mail, the high bidder may have fallen ill or gone out of town, the neighbor's dog may have eaten the check on the way to the mailbox, or any number of legitimate reasons. Be sure to specify a time frame for receiving your response to the reminder e-mail:

Dear Buyer,

Last week you won a bottle of Scrip ink on one of my eBay auctions. The payment due date for this auction passed yesterday and I have not received a check or other payment notification. Perhaps the payment has gotten lost in the mail or you haven't been able to get to this matter yet.

I'd appreciate it if you could e-mail me within 24 hours to let me know what's going on, and whether you want to follow through with the transaction. Otherwise, I would like to re-list the item if you don't want it anymore.

Best wishes,
Greg Holden

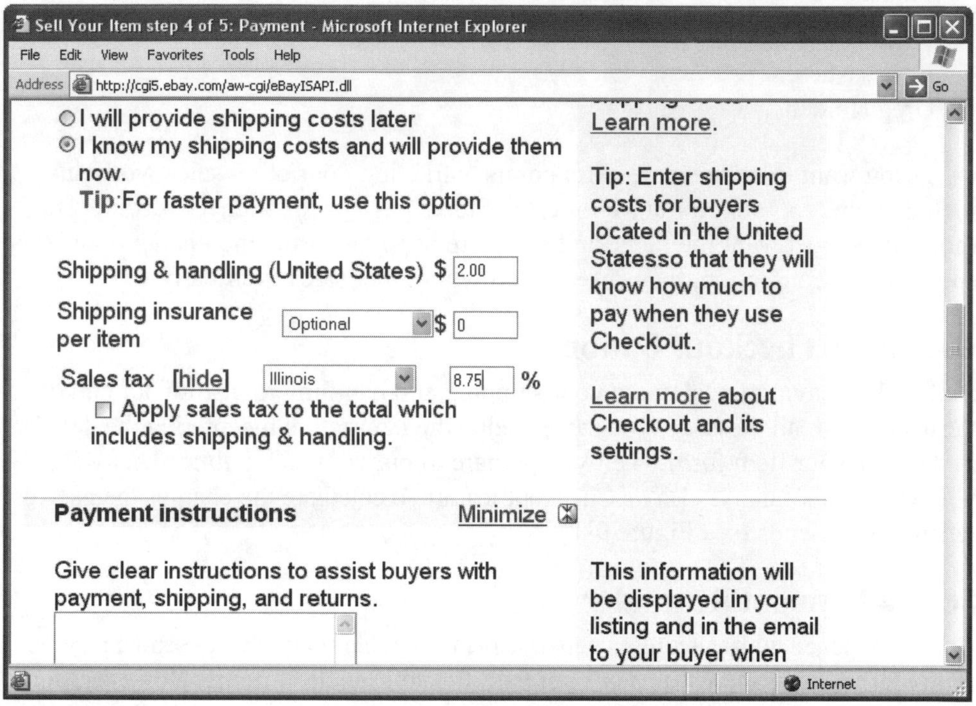

FIGURE 9-1 Help your customers by entering shipping and other charges when you create the sale.

Send a Shipping Notice

It's not technically necessary to send out a notice to a buyer from whom you have received payment stating that the item is being shipped out to them—but it helps. Tessa Hebert, a book dealer who has a page full of tips for sellers, sends a similar note. She told me that she also asks the buyer to let her know when the book has been received and is satisfied with the transaction. Such a note encourages the buyer to leave positive feedback for you after the item arrives—and many buyers need to be reminded to leave feedback.

The last step is to leave positive feedback for the individual after the transaction is complete. You don't need to receive feedback from someone in order to leave feedback for that same individual, of course. But if you want to build up your positive feedback rating, a reminder e-mail asking specifically for feedback can help.

Tessa Hebert runs a mail-order book business called Book Dealers **(http://bookdealers.home.mindspring.com)** *with her partner Bill Fulkerson. Her tips for eBay auction sellers can be found at* **http://www.mindspring.com/~bookdealers/help.html**.

Keep It Simple: Checks and Money Orders

The simplest kind of payment you can receive from bidders and buyers is in the form of a piece of paper—a check or money order. It's hard to beat these two options for simplicity and reliability. When you're just starting out, you should definitely include these methods of payment. Many sellers start out accepting checks and money orders, move up to PayPal or another payment service, and a few move on to accepting some sort of credit card payment. (See "Accept Credit Card Payments" later in this chapter.) But this chapter will focus on the two basic forms of payment first.

Accept Good Old Fashioned Paper

9

Cyberspace is great, but even for those of us who have been online for several years, it's still comforting to receive a paper check in the mail. Oddly, though, when you get to Step 4 of the Sell Your Item form (shown in Figure 9-2), the option for the PayPal, the payment service that's affiliated with eBay, is checked, but the options to accept checks or money orders are unchecked. You should check them to keep things easy and reliable for yourself and your customers.

Cashier's Checks

Cashier's checks are probably the most secure form of payment that you can receive. As soon as the customer obtains one from a bank, the money is debited from his or her account. You don't have to wait for such a check to "clear" when it arrives. However, cashier's checks carry a service charge that ranges from $3 to $5. You can't blame your customers if they don't want to send you a cashier's check. Be sure to provide other options as well.

Money Orders

Money orders, too, usually carry a service charge when obtained from a bank. The fee can be anywhere between $1 and $3. However, money orders can be obtained less expensively from a wide variety of sources. You're liable to look around your own neighborhood and find currency exchanges and stores that issue money orders. Some of the options are listed in Table 9-1

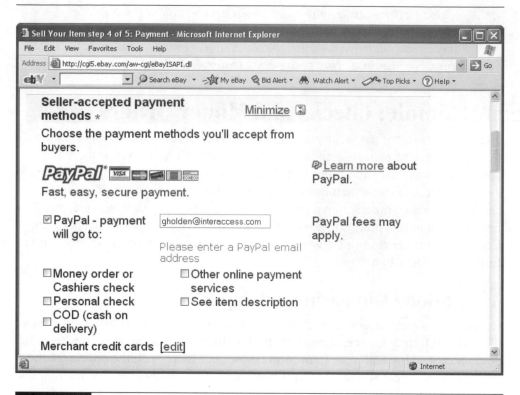

FIGURE 9-2   This area of the Sell Your Item form doesn't select checks or money orders by default.

The last option in Table 9-1—c2it by Citibank—works only if your customers have an account with Citibank already. The flat fee of $10 for international checks can be very cost-effective for larger purchases.

Money Order Source	Fee for $20 Money Order	Fee for $100 Money Order
Western Union BidPay.com	$2.95	$5
United States Post Office	$0.90	$0.90
7-Eleven	$0.99	$0.99
Payko	$3.99	$8.89
c2it by Citibank	$0.40 in U.S. ($10 international)	$2 in U.S., ($10 international)

TABLE 9-1   Options and Fees for Money Orders

> **TIP** *Your customers don't have to go to the store or bank to obtain a money order. They can obtain one online through Western Union's BidPay.com service (**http://www.bidpay.com**), as explained later in this chapter— as well as the services listed in Table 9-1.*

Personal Checks

You might ignore the check box next to Personal Check in Step 4 of the Sell Your Item form because personal checks seem much riskier than cashier's checks or money orders. It's true, money orders and cashier's checks are more secure; but personal checks are also less of a problem than you might think, and you should consider accepting them as well, while setting stringent conditions for your bidders.

One of your goals as an online businessperson should be to make life as easy as possible for your customers. If you decide to accept personal checks, you'll be giving them another option. You might save your buyers a trip to the post office or the 7-Eleven to pick up a money order. Also remember that you can (and actually *should*) specify in your auction terms that you will wait until a personal check clears before you ship out an item, even if this takes 7 to 10 days. Many sellers go through hundreds of personal checks without having one bounce. Of course, when one *does* bounce, it can be upsetting, and the experience has caused more than one seller to make auction terms even more restrictive ("I'll only accept personal checks if you have a positive feedback rating over 100," for instance).

COD (Cash on Delivery)

Cash on Delivery sounds sensible in theory. You rely on the delivery person to accept payment on delivering your merchandise. You don't have to wait for checks to clear, and you don't have to worry about credit card fees.

In practice, there are plenty of downsides to using COD. First of all, there are fees, and they can be hefty. UPS will collect payment but they will charge you $7 for the service, for instance. Suppose the driver attempts to make delivery and the individual isn't home. Then you have to wait days on end while delivery is attempted. You might have to exchange e-mails with your customer to arrange for alternate delivery; the item might simply be returned to you. You can easily wait weeks to receive your payment. It's far preferable to get a check or money order up front instead. If you insist on COD, consider using FedEx, which is flexible about delivery and pickup times, and that will overnight the money to you using— surprise, surprise—FedEx.

9

CAUTION *It should seem obvious, but I don't recommend that you accept cash from your buyers because of the danger that it can be stolen from the mail. I know that some sellers do accept cash, however, especially from overseas customers who find it difficult to deal with payment services. If something happens and payment is lost, it becomes your responsibility to explain to the customer that the money never arrived, which can easily lead to a dispute that can put your all-important reputation in jeopardy. It isn't that difficult for customers, even those who are overseas, to obtain a money order, and you should insist that they do so.*

Payment Services

If you've never been in business before, you can be excused for feeling anxious about dealing directly with customers, even if they're sending you payment in the form of checks or money orders. Many sellers and buyers alike prefer to have a "middleman" accept the money and pass it along, and sellers don't mind having the service subtract a fee for doing so. A payment service does just that: it functions as an intermediary between someone who provides goods or services and someone who pays money in exchange for them.

For eBay transactions, payment services have two big advantages:

- **Security** Payment is no longer a matter of trust when you use a payment service. The buyer knows you're going to get the money, rather than having to trust a shipper. The seller knows the payment is going to be received— and quickly, without having to wait for the mail to deliver it. (PayPal also offers fraud protection for its members.)

- **Credit card purchases** Payment services like PayPal enable customers to pay you with a credit card even if you don't have a merchant account with a bank, a Point of Sale (POS) terminal, or payment gateway software. The payment service deducts the purchase price from the customer's credit card account and transfers it to you. You become an instant credit card merchant!

A few years ago, eBay acquired a payment service called Billpoint, which was a highly regarded and reliable service. However, because of the popularity of PayPal, eBay decided to discontinue Billpoint and, in October 2002, acquired PayPal for a reported $1.5 billion in stock. PayPal is by far the most popular payment service option used by eBay sellers, though some competing services offer attractive alternatives as well.

Accept Payment with PayPal

PayPal, the payment service that is now officially part of eBay (see Figure 9-3), has gained credibility simply because it is so widely used (it's reported to have more than 17 million customers). Simply put, many sellers expect you to give them the option to use PayPal to accept payment; if you don't, there's a chance they might not bid on what you have to offer (though if you're offering something they passionately desire, they'll have no problem sending you a check or money order for it).

Before PayPal became a part of the eBay empire, sellers and buyers had to register and set up an account in order to use the service. That was the source of one customer complaint regarding PayPal—in order to use PayPal to pay a seller, buyers were forced to set up an account with the service. Now that PayPal is part of eBay, you don't have to set up a special account to start accepting payment. You only have to leave the PayPal box checked on the Sell Your Item form. (However, you *will* have to register with PayPal once the first payment comes in.) Registration is free, however.

FIGURE 9-3   PayPal sellers can accept credit payments for auction sales on an e-commerce Web site.

When you register, you'll need to choose one of two accounts: a Personal Account or Premier/Business Account. As a seller, you definitely want the Premier/Business Account because Personal Accounts may not receive credit card payments. In order to receive credit card payments, sellers are charged either a Merchant Rate or a Standard Rate. In order to qualify for the lower merchant rates, one of the following must apply:

■ You have been a PayPal member in good standing for the past 90 days, and received an average of $1,000 in payments per month over the previous 90 days.

■ You have received a competitive offer from an established merchant account provider such as First Data Merchant Services or Metavante Corporation.

■ You have proven yourself to be a long-standing eBay seller who deals in high volume, and you include your eBay User ID and password on your Merchant Rate application.

To keep yourself qualified for the Merchant Rate fees, you need to maintain a volume of $1,000 a month with PayPal and keep your account in good standing (that is, you have no unresolved chargebacks due to customers using credit cards fraudulently). The difference between the Standard Rate and Merchant Rate fees at this writing is shown in Table 9-2.

You can subtract a sizeable 1.5% from either the Merchant or Standard Rate if you qualify for Preferred Rate. To qualify for the 1.5% Preferred Rate discount, sign up for and use a PayPal ATM/Debit Card and advertise PayPal as your only online payment option—not Western Union Bill Pay, Yahoo! PayDirect, or other payment services. As a Premier/Business Account customer, you can gain access to your PayPal funds with PayPal's ATM/Debit card.

Currency in Which You Are Paid	Standard Rate	Merchant Rate
U.S. dollars	2.9% + $0.30	2.2% + $0.30
Canadian dollars	3.4% + C $0.55	2.7% + C $0.55
Euros	3.4% + €0.35	2.7% + €0.35
Pounds sterling	3.4% + £0.20	2.7% + £0.20
Yen	3.4% + ¥40	2.7% + ¥40

TABLE 9-2   Premier/Business Account Rate Fees

NOTE   *Keep in mind that PayPal's fees change from time to time and may be different by the time you read this. You can get the current fees at* **http://www.paypal.com/cgi-bin/webscr?cmd=p/gen/fees-receiving-outside**.

One particular nice thing about PayPal is that it accepts credit cards such as Discover and American Express that can be hard to accept with a conventional merchant account. Normally, even if you obtain a conventional merchant account through a bank or other financial institution, you have to make arrangements through those two credit card companies themselves to be one of their merchants.

You can configure your PayPal account so your money is transferred directly to your checking account; by check (there's a $1.50 charge for each check); or held in your PayPal account. In addition, you can print out invoices to send to your customers if you use QuickBooks; PayPal has been integrated into the QuickBooks accounting system (see Chapter 17).

PayPal also protects both buyers and sellers in a number of ways:

- It checks a buyer's address against the credit card billing address. It confirms the buyer's address and, if you ship to that confirmed address in the U.S., you are not liable for chargebacks.

- Your account is insured up to $100,000 against unauthorized withdrawals.

- PayPal verifies credit card holders by having them submit the CVV2 identification numbers printed on the back of most credit cards; the numbers force the buyer to have the actual credit card rather than using a stolen credit card number.

- Premier/Business Account holders can deny payment from any buyers who do not have confirmed addresses.

- The usual $10 fee that PayPal charges for any chargeback is waived if you fulfill the requirements in the Seller Protection Policy.

The Seller Protection Policy protects you against non-shipments, unauthorized credit card use, and chargebacks if you meet several requirements. You must have your address and checking account confirmed by PalPal with your bank, you must ship only to confirmed addresses, you must keep proof of shipping that can be tracked online, and you must ship to U.S. buyers. Seller protection and address verification doesn't apply to international transactions—which is a sore spot with many eBay sellers who want to receive payments from overseas.

9

NOTE

Some eBay users love PayPal for its convenience. Others dislike it for various reasons: the main one is cost. PayPal's fees aren't inconsiderable. Other services specifically advertise themselves as having fees that are lower than PayPal's. Another is the way PayPal handles disputes and user accounts. In fact, in September 2002 a class-action lawsuit was filed on behalf of more than 100,000 PayPal customers, alleging that the company responds slowly or not at all to disputes and complaints, thus freezing accounts for months at a time. You can read a San Francisco Chronicle article about the suit at **http://www.sfgate.com/cgi-bin/article.cgi?file=/ chronicle/archive/2002/09/07/BU232114.DTL&type=business**.

Western Union BidPay

One of the auction sellers I interviewed for this book, a gentleman with a feedback rating of more than 2400 whose User ID is decoray, specifies in his auction terms that he will not use PayPal at all. Rather, he accepts checks, money orders, and Western Union's money order payment service, BidPay (**http://www.bidpay.com**).

BidPay is simple: Sellers don't have to register with BidPay to receive money orders using the service. Registered sellers can set up accounts where they can review records of past orders and have their address verified by BidPay. However, buyers *do* need to register with BidPay so they can send you money orders. They use the BidPay.com Web site to choose a credit or debit card in order to make payment. They add any shipping fees you have specified to the amount of the money order. They also pay transaction fees as described in Table 9-3.

BidPay uses the U.S. Postal Service to send you its money orders. Once you get a confirmation e-mail from BidPay saying that the money order has been mailed to you, you have the option to either ship the merchandise immediately or wait until the money order actually arrives.

Money orders are shipped to sellers by first-class mail, and the shipping cost is included in the BidPay fees. However, buyers who are in a hurry to receive their merchandise can send you a money order by Priority Mail for an extra $6, and by Express Mail for $15.

Face Value of Money Order	Transaction Fee
$30 or less	$2.95
$30.01 to $100.00	$5.00
$100.01 to $700.00	$5.00 + 2.25% of the face value of the money order

TABLE 9-3   BidPay Transaction Fees

If you become a registered BidPay seller, you can add the BidPay logo to your auction listings as shown here.

NOTE *BidPay limits its transactions to $700 or less, including shipping fees.*

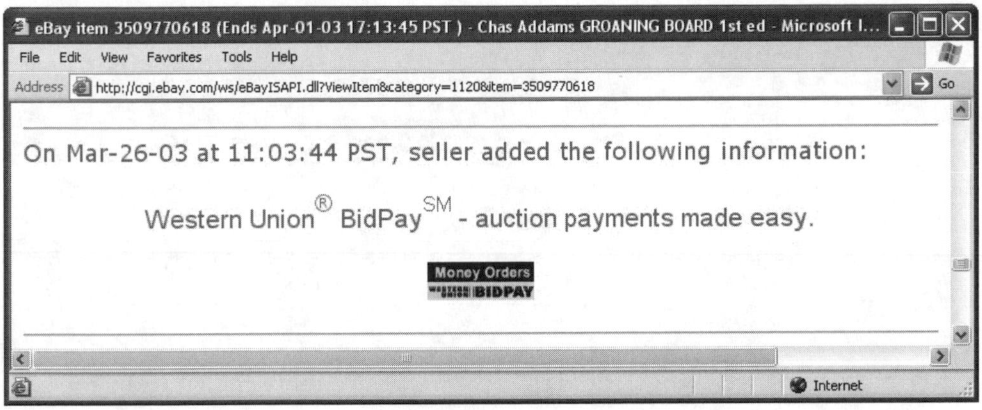

Moneybookers.com

Moneybookers.com, a London, England–based payment service, enables buyers and sellers in a variety of countries to send payments to one another. Both buyer and seller need to have accounts established with Moneybookers. It's free to establish an account, and free for the buyer to deposit money in his or her account from a bank account. To send you money, the seller pays 1% of the transaction fee or a minimum of €0.50. However, it's worth noting that while it doesn't cost anything to have money transferred into your Moneybookser.com account, it does cost money to withdraw it to a bank or other account. You'll pay a flat fee of €3.50 (the U.S. equivalent at this writing is $3.81) to withdraw a check from your account.

Accept Credit Card Payments

If you already run an antique store or other brick-and-mortar business, you probably know about merchant accounts and credit card payments. Credit card payments are ideally suited to transactions on the Web: you enter your card number and personal information in a Web page form, click a few buttons, and you're done.

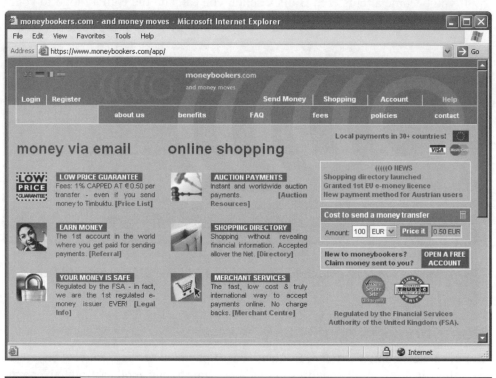

FIGURE 9-4   Moneybookers is especially good for international transactions.

Setting yourself up to accept credit card payments for your auction listings takes a little time and effort, but it isn't terribly difficult. If you're planning to do business "offline" as well as online, you may well want to establish a conventional credit card account with a financial institution. If you only plan to sell on eBay and you want to give your high bidders and buyers another way to send you payment, look to a service like PayPal to do most of the work for you. Either way, you add a new level of convenience for your shoppers. Being able to add credit cards to the list of payment options in your auctions lets people know that you're truly serious about selling online and providing good customer service, too.

The Conventional Way: Merchant Accounts

A *merchant account* is a special account that a commercial operation (a merchant, in other words) sets up with a financial institution. The merchant account enables a business to receive credit card payments from its customers. Your financial institution processes the order, working with the credit card network to debit the customer's account and credit yours. Along the way, the financial institution charges fees for the processing.

Traditional Bank-Based Merchant Accounts

The traditional way to obtain a merchant account is through a bank or other financial institution. You apply to the bank and provide documents that show that you are a legitimate businessperson. You also pay an application fee, which can amount to $300 or more. The bank's officers review your request for several weeks, after which time they hopefully grant you approval. You then purchase an input device that lets you send your customers' credit card numbers to the credit card network. This might be a Point of Sale terminal that lets you do "card swipes," plus a printer that can print out the receipts your customers sign. You can find inexpensive versions of such terminals on eBay for less than $50 (see Figure 9-5).

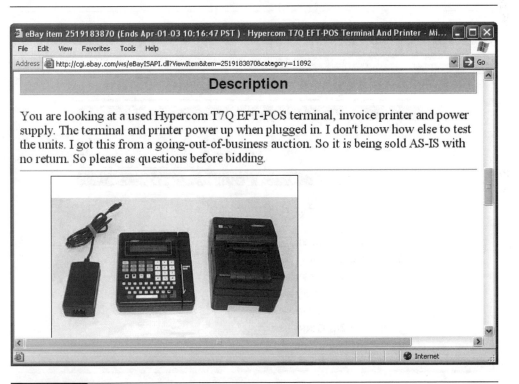

FIGURE 9-5   You need hardware like this or software to enter your customers' credit card data.

Online Payment Gateways

In the online world, you don't need a hardware terminal to submit credit card purchase information to the financial network that does the processing. Instead, you use a software program that functions as a *gateway* to the network. One program that I'm familiar with is called Authorizer by Atomic Software (**http://www.atomic-software.com**). You can either purchase and install the Authorizer software for $379 or use the online version of the service, iAuthorizer (**http://www.iauthorizer.com**).

iAuthorizer functions as a payment gateway: it allows you to add a "Pay Button" to one of your Web pages so customers can send their payments to you. This means you need to set up a Web site with a payment form where your auction customers can go to pay for what they've purchased. If you already have an online store, and you want your customers to be able to make purchases there as well as on eBay, this is a convenient way to do it. iAuthorizer adds the button "Submit for Secure Processing" to one of your forms, as shown in Figure 9-6.

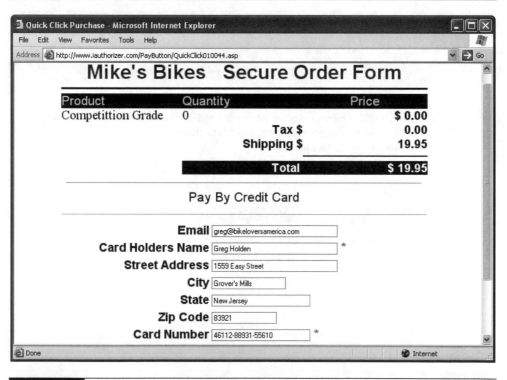

FIGURE 9-6   If you only do business online, you can sign up to use a payment gateway.

Whether you use a bank or another service, credit card merchants are assessed a number of fees for being able to process their customers' credit cards. Typically, the fees look like the ones shown in Table 9-4.

Keep in mind that the fees listed in Table 9-4 vary quite a bit depending on what financial institution you decide to use. Banks tend to be more expensive than companies that specialize in providing merchant accounts to online merchants. Companies like 1st American Card Service (**http://www.1stamericancardservice.com**) or Merchants' Choice Card Services (**http://www.swipethecard.com**) don't charge an application fee. But they do charge Internet fees, discount fees, and so on.

NOTE   *When you enter the world of merchant accounts, the term* discount rate *gets thrown around a lot. This term is quite misleading. It sounds like you're saving money on something, but actually, it's just a discount from your revenue that goes to the bank or credit card company—in other words, a fee.*

Merchant Account Alternatives

The procedures and fees described in the preceding section definitely add a new level of complexity to your eBay sales. There must be an easier way to accept

9

Fee	What It Is	Amount
Discount rate	Usage fee charged by banks and merchant account companies	1 to 4 percent of the transaction
Monthly premium	Monthly charge for having a merchant account	$30 to $70
Per transaction fee	Charge for each transaction	10 to 30 cents
Monthly statement fee	Fee charged for sending the merchant a monthly account statement	$5 to $10
Internet fee	Fee charged for conducting credit card transactions on the Internet	2 to 3 percent of each transaction
Monthly minimum processing fee	A minimum charge for using the financial institution's services	$15 to $30
Gateway processing fee	A fee charged by a gateway service for processing transactions online rather than via a POS terminal	$20 to $40 per month
Chargeback fee	Fee charged by a credit card company if you process a fraudulent purchase—a purchase using a stolen credit card	$15 or more

TABLE 9-4   Typical Merchant Account Fees

credit card payments, right? Happily, a number of services are available that streamline the process of accepting credit cards, and some suggestions are described here:

- **Yahoo! PayDirect (http://paydirect.yahoo.com)**   This service enables you to receive payment for auctions, other purchases, dinner you bought for your friends when they were short of cash—anything. The fee structure is similar to PayPal's: you can sign up for free for either a Personal Account or Professional Account. The Professional Account, however, is the only one that allows you to receive credit card payments. In order to receive money, however, you have to pay a fee that ranges from 2.2% to 2.5% of the transaction + 30 cents.

- **Costco Internet Card Processing**   Costco, the warehouse store my kid and I enjoy regularly, offers a variety of membership packages. If you obtain an Executive Membership, you can obtain credit card processing status through Nova Information Systems. You are charged 1.57% per Visa or MasterCard transaction plus 21 cents. Not only that, but you can process transactions through an Internet gateway as well. Find out more by going to **http://www.costco.com/**, clicking **services**, and clicking **Merchant Credit Card Processing**.

- **VeriSign Payflow Link (http://www.verisign.com/products/payflow/ link/index.html)**   Once you obtain a merchant account from a financial institution, you can use Payflow Link as a gateway service that enables you to process credit card transactions online. You add a link to VeriSign's Web site that enables customers to fill out forms in order to make purchases. The service costs $179 to set up, with a monthly fee of $19.95.

In addition, if you sign up for an account to sell online with Microsoft bCentral (**http://www.bcentral.com**), you pay $24.95 for monthly hosting. For an additional $24.95, you can sign up for Commerce Manager, which enables you to sell on eBay and in other marketplaces and accept credit card orders as well.

Verify Credit Card Data

If you accept credit card payments only for Internet-based transactions, you don't need to purchase and set up a POS terminal to communicate with the credit card network—after all, people aren't going to be sending you their actual credit cards to swipe, and you aren't going to be printing out receipts for them to sign. Both of these things—receiving the actual credit card, and having the customer sign the card in front of you so you can compare his or her signature to the one on the card—are safeguards for you, the seller. They enable you to verify that the person making the purchase is actually the cardholder and not someone who has stolen the card.

How do you process transactions and verify the cardholder's identity in an Internet transaction? You're at a disadvantage because you never see who you're dealing with, and you don't get a signature to ensure someone's identity. In that case, you need to use credit card processing software to do the verification for you. The software compares the cardholder's billing address to the shipping address that the customer gives you. iAuthorizer (**http://www.iauthorizer.com**) performs verification and processing, as does ICVerify (**http://www.icverify.com**).

If the two addresses are different, of course, that doesn't necessarily mean the card is being used fraudulently. Someone might be purchasing a gift for someone else, or the cardholder might have moved recently. But if the addresses vary dramatically (for instance, if the billing address is in Oregon and the shipping address is in Bolivia), you should call the cardholder to verify that the transaction is legitimate. If there's no problem, the cardholder will be glad you checked. If there is a problem, you save the cardholder a fraudulent purchase and yourself a chargeback fee.

Currency Conversion

The question of what currency to use when you sell isn't one you need to be overly concerned about. You should pick the currency that is easiest for you to use: your own. However, if you do need to calculate different currencies, keep in mind that each one of eBay's international sites has its own currency conversion utility. They all use the same basic program, but by picking the version that is specific to your own country, you immediately see your native currency highlighted. If that doesn't seem like a big enough advantage to you (it doesn't to me), use the eBay Universal Currency Converter (shown in Figure 9-7) on the U.S. eBay Web site, **http://pages.ebay.com/ services/buyandsell/currencyconverter.html**.

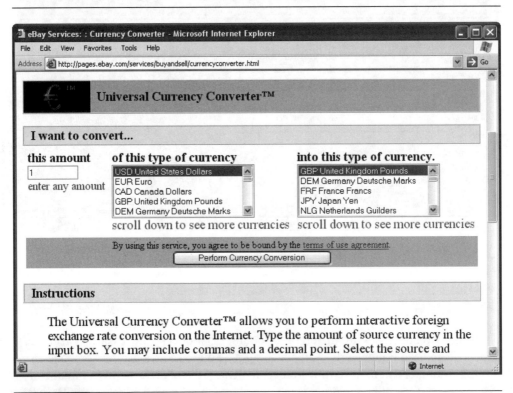

FIGURE 9-7   eBay's Universal Currency Converter

Where to Find It

- **PayPal**
  http://www.paypal.com
  Home page of eBay's payment service, where you can sign up for a seller's account.

- **Western Union BidPay**
  http://www.bidpay.com
  A service that enables buyers to mail money orders to auction sellers.

- **eBay Universal Currency Converter**
  http://pages.ebay.com/services/buyandsell/currencyconverter.html
  Online utility that enables you to quickly convert different types of currency.

9

Chapter 10

Make Sure Your Goods Reach Their Destination

How to...

■ Pack your merchandise so it arrives safely

■ Pick the right shipping options

■ Send your items overseas

■ Be aware of language differences

■ Calculate time-zone differences

■ Observe customs and export requirements

Packing and shipping are among the least glamorous aspects of selling on eBay (they rank right up there with accounting and taxes), but they're among the most important as well. A poorly packed item that is broken in transit, or something that gets lost, can effectively destroy a sale and damage your reputation as well.

To be a successful eBay seller, you need to be a successful eBay shipper. If you don't pack your items correctly, they can break in transit, which can force you to give refunds to your buyers and possibly to get negative feedback as well. It's easy for new sellers to underestimate the time and care they need to take when packing and shipping, whether across the state or across the globe. Often, sellers don't realize they need to be doing things differently until trouble occurs. One goal of this chapter is to help you avoid packing and shipping problems before they arise.

Another goal is to make you aware of issues surrounding selling and shipping to foreign buyers. You *can* decide you're only going to sell domestically, but you'll cut off a large part of your potential market in the process. One of the strengths of selling on eBay is the ability to reach across national boundaries. Along with that power, though, comes additional responsibility: you need to be aware of language, time-zone, and other differences that apply when you deal with a worldwide auction audience. Understanding customs and other requirements you may need to observe when shipping your goods internationally is also a good idea, so I discuss those considerations in this chapter, too.

Pack n' Ship Like a Pro

I have to confess that I wasn't originally planning on including detailed information about packing in this book. But almost every eBay seller I interviewed included the admonition "Pack carefully!" among their list of tips for new sellers like you.

Pack It Right

You'll find that the more you sell on eBay, the more time you'll be spending with boxes, tape and labels, and heading back and forth to the post office or private shipping companies. It's *good* to spend a lot of time on packing, in fact, though you probably won't think so at first. The packages you send to your customers are the only tangible form of contact you're going to have with them. If your package is going overseas, it's almost certainly going on an airplane. It'll be traveling not in a plush first-class reclining seat with a cocktail on its tray table, but in a crowded cargo hold, buffeted by lots of luggage. It may get wet and battered before it reaches its destination.

When you're packing, pretend that your customers are looking over your shoulder, and that you're going to hand the package to them in person. Packing and shipping are two of the criteria sellers usually consider when they leave feedback. As you are packing, keep in mind the principle good packing = good feedback, and keep the following in mind:

- Use strong boxes. Don't skimp on boxes that have already been used, that are falling apart, and that make you look cheap.

- Many sellers use the U.S. Postal Service's Priority Mail service so they can take advantage of the high-quality Priority Mail boxes, which the USPS provides free for you to pick up at a postal facility or by calling 1-800-610-8734. You can also order the boxes through the USPS's Postal Store Web site (**http://shop.usps.com/cgi-bin/vsbv/postal_store_non_ssl/home.jsp**).

- Use lots of packing material. Make friends with bubble wrap and those little white packing peanuts, and fill all available empty space.

- Put a protective barrier between separate pieces. If what you're shipping comes in separate pieces, insert a slab of cardboard in between.

- Double-pack if necessary. For especially fragile and precious items, surround a box with packing material and put it within another box for extra protection.

- Include a note. Some sellers include notes pointing out any flaws that were on the merchandise before it was shipped, so it's clear to the buyer that that particular damage did not occur in transit.

10

If you want some suggestions on how to ship some *really* delicate items, look up another, very different type of online auction site: Eggbid.com. You'll find detailed instructions on how to ship eggs through via Priority Mail (see Figure 10-1) so they arrive safely and even able to hatch chicks (**http://www.eggbid.com/help/ packeggs.cfm**).

Find Packing Material

When you conduct an ongoing business, you're going to need a lot of packing materials. eBay sellers are pretty resourceful when it comes to packing material. They find boxes from any number of sources. The busier sellers I know scrounge for recycled packing materials. Some budget-conscious sellers look for paper,

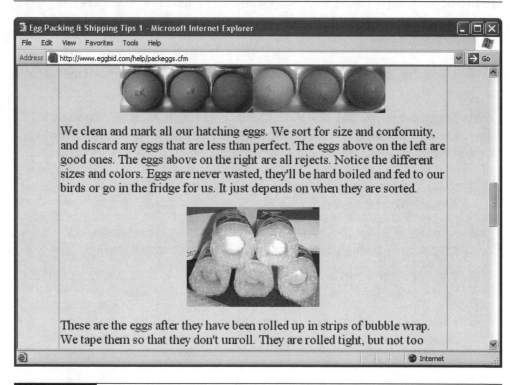

FIGURE 10-1   If you can ship eggs safely, you can probably ship just about anything.

bubble-wrap, and peanuts wherever they can be found—even in the trash. Here are some suggestions of the kinds of materials that are sure to come in handy:

- **Goo Gone**   You'll probably need to remove old mailing labels at some point, and this stuff is great at removing adhesive residue from stickers and labels. It can be messy, however. You can also tape white paper over the old mailing labels.

- **Bubble wrap**   This is a plastic product that contains little bubbles of air that protect what you pack. Bubble wrap can be expensive if you buy it in small quantities. Shop around on eBay and at online packing supply houses like Fast-Pack.com (**http://www.fast-pack.com/bubblewrap.html**) and buy the biggest roll you can afford so you don't have to buy it again for a while.

- **Packing peanuts**   These little white peanut-shaped items are handy for packing irregularly shaped objects in boxes. Storing them can be a pain, but consider hanging them in trash bags around your garage or basement.

- **Shipping tape**   You'll need clear tape that's two or three inches wide to seal boxes if you use a shipping method other than Priority Mail (in which case you can use their free packing tape). Be sure to cover the mailing label with the clear tape to protect it from the rain.

- **Plastic bags or newspaper**   Use these to wrap the merchandise inside the box. The plastic bags, in particular, will protect an item from any moisture that seeps inside.

- **Bubble envelopes**   If you ship out flat merchandise such as magazines or posters, these bubble-wrap–lined envelopes are terrific for protecting your goods.

A trip to the local office supply store will suggest many other kinds of tubes, triangle-shaped containers, and specialty boxes you can use to ship odd-shaped items.

10

NOTE   *Packing material such as the usual "peanuts" piles up in garbage bins and landfills. Consider using ecologically friendly materials such as biodegradable peanuts made from rice. You can also find plastic bags that you inflate with air, which saves money on shipping.*

Many sellers simply use the USPS's Priority Mail for all of their shipping needs. They have packing materials shipped to them for free in bulk; they use the free labels and tape; they take the finished boxes to the post office on a regular schedule, and they even make friends with the employees who get to know them well. It's a quick and economical shipping method that's hard to beat. eBay has a page on its Web site (**http://pages.ebay.com/USPS/supplies.html**) that leads sellers to the Priority Mail site so they can order supplies or track shipping costs. Or you can order supplies from the USPS's own Postal Store (see Figure 10-2).

With all this talk about packing materials, you might well ask how much the packing costs and whether you can pass the cost along to your customers. Yes, you can, but be upfront about it, and don't gouge buyers by tacking on a big "handling fee." You don't want someone to have to pay $15 in shipping costs for an item that only costs $10 to $20 begin with, for instance.

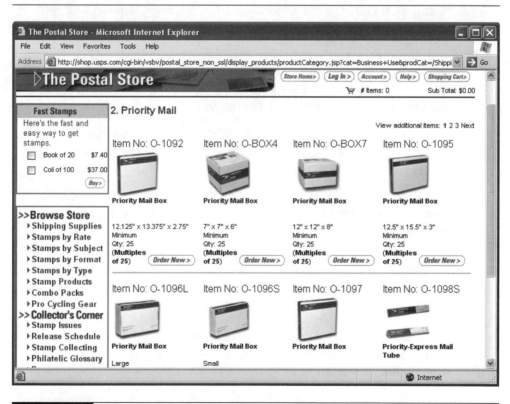

FIGURE 10-2 You can order Priority Mail supplies online for free.

TIP *You can go directly to the USPS's Priority Mail Shipping Supplies Online page (**http://www.usps.com/shipping/prioritymail.htm**) for more information.*

eBay Bestsellers
Don't Skimp When You Ship

decoray, a highly experienced eBay seller who has a feedback rating of more than 2300, and says he has sold as many as 6,000 items through the auction site, is known for unusual items of high quality. "I try to get things that are uncommon or one of a kind in order to stand out from the other listings and attract bidders." At the time we spoke, he was selling a Royal Copenhagen porcelain bowl with a figure of a lobster on it; many old "magic lantern slides" depicting Native Americans and cowboys from the old West; and a cardboard store display depicting several bottles of Kingsbury beer, among other things.

decoray has been in the antique business since 1976: "All those things that never sold in my antique store, I can sell on eBay," he laughs. He has been on eBay for five years. He is not a full timer, yet, he still puts in about 40 hours, part time, six days a week. Much of that time is spent packing and doing other post-sale activities, he points out.

decoray is also known for taking care with his shipping. That doesn't mean that everything he wants to sell should be shipped, however. "Ask yourself: Is your item actually suitable for eBay?" he asks. "If it is bulky, if it has flaws that are difficult to describe, or things that have a purely regional interest, you might want to sell it in your own area through a live auction rather than anywhere else. For instance, if I had a lamp with a stained glass shade worth $2,000, I wouldn't want to ship it in the first place. I'd try to sell it locally rather than deal with the trouble of packing and potentially having to make an insurance claim if something happened in transit.

"Prospective eBay sellers should realize that you will spend a lot of time on each item: producing good photos or scans, writing descriptions, following up on e-mails, as well as shipping and packing. A good rule of thumb is it will take you an hour per item from start to finish. There are five steps to any eBay sale: Having procured the item, you photograph it; you list it; you complete the auction; you ship the item out. I like to do some really creative packing. If you sell 50 items a week, you can estimate that it will take you 50 hours to sell and ship everything out.

"When you are packing, assume the worst. Try to imagine what you need to prevent happening to your item. Take as much time and use as much packing material as necessary to send it to the buyer. Don't skimp on anything.

"If you sell books or records or tapes, the Post Office offers the Media Mail rate, which used to be called Book Rate. You can use it to send a very heavy book very inexpensively. You should note in auctions that you have the option of a low shipping price. I tell people that I can ship by media mail or priority mail.

"When an item doesn't attract any bids, try relisting it and lowering your opening bid. If I feel it should have sold for my opening price, I relist it at 20 percent lower. Everybody has things that don't sell, but I tend to sell 60 to 85 percent of the things I list, depending on the time of year.

"Only about one percent of my customers turn out to be deadbeat bidders. That's due to the beauty of the feedback system. When I sell something to somebody who has good feedback, I send one e-mail and don't worry about it until quite a bit of time has gone by with no payment. But if the high bidder is someone who has low feedback, I word my initial e-mails so they have to reply. If I don't get a prompt reply, I know I might be in for some problems."

Because he spends so much time and care on preparing sales listings and on packing and shipping, decoray is selective about what he puts up for sale. "When you have something to sell, do a search for it on eBay first and see if it is really worth listing. If there are already 30 or 40 of the same things up for sale, don't bother. Take it to the resale shop; give it to your uncle; donate it to the church rummage sale. Don't waste your time. Junk is junk wherever it is, on eBay or wherever. On the other hand, if you have something really good, it doesn't really matter what the minimum bid or reserve price is—you'll sell it on eBay, usually for close to what it's worth."

Shipping

Before you start to sell anything on eBay, give some thought to how you are going to ship it out after you sell it. Scout the nearest postal facility and private mail stores. If you have such a facility right around the corner and there's a convenient parking lot, you might prefer to travel there for shipping. If your post office is small and parking is a problem, it might be better to set up an arrangement with United Parcel Service or Federal Express to provide pick-up service.

The following sections compare the services and suggest things to think about when it comes to setting up accounts, obtaining insurance, and the like. Since the rates and requirements are changing all the time, you're best off visiting the shippers' respective Web sites to determine current costs and procedures.

The Big Three Shippers

Most eBay sellers settle on one of the big shipping services to handle all of their needs: Federal Express (FedEx), United Parcel Service (UPS), and the United States Postal Service (USPS). They find it simpler to get one set of shipping statements, for one thing. For another, having to travel to only one facility at a set time each day or each week simplifies the whole week's activities—which can be pretty busy if you are selling dozens of items each week, and some of your time is spent shopping to build up your inventory (see Chapter 3).

United States Postal Service

The big advantage of using the good old USPS is convenience. You don't need to open an account to start shipping; anyone can come into a postal facility, order supplies, obtain stamps, and ship out merchandise.

The most popular form of shipping used by eBay sellers is Priority Mail. It's popular not because of cost (at higher weights, it can get quite expensive) but because shipments only take a couple of days, and the USPS gives out free shipping supplies if you use this service. Priority Mail is ideal for one- and two-pound packages. However, you have to pay extra fees if you want tracking numbers or delivery confirmation—services that FedEx Home Delivery and UPS provide for free.

If you want to help your customers really save some bucks and you are shipping out books, cassettes, videos, or computer readable media, give them the option of shipping out Media Mail. You'll have to provide your own packing materials, and the time to ship can be six to seven days, but the cost savings can be huge at weights of ten or twenty pounds or more. If you've got something that doesn't fit into the media mail categories and that weighs up to 70 pounds, you have to send it parcel post, but the rates are much more expensive than FedEx Home Delivery.

10

NOTE   *Items weighing more than 70 pounds can be shipped by FedEx Ground or by UPS. UPS requires special "heavy package" stickers (see UPS's suggestions for heavy packages at **http://www.ups.com/using/services/intlforms/help/ us_eng_expdoc_sed_help.html**).*

Federal Express

FedEx is regarded as being more expensive than USPS, and for one- or two-day service, it generally is. But some services that were created when FedEx acquired Roadway Package Service (RPS)—FedEx Ground and its subdivision, FedEx Home Delivery—provide good, cost-effective alternatives to the USPS for eBay sellers. Along with cost, an advantage is that FedEx gives you software called Ship Manager that you can use to print out labels.

You do need to set up an account to use FedEx, but it's easy to do so through the FedEx Web site (**http://www.fedex.com**). Your package can be delivered right to someone's doorstep in one to five business days, depending on where it's going (deliveries to Alaska and Hawaii take three to seven business days). Packages up to 150 pounds each for Ground service and 70 pounds for Home Delivery are allowed. If you use FedEx Ground or International Ground, you can have the shipper collect the money from your customers when the items are delivered—FedEx even accepts cash. Extra service options for evening delivery or signature delivery (requiring someone to sign for the package so you have proof it was delivered) are available for additional charges.

United Parcel Service

UPS is the shipper of choice for at least one of the big-time eBay sellers I profiled because, for an extra fee of $7 to $16 per week, you can arrange for UPS to make a daily stop to pick up your outgoing packages. (Even if you only shipped occasionally with UPS, you could have a driver pick up an individual package or two for an extra fee of $4 per package).

You can drop off packages at a UPS shipper without opening an account if you want to, but opening a simple Internet account (**http://www.ups.com/bussol/solutions/internetship.html**) enables you to print out your own bar-coded labels so you can save some time. To get started, go to the UPS home page (**http://www.ups.com**), select your country from the drop-down list presented on the home page, and click the link **MYUPS.COM**.

How Much Will It Cost?

It's a good idea to give buyers a couple of shipping options rather than just one, so they can feel they have a choice in the matter. Very few eBay sellers give customers the option of sending packages overnight. FedEx Home delivery, UPS residential, USPS Priority Mail, and USPS ground mail are the among the most common options. Table 10-1 compares shipping costs for a package being sent from my ZIP code in Chicago (60657) to one in Los Angeles, California (90011). Insurance is not included; nor is a delivery confirmation.

Delivery Service	2 lbs.	5 lbs.	10 lbs.	20 lbs.
USPS Priority Mail (2 days)	$5.40	$11.00	$16.30	$28.75
USPS Bound Printed Matter (6 days)	$2.38	$3.46	$5.26	N/A
USPS Media Mail (6 days)	$1.84	$3.10	$4.84	7.84
USPS Parcel Post (6 days)	$4.49	$8.64	$14.17	$20.05
UPS Ground (4 days)	$4.65	$13.09	$15.28	$22.38
UPS 3-Day Select (3 days)	$8.65	$20.45	$27.66	$41.77
UPS 2nd Day Air (2 days)	$11.88	$23.80	$35.07	$54.56
FedEx Home Delivery (4 days)	$5.82	$6.77	$8.35	$13.41

TABLE 10-1   Shipping Costs Compared

NOTE   *The cost of shipping goes up dramatically if you use a third-party shipper such as Mailboxes Etc., because they add fees on top of what UPS, FedEx, or the USPS charges.*

It can be difficult, if not impossible, to give exact shipping costs in auction listings because, usually, the cost varies depending on the distance being shipped. Sellers who live in the central United States have an advantage, particularly if they ship by Priority Mail, because the distance to the various perimeters of the country is more or less similar. But someone who lives in Seattle might run into dramatically different costs to ship to California, as opposed to Florida.

As you can see from Table 10-1, while Priority Mail is convenient in terms of packaging, and economical for 2-pound or 5-pound packages, don't overlook the relatively new FedEx Home Delivery service (see Figure 10-3), which takes a couple of days more but provides an excellent value for larger packages. On the other hand, if you are shipping books, Printed Book Rate is a good choice. For media such as DVDs, videotapes, or CD-ROMs, the Postal Service's Media Mail is a good value as well.

NOTE   *You can use a variety of online calculators to quickly determine the most economical way to send your package. The USPS's Online Calculator is at **http://pages.ebay.com/usps/calculator.html**. The UPS Service Center online calculator is located at **http://www.servicecenter.ups.com/ebay/ ebay.html#qcost**. FedEx's Rate Finder is at **http://www.fedex.com/ratefinder/ home?cc=US&language=en**.*

10

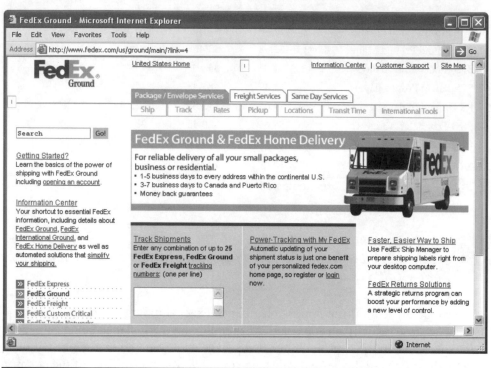

FIGURE 10-3 FedEx Home Delivery is an economical choice for many packages.

Because you can't predict what method your buyer will choose and what the cost will be, mention in your auction listings that buyers should e-mail you for exact shipping costs. One way to get more or less exact is to obtain an accurate set of postal scales you can use at home (see Figure 10-4). Make sure the model you buy can handle the weight you expect to ship; the one in Figure 10-4 handles packages up to 10 pounds.

Obtaining Insurance

Suppose you send something to a buyer and, despite your best efforts to pack it carefully, it somehow gets damaged in transit. If you did not insure the item beforehand, you would probably have to work out something with the buyer—you might have to give the buyer a discount on the purchase price, or perhaps a total refund. Insurance coverage can help defray the cost of such refunds. Insurance procedures vary depending on the shipper you use:

■ If you ship with the USPS, you have to pay extra to insure your item. Fees have risen dramatically in recent years, too (see Table 10-2).

■ If you ship with UPS or FedEx, your merchandise is automatically insured for up to $100. You pay extra if you want to insure an item for a higher amount.

An attractive alternative to the insurance provided by the three big carriers comes from Universal Parcel Insurance Coverage (U-PIC), a company that regularly insures packages. U-PIC offers two types of coverage: an Online Ordering program and an Offline Standard program. The Online Ordering program is for occasional shippers who send out a single package once in a while. The Offline Standard program is for sellers who average 100 packages per month. You can realize big savings over

FIGURE 10-4   Get an accurate set of postal scales so you can estimate shipping costs for your customers.

the USPS insurance costs, as shown in Table 10-2. The table shows the insurance fees that the USPS charged for Priority Mail and other types of mail at this writing. These fees are in addition to the regular shipping charges. They don't include delivery confirmation, registered mail, or other add-on services.

> **TIP**   *You can contact U-PIC through a toll-free number (1-800-955-4623) or by visiting its Web site (**http://www.u-pic.com**). U-PIC suggests that you include a copy of your policy in each box you send out, so buyers know the merchandise is insured and that the insurance cost is included in the total fee you charge them. By all means, read the terms of insurance when you insure an item. The terms may restrict liability if you don't package the item according to the insurance company's guidelines.*

Reach Overseas Buyers

One of the most exciting moments for many online merchants occurs when they receive their first order from overseas. That's when a host of new concerns pops up, too: How do you ship this order to Australia, Norway, Mexico, Japan, or other overseas countries?

Generally, high bidders and buyers on eBay pay additional costs that may apply, such as duties, taxes, and customs clearance fees. For example, international rates may or may not include pickup and door-to-door delivery with customs clearance. Some carriers will offer customs and brokerage services to help you learn more about what you need to tell your buyers about additional charges, duties, and taxes. An "extended area surcharge" may also apply to your buyers depending on their international locations.

To get started with shipping to overseas buyers, check the appropriate options in the Ship-to Locations section of the Sell Your Item form. You don't have to ship to every country in the world. The "Will ship worldwide" option forces you to

Insurance Coverage	USPS Fee	U-PIC Online Ordering Program	U-PIC Offline Standard Program
$0.01 to $50.00	$1.30	$1.00	$0.75
$50.01 to $100.00	$2.20	$1.00	$0.75
$100.01 to $200.00	$3.20	$2.00	$1.50
$200.01 to $300.00	$4.20	$3.00	$2.25
$300.01 to $400.00	$5.20	$4.00	$3.00

TABLE 10-2   USPS and U-PIC Insurance Fees

accept potential purchases from everyone in the world. You may want to stick with countries from which it is particularly easy to ship from the United States, such as Canada, to which the U.S. Postal Service will ship.

CAUTION   *Don't check "Will ship worldwide" if you sell computer software that uses encryption or other potentially sensitive items. You may be prohibited from selling to certain nations. (See "Be Aware of Export Restrictions" later in this chapter.)*

NOTE   *Colloquial evidence gleaned from the eBay Global Trading message boards indicates that some countries are more prone to have fraudulent sales than others (for instance, Indonesia). Check out the boards before you say you'll accept shipments from everywhere in the world.*

CAUTION   *Beware of international sellers who ask you to FedEx something they buy with a credit card. Occasionally, they will want you to ship FedEx so the item arrives before the stolen credit card number is canceled.*

10

Shipping to Canada

Shipping to Canada from the U.S. might seem straightforward because it's just over the border. Not so. Although the North American Free Trade Agreement (NAFTA) made trade between the United States, Canada, and Mexico flow more easily, that doesn't mean it's less expensive. In Canada, buyers are responsible for paying duty fees, a Goods and Services Tax (GST), and applicable customs brokerage fees in addition to the cost of the merchandise you sell them. Buyers generally pay these fees upon receipt of your shipment (although you can arrange to have UPS bill them beforehand. It's a good idea to tell your Canadian buyers that they may be charged additional fees once they receive your package.

If you expect to sell frequently to Canada, you may want to call UPS at 1-800-PICK-UPS to obtain a Non-Resident Importer (NRI) Account. The U.S. seller can then bill the customer up front for duties and taxes, as well as shipping and handling.

To find out more about Canadian customs charges, visit the Canada Customs and Revenue Agency at **http://www.ccra-adrc.gc.ca/customs/menu-e.html**.

Language Considerations

Your ability to reach bidders in Japan, Chile, or other countries is greatly enhanced by the use of simple, clear language in your auction descriptions. After all, the important thing is that your buyers understand exactly what you have to offer and what its best features are. Your use of slang may give the residents of your own country a chuckle, but it can leave many more people scratching their heads and clicking on to the next auction listing. (Consider what a translation of "putting someone in stitches" might look like.) Keep your language simple so people from all parts of the world can understand you.

If you do not speak the same language as one of your bidders and you get e-mail that seems garbled or that is in a foreign language, you may want to use an online translation service to translate key phrases. You can also use such a service to translate your English into someone else's language. Some translation services are available free on the Internet, but they are not 100 percent accurate. If you use such a service, provide simple, grammatically correct phrases free of abbreviations to maximize the chance of an understandable translation.

How to ... Use Babelfish to Communicate with Foreign eBay Users

Babel Fish, a service of the search site AltaVista, is particularly easy to use. You don't always get a high-quality translation, and if you have to translate anything complex or dealing with financial information, you're better off with a human translator. But the service is free and works for very simple statements. Follow these steps to get your own instant translation:

1. Enter the address for the Babel Fish Web site (**http://babelfish .altavista.com**) in your browser's Address box and press ENTER to connect to the site, as shown next.

2. Type or paste the text you want to translate in the "Translate a block of text" box. To have the service translate an entire Web page, enter the URL in the "Translate a Web page" box. (Remember, the shorter and simpler the text, the better your results.)

3. Choose the translation path (that is, *from* what language *to* what language) from the drop-down menu beneath the text box. Your selected option appears on the drop-down menu. At this writing, Chinese, English, French, Japanese, Korean, Spanish, German, Italian, and Portuguese, and Russian-to-English (but not English-to-Russian) are covered by the service.

4. Click the **Translate** button.

5. As quick as you can say, "Welcome to the new Tower of Babel," a new Web page appears onscreen with the translated version of your text.

10

Use One of eBay's Global Sites

For the most part, you'll probably want to use the main (U.S.-based) version of eBay (**http://www.ebay.com**) to create your auction listings, but if you live in a country where eBay has a Global Site and you want to reach potential buyers in that country, consider listing on that version of eBay. At this writing, eBay has sites in countries such as Argentina, Canada, Mexico, Italy, Taiwan, and New Zealand.

One advantage of using such sites is that some members may accept payment in their own currency. Another is that if you are fluent in Spanish and you have an object of national interest (such as an antique version of that country's flag, or a book describing that country's history in the local language), you'll be able to reach local bidders through the Global Site. You might sell on, say, MercadoLibre Mexico, the Mexican affiliate of eBay (shown in Figure 10-5).

FIGURE 10-5   If you live in a Spanish-speaking country, you may find it more convenient to sell on MercadoLibre Mexico.

Observe Time-Zone Etiquette

If you are trying to attract bidders from around the world, try to schedule your auction so that it ends at a time when the largest number of potential bidders are available. Although it's true that proxy bidding (in which a bidder enters a maximum bid amount rather than the minimum increment, so that eBay automatically places bids until the specified maximum amount is reached) makes it unnecessary for bidders to be present at the end in order to place a last-minute winning bid, it's often the last hour or two of an auction that sees the most action.

I once had to schedule a chat event so that the largest number of participants around the globe would be able to participate easily. The company that provided the chat software suggested Saturday around 2 P.M. Central Standard Time as an optimal time for the event. That way, in Europe, it's Saturday evening, while on the West Coast and as far west as Hawaii, people can still participate without having to stay up until the "wee hours." You can determine the difference between eBay's official time and time zones around the world at the Time Zone Conversion page, shown in Figure 10-6.

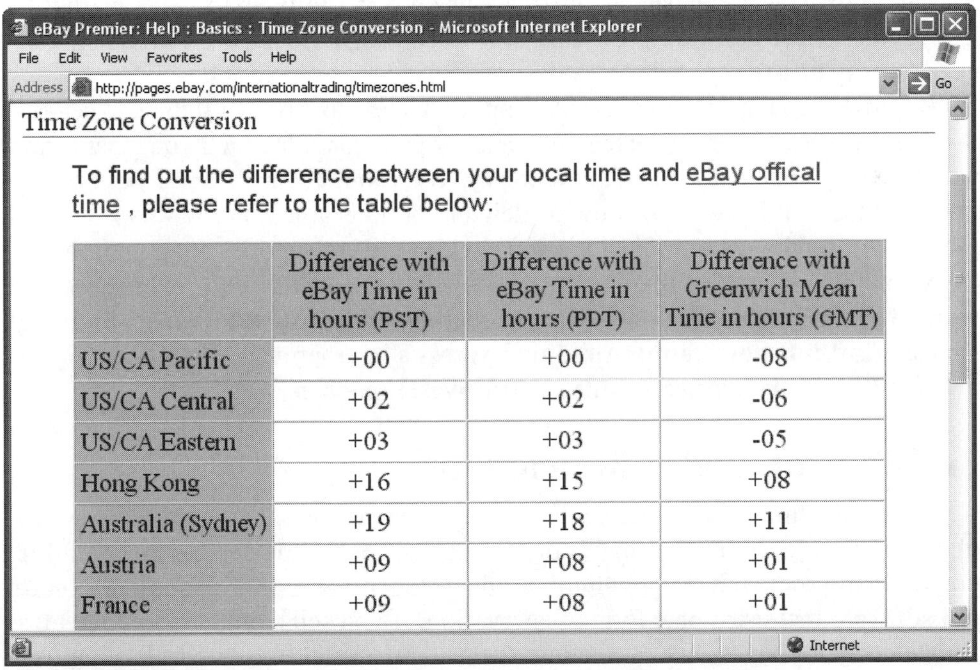

10

Time Zone Conversion

To find out the difference between your local time and eBay offical time, please refer to the table below:

	Difference with eBay Time in hours (PST)	Difference with eBay Time in hours (PDT)	Difference with Greenwich Mean Time in hours (GMT)
US/CA Pacific	+00	+00	-08
US/CA Central	+02	+02	-06
US/CA Eastern	+03	+03	-05
Hong Kong	+16	+15	+08
Australia (Sydney)	+19	+18	+11
Austria	+09	+08	+01
France	+09	+08	+01

FIGURE 10-6   How close are you to eBay time? Find out on this page.

Observe Customs Requirements

When you sell to a customer who lives in another country, you or your customer may be subject to customs charges before the shipment can be completed. Customs usually comes into play when items are valued at several hundred dollars. In addition, you may need to fill out a variety of documentation, including

- A commercial invoice, a form that a shipping company needs you to fill out if the item you're shipping is bigger than a printed document and is going overseas. You can find a sample on the UPS Web site (**http://www.ups.com/ using/services/intlforms/help/us_eng_expdoc_sed_help.html**).

- A Shipper's Export Declaration (SED), which is required by U.S. Customs if the item you are planning to ship by mail is valued at more than $500 (or, for items that are to be shipped by other means, more than $2,500).

The SED requires you to fill out your name, address, and either your Social Security number or Internal Revenue Service Employer Identification Number (EIN), if you have one. You also have to report what you're shipping and where it is going to. You'll find detailed instructions on how to fill out the SEC on the U.S. Census Bureau's Web site (**http://www.census.gov/foreign-trade/www/ correct.way.html**).

Because such requirements can be complex, it's best to rely on a shipper to act as a customs broker and handle the requirements for you—or at least tell you what forms you have to fill out and what you have to pay. You can find out about Global Priority Mail and the USPS's other worldwide delivery options at **http://www.usps.com/ global/sendpackages.htm**. FedEx's worldwide delivery services are popular with eBay sellers, and are described at **http://www.fedex.com/us/about/overview/ worldwide**. UPS's international shipping section is at **http://www.ups.com/using/ services/intl/intl-guide.html**. Airborne Express's International Shipping section is at **http://www.airborne.com/IntlSvcs/IntlSvcsHome.asp**.

Be Aware of Export Restrictions

If you are planning to sell your goods and services overseas, you need to be aware of any trade restrictions that may apply to your business. You need to be careful if you trade in foodstuffs or agricultural products (such as seeds or plants), or if you sell software that uses some form of encryption. If you sell computer equipment, and any of your buyers live in a country with which your own country has imposed trade restrictions, you might get in trouble, too.

It pays to take a few minutes to read the U.S. government's export restrictions. You could incur a sizeable fine for exporting to a Denied Person, Specially Designated National, or Restricted Country. You'll find a current list at the Bureau of Industry and Security Web site (**http://www.bis.doc.gov/ComplianceAndEnforcement/ index.htm#LTC**).

Where to Find It

- **eBay's International Trading message board**
  http://forums.ebay.com/db1/forum.jsp?forum=31
  Discussion board devoted to tips and problems associated with selling or buying overseas.

- **eBay's International Trading Web page**
  http://pages.ebay.com/internationaltrading/index.html
  A welcome page devoted to users who are interested in buying or selling overseas.

- **eBay's gateway page for USPS services and supplies**
  http://pages.ebay.com/USPS/supplies.html
  Links to the USPS postal calculator and to the Priority Mail site.

- **United Parcel Service online rate calculator**
  http://www.servicecenter.ups.com/ebay/ebay.html#qcost
  Calculate rates online for ground and other shipping options

- **FedEx Rate Finder**
  http://www.fedex.com/ratefinder/home?cc=US&language=en
  Calculate rates for FedEx Ground, FedEx Home Delivery, and other shipping options.

10

Chapter 11

Meet Other Auction Hounds

How to...

- Use feedback to your advantage as a seller
- Support your business with effective e-mail
- Get help and advice on message boards
- Meet other sellers in the eBay Café
- Share your wares at eBay "Street Faires"
- Give to charitable causes and help out fellow members

Many Web sites, particularly those that depend on selling goods and services to the public, proclaim that they have a community of visitors. By attracting a set of regular visitors and providing ways for those visitors to interact with one another, they keep those individuals on their site longer than they otherwise would. The longer visitors stay on site and the more they see the site as a resource, the better the chances that they will spend money on the site or use the site's resources in some way.

eBay frequently describes the people who buy and sell on its site as a community, and for the most part, this is an accurate description. Perhaps the most surprising thing about eBay—the thing that keeps it running smoothly—is the fact that it depends on people behaving in a trustworthy and courteous manner and helping one another.

By becoming a fully participating member of the eBay community, you gain all kinds of benefits. You can get questions answered by experienced buyers and sellers who are happy to pass along their experiences, both positive and negative. You become a better and more effective seller. Like the sellers I know, you can meet some wonderful and interesting people, some of whom may turn out to be friends with whom you interact outside of eBay's world. This chapter describes how to interact with the people you meet on eBay, and how to take advantage of eBay's community-building features to make your time on eBay more fun, and hopefully, more profitable as well.

Use Feedback to Your Advantage

Feedback makes the world go 'round—in this case, the world of eBay—and it's especially important when you set up shop as an eBay seller. You're probably at least somewhat familiar with the feedback system, and you got some general information about feedback in Chapter 2. This section passes along some tips for using feedback in a way that contributes to eBay's community while helping you succeed in your eBay business.

Be Courteous, Be Specific

When you give feedback on buyers, remember that your comments are likely to remain online for many months—if not years. The feedback you leave reflects on your reputation as a seller, just as the e-mail you send to customers. Which of the following examples makes you look better as a seller:

- Jerk did not pay up despite 20 emails!!! I curse you!

- Super-fantastic speedee payment!!! Wonderful buyer!!!

- Buyer's check received in three days; smooth transaction.

The third example is without doubt the most boring. It's also the most businesslike and factual, however.

NOTE *If you ever change your mind about the feedback that you leave, you can always amend your comments to clarify what you said. You can also make a rebuttal about feedback that others leave for you. You can find out how to do so at* ***http://pages.ebay.com/services/forum/feedback.html***.

11

Encourage Positive Feedback

When you buy on eBay, feedback is important because it has a bearing on how much sellers can trust you to come through and complete your part of a transaction. But when you sell on eBay, feedback becomes even more important. For example:

- You can set up an eBay Store. You can't create a store until you have a feedback rating of at least 60 and have gone through the ID Verify program (see Chapter 7).

- You can become a Power Seller. A Power Seller is someone who generated at least $1,000 of income from eBay sales in the past three months, who has at least 100 different feedback results, 98 percent of which are positive, and who contacts buyers within three business days after a sale closes. (Other Power Seller requirements are listed at **http://pages.ebay.com/ services/buyandsell/powerseller/criteria.html**.)

■ **You get more business.** A number of sellers who make a full-time living on eBay told me that when you get to a very high feedback level—around 1,200—you start to get more bids. People are drawn to that big feedback number next to your name.

Your goal as a seller, then, should be to get everyone who buys from you to submit feedback. How do you induce buyers to do this? People's natural inclination is often to speak up only when they have a complaint, not when things go smoothly. You may need to insert a slip of paper in the box with each piece of merchandise. The paper might say something like this:

I hope you are completely satisfied with your purchase and that it arrives in good condition. If it does not, or if you are unsatisfied for some reason, please contact me. If you are satisfied, please leave feedback for me at your earliest convenience.

You can tailor such a message to fit your own Terms of Sale. If you decide to offer a refund in case someone is dissatisfied, state as much. Also add a reminder to send feedback in the e-mails you send your high bidders/buyers.

NOTE   *Don't leave feedback for a buyer until you are paid for your merchandise and until the buyer leaves feedback for you. Withholding feedback can serve as a way to encourage a buyer to complete a transaction or respond in some way.*

Observe Good E-Mail Manners

The Web allows you to sell your items and to contact other users through message boards, but e-mail is arguably the most important way you can establish close connections with buyers and sellers alike. When I buy on eBay, I always try to send an e-mail inquiry to the seller just to let the person know I am a serious bidder, and to evaluate the seller's level of responsiveness. I know others do this, too. The way you present yourself via e-mail has an effect on your sales.

Because e-mail is such an important part of your eBay business, it pays to take some simple, yet effective steps to make your e-mail communications more effective. The following sections describe some easy-to implement techniques for maintaining contact with prospective bidders and current customers.

Say Hello and Goodbye

E-mail is so convenient that it's alarmingly easy to overlook the basics—the kinds of things your mother told you to do when speaking to people on the phone. I may be overly sensitive, but omitting a salutation such as "Hello," or "Hi" at the beginning of an e-mail sends me a troubling message—that someone doesn't really respect me. Also, don't forget to say Best Wishes, Sincerely, or whatever at the end of a message, or someone might think you're mad at them. You can't convey emotions by gestures or facial expressions when you're using e-mail. You need to depend on a little extra effort to build goodwill.

TIP

If you send out e-mail with misspellings or grammatical errors, it indicates that you were in a hurry and didn't think it was worthy of your highest level of attention. Outlook Express and Netscape Messenger both include spell-checkers that you should use before you send a response to a bidder or buyer. In Netscape Messenger, click the Spell button in the Compose toolbar before you click Send. In Outlook Express, select Tools | Options, click the Spelling tab, and click the box next to Always check spelling before sending.

Add a Signature File

A *signature file* is a bit of text that is appended to the bottom of your e-mail messages (as well as the messages you post on Internet newsgroups). It gives the recipient detailed information about who you are, where you work, and how to reach you. A signature file (commonly called a *sig file*) can be as simple as your name and phone number, or as long as your eBay User ID, a link to your eBay Store or About Me page, street address for sending in that all-important check, and so on.

If you save your signature file as a separate text document, you don't have to type it every time you send e-mail. Your e-mail software lets you specify the signature file to append to your mail.

Use Smileys

Earlier in this chapter (in the section "Say Hello and Goodbye") I mentioned how difficult it is to register emotion in e-mail. That's not totally true. It's easy enough to register negative emotions like anger and disgust with ALL CAPS, or lots of exclamation marks!!!! But it's difficult to register other emotions like amusement, surprise, or sadness.

How to ... Save a Unique Signature File

1. First, open a text editor such as Notepad or WordPad (for Windows users), SimpleText (for Mac users), or Microsoft Word.

2. Type the hyphen or equals sign key a few times to make a dividing line between the body of your e-mail message and your signature.

3. Type some information about yourself, such as your name, your eBay ID, your business name, your phone number, your Web site URL, and so on. Press Return or Enter after each line. Signature files are anywhere from three to seven lines long.

4. Choose File | Save. When the Save As dialog box opens, name the file and save it in a folder on your hard disk. Make sure the name ends with the .txt (plain-text) filename extension so you can locate it more easily.

5. Next, start up your e-mail program. (This example uses Outlook Express.) Choose Tools | Options, and click the Signatures tab.

6. Click File, and then click Browse. When the Open dialog box appears, locate your signature file on your hard disk. Click the file, and then click Open.

7. When the Open dialog box closes, the path leading to the signature file appears in the File box. Check the box next to "Add signatures to all outgoing messages."

8. Click OK.

Now, when you compose an e-mail message, your signature file appears automatically at the bottom (see the following illustration). This signature file tells other eBay participants who you are and how to reach you. You can delete the message if you don't want it to appear with the particular message you are preparing to send.

As time goes on, I see fewer and fewer *emoticons*—graphic images created by typing keyboard characters—and I think it's a shame. Emoticons are typographical representations of things like smiling faces used to annotate a text with a suggestion of how you feel about what you're writing ("That was meant to be a joke." "What a surprise!"). Used sparingly, they can add a personal touch to your e-mail.

TIP *You'll find an extensive list of emoticons at **http://www.computeruser.com/ resources/dictionary/emoticons.html**. Let your imagination wander at what you can say to legitimately use "starry-eyed angel" or "hats off to you!" for instance.*

eBay Bestsellers
She Gets By With a Little Help from Her eBay Friends

Sheila Schneider checks her e-mail "six or seven times a day" and takes the time to respond to each inquiry she receives from her bidders, no matter what the question is. She once took the time to explain to someone how to leave feedback for her. She knows how important it is to be a helpful member of the eBay community.

"I find that people really appreciate you helping them through things," comments the Portland, Oregon resident, who has been selling on eBay since November 2002. Schneider, herself, has received some helpful answers from the eBay message boards, so she is no stranger to how eBay members support one another.

"I use the message boards for questions that come up, and I have found them to be very helpful. After the holidays, I posted a message asking if I should try to sell anything in the week after Christmas and before New Year's. Several people answered who are power sellers, saying that yes, people are visiting their families and have time on their hands. It turned out to be my most productive sales period ever."

The product-specific message boards attract committed collectors who are only too eager to share their often-encyclopedic knowledge, she ad. "I went on the glass board asking about a particular pattern I wasn't familiar with. One person not only told me about the pattern, but sent me four photos of it. The people who have answered my questions are extremely nice. There's a group of friends who 'meet' there every day, and they seem to know each other."

Sheila also exchanges daily e-mail messages with her friend Jo Stavig in Chicago, whom she describes as her "co-worker." The two exchange tips and tricks about selling. Like her friend Jo (who is profiled in Chapter 2), Sheila used to sell collectible pottery and glass in antique malls, but she's having so much fun selling on eBay that she's beginning to make it her full-time occupation.

"Some of the items I've sold on eBay were things that sat on the shelf in the antique mall for a year. Some of it sold for beyond the prices I had it listed in the antique mall. Your audience on eBay is just so much greater. It's kind of cool to think that people all over the world can see your stuff. My eBay business is allowing me to a) pay my own bills and b) purchase more stuff to sell. Not raking in the dough just yet, but I'm beginning to see that I could make a lot of money."

Sheila passes along the following tips for sellers:

- "I only leave positive or negative feedback, never neutral. The one time I left neutral was when I bought a cookie jar which came to me broken in the mail; the seller turned around and gave me a negative feedback."

- "Never use a flash when photographing items, leaves too much glare. I have a couple of cheap spotlights I bought at the local fix-it store; I use those, and my backdrops are scraps of material I've picked up at garage/estate sales for 25-50 cents."

- "I almost always include a Gallery picture in my auction listings unless the item is super inexpensive and it just doesn't make sense to pay the extra quarter."

- "I learned a great deal from attending the eBay University when it came to my area. It was inexpensive and fun."

- "Priority mail is the best and safest method I have for shipping breakables. You get the boxes for free and they handle what they ship with care."

Her most exciting sale? A tiny chrome table that had been sitting in the basement for sixteen years, and that she hoped to sell for $50. "The night before the sale ended I checked it and it was at $50, and I was happy. The next morning I looked and I thought I was seeing things—the final bid was $350."

11

Frequent eBay's Message Boards and Cafés

Aside from books like this one, the best places to learn insider secrets about eBay are through the extensive message boards eBay provides its members. Message boards provide eBay users with similar interests a place to hold online discussions. On a message board, communication doesn't occur in real time as it does in a chat room. You have a bit more lag time between posting a message and viewing it. You'll find several types of boards listed in the Discussion Board page shown in Figure 11-1.

Some of the most useful selling tips are presented in eBay Expert Member Workshops, which are found by clicking **Workshops** near the bottom of the Boards page or by going directly to http://forums.ebay.com/db1/forum.jsp?forum=93.

FIGURE 11-1 Discussion boards give eBay members a place to meet and greet and post questions and comments.

Workshops are conducted not by eBay staffers but by sellers. The one shown in Figure 11-2 provided a variety of tips on spicing up sales descriptions without having to learn HTML. The really nice thing about these workshops is that they are archived; you don't have to be present at the time they were originally held in order to read what was discussed.

The discussion boards are divided into several general categories. The Community Help Boards include many subjects of interest to sellers. The Packaging & Shipping board might sound boring, but not if you've recently had an item returned because you didn't ship it carefully enough. The Category-Specific Boards are great if you have a question that only an expert seller of Dolls, Comics, or Needle Arts and Vintage Textiles can answer. The General Discussion Boards or the well-known eBay Café (http://chatboards.ebay.com/chat.jsp?forum=1&thread=1), is the place to go to get to know people and talk about anything that's on your mind. Lots of people visit these boards every day and greet one another like the old friends they are.

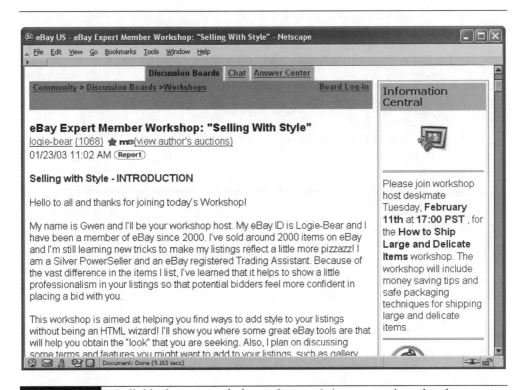

FIGURE 11-2   Individual users regularly conduct workshops on topics related to eBay selling.

> **NOTE** *eBay uses the term "chat room" to describe many of its discussion areas, but this is misleading. Chat rooms, which are well known to teenagers around the world, enable participants to type messages to one another in real time. eBay's discussion areas function like message boards. There's a lag time between comments. The discussion doesn't move as fast as it does on chat rooms, but it tends to be more focused.*

Sometimes, events are staged on discussion boards by eBay members themselves. For instance, under the General Discussion Boards you'll find a board called The Park. Click on it and look for a message topic called either eBay Street Faire or Share-Your-Wares. These are announcements of scheduled sales in which eBay members can sell and shop together. During a Street Faire, eBay sellers from specific categories (sometimes, from all categories) get together and list items for sale.

11

eBay Bestsellers
The Good, the Bad, and the Neutral

There are a few bad apples in every barrel, and eBay is no exception. Another seller, Steve Brothers of Silk Road Trading Concern, has this to say about the people he's met on eBay:

"We have made some good friends through eBay. The majority of our clients are good people and interesting too, but there are a handful of individuals who we have become very close with. eBay has good, bad, and neutral people. We have been quite fortunate to have had very few bad experiences. I think the nature of our items attracts people with a spiritual orientation and those folks are generally conscientious folks who are making efforts to evolve and cultivate compassion, gentleness, and positivity in general."

"We haven't really become close with other sellers, but we have become great friends with a couple of clients. Two in particular come to mind. One doesn't shop on eBay anymore but though we may not be in frequent contact like we were previously, we do stay in touch and have met in person. The second is a gentleman (and his wife) from Atlanta. First-class people, and here again, though he doesn't buy from us very regularly any more, we are in e-mail contact a couple times a week on average. We are very close and indeed our relationship 'outgrew' the confines of eBay.

"But frankly, eBay is not always such a pleasant place. We are grateful for the opportunity it has provided us, but eBay and the clientele have changed a bit over the past couple of years. More neutral-to-unpleasant individuals and experiences seem to have come to the community but, nonetheless, it is a great venue where one is still apt to meet some of the real gems of humanity. That sounds a bit extreme I realize, but really interacting with a couple of these top-notch personalities really does make it all worthwhile."

For instance, in a Street Faire held just before St. Patrick's Day, members were encouraged to post anything they had for sale that was green. Listings of green ties, turtle bracelets, and even a green-colored juicer were offered, and members had great fun commenting on one another's merchandise.

Learn Newsgroup Etiquette

eBay's Café and other message boards aren't the same as the newsgroups that populate the area of the Internet known as Usenet. The set of rules called "Netiquette" that is widely employed on Usenet (short for User's Network, the system of discussion groups that you access through your account with your Internet Service Provider) can help you use eBay's message boards more effectively. The following sections give you some tips on how to do good messaging.

Messages Don't Go Away Quickly

It's so easy: You only need to click Send, and that message board posting is on its way to one or more individuals, carrying all of your emotion with it. But stop and think before you click. An angry message that you regret later can invite angry responses and possibly unwanted interactions from other eBay participants.

Stay on Message

Simply staying "on topic" by reading other messages and getting a feel for a group before you start participating is always a good idea. Often, the discussions on a message board have little or nothing to do with what eBay has stated as the purpose of the board. Members decide what *they* want to talk about instead. In general, it's a good idea to post messages that offer something in the way of advice or personal experience to other participants. If you're able to be helpful, you'll generate goodwill, and your presence in the group will be welcomed.

> **TIP**
>
> *When you sign up for an account on AOL, you have the ability to create multiple screen names. The screen names are used to identify you, not only in chat rooms but in your AOL e-mail addresses. If you want to maintain some privacy and separate your social time in the chat rooms from your business time on eBay, consider creating two or more User IDs, one for chat and one for selling.*

11

Send Emergency Messages

eBay's Emergency Contact board (http://chatboards.ebay.com/chat.jsp?forum= 1&thread=81) is the place to go if you need to contact someone and you haven't been able to do so through the eBay e-mail system. Surprisingly, very few if any of the messages posted on Emergency Contact are actually from one individual attempting to contact another one, which is the message board's stated purpose. Users themselves have turned it into a place where they can get help if they're in a hurry.

Suppose you are in the process of uploading image files in order to list an item for sale and something goes wrong. Suppose you've tried over and over to change your User ID, your password, or your e-mail address, and nothing seems to work, and you're at your wit's end. Many users who don't want to contact eBay for one reason or another turn to Emergency Contact.

TIP   *If you really need help, contact eBay directly by clicking the Live Help! button that appears on many eBay pages or going to **http://pages.ebay .com/help/basics/select-support.html**.*

The Emergency Contact board can be an unsettling yet eye-opening place because it frequently contains messages about the many ways in which eBay users can be scammed by unscrupulous individuals who are attempting to "take over" their user accounts or trick them into giving out their PayPal passwords, yet, it's a good way to learn about the many pitfalls and problems you can run into on eBay.

TIP   *Emergency Contact frequently posts messages by users who have been tricked, or almost been tricked, into giving out their eBay or PayPal passwords. Don't be fooled by any e-mails that ask for such information.*

Give to Charitable Causes

eBay regularly conducts a variety of charity auctions, and your organization can sell on eBay as a way of raising funds. You can list charity auctions at **http:// pages.ebay.com/charity**.

There's also a Giving Board (http://chatboards.ebay.com/chat.jsp?forum= 1&thread=59) where people can give to other eBay members in need. When I checked, there was a long series of messages in response to a plea from a user who needed money for diapers and diaper wipes. Some users were skeptical, but some offered advice as well as monetary support.

Where to Find It

- ■ **eBay Discussion Boards home page**
  http://pages.ebay.com/community/boards/index.html
  Links to all of eBay's discussion boards.

- ■ **eBay Emergency Contact board**
  http://cgi3.ebay.com/aw-cgi/eBayISAPI.dll?ViewBoard&name=emerg
  Supposed to be a place where members can find one another in an emergency, but it's commonly used as a problem-solving forum.

■ **eBay Charity auctions**
http://pages.ebay.com/charity
List of current auctions being conducted to benefit charitable causes.

■ **eBay General Support form**
http://pages.ebay.com/help/basics/select-support.html
A form you can fill out to submit a question to eBay's Customer
Support staff.

11

Part IV

Sell Specialty Items on eBay

Chapter 12

Drive Home the Deal on eBay Motors

How to...

- Spruce up your vehicle to attract bidders

- Set a reserve or Buy It Now price

- Create descriptions and photos that sell

- Arrange for inspections

- Transfer the title

- Deal with deadbeat bidders

- Receive the money and ship the vehicle

- Have eBay manage the sale for you

It's downright easy to sell and ship small-scale treasures such as a toy doll or a family of Simpsons Pez dispensers on eBay. You take some photos, receive bids, pack the items in a box, and ship them out to the lucky winner. But what if you need to unload a six-year-old station wagon, a twenty-five-foot yacht, or that spare jet airplane you simply don't need any more? Just try to park your vehicle outside the local Mailboxes Etc. and ask them to "wrap it up." They're more likely to wrap you up and ship you off to the funny farm.

Things do get complicated when you need to auction off a car or other motorized vehicle, but sellers use eBay every day to unload their wheels, not to mention related parts and accessories. eBay has come up with some services and shortcuts that are designed to streamline the process on a specialized auction site called eBay Motors (**http://pages.ebay.com/ebaymotors/index.html**). You'll find everything you need to handle the special challenges involved in selling motor vehicles online. These include

- How can you induce a buyer to bid thousands of dollars for a vehicle when they can't "kick its tires"—in other words, when they can't get up close and personal with it?

- How can you be sure you are going to get paid by a customer you may never meet in person?

- How do you get the vehicle to an out-of-state buyer? Who pays for shipping? What happens if the item is damaged in transit?

In this chapter, you'll learn how to drive smoothly through such roadblocks with the help of eBay Motors. As one long-time seller commented on the eBay Motors message boards, the trick is to "sell yourself…the rest is easy."

Get into Gear

eBay Motors has become a popular sales channel on the world's most popular auction site. Some vehicles sell better than others, however, and some sellers tend to get better sales results. Knowing what to expect and what you can gain by auctioning off your vehicle on eBay (as opposed to one of the other long-established sites such as Autobytel and Cars.com) can decrease the chances that what you hope to be a smooth sale will turn into a bumpy ride.

The big benefit of selling a car online is the ability to gain a nationwide audience for that vehicle. If your car is a collectible or rare item, you might even attract buyers from overseas. You also get the benefit of eBay's built-in inspection, shipping, payment, and buyer protection services, which make bidders feel at ease.

NOTE   *You can sell vehicle accessories such as tires, hubcaps, or seat covers on eBay Motors. You can even sell parts, which can be difficult to locate for some older and unusual vehicles.*

Who Should Sell

eBay Motors is a good choice if you are an established seller who has accumulated good feedback ratings. An established auto dealer who already has experience with financing and selling cars and who has successfully completed sales also inspires confidence. Mention any business experience you have, even if it isn't directly related to automobile sales; bidders will want to know that you are someone who is already aware of the need to build and maintain trust among a group of customers.

If you are an existing auto dealer, you can build an extra level of trust by obtaining a seal of trust from SquareTrade (**http://www.squaretrade.com/cnt/jsp/index.jsp**). If you qualify, you can obtain a graphic seal icon that appears next to your eBay auto listings. Anyone who sells on eBay can obtain a SquareTrade seal, and any eBay user can use SquareTrade for dispute resolution, as described in Chapter 16.

TIP   *eBay's new Help format appears in a small popup window. If you'd rather read a conventional Web page full of tips on selling vehicles, visit eBay Motors Canada's Simple Guide to Successful eBay Motors Selling page at* **http://pages.ebay.ca/ebaymotors/help/sellerguide/sell_vehicles.html**, *or the main eBay Motors Help page at* **http://pages.ebay.com/ebaymotors/ help/sellerguide/sell_vehicles.html**.

12

What to Sell

What you sell on eBay Motors also has a bearing on whether bidders meet your reserve price or Buy It Now price. If you can, pick a *marketable* car to sell. A marketable car is not a "dime a dozen" model. It is unusual, rare, or notable for some other reason (such as its superb condition, its age, and so on). eBay has always been the perfect place to market rare, collectible, or one-of-a-kind items. Things like a Batmobile from a Batman movie, a tiny Corbin Sparrow of the sort seen in the Austin Powers series of movies (shown in Figure 12-1), or a Lamborghini Countach sports car are bound to get bids.

eBay may be just about the only place where eager collectors or automobile enthusiasts can locate antique or limited edition vehicles. You won't have any trouble getting bids on them. For autos that are widely sold and readily available at local auto dealerships or through local newspapers, you need to take care writing extra-good descriptions and taking plenty of photos to make your vehicle stand out from the crowd.

FIGURE 12-1   Unusual or collectible vehicles sell best on eBay Motors. This one's description is especially complete and honest.

"Motors" Doesn't Necessarily Mean "Wheels"

When you hear the name "eBay Motors," you might think this is only a place to sell cars, trucks, SUVs, and the like, but eBay Motors is for any kind of vehicle that runs with a motor. That includes houseboats and yachts, or even toy cars. At this writing, a houseboat in Fiji was for sale, as well as a 52-foot yacht. You might even put a "land yacht"—otherwise known as a motor home—up for sale as well.

TIP   *eBay keeps track of "hot items"—items that are selling especially well at the current time. Go to the Community: Discussion Boards page (**http://pages.ebay.com/community/boards/index.html**), click **Hot Items**, and click the link **eBay Motors Category - *HOT* items information**.*

Dollars and Sense

eBay Motors sales are "big" in terms of the sale items themselves—which, after all, might weigh a couple of thousand pounds and span ten feet or more in length. The sales price of your vehicle will (hopefully) be as big as you want as well. What about other money matters, such as the fees you pay to eBay to conduct and complete a sale? These and other big money matters are discussed in the sections that follow.

Determine the Vehicle's Value

Before you can sell, you need to have an idea of the vehicle's value so you can set a reserve price or Buy It Now price. One way is simply to search completed auctions on eBay itself.

1. Go to the eBay Advanced Search page (**http://pages.ebay.com/search/items/ search_adv.html**).

2. In the Search box, enter a keyword or two that describes the kind of vehicle you're hunting for. (Adding the year of the vehicle in the form YYYY will help narrow down your search.)

3. Choose "Automotive-eBay Motors" from the Category drop-down list.

12

4. Check the box next to "Completed Items only."

5. Choose "Items ending first" from the "Sort by" drop-down list.

6. Select any other options you want to specify, such as a geographic region, or sorting option.

7. Click Search.

You can scan the list of completed sales for cars that match the one you want to sell. Hopefully you'll have enough results to be able to take an average and get a reliable value.

As an alternative, you can have an eBay Trading Assistant handle the sale for you. You fill out a registration form, and you provide detailed information about cars you wish to sell. After that, someone will then contact you by e-mail or phone to ask you questions about the car. The service will then help you to determine the value of the car you want to sell.

The advantage of having eBay set up your auto sale is that they then take responsibility for how the sale is conducted. It costs more to use a listing service but it shows the buyer that you really care about selling the car to a satisfied customer.

TIP *You can also hire an eBay Trading Assistant to handle the sale for you from start to finish. Search for an assistant in your area at http://pages.ebay.com/tradingassistants.html.*

Choose Your Sales Format

The classic eBay sales—the ones with which everyone is familiar—are auctions that last for three, five, seven, or ten days. But at the end of the auction, the highest bidder wins if there is no reserve price. If a reserve price has been set, the high bidder wins if his or her bid matches or exceeds the reserve.

However, you may want to dispense with the auction format altogether and simply set a fixed price for your vehicle. If someone offers to meet the price, they agree to purchase it immediately. Or you may want to sell cars or related accessories through an eBay Store like Truck and RV Supply, shown in Figure 12-2.

(See Chapter 5 for more on how to set up an eBay store.) The options available to you for conventional eBay sales listings are described in the sections that follow.

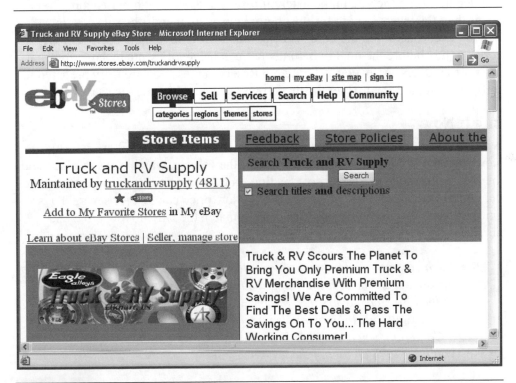

FIGURE 12-2 You can gain more attention for your vehicle-related sales by presenting them in one place—an eBay Store.

Reserve Price

If you want to obtain a minimum amount for the vehicle you are selling, by all means specify a reserve price. Suppose, for instance, you specify a reserve price of $5,000 for a car. If the high bidder reaches $3,999, you aren't obligated to complete the sale. You can relist or try to sell the vehicle at a later date.

No Reserve

A No Reserve auction is one in which the high bidder wins no matter what the bid is. That's because the seller has not specified a reserve. Such sales have an air of excitement about them; they typically attract attention on eBay from bidders looking for rock-bottom prices.

Auto sellers frequently choose a No Reserve format because they are unsure of how much a vehicle is worth. They simply want to see how much they can get for a vehicle. Many let the sale end and take the high bid, no matter what it is. However, when the close of the auction approaches, other sellers evaluate the current bidding and decide to end the sale immediately if it seems like the high bid is going to be lower than they were hoping for. Just before the auction ends the sale is stopped, leaving everyone out in the cold. They sometimes remove their eBay listings abruptly just before the final bids come in. Such behavior, while technically legal, frustrates bidders. Also, don't choose No Reserve unless you are truly prepared to sell your vehicle for whatever the market will bring at the time the sale occurs.

Buy It Now

A Buy It Now sale is one with which auto dealers should be familiar. In a Buy It Now sale, the seller chooses a fixed price for the vehicle, which stays in place until the first bid is made in a no reserve auction. In a reserve price auction that includes the option of a Buy It Now price, the Buy It Now price can last for several days. Until the reserve price is met, any bidder can match the Buy It Now price and purchase the vehicle immediately.

NOTE *Each version of eBay has its own eBay motors area. eBay Canada, for instance, has one at **http://pages.ebay.ca/auto-index.html**. You should sell in the eBay that covers the country where you live. That doesn't mean you have to sell only to individuals who live in your own country, however. As a Canadian, you can sell to U.S. buyers or people in other countries, but you have to figure about the exchange rate.*

eBay Store Sale

If you're not comfortable with a sale that lasts ten days or less, create an eBay Store and advertise your vehicle there. You specify a set price for the vehicle, so there's no bidding and no reserve. You can have the vehicle for sale for 30, 60, 90, or even 120 days.

Choose Marketing Add-Ons

eBay Motors is a popular area of the eBay marketplace, and it can be difficult for a vehicle to stand out from the crowd. If your vehicle isn't noteworthy because of its manufacturer, age, speed, or other desirable qualities, consider some formatting add-ons that eBay provides to get extra attention.

Gallery Featured

Gallery Featured items appear with a thumbnail image right on the eBay Motors portal page. Often, sellers feature vehicles that are especially desirable and expensive. If the sale price is $30,000 to $40,000, for example, what's a few extra bucks to get the added attention?

You pay extra for such exposure: the Gallery Featured fee is $99.95 for vehicles, and $24.95 for items that aren't vehicles themselves, such as automobile memorabilia.

Category Featured

With Category Featured, the listing appears at the top of the specific category in which you want to sell it. For instance, if you are selling a motorcycle and you want to feature it at the top of the eBay Motors Motorcycles listings, you pay a Gallery Featured fee. However, if you are selling a Yamaha motorcycle and you want it to be included in a "short list" of Yamahas that appears at the top of the first page listing all the Hondas that are currently up for sale, you pay a Category Featured fee of $14.95.

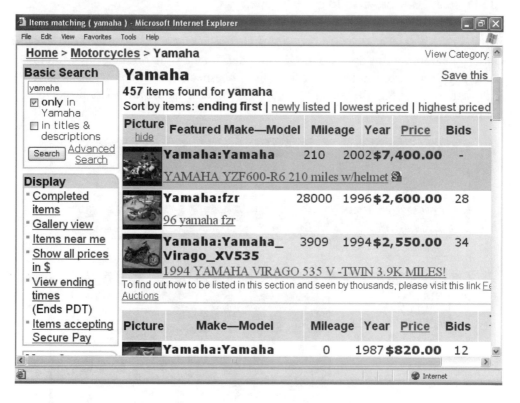

Highlighting

To my mind, Category Featured listings are difficult to read and don't really call attention to sellers who search by using eBay's Search feature. On the other hand, if you highlight your listing, you can make your listing stand out in a sea of other listings. Vehicle listings are highlighted in a bright color (for instance, purple). Another option is to make your listing stand out in bold type. Both highlighting and bold listings are shown in Figure 12-3.

Highlighting costs an extra $5, while bold listings are only $2 extra. You can also combine the two add-ons. Keep in mind, though, that the listings that appear on either side of yours might be bold and/or highlighted, so they may not stand out as much as you hoped.

Know What You'll Be Charged

You may not know what your item will sell for before you start an eBay auction, but you can calculate the seller's fees you'll have to pay. Some costs are fixed,

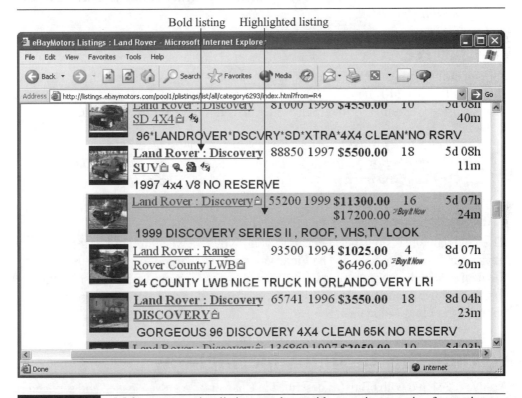

FIGURE 12-3   Make your auction listing stand out with some inexpensive formatting add-ons.

12

while others depend on the type of sale you want to conduct. The fixed fees are listed in the table that follows.

Vehicle	Insertion Fee	Final Value Fee
Cars, boats, airplanes, RVs, snowmobiles, and items listed in "Other Vehicles" category	$40	$40
Motorcycles	$25	$25

> **TIP** *In addition, you are charged a fee of from 50 cents to $2.00 if you list an item with a reserve price and the item doesn't sell. If it does sell, you are refunded the reserve price fee. You can review the current fees for selling on eBay Motors at **http://pages.ebay.com/ebaymotors/help/sellerguide/selling-fees.html**.*

Insertion Fee

The Insertion Fee is the fee eBay charges you for putting your sale online. The Insertion Fee is non-refundable; you pay it even if your item gets no bids, if your reserve price is not met, or the high bidder does not pay you for the item.

> **NOTE** *The charge for the Insertion Fee doesn't apply to items sold on eBay outside of eBay Motors. On other parts of eBay, you can relist the item for free if you are able to sell it the second time around.*

Final Value Fee

The final value fee is what eBay charges you if you receive a high bid or if someone pays your Buy It Now price. The Final Value Fee is charged to you whether or not the deal is actually consummated—if someone is the high bidder but doesn't follow through with a deposit or doesn't like the car when it is delivered, you are still charged the Final Value Fee.

Drive Onto the Auction Superhighway

You've registered with eBay (as described in Chapter 2). You've cleaned and serviced your vehicle, and taken some clear digital photos (as described in Chapter 8). You've chosen an auction format and picked some marketing add-ons. Now, you can create your auction listing and publish it online, as described in the following sections.

Write Sales Descriptions That Sell

Some cars sell themselves because they're rare. Most, though, need some help from you in the form of clear photos and good descriptions. Bidders go into eBay Motors with a skeptical attitude. They are accustomed to buying autos or boats through newspaper ads or brick-and-mortar dealerships. You have to convince people they should trust you by providing accurate, honest descriptions of what you have to offer.

TIP *Include lots of photos with your descriptions. You can hardly include too many. Make sure they are sharp and well-lit. If the color isn't quite right in a photo, say so ("the color in the photo has a reddish cast but the real color is purple"). You don't want people to be surprised in any way when the vehicle is delivered.*

Honesty is the best policy when it comes to descriptions of vehicles on eBay Motors. Telling your bidders about any problems with your vehicles and describing both the good and not-so-good aspects of the vehicle helps you as well as your potential customers. It helps you because it reduces the chances that buyers will be stricken with "buyer's remorse" after the sale ends (as explained in the section "Buyer's Remorse" later in this chapter.)

Of course, your descriptions shouldn't all be about problems. You need to emphasize everything that's positive about your vehicle. Be an enthusiastic booster and try to generate some excitement among your bidders. Here are some examples of the good points you might emphasize:

- Low mileage

- Special options like leather upholstery or extra seats on SUVs

- The fact that you're the only owner, if that's applicable

- If the vehicle has an extended warranty

- If the vehicle has been certified by an organization such as Carfax (**http://www.carfax.com**)

Buzzwords like "Sporty," "Like New," and "Sharp" aren't specific and descriptive; they're overused. Facts about the vehicle count for much more.

12

TIP

Before you start the sale, check your vehicle's warranty information to verify that the warranty may be transferred to the next owner. If the warranty information is transferable, that makes your vehicle more desirable, and you should mention this in your description.

Arrange for a Vehicle Inspection

Bidders who don't live near you need to trust you when it comes to an accurate description of your vehicle, or verify your description with an inspection by a third party. You can either pay for an inspection yourself and include the inspection results with your auction listing, or allow the high bidder/buyer to conduct an inspection before the sale ends.

   If you include a vehicle inspection report with your listing, you are more likely to get serious bids. You can schedule an inspection either yourself, by taking the vehicle to a local car dealer, or by contacting the inspection service that's affiliated with eBay, Vehicle Care Management Corp. (**http://pages.ebay.com/ebaymotors/ services/inspection/inspection.html**). You can choose from one of three different types of inspections, as shown in Table 12-1.

Level	What Is Covered	Price	When to Choose
Level 1	The inspector looks at the interior and exterior but doesn't actually drive the car; any damage is reported and photos of damage are taken.	$80.00	When the vehicle is really new and there is not likely to be an issue about how well the motor works. Otherwise spend a few bucks more for the Level 2 or Level 3 inspections. A report is sent to prospective buyers and sellers, but it's up to you to e-mail it or include it in your listing.
Level 2	Everything in Level 1, plus a more detailed inspection that looks more closely at lights, switches, CV boots, joints, or oil or fluid leaks. A two- to five-mile test drive is included.	$90.00	A report is generated that can be e-mailed or faxed to purchasers, but it's up to you to include it in your auction listing.
Level 3	Everything in Level 1 and 2	$99.99	The extra $9.99 enables the inspector to post a link to the report online; you can make a link to the report that you can include in your auction listing. Choose this if you don't want to scan or post your own files online.

TABLE 12-1   Automotive Inspection Types Offered by eBay

Which type of inspection is right for you? If you expect to sell your car for hundreds or perhaps even thousands of dollars, I don't see why you would choose Level 1; choose Level 2 if you want to save $10 and post your inspection online; choose Level 3 if you're in a hurry and you don't mind spending $10 to have the file posted online.

> **CAUTION** *Inspections by Vehicle Care Management Corp. can be conducted anywhere in the continental United States. However, if the inspector has to drive more than 100 miles to get to you, you'll be charged for mileage. Work out beforehand how much everything is going to cost so you aren't surprised.*

> **TIP** *You don't have to have eBay do an inspection. If you are already affiliated with an inspection service you may use them as well. Or, arrange to take the vehicle to a local dealer (if you are buying a BMW, take it to a local BMW dealer) and have them do an inspection.*

Let the Sale Begin

Once you have chosen the sale format, created your description, and taken photos, you put your listing online as described in Chapter 3. During the sale, be sure to answer questions from bidders promptly and thoroughly. Based on the questions you receive, you may want to add further descriptions or new photos to your auction listing.

> **NOTE** *Even while the sale is continuing, if you have second thoughts about your reserve or Buy It Now price, you can lower the selling price. You might want to do this if your vehicle doesn't seem to be attracting much attention.*

12

Be Up-Front About Fees

Auto sales require purchasers to handle more fees than other small-scale items sold on eBay. You need to be up front about explaining those fees so the buyer isn't surprised when it comes time to close the deal. For instance, your state probably requires the buyer to pay a fee for documentation, administration, a temporary license tag, and notary services. Besides that, the buyer may have to pay tax and license fees in his or her home state. It's a good idea to mention that buyers are responsible for researching and paying such fees—not you.

Complete the Transaction

After the sale ends, you should contact your high bidder within three business days. Check your e-mail or phone on a regular basis. If you don't get an e-mail message from the high bidder within the three-day period, you can move on to the next highest bidder—or place the vehicle up for auction again.

What If You Run Into Problems?

There's a reason for the inspection, warranty, insurance, escrow, and other services provided by eBay for vehicle sales. The reason is simple: fraud. Since you're an honest seller, I won't go into the fraudulent, inaccurate descriptions that buyers sometimes encounter. Sellers, too, can run into problems completing a sale.

Nobody Meets Your Price

Normally, if none of your bidders meets your reserve price, you don't have to sell. You withdraw the item and resell it some other time. On eBay Motors, however, you have another option. You are allowed to lower your reserve price or your Buy It Now price so you don't have to resell. Suppose you work at an auto dealership, and you

Did you know?

Under Bidders Can Be the Underdogs

The term *under bidder* refers to anyone other than the high bidder. An under bidder, in other words, is someone who just didn't bid high enough. Usually, you can't sell to an under bidder if the deal falls through with the high bidder. But eBay has a new Second Chance Policy in which you can sell to under bidders if the high bidder can't complete the purchase. You can pick any or all of your under bidders; you can also set your price for the Second Chance Offer. If you have two identical items for sale and you only offered one for sale on eBay, you can use the Second Chance Offer to sell the other item to someone else. You can do this up to 60 days after the auction ends. After you are certain that the high bidder is not going to complete the deal, go to your closed auction listing on eBay and click Bid History. Then choose the under bidders to whom you want to send the second chance listing.

have to pay a monthly fee to keep a car on your lot. Relisting the item means you have to pay another monthly fee; by selling right away at a lower price, you not only save yourself some time and trouble, but you might save a little money as well because you don't have to pay that extra month's rent.

Buyer's Remorse

Buyer's remorse occurs when someone places the high bid or pledges to pay a Buy It Now price, but then decides to back out of the deal. Sometimes, buyers back out before they pay anything. Other times, they pay a deposit, but then fail to pick up the vehicle. The new eBay Motors message board occasionally receives messages from people who sell a car and receive a deposit from a high bidder, and then still run into problems. Examples include

- Someone who actually drove hundreds of miles to pick up a car and who was unhappy with its condition upon seeing it, and who stalked away angrily without paying

- One person who threw a fit, kicked the door of a 1953 Buick, and said he would forfeit the deposit

- Another who never showed up at the appointed time to pick up the vehicle

If you run into trouble or need to contact eBay Motors about something, you can send an e-mail message to motors-support@ebay.com. Or, post a message on the eBay Motors discussion board. If you are so inclined, you can take a buyer to small claims court. Many problems with completing transactions are covered by Uniform Commercial Code section 2-708, so you could conceivably sue buyers who refuse to pay for a deposit or at least part of the purchase price.

Receive Payment

You pretty much need to assume that you are going to use a payment or escrow service (see Chapter 9) to handle the transaction because such a large amount of money is involved. Also, you have taken the time and effort to prepare the vehicle for sale, so you need to safeguard that the sale will be transacted successfully and you won't become a victim of fraud.

Requiring a Deposit

It's the rule, rather than the exception, for auto sellers on eBay to ask the high bidder or purchaser for a deposit. A deposit is considered "earnest money." It demonstrates

12

that the buyer is serious about wanting the vehicle and will be likely to follow through. You have two options:

- Require a deposit right in the listing. This way you can require any deposit you want. Deposits range anywhere from $200 or $250 to 25 percent of the purchase price.

- Automatically require a $200 deposit from the seller through eBay Payments. You need to be a member of eBay Payments to use this service, and so does your high bidder.

Using a Payment or Escrow Service

Payment services like Pay Pal give you a good opportunity to receive payment for vehicles you sell on eBay Motors. Not only that, but some services will also handle the transfer of title and registration for a small fee. You are required to disclose the accurate odometer reading, and in California, you have to provide a certificate stating that the vehicle has passed smog checks as well. An escrow service such as eBay's affiliate Escrow.com will handle the paperwork along with handling payments.

Escrow.com, in fact, provides a set of services that are collectively called Secure Pay, and that are designed to protect eBay Motors buyers and sellers alike. The system works as described in the upcoming sidebar "Use Escrow.com to Protect Your Payments."

It's up to you and the buyer to determine who will pay the $22 transaction fees (and any extra fees for wire transfers), or whether the fees should be split between the two of you.

Transfer Title

Once payment is received, you need to transfer title to the vehicle to the seller. Check with the state where the buyer lives to determine how quickly this needs to be done. Many states require titles to be transferred within 21 days after purchase; however, Minnesota requires title transfer within 10 days. Check with your own state's Department of Motor Vehicles to verify the current requirements.

> **TIP** *You'll find a state-by-state list of links to Department of Motor Vehicles Web sites at **http://www.magnatize.com/magnatize/dmv.html**.*

If you are able to meet with your buyer in person to receive payment and transfer title, it is obviously the best way to seal the deal. If you can't, you can then require that the seller pay you in full before you sign over the title.

How to ... Use Escrow.com to Protect Your Payments

1. Buyer and seller must register with Secure Pay at **http://pages.ebay.com/ebaymotors/services/securepay.html**.

2. Buyer and seller agree on price, shipping, and other terms of the purchase.

3. The buyer pays Escrow.com for the purchase.

4. Escrow.com notifies the seller that payment has been received, and the seller ships the merchandise.

5. The buyer receives the merchandise and inspects it to make sure it is acceptable (the buyer is given a set period of time in which to accept or reject the purchase).

6. If the purchase is acceptable to the buyer, the seller is paid by Escrow.com. If it is not acceptable, the buyer must pay to have the vehicle shipped back to the seller.

Let Buyers Decide How to Ship

12

Shipping is getting to be more and more popular among people who buy cars. eBay is affiliated with Dependable Auto Shippers (DAS): **http://www.dasautoshippers.com**. You can visit the company's Web site for an instant quote.

Before you prepare to ship, you need to prepare the vehicle. As with any eBay sale, your goal is to ensure that the customer will be satisfied when the vehicle arrives. You don't want the customer to have any unpleasant surprises—especially with such high-priced items. You need to do some simple but obvious things:

- Wash the vehicle. Before you deliver the vehicle to the shipper, make sure it's in good condition so the shipper can inspect it easily.

- Keep the fuel level low. Make sure the fuel level is less than half of a full tank to keep the weight of the vehicle down. The lower the weight, the lower the shipping cost.

- Clean out your personal items. This keeps the weight down and ensures that you won't have anything stolen, too.

- Keep the vehicle profile compact. Retract antennas, remove luggage racks. Be sure to turn off car alarms as well.

TIP   *Many auto dealers that sell on eBay handle shipping with their usual provider, but pass the cost on to the customer. As an alternative, you can suggest that customers get their own quote from a site like the Internet Directory of Automobile Transporters (**http://www.movecars.com**) and give them the option to arrange for shipping themselves.*

Pay Your eBay Fees

When all is said and done, you need to pay your eBay fees and settle up with the purchaser or with your payment or escrow service. Remind your purchaser to send feedback about the sale so you can develop a good feedback rating, which encourages more auto buyers to place bids with you.

CAUTION   *Most states will allow you to sell up to five autos per year. However, if you sell more than five autos per year, you may be required to obtain an auto dealer's license. Check with your state to make sure you're operating within the law.*

Where to Find It

- **eBay Motors portal page**
  http://pages.ebay.com/ebaymotors/index.html
  Links to all categories on eBay Motors, as well as links to the Help area.

- **Fees for eBay Motors**
  http://pages.ebay.com/ebaymotors/help/sellerguide/selling-fees.html
  How to calculate Insertion Fees and Final Value Fees; when and how to pay your eBay seller's fees

- **eBay Motors How to Sell—Vehicles page**
  http://pages.ebay.ca/ebaymotors/help/sellerguide/sell_vehicles.html
  A link to a Seller's Checklist and other tips on how to sell on eBay Motors

- **Contact support for eBay Motors**
  motors-support@ebay.com
  E-mail address for the eBay Motors support staff

Chapter 13

Auction Off Business Goods and Services

How to...

- Procure business supplies at bargain rates
- Sell off excess inventory
- Limit sales to purchasers in your area
- Offer wholesale lots for sale
- Comply with government regulations when needed
- Provide your services as a freelancer
- Post projects on eLance

Perhaps you've seen the commercial in which two companies have just completed a transaction on the Internet. One supplier claps his hands in glee—he's just located a buyer for his product. Cut to another businessperson who crows happily to an employee that they've just found the supplies they need at a bargain price. The two leave their respective buildings and simultaneously cry "Thank you!" to the heavens— and wind up greeting one another in person. Their businesses, it turns out, were located right across the street from one another all along. All they needed was a way to make a connection. eBay's Business & Industrial area provides just such a place to meet and do business.

eBay isn't just for individuals who want to auction off personal goods to other individuals. The eBay marketplace can work just as effectively for businesses that need to connect with other businesses, which, as you might expect, are called Business-to-Business (B2B) transactions. If you want to cut costs by procuring supplies at more reasonable prices than before, you might find a cheaper supplier through eBay. This chapter discusses four eBay resources that enable businesses to trade more effectively: the Business & Industrial area, the Wholesale Lots area, eBay Local sites, and eLance.

Through the Business & Industrial area (**http://pages.ebay.com/catindex/ business.html**, shown in Figure 13-1), eBay hopes to function as a B2B marketplace. According to an article in eWeek (**http:// www.eweek.com/article2/0,3959,849126,00 .asp**), business transactions account for more than $1 billion in sales on eBay each year.

A B2B marketplace is a place where companies can trade every kind of equipment—everything from laser interferometers to Ginsu knives—with other companies. You're likely to find tractors and other agricultural equipment, building

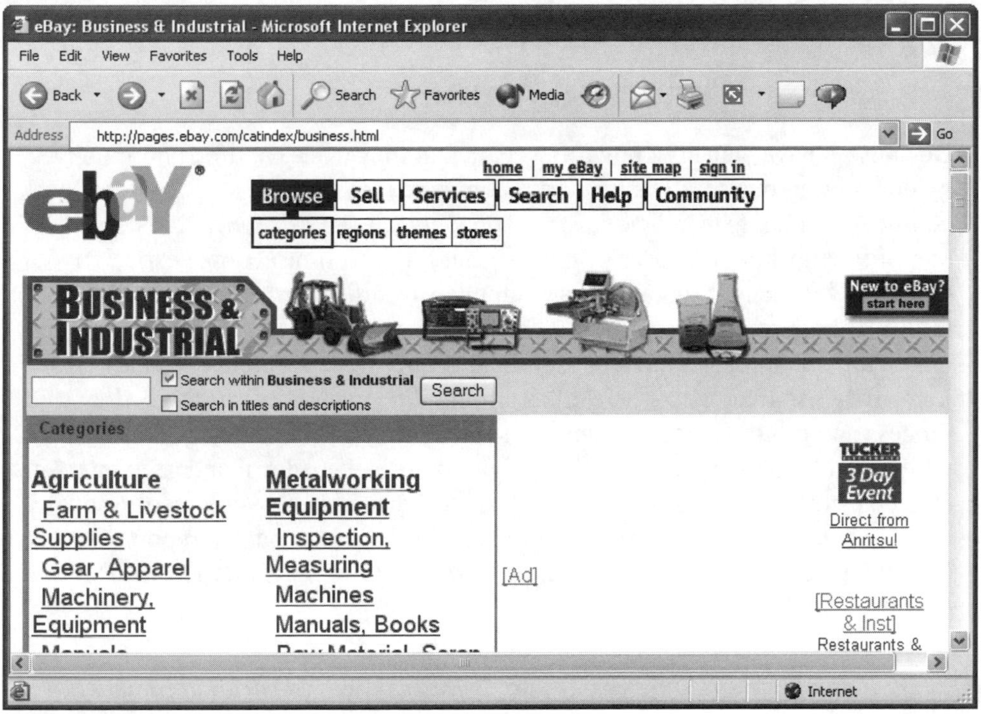

FIGURE 13-1   eBay's Business & Industrial area

and construction materials, restaurant supplies and food services, electronic components, health care supplies, lab equipment, printing, metalworking, retail fixtures, and myriad other items.

Buy or Sell Business Supplies

There's nothing wrong with professionals who specialize in purchasing or with purchasing departments. They save money for many large organizations, and they ensure that quality goods are obtained at reasonable prices. For small-scale purchases of essential supplies or services that a business needs to order periodically, however, it can be faster and more cost-effective to put some level of control in the hands of individual employees and let them procure goods over the Internet. In fact, purchasing professionals also commonly save time and money for their companies by doing supply procurement online through venues like eBay.

Did you know?

E-procurement Saves Time and Money

Businesses have actually known for years that they can save time and money by conducting business-to-business e-commerce: online transactions between companies rather than individuals. *E-procurement* is a flashy term that describes one of the most popular uses of the Internet for B2B transactions, especially those in which a company purchases supplies over the Internet rather than using traditional paper purchase requests. Most of the companies that do procurement online are obtaining indirect goods—maintenance, repair, and operations (MRO) items they use internally—as well as commodity-type or direct goods they can process and resell. E-procurement can save your company both time and money while maintaining approval and oversight to push costs down and efficiency up. Business-to-business transactions accounted for more than 94 percent of all e-commerce in the year 2000, according to a U.S. Census Bureau report released in early 2003 (**http://www.census.gov/eos/www/papers/estatstext .pdf**).

TIP   *If you have questions about eBay's Business & Industrial area, you have two options. Visit the Business & Industrial discussion board (look for a link to the board on the Wholesale Lots home page: **http://pages.ebay.com/ catindex/catwholesale.html**), or e-mail business@ebay.com.*

Benefits of Buying Supplies Online

Going online to procure stock brings about cost savings. The e-marketplaces you use can charge lower prices because they're aggregating purchasing volumes. E-procurement gives you these additional advantages:

- **Control**   Your employees can purchase their own supplies online (with the appropriate approvals).

- **Streamlining**   You can conduct paperless procurement, thus saving the cost and time involved in generating the usual purchasing documents.

- **Savings**   You can snatch bargains by bidding on supplies at auction.

- **Automation**   Your preferred suppliers can set up automatic inventory control systems to help you to replenish stock and set up packages of supplies based on previous orders.

■ **Reliability**   Following standard ordering procedures and filling out forms at electronic marketplaces prevents errors that can arise from entering data by hand.

Businesses frequently need to sell off equipment. A medical supplier might have a batch of twenty unused stethoscopes that would be perfect for a hospital; an industrial supply company might need to sell off a forklift or a set of tools; a furniture supply house might want to sell lighting, shelving, or other items that practically every business needs.

Table 13-1 lists actual final auction prices taken from eBay's Completed Auctions listings. They indicate the kinds of office equipment deals that bidders have secured for their companies. (You aren't guaranteed to get the same prices yourself.)

Benefits of Selling Off Excess Inventory

Are you unsure what constitutes a reasonable price for items that you have never ordered before? Consider letting the market decide the price by posting your sale on eBay.

The Business & Industrial area can give your company a way to unload stock it may have had trouble selling previously. If you are already a registered eBay seller, the steps involved in selling business supplies are the same as on other parts of eBay. The advantage of selling on Business & Industrial is that buyers go there looking for office supplies, tools, and manufacturing equipment. The best items to sell are commonly used supplies that are in good condition and that you don't mind selling at a fraction of the original list price. Heavy equipment like forklifts, lumber, or construction-related items sell well. You also are likely to have more immediate results. It takes less time to sell on eBay than it would to place an ad in a trade journal and wait for a response from a potential buyer.

13

Item	List Price	Business & Industrial Price
Herman Miller Aeron chair size B black	$800	$476.51
Topcon RLS1B Self-Leveling laser level	$1995	$705.77
Turbotorch self-lighting swivel head torch tip	$139.60	$32.03
Tektronix TDS744A oscilloscope	$7,695 (refurbished)	$5,825

TABLE 13-1   Business & Industrial Auction Examples

FIGURE 13-2   eBay provides this newsletter for companies that sell in the Business & Industrial category.

You can get selling tips on eBay's Business & Industrial newsletter (**http:// www.ebay.com/Binewsletter/ Vol1Issue1.html**), shown in Figure 13-2.

Unload "Lots" of Items at Once

Suppose your store is closing or you are discontinuing a line of clothing. You are left with dozens or perhaps even hundreds of items. Or you find yourself with a pallet containing 85 refurbished computers. What can you do? Put them up for auction on eBay's Wholesale Lots area. Wholesale Lots is an area especially designated for companies that need to sell a group of items as a single item (in other words, a *lot*).

You can find the Wholesale Lots listings on eBay in one of two ways:

■   Go to the Wholesale Lots Web page (**http://pages.ebay.com/catindex/ catwholesale.html**), shown in Figure 13-3. If you're looking for a particular type of item, you can click through sets of categories here and hopefully find what you want.

■ Go to the eBay Stores home page (**http://www.stores.ebay.com**), enter "Wholesale Lots" in the Search Stores box, and click **Search Stores**. This presents you with a listing of all current eBay Stores listings that have the words "Wholesale Lots" in the title. If you're in a hurry, try this first; if you don't find what you need, go to the Wholesale Lots page listed above and do a lengthier search (bay.com/stores/category31578/).

If you expect to deal in wholesale lots frequently, it's a good idea to open an eBay Store. It's located in the Wholesale Lots category, along with creating individual listings in the Wholesale Lots area. Because an eBay Store is essentially a gathering of all of your sales in one set of Web pages, you won't be repeating yourself. Instead, you'll be getting exposure in two areas.

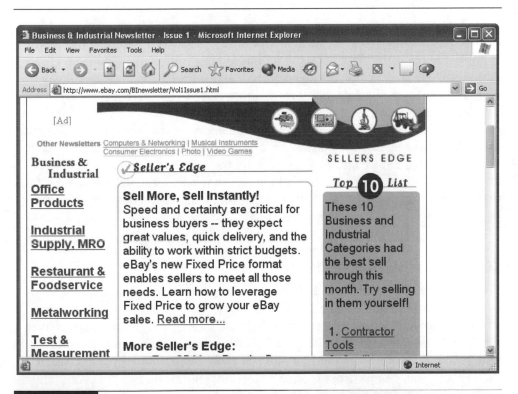

13

FIGURE 13-3   You can sell a group of items all at once in Wholesale Lots.

Many wholesalers obtain lots of items at a bargain price and hope to sell the lots all at once on eBay to gain a profit. The primary categories included in Wholesale Lots at this writing are:

- **Home, Living, and Hobbies**   This category includes items that are frequently sold as lots, including clothing and collectibles.

- **Computers & Electronics**   This category is found in Business & Industrial, Half.com, and the general eBay sales area, so make sure you only sell lots of computer equipment here.

- **Business & Industrial**   This can include tools, restaurant supplies, and MRO items.

- **Media**   Subcategories here include books, movies, and music. Again, make sure you only sell in Wholesale Lots if you have groups of items. For books, CDs, or movies, see Half.com, which is described in Chapter 14.

Often, companies are left with orders that they can't fulfill, and they need to clear out their inventory to make room for new products to sell. In either case, Wholesale Lots is the place to do the selling. If your priority is to unload a group of items all at once, list them with no reserve and see what the market will pay for it. The key is to be prepared to sell for as low a price as possible: buyers come to Wholesale Lots looking for real bargains and deep discounts.

To sell in Wholesale Lots, first go to the category where you want to sell your lot of items. For instance, if you have a leftover batch of 100 teddy bears, go to the Wholesale Lots home page, click **Dolls & Bears**, and open a page where lots of dolls and bears are being sold, such as the one shown below. Click the link **Sell in this category** on the right side of this page. Follow the instructions on subsequent pages to sign in and list your own lot for sale.

Look for Local Buyers

When you are attempting to sell off large lots of goods or heavy machinery such as farm or construction equipment, it's generally best to attract a wide audience of bidders so you can get the best price. You can then ship the goods to the buyer. However, if you're trying to sell heavy, bulky items and you are in a hurry, finding a shipper and arranging for transportation can take more time than you have. In such cases it can be practical to locate a buyer in your local area. That way, your buyer can pick up the merchandise and pay you for it in person. Even though you may restrict your potential customer base, you don't have to worry about packaging

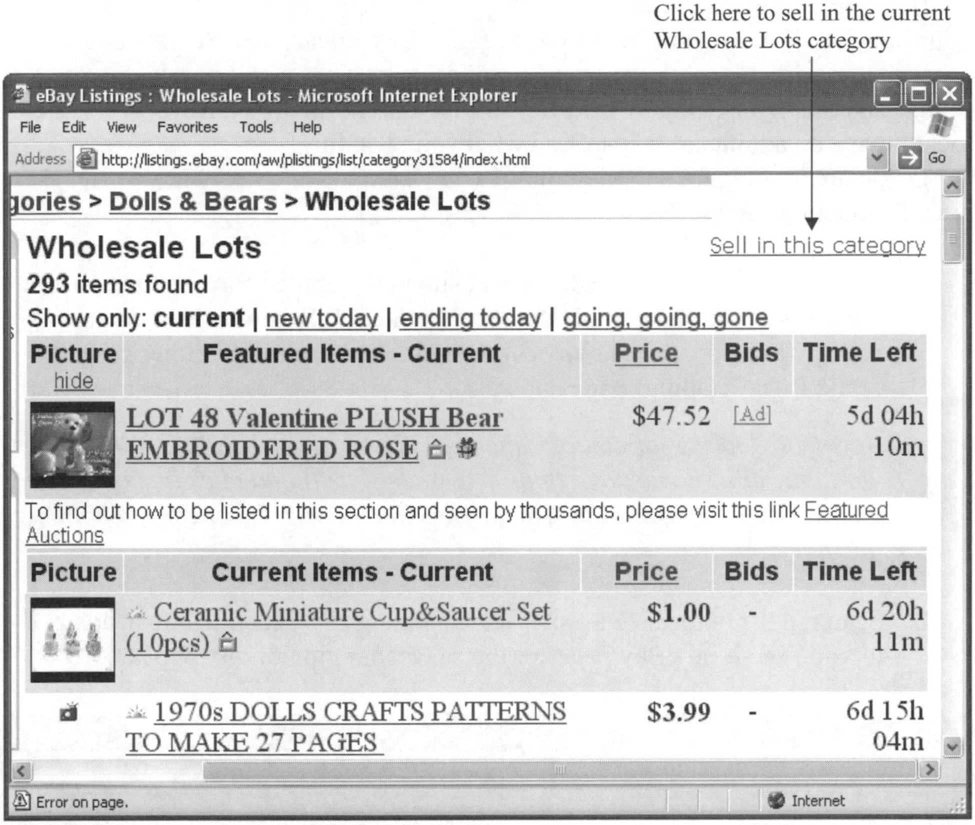

Click here to sell in the current
Wholesale Lots category

FIGURE 13-4   If you have large quantities of identical items to sell, list them in Wholesale Lots.

and shipping. Occasionally, sellers specify in their descriptions that they will only sell locally with a phrase such as:

I will not ship this item; it is available for local pickup only..."

Such a statement can potentially cause conflicts with bidders, however. Let's say that a bidder really wants what you have to sell and turns out to be the high bidder. The one little detail is that he or she doesn't live in your specified area. That individual could possibly claim not to have seen the requirement to live in a particular area. Then a nasty argument could be the result.

A more reliable method of finding buyers in your area is to click the radio button next to **Will arrange for local pickup only (no shipping)** in Step 4 of 5 of the Sell Your Item form. You also need to provide pickup instructions in the Payment Instructions box on the same page.

13

If you are especially interested in local buyers being able to find and bid on your merchandise, list your item in one of the eBay Local sites. Such sites are specific to a particular metropolitan area or country. They don't restrict buyers to that region; anyone in the world can still bid on your item. However, you give local buyers an additional way to find what you're selling.

If you are looking for supplies, and if you want to locate items in your local area, follow these steps:

1. If you're looking for an eBay Local site in the United States, you can go to the eBay home page, click **Buy**, and then click **Regions**. You can also go directly to **http://pages.ebay.com/regional/hub.html**. In either case, the eBay: Local Trading! page appears.

TIP *If you are looking for an eBay site in a country other than the United States, go to the eBay home page (http://www.ebay.com) and click one of the links to international eBay sites listed in the Global Sites box near the bottom of the page.*

2. Scan the list of local eBay sites shown below and click the one nearest to you. The local eBay page for the selected region or city appears.

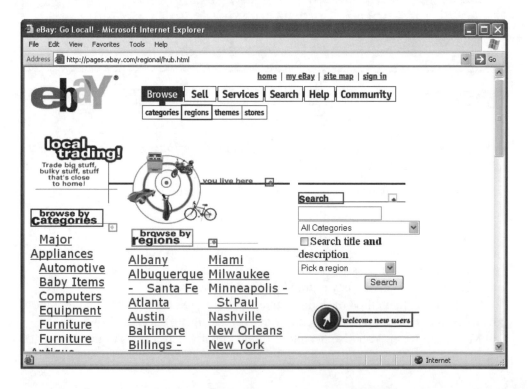

3. If you are shopping for business supplies, either search through the list of categories, or enter a search term in the Search box. (If you do a search, make sure the button next to the city or region is selected so your search is limited to items in the selected area.) If you're selling, click the category that applies to the merchandise you want to sell. For instance, under the category Equipment, you might click **Office** if you're trying to sell off furniture or copiers.

4. Continue clicking through subcategories until you locate a page that is specific to the item you want to sell and that has the link **Sell in this category** on the right side of the page.

5. Click **Sell in this category**. On subsequent pages, you sign in and list your item for sale just as you do on other parts of eBay.

You should note that just because you are selling in, say, the Orlando, Florida, version of eBay doesn't mean you'll get buyers who live in or near Orlando, Florida. There's no requirement that bidders have to live in a local eBay region in order to place bids on items that are sold on the local eBay Web site. It *does* mean that, if you're shopping for supplies, you'll find sellers who are in or near Orlando. It also means you'll be competing with other sellers in your local area.

CAUTION *Most people don't restrict their buyers to a particular area because it's possible to ship very large items, including cars and other vehicles such as tractors, anywhere in the world. For some heavy building materials, you might want to specify that you will only ship in the United States, which is a restriction commonly seen on eBay listings.*

13

Buy Government Surplus Materials

If you're a bargain hunter like me, you've probably scoured surplus stores and warehouses looking for coats, camping equipment, and other surplus items the U.S. government needs to sell. Now, both federal and state government agencies are turning to eBay to auction off excess property. For instance, the Oregon Division of Administrative Services (DAS) manages auctions for a variety of government offices and reportedly takes in more than $100,000 per week through eBay auctions. You'll find links to its eBay auctions at **http://tpps.das.state.or.us/surplus/auction .htm**. The department reported that it gets higher prices through eBay auctions than through traditional surplus merchandise auctions. For instance, a K2 bike that fetched $300 at a traditional auction sold for $1,035.99 online. A Toshiba VCR that sold for $50 at a traditional auction brought $139.05 on eBay.

NOTE   *Even the U.S. Post Office has, in the past, used eBay to sell items that were found to be undeliverable for some reason or that had been returned to their senders. However, the attempt to unload such merchandise through eBay was suspended and reviewed as a result of deadbeat bidders who never paid for or picked up their merchandise. When I checked, the Post Office had no items for sale on eBay through its previous User ID usps-mrc-everythingelse.*

Government entities can sell through the Business & Industrial area on eBay, but they need to follow regulatory procedures for buying and selling goods and equipment. Often, state agencies can't sell directly through eBay, but need to sell through an office such as the General Services Commission (Texas). If you work in a state agency, you may have to make a formal declaration stating what property you are going to declare as "surplus." You may also need to advertise the surplus merchandise locally before you offer it online. Check with your own general services office before you post online.

Buy and Sell Professional Services on eLance

If you're a freelancer or contractor, you probably already use the Internet to look for work. You may have used a service called eLance that enabled employers to post projects for which they needed freelance help. In response to such postings, freelancers would bid on the jobs and the employer would be able to choose the bidder based on price and other considerations.

Like Half.com (see Chapter 14), eLance became extremely popular and is now affiliated with eBay. A story on PR Newswire reported that the number of projects outsourced through eLance grew by more than 55% during 2002 as more than 30,000 small businesses used the service. (On eBay, it now goes by the awkward-sounding name eBay Professional Services – eLance, but for the purposes of this chapter I'll just call it eLance.) If you use eLance, you can buy or provide professional freelance services. eLance brings businesses and service providers together like the want ads or employment agencies, with the help of a few special features:

■ **Feedback**   You can check out employers and freelancers to see what kind of feedback has been left for them.

■ **Interactivity**   Employers can place their ads before the eager eyes of freelancers in a matter of minutes; freelancers can place bids almost immediately. eLance lets participants communicate and collaborate online, too.

■ **Competition**   Freelancers bid on jobs that providers offer, so employers get the best prices, and freelancers have the advantage of being able to find work.

There's another big difference between eLance and more traditional ways of finding work: You have to pay to list yourself as a service provider, if you go over an allotted number of bids per month, and if you get a job, too, as explained in the next section.

NOTE   *You'll find eLance in two places. You can go to **http://www.elance.com**, or **http://pages.ebay.com/professional_services/index.html**.*

Benefits for Businesses that Need Freelancers

Like the Business & Industrial area, eLance brings businesspeople together. In this case, services such as writing, design, accounting, and consulting are being traded rather than tools, photocopiers, or other objects. Businesses that have projects they need done by outsiders make those projects available on eLance. On the other side of the equation, freelancers who are looking for work market themselves and bid on projects.

Suppose, for instance, you need to have a logo designed for your company. (Web page creation and graphic design are, in fact, two of the most popular services "sold" on eLance.) Here's how the system would work for you:

1. Open an eLance account so you can send payments to service providers or pay transaction fees.

2. Post a description of your project online (see Figure 13-5). You either solicit bids or offer the project at a fixed "Buy Now" price.

3. Freelance service providers post bids—sometimes, within hours or even minutes of the project going online. You review the bids and check on the providers' bids, feedback ratings, and sample work.

4. You can ask bidders questions by posting messages on eLance's private message boards. You then choose the freelancer you want based on the individual's qualifications and the amount of the bid.

5. The service provider does the work; when the work is done eLance charges the selected freelancer a transaction fee of 8.75 percent of either the invoiced amount of the job or the original bid amount (whichever is greater). You use eLance's billing and payment services to complete the transaction.

13

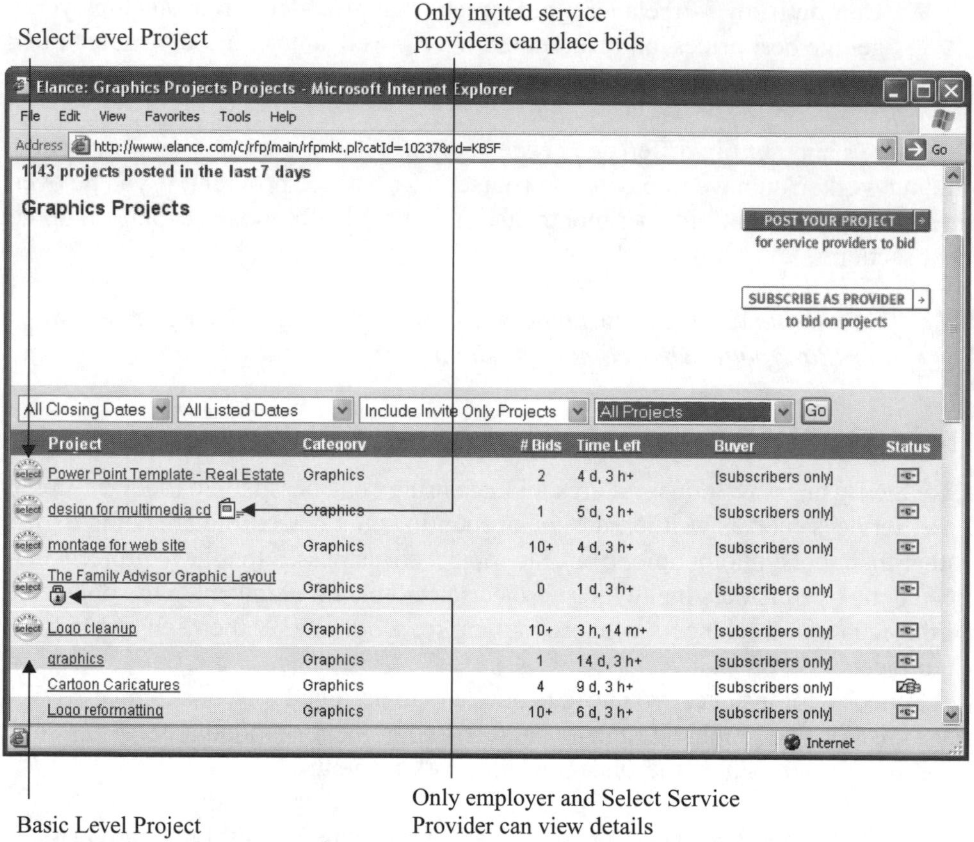

Select Level Project

Only invited service
providers can place bids

Elance: Graphics Projects Projects - Microsoft Internet Explorer

File   Edit   View   Favorites   Tools   Help

Address   http://www.elance.com/c/rfp/main/rfpmkt.pl?catId=102378rld=KBSF   Go

1143 projects posted in the last 7 days

Graphics Projects

POST YOUR PROJECT
for service providers to bid

SUBSCRIBE AS PROVIDER
to bid on projects

All Closing Dates   All Listed Dates   Include Invite Only Projects   All Projects   Go

Project	Category	# Bids	Time Left	Buyer	Status
Power Point Template - Real Estate	Graphics	2	4 d, 3 h+	[subscribers only]	
design for multimedia cd	Graphics	1	5 d, 3 h+	[subscribers only]	
montage for web site	Graphics	10+	4 d, 3 h+	[subscribers only]	
The Family Advisor Graphic Layout	Graphics	0	1 d, 3 h+	[subscribers only]	
Logo cleanup	Graphics	10+	3 h, 14 m+	[subscribers only]	
graphics	Graphics	1	14 d, 3 h+	[subscribers only]	
Cartoon Caricatures	Graphics	4	9 d, 3 h+	[subscribers only]	
Logo reformatting	Graphics	10+	6 d, 3 h+	[subscribers only]	

Internet

Basic Level Project

Only employer and Select Service
Provider can view details

FIGURE 13-5   eLance projects are posted on lists organized by the type of
service needed.

6.   Once the project has been completed to your satisfaction, you post feedback
about the quality of the work and of the freelancer. Your feedback then
becomes part of the freelancer's overall feedback rating.

For employers, one of the big advantages of using eLance is the fact that you
can draw upon a large pool of freelance service providers, and get competitive
prices for the project you need done. You don't have to go out and seek professionals
yourselves; rather, they come to you. Simply posting a job on eLance is free. When
the bids come in, you don't need to pick anyone at all; you can decide not to use
anyone's freelance services.

TIP *You can pay an extra listing fee to have your project listed at a Select Level rather than the plain old Basic Level listing. A Select Level listing can be bid on only by providers whose credentials have been verified by one of two third parties, US Search or Square Trade, so you're more likely to find someone who's reliable. You gain the opportunity to "pre-screen" providers by asking them three questions before a provider can bid on a job. However, you must place a refundable deposit of $25 in order to place a Select Level bid, and projects at the Select Level are subject to minimum bid requirements—$300 for a graphic design job, $550 for Web design and development, and so on. See the eLance Help files for more specific information.*

Benefits to Freelancers

If you're a freelancer, eLance has the obvious benefit of bringing you projects you can consider and bid on. Once you register with eLance, you need to post background information about your experience and qualifications on a profile page. This page also includes the history of previous projects you've completed on eLance as well as your feedback rating.

eLance is convenient, but it isn't free. You do pay an 8.75 percent fee to eLance if you are chosen, however. If the fee for the job turns out to be $1,000, this fee amounts to a not-inconsiderable $87.50. In addition, you must pay a monthly fee to subscribe as a bidder. A Basic Subscription costs $70 per month and gives you 80 free bids per month. Any bids that go over your number of free bids are subject to bid fees. A Select Subscription gives you 120 free bids per month and costs between $75 and $250 depending on the category of the jobs you want to see. As a freelancer, you are rated based on the feedback you receive when you complete a project. The feedback ratings are listed in Table 13-2.

Rating	What It Means
5.0	Extremely satisfied
4.0	Very satisfied
3.0	Satisfied
2.0	Not satisfied
1.0	Extremely unsatisfied

TABLE 13-2   eLance Feedback Ratings

13

Feedback is calculated by service buyers based on quality of work, responsiveness, professionalism, subject matter expertise, adherence to the budget, and adherence to the schedule. eLance functions as a go-between where payment is concerned; you submit invoices to eLance, the buyer of your services submits payment to eLance, and eLance forwards payments to you.

While you are doing the work, you can make use of a file-sharing area called Work Space that eLance provides, where you can upload files and virtually present them for review. You can also use the Work Space area to exchange messages and do scheduling.

eLance includes a category of freelancers called Select Service Providers. To be given this designation, you have to pay a listing fee and receive "verification" that you are a reputable provider.

Where to Find It

- **Business & Industrial Newsletter**
  http://www.ebay.com/BInewsletter/ Vol1Issue1.html
  Lists of "hot items" that sell well in the Business & Industry category; profiles of businesspeople who buy and sell supplies on eBay

- **eBay Business & Industrial area**
  http://pages.ebay.com/catindex/ business.html
  eBay's business-to-business marketplace.

- **eBay: Professional Services - eLance**
  http://pages.ebay.com/ professional_services/
  Offer your professional services online through eBay

- **eBay Wholesale Lots**
  http://pages.ebay.com/catindex/ catwholesale.html
  Lists of items for sale as wholesale lots.

Chapter 14

Fix Your Price on Half.com

How to...

- Set a competitive fixed price for your sales items
- Take advantage of Half.com's database of sales images and specs
- Specify shipping options for your customers
- Build positive feedback by providing good customer service

Half.com makes selling as simple as putting on a garage sale, but without any haggling over prices, attaching sticky labels, or cleaning your garage. Half.com even helps provide you with images for the items you want to sell, and handles the payment processing, too. If you find reserve price and Dutch auctions confusing, you don't like the auction process, or you just want to sell your old textbooks, CDs, and electronics items quickly and simply, Half.com is the place for you.

Half.com is a unique place. You visit Half.com on eBay in order to sell your merchandise at reduced price. But that's not all. You can get in your car and drive to Oregon. There, you'll find the real town called Half.com (a.k.a. Halfway) shown in Figure 14-1. In 2000, Half.com (the company, that is) persuaded the town of Halfway, Ore. (pop. 345), into renaming itself Half.com, Oregon, in exchange for $75,000 and 22 computers. The move made national headlines and made Half.com one of the most popular sites on the Internet. Before long, Half.com (the company) was purchased by eBay.

NOTE   *There's a reason why Half.com looks and feels different than other parts of eBay. Half.com was started by an entrepreneur named Josh Kopelman. Since you're an online entrepreneur yourself, you may want to read the full story of Half.com at* **http://corp.half.com/pressfiles/time_magazine_02_05_01/ time_magazine_02_05_01.html**.

Half.com is a highly successful part of eBay because it provides real bargains without the uncertainty of auctions. It supplements eBay's usual auctions with fixed-price sales. You see something for sale, you pay the price, you simply buy it, and you're done.

For sellers, Half.com provides a far different experience than selling on eBay. Half.com's sales are not scheduled to end at a specified time, like eBay's auctions. Rather than individual listings grouped by time or type of merchandise, Half.com groups all items with the same book title, game title, DVD title, by different sellers on the same page. Sellers have very little opportunity to stand out from the crowd, unless they set a price that's slightly less than the other instances of the same item

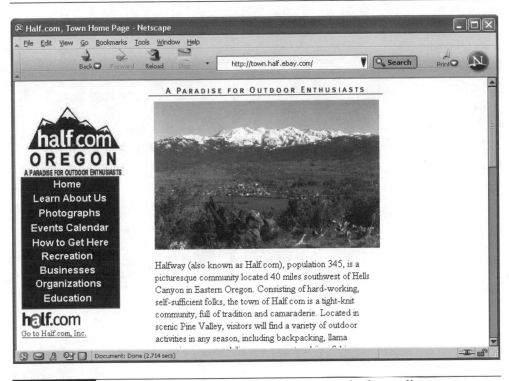

FIGURE 14-1   Half.com: Not just an auction site, but a scenic place to live, too

that are already up for sale. They can also write a better description of their item, though only the first few words of that description appear on the sales page.

On the up side, Half.com, unlike eBay, functions as an intermediary with regard to payments. The company bills the buyer and pays the seller, which means there's no danger that a seller will have to deal with a bounced check. If you are looking for certainty and a bit of extra security and don't mind having your sales items look like everyone else's, Half.com is for you.

As you can see from Figure 14-2, Half.com's virtual home on the Web isn't in Oregon but at **http://half.ebay.com**, and the emphasis is on easy-to-transport entertainment-related items.

As a Half.com seller, your main responsibilities are to describe your item accurately, set a reasonable price, and ship it out quickly when it's purchased. That's all there is to it. The step-by-step process is outlined in the sections that follow.

14

Buyers can place pre-orders
that you can fill

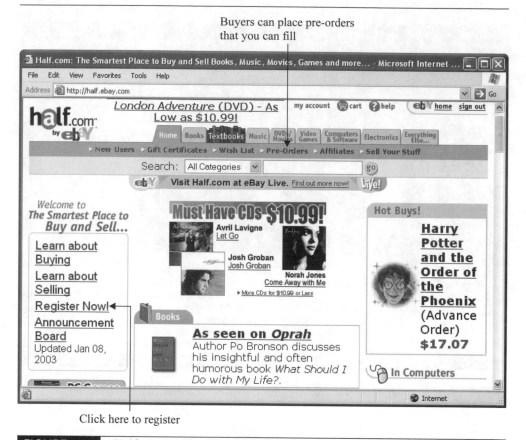

Click here to register

FIGURE 14-2 Half.com's virtual home on the Web

Step 1: Become a Member

Some parts of eBay are perfect for businesses (such as Business & Industry, described
in Chapter 13), but Half.com is the ideal place for individuals who want to make a
few extra dollars by cleaning out books, CDs, or games that are cluttering their shelves.
As a freelance writer, for instance, I get plenty of sample books from publishers.
They tend to languish in boxes unless I sell them. The following sections show how
I set up one of my own sales on Half.com.

NOTE

If you are already a member of eBay, you do not have to become a member of Half.com. You can use the same User ID and password for your Half.com account. If you do use the same User ID and password, all your feedback from both sites will be collected in a single set of feedback. However, you may want to keep two different User IDs in case you sell on eBay as part of your business, and on Half.com to get some additional personal income, for instance.

If you need to create a Half.com account, click the **Register Now!** link on the Half.com home page and follow the instructions on subsequent pages. If you already have an eBay account, and you don't want to create a separate Half.com account, click **My Account** near the top of the Half.com home page.

CAUTION

Only residents of the United States can buy and sell on Half.com at the time of this writing—a restriction that does not apply to other parts of eBay.

Provide Your Seller Information

Once you have an account, You click **My Account** on the Half.com home page. Then, click **Become a Seller** under the heading My Account. On subsequent pages, you provide Half.com with your address, phone number, and credit card information. As Half.com points out, the credit card information is used to verify your identity. It also might be used to charge you money in case you are found liable as a result of a dispute, or if you have not followed through on a sale.

Next, on the "Create Seller's Account: Step 2 of 2" page shown in Figure 14-3, you specify how you want to be paid by Half.com when you sell something. This is one of the best advantages of using Half.com for selling—you are paid by Half.com, not the buyer. You can be paid either by a paper check or direct deposit. Direct deposit is generally preferable, because Half.com charges you a $1.50 handling fee for each check. If the item you're selling costs less than $10, for instance, that $1.50 is a substantial part of your profit, after all.

Once you specify a payment option, you choose the default option for how you want your items to be shipped. This might seem confusing at first, because you are the one who will actually pack up your book or CD, take it to the post office or shipping company, and send it out. Keep in mind that, at this point, you're only specifying what you consider your "first choice" shipping option. You and your buyer can

14

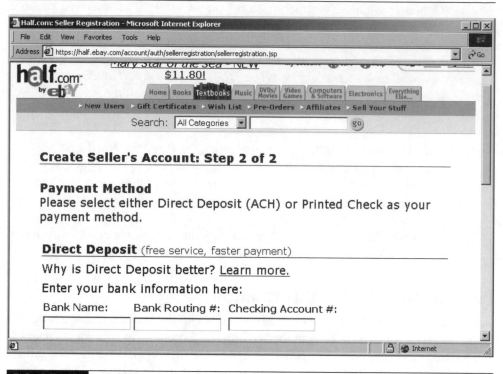

FIGURE 14-3   Half.com pays you either by check or direct deposit into a checking account.

work out a different option after the purchase is made. You only have two options: you can specify at the U.S. Postal Service's Media Rate (which typically takes four to twelve days) or at an expedited rate (two to eight days). Choose Media Rate if you want your customers to save money and you don't think they'll mind waiting a week or more to receive what they've purchased.

TIP   *Half.com reimburses you for shipping charges. See the section "Ship Your Goods Promptly" later in this chapter for a more detailed explanation.*

Once you've chosen the default shipping option, click the Register button at the bottom of the page. Your browser then displays a page with the heading Welcome [your user name]. You can now put up merchandise for sale as described in the sections that follow.

Step 2: Pick a Sales Category

Once you've become a registered Half.com user, it's time to do some detective work. Look around Half.com and check out the kinds of items that are already up for sale. Do a search to determine whether or not someone else is selling that college textbook or DVD you need to off-load. If you find that item is already up for sale, you needn't be discouraged. You can still put your own stuff up for sale at any price you want to set. Your price can be the same or even lower than your competitors' price tags; it can also be higher than the price of competing items.

Next, do some scouring around your own house and gather up some goodies you can potentially sell. You can't sell just anything on Half.com. Although the range of items that are put up for sale on Half.com is continually growing, shoppers go there expecting to find new or almost-new books, music, movies, or games. The full range of items sold on Half.com at this writing is as follows:

- **Books**   Half.com started primarily as a place to sell books, and these are still the most common sales items you'll find there. Students selling textbooks, bookstores selling remainders (leftover books that didn't sell), and authors unloading sample copies are ideal sellers. Even eBay's CEO Meg Whitman has reportedly sold her old Princeton textbooks on Half.com.

- **Music**   Music is already a popular sales category in eBay and many other online venues. You can only sell CDs on Half.com; music recorded on other media—from LPs, to cassettes, to piano rolls, to laser discs—should be sold on eBay. (You can sell audio books on cassette, though.) When you sell, you list the Universal Product Code of the CD as found on its jewel box. If the CD has an ISBN as well as a UPC, only list the UPC.

- **Movies**   These can be DVDs or VHS videotapes. Best sellers include boxed sets, recent releases, and tape or disk versions of programs that originally appeared on TV.

- **Games**   These are games that can be played on Game Boy, Nintendo, Xbox, or other consoles. (PC games are sold under the Computer Software category, however.)

- **Electronics**   These include game consoles such as Game Boy or Nintendo, digital cameras, DVD players, camcorders, and the like.

14

- ■ **Computers**   This category includes not only computers but peripheral devices such as scanners, monitors, and printers, as well as software.

- ■ **Everything Else**   This catch-all category includes sporting goods, garden items, jewelry, musical instruments, office furniture.... You'd better scan the list yourself to get an idea of what you can sell here.

Don't turn to Half.com to try to unload antiques, furnishings, heavy equipment, or items that are several years old and more likely to appeal to collectors—you'll have better luck selling those on eBay itself.

Find the Item Code

Virtually every book published by a commercial publisher has a number code. To begin, you need to look up the ISBN or UPC number code for the book or books you want to sell. ISBN stands for International Standard Book Number. UPC stands for Universal Product Code. They are "standard industry inventory numbers," found on all books, often expressed as bar codes. You'll find examples of ISBN numbers on the back of the book you're reading right now, and on Half.com's Start Selling Books page (**http://half.ebay.com/help/sell_books.cfm**), shown in Figure 14-4.

Listing Multiple Items

If you have more than one item to sell, just look up the ISBN or UPC numbers and enter them on the multiple listing form shown in Figure 14-5. Note: The original idea behind Half.com was that no book sold on the site would cost more than half its list price. That rule isn't strictly observed today, just as books aren't the only thing you'll find on Half.com. You *can* sell items for more than half of list price, though eBay doesn't recommend it.

Research the Competition

In my case, I have a box full of sample books given to me by the publisher of a book I wrote about the literary heritage of Chicago called *Literary Chicago*. The books are new, and I can offer them with the author's signature, so I decided to put one up for sale to see what would happen. I did my own detective work beforehand by doing the following:

■ I wrote down the ISBN number of the book

■ I entered the book's title *Literary Chicago* in the search box on Half.com's home page to see if anyone else was selling this book. I got 57 listings in the search results with the word "Chicago" in the title; one link was to my own book.

To my surprise, I discovered that more than a dozen sellers had my book up for sale at prices ranging from $8 to $18 (considering that the list price is $15.95, this last price is pretty amazing). I noticed that Half.com did not have an image available for this book. I also noticed that, although the sales form says up to 40

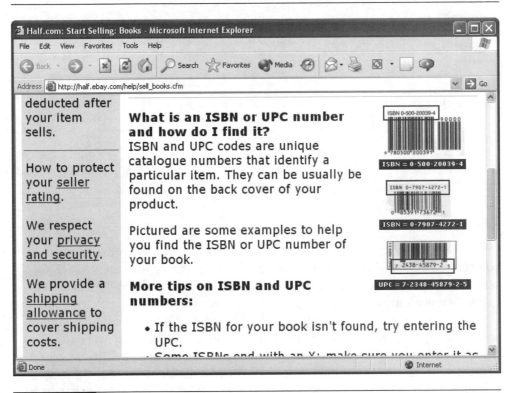

FIGURE 14-4 Examples of ISBN numbers

14

characters of a description might appear on the listing page, as few as 14 characters sometimes appear.

Set a Sales Price

If you find that others on Half.com are already selling what you want to sell, you can get a good idea of what the price should be. If not, you can research the same item on other well-known online retailing Web sites such as Amazon.com (**http://www.amazon.com**) or Buy.com (**http://www.buy.com**).

In the case of *Literary Chicago,* I had a new book that was going to compete with other new books selling for between $11 and $12. When prices are close, why does a buyer choose one seller over another? They choose a seller with lots of positive feedback. Since I don't have an eBay feedback rating in the thousands, I can't compete with long-established sellers. I do have a big advantage in that I am the author and I can provide a signed copy, however. I decided to sell my signed copy for $11.99.

TIP *How do you check what constitutes a reasonable price? If you need to compare prices at retail outlets so you can set a Half.com price, check out the Price Checker at Consumer World (**http://www.consumerworld.org**).*

Step 3: Fill Out the Sales Form

Armed with a price and the ISBN, and an idea of the competition, I started to fill out the sales form. You get to the Half.com sales form in one of several ways:

- Go to a page that lists the same item you want to sell, and click on the link **Sell Yours Now**.

- Click the **Sell** link at the bottom of any Half.com Web page (you can also reach this page by entering the direct URL **http://half.ebay.com/help/sell.cfm**), then click on the category in which you want to sell.

You then fill out the form's simple contents, which are described in the following sections.

Specify the Condition

The Item Quality ranking on Half.com is very specific and varies depending on what you want to sell. I chose the condition: Brand new. If an item you have for sale isn't brand new, you need to choose the description with care. The categories are as shown in Table 14-1.

Condition	What It Means
Brand New	New, unread, in perfect condition
Like New	Undamaged cover, no missing or undamaged pages, no writing or highlighting
Very Good	No noticeable damage on cover; no missing pages; no damaged pages; no underlining of text, no writing in margins, minimal wear and tear
Good	Minimal damage to cover; dust jacket may or may not be present; most pages undamaged, minimal pencil underlining, no highlighting, no missing pages
Acceptable	Some cover damage, binding slightly damaged; may be writing in margins as well as underlining or highlighting of text

TABLE 14-1   Condition Categories for Half.com

14

If the condition is worse than acceptable—in other words, if a significant number of pages are damaged and there are missing or stained pages, Half.com does not allow you to sell the item.

TIP   *The condition descriptions vary depending on what you're selling. Refer to the detailed list of options at* **http://half.ebay.com/help/ popup_display.cfm?helpsection=pricing#2**.

Create a Description

If writing descriptions of sales items is your least favorite aspect of online selling, Half.com is the place for you. Forget about detailed descriptions of the condition or flaws of your book, CD, or movie. Forget about explaining where you found that special something or how many times you used it. You only really need two pieces of information here:

- the ISBN or UPC number
- a standard description that describes the item's condition

That's it. You can add comments of up to 1,000 words describing an item, but this is optional. Keep in mind that only the first 40 characters of a description appear on a list of items for sale on Half.com, so these should contain the most important parts of your description. You may receive questions from prospective buyers inquiring about the condition of an item, but most of the time, you'll simply receive an e-mail message from Half.com stating that the item has been purchased and providing you with shipping information.

In my case, my biggest challenge was to state, in as few characters as possible, the fact that the book was being sold and signed by the author, and that it was brand new. I tried the following:

New! Signed by author.

I agonized over whether to list the book as Brand New (the official Half.com condition ranking) or simply New. I decided on New to make sure the word "Signed" would appear. This was only 22 characters, so there was a good chance it would all appear on the listing page. I added the following comments:

Sold by author, so signature can be personalized.

Your Listing Can be Removed?

Your listing will be removed from Half.com if you do any of the following:

- List merchandise in the wrong category

- Place ads to your own business within your description

- Place lots of similar listings in a single category which forces out your competition

Although you cannot place an ad to your business within a Half.com description, you can include a link that "points interested buyers to another Internet page that contains only more information (such as pictures, product specifications, or detailed terms and conditions) about eBay items listed by that seller."

Add an Image

In many cases, you don't have to worry about capturing an image of the item you have to sell. In many cases, Half.com is able to match the ISBN or UPC number you include with the listing to a photo that already exists in its extensive database.

Since Half.com did not have an image of *Literary Chicago* in the Add an Image section of the sales form, I clicked the Browse button and located an image of the book cover on my hard disk. Then I clicked the Continue button at the bottom of the sales form.

Finish the Listing

After you click Continue, your browser displays a Sell Your Stuff page that prompts you to enter your eBay User ID and password. Enter the information, and click **Continue**.

The Set Price and List Your Item page appears. Half.com suggests a price based on the average sales prices of similar items and the condition you described earlier. In my case, Half.com suggested a price of $12.07. I changed this to $11.99 (which looks slightly less expensive on screen) and clicked List Item. A page appeared with the heading "Thank You for Listing!"

14

After your listing is confirmed, be sure to check the listing to make sure the price and description are accurate. If you need to make changes or monitor all of your sales at once, click the **My Account** link at the top of the Half.com home page. Click Manage Inventory, and a list of your current sales appears. Click the link for the sale you want to change, and follow the steps displayed on subsequent screens to make the changes you want.

Feedback and Customer Service

When you purchase something, whether online or off, you expect good customer service. But when you sell on Half.com, you are the one who has to provide good service, because you are responsible for packaging the items you sell and dealing with your customers. It's not a difficult subject to master: Just think about how you like to be treated when you shop, and do the same.

Build a Good Seller Rating

Feedback is different on Half.com than it is on eBay: only sellers are rated, not buyers. Having a good seller rating not only attracts buyers, but it can bring you more business. You may be called upon to fulfill a pre-order—an order in which the buyer has indicated that they will accept an item as it is described in your sales catalog if you have one, in a specified quality rating, from a seller with a specified feedback score.

CAUTION   *Don't sell something you don't have the rights to sell. If you burned a CD that you or someone else purchased originally, don't try to sell that copy unless you received permission from the copyright holder to make that copy. Find out more at* **http://half.ebay.com/help/index.cfm?helpsection=vero**.

Ship Your Goods Promptly

The primary way to build a good feedback rating on Half.com is simple: ship your goods out promptly and thoroughly. Half.com suggests that all sellers insure and track their shipments. Packages shipped via Media Mail should have the words "Media Mail" written on the outside.

NOTE   *If you plan to be out of town, be sure to send Half.com a vacation notice so your listing is taken off the site until your specified return date. That way anyone who purchases your items won't experience long days until you respond.*

First-Class Service Pays Off

Andy Noise is the owner of a small brick-and-mortar music shop in Bakersfield, California. Half.com has helped transformed Andy Noise (that's the name of the store, too) from a local music outlet to a national supplier. He says he does twice the amount of business on the Internet than he does through the physical store. The store's Web site (**http://www.andynoise.com**) contains links to his auctions on eBay as well as Half.com.

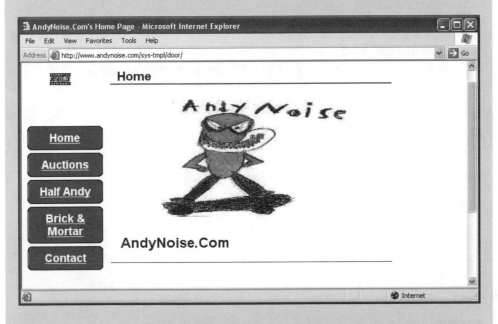

At this writing, since becoming a member of Half.com, Andy had sold 7,068 items for a total of $72,770.27.

He regularly scans CD bins to find bargain CDs he can resell on Half.com. He emphasizes the need to describe an item's condition accurately and ship out promptly. In fact, he employs a little "trickery" when shipping that helps improve his level of customer service. "My customers pay for Media Mail, and they pay for media but I always ship first class. So they get the stuff faster," he says.

As far as shipping, he uses the e-mail message he receives from Half.com as a mailing label. "Many of the home postage systems require you to enter the address to get the postage and this is a waste of time. I just cut the address off the email and tape it to the bag. That way if the address is incorrect, it is not my error." He uses 6-inch by 6.5-inch CD bubble mailers that he buys in lots of 50 on eBay. The best thing about selling on Half.com, he says, doesn't have to do with feedback or money: He's able to spend more time with his sons because he can do much of his work from his home computer.

If your item is sold, you pay the shipper to send the item out, but the buyer has to pay shipping costs. Half.com then reimburses you for the shipping based on the scale shown in Table 14-2.

For instance, if my book sells for $11.99, the following occurs:

1. The buyer pays a total of $14.98 ($11.99 plus $2.79 for Media Mail shipping).

2. Half.com charges me a 15 percent fee on the $11.99 sale price, or $1.80.

3. Half.com reimburses me $2.79 for this paperback book.

4. Half.com pays me a total of $12.79.

	USPS Media Mail	Expedited Mail
Hardcover Book	$3.25 per book	$5.45 per book
Paperback Book	$2.79 per book	$4.99 per book
Audio Book	$2.79 per book	$4.99 per book
Music	$2.49 per item	$4.99 per item
VHS Movies	$2.79 per item	$4.99 per item
DVD Movies	$2.49 per item	$4.99 per item
Games	$2.49 per item	$4.99 per item

TABLE 14-2   Half.com Shipping Reimbursement

CAUTION   *If you and your buyer have a dispute, Half.com reserves the right to make adjustments to your seller account balance in the event of a member dispute, fraud, or a lack in seller performance. If insufficient funds exist in the seller account balance, Half.com will deduct funds from your checking account, or charge your credit card.*

Where to Find It

- **Half.com Help**
  http://half.ebay.com/help/index.cfm
  General instructions on how to buy and sell on Half.com.

- **Multiple Listing page**
  http://half.ebay.com/account/list/multiList.jsp
  A form in which you can enter the ISBN or UPC numbers of multiple books you want to sell.

- **Start Selling page**
  http://half.ebay.com/help/sell.cfm
  Links to major categories (books, music, movies, games, computers, electronics, sporting goods). Each link leads you to a form that enables you to put up an individual item for sale.

Chapter 15

Get Top Dollar on Sothebys.com

How to...

- Register so you can auction fine art and antiques online
- Consign your merchandise to authorized Sothebys.com dealers
- Guarantee the authenticity of what you sell
- Create clear descriptions of your sales items
- Join in the excitement of live auctions

eBay auctions have become successful, in part, because they enable you to sell or buy from the comfort of your home; they allow you to track bidding over a period of three, five, seven days or more; and because ordinary people do the selling rather than professionals.

When you buy or sell on Sothebys.com, eBay's latest high-end auction site and the online branch of the famous British auction house, you step back in time to a place that, in many ways, resembles the world of traditional auctions. Sales are held at specific times, and they last only a matter or minutes or hours. Items are called *lots;* the winning bid is called the *hammer price*; for selected sales, bidders in real auction houses compete with bidders on the Internet.

If you are an antique dealer or have something for which you want to attract high-end bidders—bidders such as museums or well-to-do collectors who will pay tens of thousands or even more for a rare item—you may want to turn to Sothebys.com. Sothebys.com has its official home at **http://www.sothebys.com**, and this page includes links to premium auction events in its various auction houses around the world as well as its online auctions. Sotheby's eBay-affiliated home (**http://pages.sothebys.ebay.com/hp/online/index.html**) focuses solely on online auctions of fine art, rare books, desirable decorative arts pieces by Tiffany, Lalique, and others; jewelry and time pieces; historical items; and many other collectibles. This chapter examines the special requirements for selling on this premium auction site.

NOTE *eBay has operated premium auctions of its own in the past. You may be familiar with eBay Premier. In early 2002, eBay replaced eBay Premier when it entered into a joint venture with Sotheby's. The jury is out on whether Sotheby's-style auctions can work online. Sotheby's reportedly partnered with eBay after Sotheby's lost millions with its previous Web site. Many sales on Sothebys.com end without any bids being received.*

Terminology is Important

When you sell on Sothebys.com, it helps to know some of the terminology of traditional auction houses. Things are described differently in the old-style English auction houses than on eBay. For instance, Sotheby's and other traditional auction houses use the term *cataloguing* to describe the description and sale of a group of items. An individual item is called a *lot*.

Get Acquainted with Sothebys.com

Regular eBay auctions are great for moderately priced collectibles and merchandise of all sorts, but they might not be the best place to find a certain type of collector. Suppose, among the salt shakers and antique marbles you usually sell, you find a real treasure: a painting from the 1850s hidden behind what seems like a run-of-the-mill print, or a dresser made in Philadelphia in the 18th century? If you've really uncovered a valuable piece of art or furniture, and you want to attract worldwide bidders who are looking for maximum reliability and authenticity, you can go to an authorized Sothebys.com seller to put it up for auction—or become a Sothebys.com seller yourself.

What's the difference between Sothebys.com and eBay? You can get an idea of the difference the moment you visit the Sothebys.com home page shown in Figure 15-1.

As indicated by its home page (**http://pages.sothebys.ebay.com**), Sothebys.com is a more orderly and dignified place than most of the rest of eBay (or most e-commerce Web sites, for that matter). Sotheby's has its own set of requirements for sellers. Most notably, Sothebys.com sales are restricted to sellers who are already dealers in art, antiques, or collectibles. Dealers who are "old school" those who are more comfortable with traditional auction sales rather than selling online—will be happy to sign on and sell through this venue.

If you want to sell on Sothebys.com, you need to follow its rules, including:

- You must be a manager or employee of an auction house or a dealer in fine art or antiques.

- You must be able to guarantee the authenticity and condition of the items you sell.

15

FIGURE 15-1 eBay and Sotheby's have partnered to auction high-quality art and other objects.

- You need to take good quality photos of what you sell.

- You need to write clear descriptions, each accompanied by what Sothebys.com calls "a captivating additional note."

- You need to be aware of any import or export restrictions that may apply to what you are selling.

In return, Sotheby's promises, you get the prestige and reputation of Sotheby's behind you. But is that really true? Sotheby's *is* one of the oldest auction houses, founded in the mid-1700s. Sotheby's is famous for selling fine art for huge prices—for instance, Vincent van Gogh's painting *Sunflowers* sold for approximately $40 million in 1987. When you sell through Sothebys.com, you are supposed to get the power of Sotheby's auction house to attract collectors of fine art and antiques.

It's not clear to me, though, that huge numbers of those collectors are using the Internet as yet to bid at auction. It *is* clear to me that eBay is continually growing in popularity, and that valuable antiques and works of art are sold on eBay for thousands of dollars all the time. Sothebys.com gives you another way to sell high-priced collectibles, though it's not the only way. Each of the requirements for selling on Sothebys.com is described in more detail in the sections that follow.

Become a Sothebys.com Associate

If you are already "in the trade"—in other words, the business of buying and selling fine art, antiques, or collectibles—you are eligible to become an authorized seller on Sothebys.com, which the auction house calls an Associate. You do this by meeting the following criteria:

- You are a specialist in the field(s) in which you expect to offer property

- The merchandise you sell on Sothebys.com is worthy of serious interest

- Your sales items fall within one of the categories currently existing on Sothebys.com

- You have a good reputation and associate regularly with other dealers in your field

- You are familiar with the general standards for describing and selling items within your field of expertise.

How, exactly, do you prove this criteria? When I started writing this book, Sothebys.com required sellers to fill out an application form and provide references from two other dealers as well as extensive information about your own dealership. But during the editing process, the form was removed, and sellers were given direct access to the Sothebys.com Sell Your Item form (go to the Selling on Sothebys.com page, http://pages.ebay.com/sothebys/sell/index.html, scroll down the page, and click the link <u>Sell Your Item</u> to access the form). As long as you are a registered eBay user, you can list items for sale on Sothebys.com. The auction site, however, still expects you to abide by the requirements stated above.

However, if you have something very valuable to sell and you aren't a professional dealer, you can consign your item to a qualified Sothebys.com seller. (See the section "Sell on Consignment" later in this chapter.)

15

Guaranteeing Authenticity

When you are preparing a description for Sothebys.com, keep in mind that the highlighted link **Sothebys.com Guarantee** will appear with it. When prospective bidders click this link (see Figure 15-2), they are taken to a page (**http:// pages.ebay .com/sothebys/help/rulesandsafety/guarantee.html**) that extensively describes the guarantees that Sotheby's puts behind each item. One of the advantages of using Sothebys.com is the structure that Sotheby's imposes on sellers, and the requirements it places on both sellers and buyers. Buyers are likely to be serious because they are required to pay a substantial "Buyer's Premium" along with a winning bid. They also have to place a credit card on file with Sothebys.com before they can bid at all.

Multiple high-quality images usually accompany descriptions

Sotheby.com auctions usually last two weeks

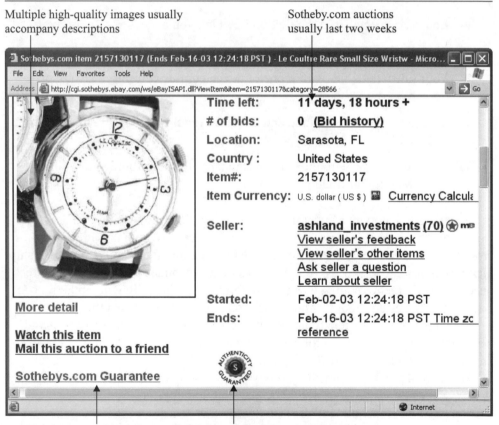

Click here to read Sotheby's authenticity and condition guarantees

FIGURE 15-2   Be sure your merchandise meets Sotheby's guarantee requirements.

Here are just a few examples:

- **Authenticity** The authenticity of an item is the accuracy with which its date and place of origin can be verified.

- **Condition** The condition needs to be accurate.

- **Refunds** If the condition and authenticity are found to have been inaccurate, the seller (not Sotheby's) will be required to provide a refund to the buyer.

CAUTION *Guarantees of authenticity aren't the only requirements for selling on Sothebys.com. The buyer pays a "Buyer's Premium" of 15% of the sale price. Sellers pay additional fees on top of that. You pay a listing fee of $5 for each item, for one thing. If a bidder meets your reserve price, you are also subject to a 15% Final Value Fee. This fee is 15% of the actual sale price plus the "Buyer's Premium." In other words, if you sell something to a high bidder for $1,000, that bidder actually pays you $1,150. However, you pay Sotheby's 15 percent of $1,150 or $172.50.*

The Longer the Description, the Better

You have to follow Sotheby's rules for creating listings and buying and selling, which tend to be more stringent than those on other parts of eBay. On the plus side, this means that you create listings that are of better quality, more accurate, and more reliable than others. They are listings that will make people feel they can invest many thousands of dollars in an item. On the down side, they make you go through more work. The elements of a Sothebys.com listing are described in the following sections.

Main Description

The main description is a short summary of the estimated value of the item being sold and a brief summary of the item's main features. This initial description should tell prospective bidders at a glance what the item is, how big it is, and its condition.

- Before you list the item, you need to make sure it does not violate the Sothebys.com restrictions. Be sure to check the Sothebys.com Requirements & Prohibitions page (http://pages.sothebys.ebay.com/help/rulesandsafety/reqs-and-restrictions.html) for a current list.

15

TIP   *The cataloguing guidelines also describe how to rate and describe particular kinds of items; be sure to review them at **http://pages.sothebys.ebay.com/help/sellerguide/cat-guidelines.html**.*

CAUTION   *Sotheby's, like other auction houses, observes an extensive set of restrictions and requirements for what it sells: you can't sell African ivory or coral, or archeological artifacts, for instance. You also can't import Rolex or other types of expensive watches. Read about the restrictions in detail at **http://pages.sothebys.ebay.com/help/rulesandsafety/reqs-and-restrictions.html**.*

Additional Information

You can add information to your Sothebys.com listings after the sale goes online, just as you can on eBay. However, Sothebys.com encourages sellers to include a "captivating additional note" with each entry when you first create it. Just what does this mean? Each auction description is divided into three main sections:

- **Estimate**   An estimate of the item's value

- **Description**   A brief summary of the item

- **Notes**   Detailed notes that describe the item's origin and authenticity and why it is distinctive and valuable.

For example, take a look at the description of a sculpture by the famous artist Henry Moore shown in Figure 15-3. At the top, you have a brief description of the item's features. The Notes section is far more extensive, and provides information about the seller as well as the item itself.

If you don't have a great deal to say about an item, don't feel obligated to include lengthy notes about it. Also, don't assume that everything you sell on Sothebys.com has to be extremely expensive. You'll find moderately priced wristwatches on the site for less than $200 or $300, just as you would on eBay, for example. The difference is that dealers and authorities in the field sell on Sothebys.com, so are more likely to get serious bidders, or bidders who are most concerned with getting what they paid for. Buyers who don't want to be swindled, in other words. Another big difference: you find buyers who are willing to pay the 15 percent "Buyer's Premium" that is added to the winning bid price and that is paid to the seller, ostensibly to cover the cost of the sale. In my opinion, this fee (which is standard

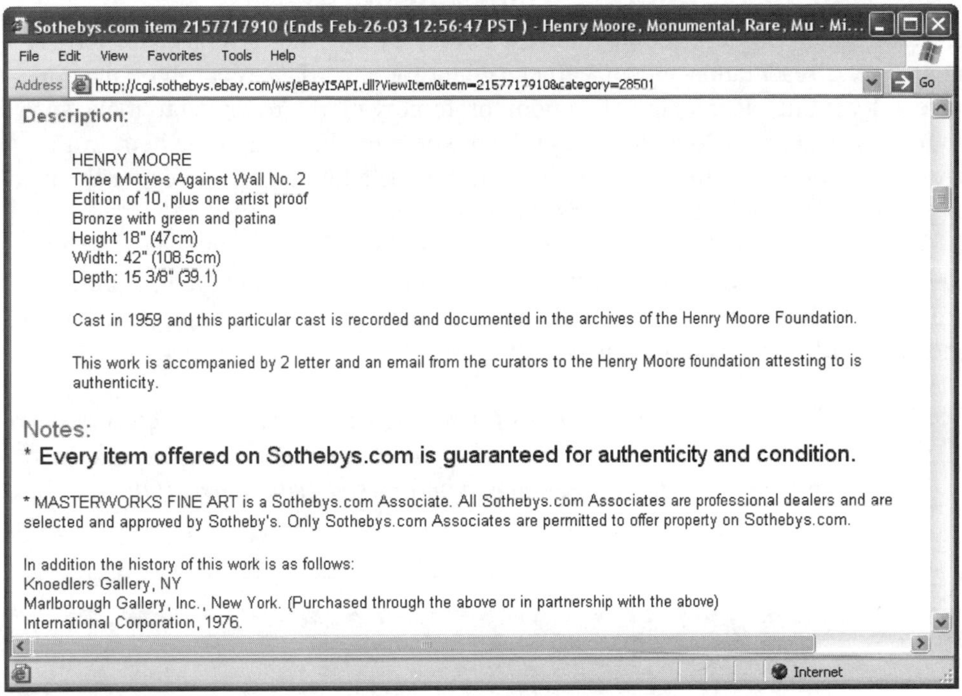

FIGURE 15-3   Many Sothebys.com descriptions include a detailed Notes section.

procedure in traditional auction sales, but not on eBay) discourages bidders, many of whom prefer to look for bargains on regular eBay auctions.

High-end sales can go on eBay, too

You don't have to sell expensive auctions through Sothebys.com, of course. Plenty of expensive items are sold on other parts of eBay all the time. Rare sports cars might go for as much as $100,000 on eBay Motors, for instance (see Chapter 12). People often turn to eBay specifically to avoid traditional auction houses like Sotheby's, Christie's, and Butterfield's.

15

Make Your Images Worth a Thousand Words

To sell through Sothebys.com, you have to play by the rules of this centuries-old auctioneer. Presentation and appearance count for a lot. That means you need to have at least one clear image of an item, preferably more. You need to make sure your images are clear and close-up. Take the time to photograph the item from several angles, if possible. You might even include a human being next to the item to give people an idea of its size, as shown in Figure 15-4.

Don't go looking for any rules about the number of photos you need to have or how big they need to be. There aren't any formulas for such things. I suggest you browse extensively through the Sothebys.com listings to see what other sellers do and gather ideas for your own presentations.

TIP   *You'll find tips and suggestions for selling rarities in the Antiques and Art category-specific newsletters. Links to these and other eBay newsletters can be found at **http://pages.ebay.com/newsletterdirectory.html**.*

FIGURE 15-4   Sellers tend to present more photos with Sothebys.com listings than on eBay.

Sell on Consignment

Chances are you aren't going to want to sell exclusively on Sothebys.com unless you're already a dealer of art, antiques, or the like. You can still sell on Sothebys.com occasionally, however. You should look around and find someone who is an approved seller who can sell the item for you on consignment. Go to the page where the current Sothebys.com Associates are listed (**http://pages.sothebys.ebay .com/buy/dealers/index.html**). Scan the list for an Associate who deals in what you want to sell. Be sure to review the seller's previous sales and pay attention to the way the business is presented online. Make sure the Associate's sales are presented the way you would want your own to appear. Look at the seller's feedback. Then approach the seller to see how well you get along. Usually, the seller's About Me page on Sothebys.com has a selection of feedback presented, as shown in Figure 15-5.

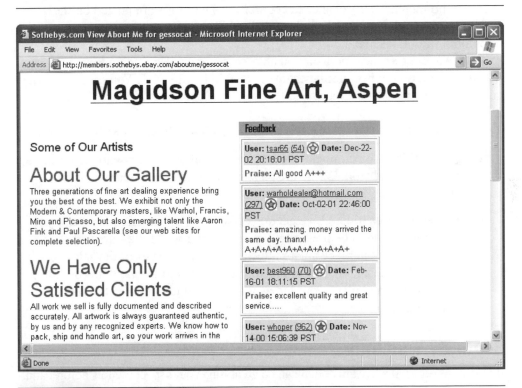

15

FIGURE 15-5   Sothebys.com uses a feedback system based on eBay's successful system.

Typically, the feedback is gushingly positive, but it can still give you an idea of whether the seller can do a good job for you.

Participate in Live Auctions

eBay auctions can be exciting right at the end, when bidding heats up and the end of the auction approaches. However, there's nothing quite like a live auction—an auction in which bidding occurs in real-time and the whole sale is over in a matter of minutes rather than days. Live auctions have been held for many decades by traditional auction houses.

When Sotheby's partnered with eBay, it gained the ability to use eBay's Live Auctions technology. Now, you can sell in live auctions that enable bidders to compete in real-time both online and at a significant number of Sotheby's auction houses in New York and London. In other words, as bidders on the Internet place bids on an item, their bids are announced to bidders assembled in Sotheby's auction houses, who then have the chance to counterbid. Their bids are posted on the Sothebys.com Web site, which enables online bidders to place counterbids, and so on until the sale is made.

Live Auctions are held both on Sothebys.com and on eBay's own Live Auctions site (**http://www.ebayliveauctions.com**), shown in Figure 15-6. You can participate in live auctions in one of three ways:

- **Just watch** This is a good way to get acquainted with what's going on.

- **Place bids** You compete not only against other bidders who are online, but against individuals who are physically present in Sotheby's or other auction houses.

- **Place absentee bids** Live auctions take place at specific times, and you may not be able to be present at your computer when the sale occurs. In that case, you can place an absentee bid before the start of the sale. You register for the auction, go to the Web page where the sale item (or "lot") is described, and place your bid as you would with a convention eBay online auction.

Begin By Watching

If you've never seen a live auction, it can be great fun. You inspect the lots beforehand, and pick out the ones on which you want to bid. Then the action starts. The tension

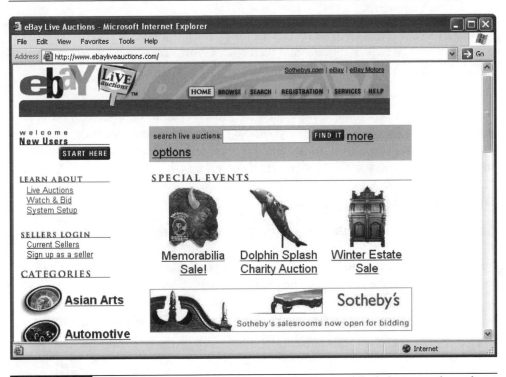

FIGURE 15-6 You can access live auctions on both eBay and Sothebys.com through this page.

mounts as you wait for your special items to come up. Your heart pounds as you place the bid and wait for counterbids.

It's just as exciting to be a "live" auction participant from the comfort of your home, sitting before your computer screen, as it is to be on the real brick-and-mortar auction floor. It's easy to check out a live auction as an observer without actually bidding in it. Follow these steps:

1. Go to the eBay Live Auctions home page (**http://www.ebayliveauctions.com/**).

2. Click **Watch & Bid**.

3. Browse through the live auction sales coming up, and find one that interests you.

15

4. Click **Sign Up**.

5. Read the terms of the auction carefully, check the box that says you accept the terms and conditions, and then click **Continue**.

6. Read the Live Auctions User Agreement, then click **Submit**.

You'll receive an e-mail message telling you that you have signed up for the sale. This message contains links that enable you to place absentee bids, if you want. Otherwise, you wait until the auction begins, then go to the Live Auctions site and click on the auction to view what's going on.

Place Absentee Bids

Absentee bids go against the purpose of live auctions. After all, live auctions are supposed to bring bidders together at the same time so they can compete against one another. Absentee bids give you a chance to beat the time constraints that those auctions impose, however. Here is how absentee bids work:

1. First, you register to participate in a live auction. After you're approved, go back to the lot page and input the maximum amount you are willing to pay for that lot—that is your absentee bid.

2. You and any other approved bidders place absentee bids up to one hour before the live event begins. Suppose you bid $750 for an item, another bidder named Jill bids $450, and Frank bids $300. The bid increment is $50.

3. When the auction starts, eBay calculates all the absentee bids and determines the winning absentee bid: The winning absentee bid equals the second highest bid plus one bid increment: In this example, you are the winner at a $500.

4. When the live bidding starts, the auctioneer is told that there is an Internet absentee bid of $500. Other bidders in the auction house can then bid against you during the time period of the live auction.

If the live auction bids do not exceed your maximum bid of $750, you are the winner. However, if someone in the live auction period bids more than your maximum of $750, they win, not you.

NOTE   *Read the requirements for the live auction carefully if you plan to bid. Some sellers require you to provide credit references or place a deposit of as much as 20 percent of your likely bids before you can even begin to participate.*

Get Ready for Real-Time Auction Action

You need to make sure your computer is equipped to handle real-time activity such as real-time auctions. You need, at minimum, a Pentium II processor and a central processing unit running at a speed of at least 350MHz; a 56K modem or a direct DSL or cable modem connection; 64MB RAM; Windows 95, 98, or NT; and Internet Explorer 4.01 or Netscape Navigator 4.03 or later.

In addition, you need to make sure your Web browser is set up to process Java applets—miniature programs that enable you to interact with Web sites in real time. In Internet Explorer, you enable Java by following these steps:

1. Click Tools | Internet Options.

2. Click the Advanced tab.

3. Do one of the following: If you are using Internet Explorer 6, scroll down to the Java section and make sure the option "Use Java 2..." is checked. If you are using an earlier version of Internet Explorer or if your Advanced tab options are different, scroll down to the Microsoft VM section and make sure the "JIT compiler for virtual machine enabled" option is checked.

4. Click OK.

5. Click File | Exit to quit Internet Explorer, then restart Internet Explorer to take advantage of the new settings.

If you use Netscape Navigator, click Edit | Preferences, click Advanced, and check the box next to Enable Java. You can read more about the live auction requirements at **http://pages.liveauctions.ebay.com/help/before/lasystem.html**.

15

Where to Find It

- **Sothebys.com online auctions home page**
  http://pages.sothebys .ebay.com/hp/online/index.html
  Current catalogues and lots being sold at auction.

- **Sotheby's Appraisal Services**
  http://search.sothebys.com/ services/appraisals/
  Contact information for Sotheby's appraisers who can tell you how much something is worth. (Be sure to use the forward-slash at the end.)

- **eBay Live Auctions**
  http://www.ebayliveauctions.com
  Links to upcoming live auctions on eBay or Sothebys.com.

Chapter 16

Protect Yourself and Your Customers

How to...

- Create a list of pre-approved bidders
- Investigate first-time bidders
- Build credibility with ID Verify
- Give your sales the seal of approval
- Use encryption to verify your identity
- Encrypt your e-mail messages
- Offer a warranty
- Steer clear of prohibited items
- Shy away from shill bidding

As a seller, you might think at first glance that bidders are the ones who are in control of eBay auctions, not you. On the surface, at least, it seems like your job is to present the items for sale and simply wait until the bids come in. You can't control who places the top bid, and you can't ensure whether the purchaser is a reputable individual or not.

Or can you? Actually, you have more control than you think as an eBay seller. You can choose the individuals you want to bid on your items. You can ensure what you sell. You can tell potential buyers you care about their safety by entering the SquareTrade program, or by obtaining a digital certificate that verifies your identity. If you're looking for an extra measure of security, you can even encrypt your communications with your customers. You can also keep sales running smoothly by avoiding the sale of items that are prohibited or questionable. This chapter discusses different ways in which you can control who bids and buys what you put up for sale, and how you can ensure that the transaction goes smoothly.

Control Bidders and Buyers

Most auctions work by attracting as many interested bidders as possible to gain the highest purchase price. When you attract everyone, however, that also means you attract not-so-good bidders as well as good ones. The bidders who fall into the not-so-good category are ones who turn into deadbeats and don't follow through with purchases. In order to avoid the deadbeats and permit purchasers who have bought from you in the past and whose qualities you are familiar with, you may want to add a note to your auction description, or create a pre-approved list of buyers, as described in this section.

Add a Note to Your Description

One of the most effective ways to avoid attracting bidders who are likely to cause problems (to retract their bid at the last minute or simply fail to follow through with a transaction) is to include an advisory note in your auction description. Such a note might read as follows:

> Bidders with overall negative feedback, no feedback, or more than *x [fill in the blank]* negative feedbacks in *[fill in a period of time]* will be removed from the auction.

Such a note is generally pretty effective in discouraging bidders you don't want. If the final bidder is someone who ignored that part of your Terms of Sale, then you can just offer the item to the second bidder instead, because the final bidder ignored your terms.

Creating a List of Approved Buyers

In their quest to get the highest price possible, most sellers don't think about ways to limit the number of bidders who try to win their auctions. However, you do have the ability to create a list of approved individuals—people you have identified as being eligible to bid on your items. The feature works like this:

- You specify the pre-approved list of eBay members who can bid on your item or purchase it using the Buy It Now feature.

- Anyone who is not on your list must e-mail you for approval before they can bid; you can screen bidders by asking questions about their background or what they plan to do with your item.

- You can create a pre-approved list for each item individually, so your other sales can be restricted if you wish.

- While a sale is ongoing, you can add and delete pre-approved bidders or buyers.

16

This idea of limiting who can bid on your sales might seem to contradict the concept behind auctions, but creating a pre-approved list does have an important purpose. For one thing, if the items you want to sell are special in some way—such as objects that are used in religious worship—you might want to screen bidders beforehand to make sure they're going to respect the purpose intended. Some eBay sellers use a pre-approved list for bidders who express an interest in purchasing two or more of their sales items at the same time, as described in "Joining Sales with a Pre-approved Bidder's List" later in this chapter.

CAUTION   *The obvious problem with creating a pre-approved list of buyers is that you won't get as many bids as you would otherwise. eBay users, for the most part, don't like to be told what to do. They prefer the freedom of being able to bid or sell without restrictions. Some will be completely turned off by the pre-approval requirement and not e-mail you. On the other hand, those who do e-mail asking for approval are likely to be serious purchasers rather than deadbeat bidders.*

Create the List

To create a list of pre-approved bidders, you first offer your item for sale on eBay. Then, follow these steps:

1. Go to the login page for creating a set of pre-approved buyers (**http://cgi3.ebay.com/aw-cgi/eBayISAPI.dll?PreApproveBidders**).

2. If you are prompted to (in other words, if you aren't already logged in), enter your eBay User ID and password, and click the Sign In button.

3. When the eBay Pre-Approve Bidders/Buyers page appears, read the brief introduction, then click **Add a New Item**.

4. When the next page appears, enter the eBay item number of the sale item you want to restrict in the Item No. box.

5. In the box labeled "Add or remove pre-approved bidders/buyers", enter the User IDs of the bidders or buyers you have pre-approved, as shown in Figure 16-1.

6. Click **Submit Item**.

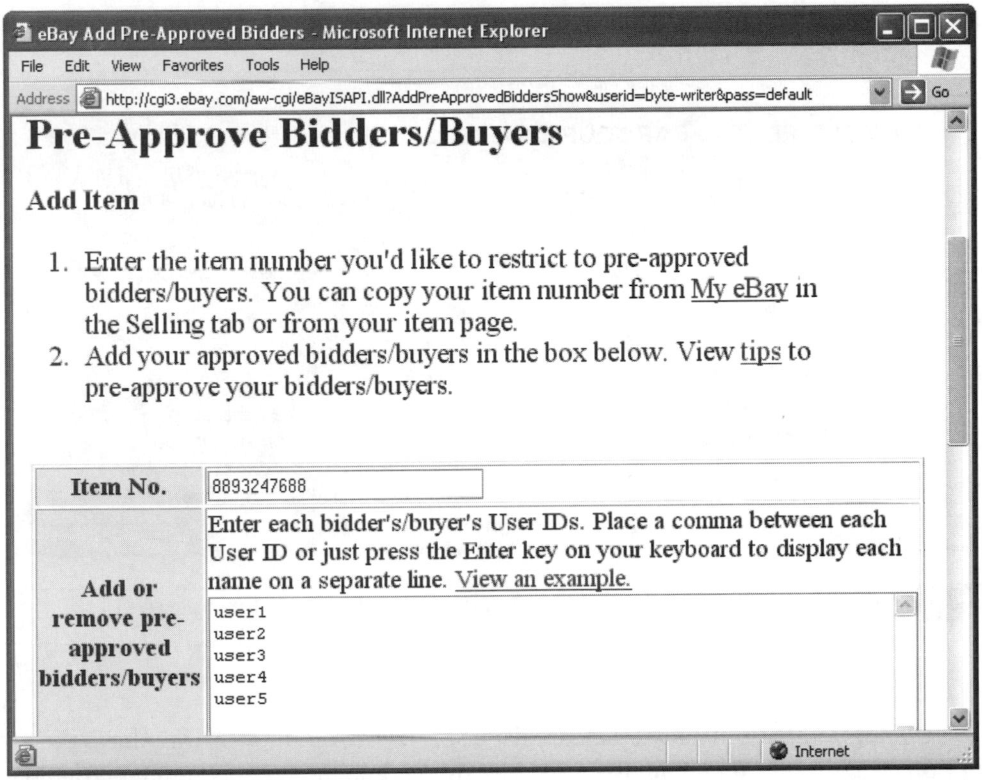

FIGURE 16-1 You create a list of pre-approved bidders or buyers after your sale has gone online.

When the list has been created, the notice shown in Figure 16-2 appears in the area where bidders would normally begin the bidding process.

When prospective bidders click on the link shown in Figure 16-2, they are asked to sign in with their eBay User ID and password. They then are prompted to contact the seller to bid on the item. When you receive that e-mail, you can evaluate whether the bidders are ones you want to permit. You can ask them to register with eBay's ID Verify program (see the section "Use ID Verify" later in this chapter). You can ask for their feedback history and why they are interested in your item. If they seem serious and trustworthy, you can add them to your list. Only then will the individual be able to bid.

16

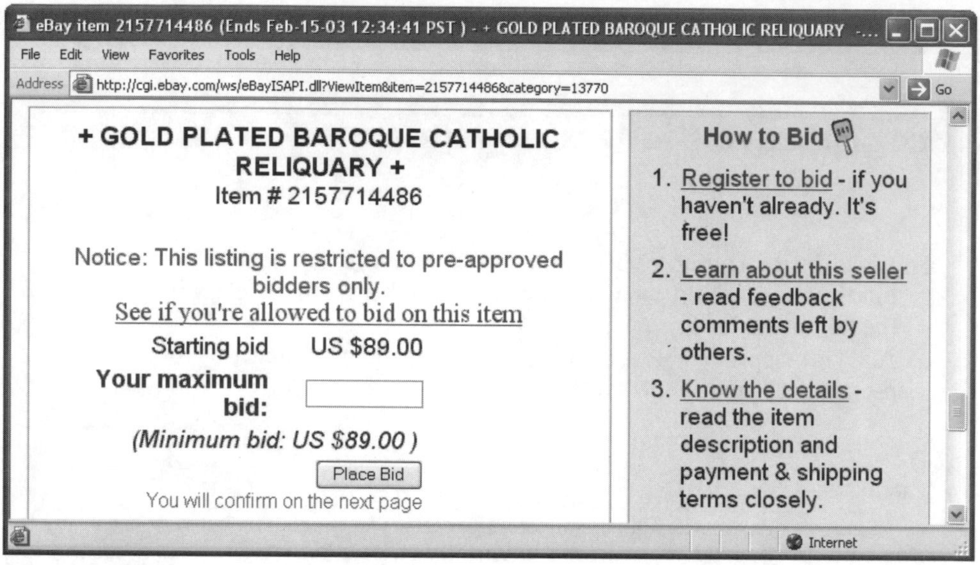
eBay item 2157714486 (Ends Feb-15-03 12:34:41 PST) - + GOLD PLATED BAROQUE CATHOLIC RELIQUARY -...
File Edit View Favorites Tools Help
Address http://cgi.ebay.com/ws/eBayISAPI.dll?ViewItem&item=2157714486&category=13770
Go
+ GOLD PLATED BAROQUE CATHOLIC RELIQUARY +
Item # 2157714486
Notice: This listing is restricted to pre-approved bidders only.
See if you're allowed to bid on this item
Starting bid US $89.00
Your maximum bid:
(Minimum bid: US $89.00)
Place Bid
You will confirm on the next page
How to Bid
1. Register to bid - if you haven't already. It's free!
2. Learn about this seller - read feedback comments left by others.
3. Know the details - read the item description and payment & shipping terms closely.
Internet

FIGURE 16-2 If you want to restrict access to a sale, eBay adds this note to your description.

Even if you have already created a list of pre-approved bidders, you have the option of adding or removing names at any time while the sale is ongoing. To add a name, go to your list of pre-approved bidders and add the User ID of the new bidder on a new line. Or, you can separate each of the names on the list with a comma, colon, semicolon, or even a single blank space.

TIP *It's a good idea to explain in your item's description that you are pre-approving bidders, and to describe the criteria for approving new bidders.*

You can also change your mind and open up your sale to all bidders rather than a selected list while the sale is still going on. You might want to open up the sale if your item is attracting more interest than you expected, for instance. You do this by clicking the **Deactivate** link on the Web page that lists your pre-approved bidders.

Joining Sales with a Pre-approved Bidder's List

You might also want to use a pre-approved bidder's list to combine two or more of your sales so you can ensure that those items will go to a particular bidder. I've seen this done by a seller who specializes in Laura Ashley items. This seller charges $22 for shipping domestically; however, this is a flat rate and doesn't depend on weight. If someone expresses an interest in several different items, the seller will take those items and create a pre-approved bidder's list that includes only the interested buyer. That way, the buyer can buy two, three, or more items at once and save on shipping charges. The point of using a pre-approved bidder's list in this case is that it ensures that one person will get the items, since that person is the only bidder on the list. This is an unorthodox—and clever—way to use the pre-approved bidder's list feature to boost sales.

Contact Buyers Who Make You Nervous

Suppose you are nearing the end of a sale, and the current high bidder is someone who has zero feedback and appears to be a first-time buyer. You might wonder whether the individual is really serious about following through with the sale, and really understands how the auction process works. You don't want the buyer to turn out to be a deadbeat. What can you do?

Rather than waiting for the sale to end and crossing your fingers in the hope that the buyer will complete the transaction, take a proactive approach. Don't come right out and ask if they are serious about their bid. You might be perceived as confrontational and unfriendly, and you may provoke exactly the response you're trying to avoid. Rather, ask the person if he or she needs any help or advice. Simply remind the person that you will be happy to answer any questions they have about the object, such as shipping options. Their response may well indicate how serious they are. At the very least, you will convey that you are in charge of your sales and that you care about how they proceed.

TIP   *You can also control the sale by making a Second Chance Offer to bidders who didn't meet your reserve price or Buy It Now price. A Second Chance Offer is a feature of eBay that enables sellers to sell to a bidder at the bidder's highest bid amount, even if that bid amount did not meet the reserve price. Keep in mind, though, that some bidders intentionally bid low in the hope that you'll lower your price through a second chance offer. Find out more in Chapter 4 and at **http://pages.ebay.com/help/sellerguide/ faq-personaloffer.html**.*

16

Build Your Credibility

eBay bidders are hopeful, but they don't take good deals or descriptions that they read online for granted. Every bit of documentation that you provide helps induce them to bid. The more effectively you can convey that you are a reliable businessperson, the more bids you'll get. How do you prove you are who you say you are? Feedback helps, but what if you don't yet have a lot of feedback? You can't show your state ID or passport to someone online, but you can display a seal of approval from a third party that verifies that you are a reputable business, and you can give buyers or other sellers you meet an electronic document called a *personal certificate*.

Obtain a Seal of Approval

Some eBay businesspeople stand out from the crowd and indicate their commitment to good customer service by adding a seal of approval to their descriptions, their About Me pages, or their eBay Stores. The Better Business Bureau Online (BBBOnline) and SquareTrade are two companies that provide seals of approval. In the case of both the BBBOnline and SquareTrade seals, you need to spend some money to obtain and keep displaying the symbol, but you can take advantage of the organization's dispute resolution services. When you have an independent organization verify your identity and your reputation, you increase the chances that someone will bid on your items rather than those of your competitors.

BBBOnline

The BBBOnline Reliability Seal (**http://www.bbbonline.org**) is intended for existing businesses that are already members of their local Better Business Bureau. The seal tells prospective customers that you will handle complaints and returns fairly and promptly, that you will use the BBB's dispute resolution services if needed, and that you observe the BBB's Code of Online Business Practices. The Code states that you will not use deceptive or misleading practices, that you won't disclose details of your transactions with your customers, and that you'll answer questions and resolve complaints in a timely and responsive manner.

The Junction Antique Mall's About Me page includes BBBOnline reliability seals, as shown next.

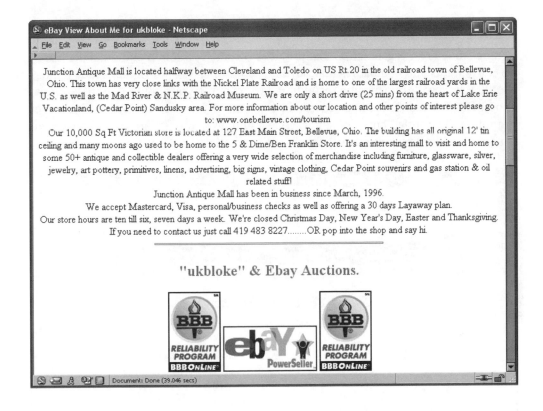

TIP *You can read a summary of the Code of Online Business Practices at* ***http://www.bbbonline.org/reliability/code/principle.asp***.

In order to apply for the BBBOnline seal, you need to provide the BBB with your company's street address and telephone number, you need to have been in business for at least one year, and you need to pay a licensing fee that varies by location. If you run an e-commerce Web site that's a spinoff of an existing brick-and-mortar business and you also sell on eBay, the BBBOnline seal is perfect. If you are an individual who sells on eBay on a part- or full-time basis and you don't own your own business, turn to the SquareTrade seal of approval.

16

SquareTrade

SquareTrade is an organization that provides dispute resolution and other services for individuals and companies that buy and sell online. One of SquareTrade's most useful services, online dispute resolution, is a resource you should definitely know about. Dispute resolution is discussed in Chapter 19. Keep in mind that, if you ever run into a disgruntled buyer or seller, you should go to the SquareTrade home page (**http://www.squaretrade.com**) shown next and click the eBay link.

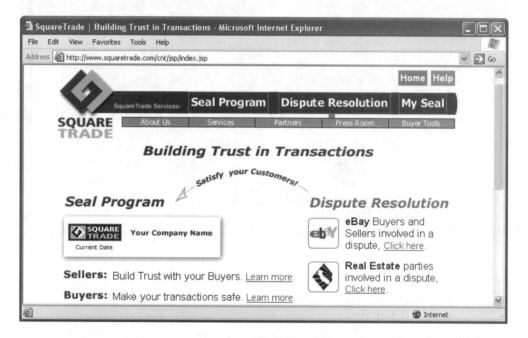

To build credibility, you can also apply to obtain a SquareTrade Seal. SquareTrade claims that as many as 10,000 eBay users display such a seal on their auction listings, About Me, or eBay Stores pages. An example is shown in Figure 16-3.

You can try SquareTrade free for 30 days. During that time, you can see if you receive more bids when your auctions display the SquareTrade logo, as SquareTrade claims. If you decide to stay in the program, you pay a $7.50 monthly fee. Of course, you have to fill out an application form and go through an approval process first. During the approval process, SquareTrade checks the following:

- Verifies your identity
- Reviews your selling history

- Checks your feedback
- Checks for dispute resolution problems

TIP *You might consider signing up with SquareTrade for free for 30 days and conducting a pseudo-scientific test. Place the logo on some of your sales and leave other sales logo-free. Then you can compare the response.*

SquareTrade's Web site claims that negative feedback is reduced by as much as 43 percent when you add the logo, and that you not only receive more bids, but the purchase price goes up as well. Take these claims with a big grain of salt. It's hard to quantify the benefits of added credibility. Enrolling in the seal program, however, does bring you tangible benefits, including the ability to receive seller activity reports from SquareTrade that graphically depict your sales activity over a period of time. As a seal holder, you also give your buyers $250 worth of fraud protection from SquareTrade as well.

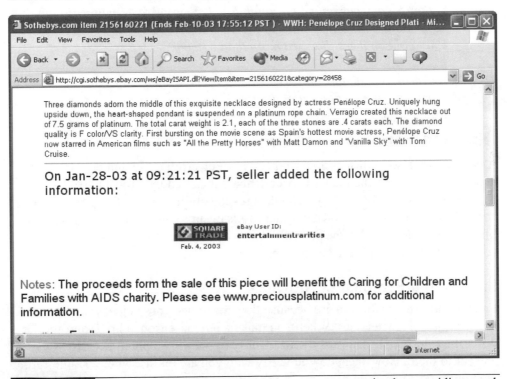

FIGURE 16-3   The SquareTrade Seal tells bidders you are committed to providing good customer service.

16

Use ID Verify

How do you know who is actually placing a bid on your merchandise? By the same token, how do your bidders know who *you* are? You can use the ID Verify program to know for sure. ID Verify is an identity verification service available to eBay users. Your personal information is checked against databases of consumers and businesses for consistency. The company that does the checking—Equifax Secure, one of the nation's largest credit verification companies—only verifies your identity against existing information in their files, and not performing a credit check. ID Verify isn't just an option for telling people who you are. eBay requires that you use ID Verify before you can offer anything for sale on a Buy It Now basis.

To initiate the verification process, go to the ID Verify: Accept Terms page (**http://pages.ebay.com/services/buyandsell/idverify-terms.html**), and click **I Agree**.

> **TIP** *ID Verify is a good alternative to getting a SquareTrade seal, which carries monthly fees. ID Verify, in contrast, only carries a one-time fee of $5. You need to go through ID Verify in order to place a bid on Sothebys.com, buy an item through Buy It Now, or sell anything in the eBay Mature Audiences category. Plus, your ID Verify status enables you to bid on items that cost more than $15,000.*

> **CAUTION** *ID Verify is available only to residents of the United States and U.S. territories, not to international users.*

Obtain a Personal Certificate

A *certificate*, also known as a Digital ID, is an electronic file that ensures your identity to others on the Internet. A certificate is issued by a third party called a *certification authority (CA)*, which takes responsibility for verifying the owner's personal information. The owner's identity is ensured by the use of encryption. Like the seals described in the preceding section, you need to purchase and maintain your certificate through a licensing fee.

Understand Personal Certificates

Your friends know who you are because they recognize your voice, your face, and other unique characteristics. When you make a purchase from a brick-and-mortar store, the salespeople can verify your identity by viewing a photo ID card you present to them. How, then, do you verify who you are online, where people can't see you in person?

When you obtain a certificate, the CA gives you a license to use a mathematical formula it owns, called an *algorithm*. You use the algorithm to generate a very long series of encrypted characters called a *key*. This initial key is called a *private key* because you are supposed to keep it secret and never share it with anyone. Once you have the private key, you use it to create a new key called a *public key*. The public key is freely exchanged with people who want to verify your identity; it's what verifies your identity to customers or others you meet online.

Certificates are commonly used by businesses to verify their own identities and to provide information about where they are located. You have to remember to keep your certificates up to date by paying the regular license fee, however. Half.com has its own certificate, issued by the CA VeriSign (see Figure 16-4). To my surprise, when I viewed the certificate, I discovered it had expired.

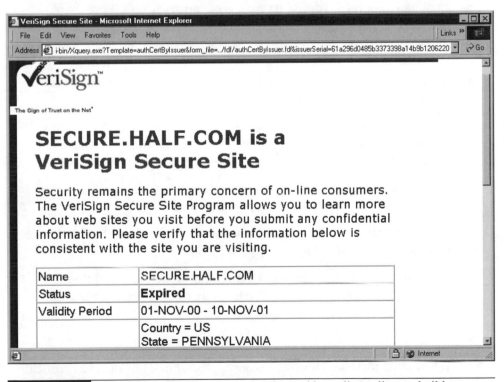

16

| FIGURE 16-4 | Digital certificates are commonly used by online sellers to build credibility—but keep them up to date! |

Obtain a Personal Certificate

You may want to obtain a certificate if you operate an online business Web site in addition to your eBay auctions. You can include a link to your Web site on your eBay Store page. Visitors to your site can elect to receive your certificate to verify that your business is real and that you are who you say you are.

It's surprisingly easy to obtain your own certificate. You apply to and pay a license fee to a CA such as VeriSign. A VeriSign Class 1 Digital ID, which you can use to authenticate yourself in e-mail, news, and other interactions on the net, costs $14.95 per year, and you can try it out free for 60 days. To get a VeriSign certificate, follow these steps:

1. Launch your Web browser and go to the VeriSign, Inc. Digital IDs for Secure E-Mail page (**http://www.verisign.com/products/class1/index.html**).

2. Click the link **Try a Digital ID FREE for 60 Days**.

3. Read the introductory information on the Personal Digital ID Enrollment page, then click Enroll Now.

4. If your browser displays a dialog box asking if you want to download a certificate installer, click OK.

5. Fill out the form on the first enrollment page. Click the button next to "I'd like to test drive a 60-day trial Digital ID for free." Read the Subscriber Agreement, and then click **Accept**.

6. Check your e-mail inbox in a few minutes for a message entitled "Trial Class 1 VeriSign Digital ID Pickup Instructions."

7. Click and hold down your mouse button and scroll across the PIN to select it; then choose Edit | Copy to copy the PIN.

8. Go to the URL for the Digital ID Center that is included in the e-mail message, and paste your PIN in the text box next to Enter the Digital ID Personal Identification Number (PIN).

9. Click Submit.

10. When the Certificate Download page appears, click Install. The certificate is downloaded to your computer.

To view the certificates you obtain using Internet Explorer 6, choose Tools | Internet Options, click the Content tab, click the Certificates button, click the certificate you want to view, and then click the View button. VeriSign's certificate is shown in the next illustration. If you use Netscape Navigator, choose Edit | Preferences to open the Preferences dialog box, click the arrow next to Privacy & Security, click Certificates, and click Manage Certificates.

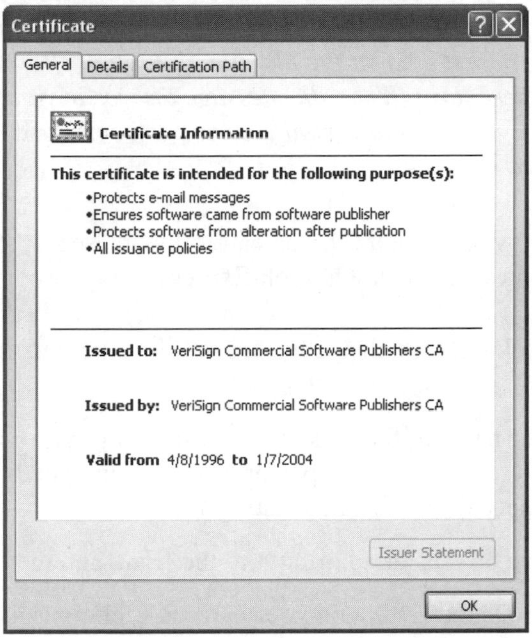

NOTE *VeriSign is well-known, but has drawn complaints for their aggressive marketing techniques and the way they manage customer information. They aren't the only Certificate Authority around, though. Also look into RSA Security (**http://www.rsasecurity.com**) and Thawte Consulting (**http://www.thawte.com**).*

Secure Your Communications

Once you have obtained a Digital ID, you can use it to ensure your identity to those with whom you do business. You may want to do one of two things:

- **Send a digital signature.** You can attach your Digital ID to your e-mail messages so you can assure the recipients that the message is really coming from you.

- **Encrypt your e-mail messages.** You can use the personal key that is part of your Digital ID to ensure that only the intended party can read it.

16

CAUTION   *You can only encrypt or digitally sign messages that you send using your e-mail software, such as Outlook Express, Netscape Messenger, or Eudora. You can't attach your Digital ID to e-mail you send through eBay's usual system for contacting other eBay members, because such messages are sent through a Web page interface rather than e-mail software. If you want to send encrypted communications to someone, you'll have to first contact the individual through eBay's "contact an eBay Member" form. When the message arrives in your e-mail inbox, you can use your regular e-mail software to compose a digitally signed or encrypted message.*

Once you obtain your Digital ID, you can follow these steps to send encrypted or digitally signed messages with Outlook Express:

1. Open Outlook Express, then choose Tools | Address to open the Address book.

2. Highlight the name of the person to whom you want to send a signed or encrypted message. (If the person is not yet included in your Address Book, you need to create a new listing.)

3. Click the Digital IDs tab to bring it to the front, and then click Import.

4. Locate your Digital ID file on your hard disk, click its name, and then click Open.

5. Your certificate appears in the box labeled "Digital IDs associated with the selected E-Mail address." Click OK. The Properties dialog box closes.

6. In the Address Book, highlight the recipient's name, click the Action toolbar button, and choose Send Mail from the menu that appears.

7. When the New Message window appears, click the Tools toolbar button, then click either Encrypt (to encrypt the message) or Digitally Sign (to digitally sign it).

8. Finish composing your message, and click Send to send it on its way.

NOTE *You can also use a popular program called Pretty Good Privacy to encrypt your e-mail messages. However, the recipients also have to have PGP installed so they can exchange public keys with you. You then attach the public keys to the e-mail messages you exchange. (This is the best way for Macintosh users to be able to encrypt e-mail messages and files.) Pretty Good Privacy is available in two versions: freeware and commercial. The freeware version is distributed by the Massachusetts Institute of Technology at **http://web.mit.edu/network/pgp.html**. The commercial version is available at **http://www.pgp.com**.*

Keep Your Transactions Trouble-Free

It isn't possible to eliminate all problems from eBay auctions because you can't always predict what your bidders will do. However, you can minimize the number of disputes or problems you encounter by following a few simple practices.

For instance, even if you sell your items in good condition, you can point out to your customers that warranties are available for eBay purchases for nominal fees. You can also avoid trouble for yourself by avoiding the sale of items that are prohibited by eBay or by state or local laws. You can protect your buyers by avoiding shill bidding, and by not selling questionable items that can get your purchasers in trouble at some point after the sale.

Offer a Warranty

A warranty is a contract or guarantee to perform specified duties or services. In terms of consumer products, a warranty is a guarantee that a product will perform satisfactorily during a specified period after purchase. eBay sales items come in a virtually limitless range of ages and conditions, and most are far from new. Your high bidders or buyers, however, aren't necessarily looking for merchandise in perfect condition. They just want what they purchase to be in the condition you described.

Anyone who purchases a computer- or electronics-related item, a video game, or a musical instrument on eBay has the opportunity to purchase a warranty through eBay's Warranty Services program. The warranties include one year of coverage on most new, used, or refurbished items. They are provided not by eBay itself but by a partner organization, N.E.W. Customer Service Companies, Inc. Buyers aren't

16

the only ones who benefit from this program. If you display a Warranty Services banner on a sale, like the one shown in Figure 16-5, and your high bidder or buyer purchases a warranty, you earn a cash bonus. For items that sell for $200 or less, you get a bonus of 25 percent of your eBay Final Value Fee; for items that sell for more than $200, your bonus amounts to 50 percent of your eBay Final Value Fee.

TIP
Residents of Maine, Oklahoma, Alaska, Guam, or Puerto Rico cannot have the items they sell covered by Warranty Services due to state regulations. You can find out more about eBay's Warranty Services and how they can benefit sellers at **http://pages.ebay.com/help/warranty/seller_overview.html**.

You can add a warranty graphic to your sales page by going to the How to Offer Warranties page (**http://pages.ebay.com/help/warranty/how_to_offer.html**), reviewing the types of graphic banners that are available, and copying the HTML code for the one you want. You then copy the HTML code into the description for a sales item. You can also add the banner to your About Me or eBay Store pages.

FIGURE 16-5   If you offer a warranty, you can add this banner to your sales description.

Don't Sell Anything Illegal

While I was working on this book, the space shuttle Columbia broke up while entering Earth's atmosphere, dropping wreckage over several states. Incredibly, only a matter of hours after the disaster, supposed pieces of the shuttle were offered for sale on eBay. Those items were quickly removed by eBay. Two Texas residents were subsequently arrested and charged with theft of government property. Government officials did not make clear whether the two persons were the ones who put the items up for auction, but the charges carry maximum penalties of a $250,000 fine and ten years in prison.

This is a dramatic example of what can happen if you sell, or attempt to sell, the wrong things on eBay. You need to be aware of what you can't sell, and what your own home state considers to be prohibited items. You are subject not only to federal regulations but to your own state's regulations governing business transactions. The following sections describe how to keep out of trouble by simply being aware of what you can't sell on eBay.

TIP *Some truly outrageous (and illegal) items have been put up for sale on eBay over the years. For instance, during the year 2000 presidential election, someone allegedly attempted to auction off votes on eBay as a political protest, which prompted an investigation by the U.S. Justice Department (read about it at **http://www.cnn.com/2000/TECH/computing/ 08/18/internet.vote**). One California man attempted to sell his own family (**http://www.signonsandiego.com/news/state/20030111-0449-ca-ebayfami ly.html**). Human kidneys, used dentures, and souvenir debris from the World Trade Center have also gone up for auction (**http://abcnews.go.com/sections/ us/WolfFiles/wolffiles231.html**). You can find out what your own home state does not allow you to sell by contacting your state's Department of Commerce.*

Stay Away from Prohibited Items

Prohibited items are banned from sale from eBay. In some cases, trying to sell illegal items can get you in trouble with law enforcement authorities. Trying to sell other items may not be strictly illegal, but can get either you or eBay (or both of you) in trouble in other ways. Examples are shown in Table 16-1. I've divided the items into two columns. The column on the right lists some items that you might not realize are illegal to sell in some states or that are heavily regulated.

16

Obviously Illegal Items	Not-So-Obvious Illegal Items
Alcohol (However, you can sell alcohol on eBay if the container has not been opened, the buyer is over the age of 21, and the container is considered collectible, with a value exceeding the alcohol's retail price. In other words, rare bottles of wines or cans of beer that aren't available in retail stores can be sold.)	Human parts and remains. Just about the only thing you can sell that contains human body parts on eBay are lockets or other jewelry that contain human hair, or skulls and skeletons that are used for educational purposes. Everything else is prohibited.
Counterfeit Currency and Stamps	Travel-related items: Don't try to sell airline tickets, vacation packages, or lodging unless you're licensed to do so and are in the Seller Verify by SquareTrade Program.
Credit Cards	Catalogs and URL Sales: You can't list sales catalogs or Web sites that sell items directly—unless you're trying to sell a 1901 Sears, Roebuck catalog or other collectible item.
Tobacco	Animals and Wildlife Products: No, you can't sell your baby bunnies or kittens on eBay. You can't sell stuffed migratory birds such as ducks, geese, or owls, either. You can't sell animal pelts, bear-related products, or items that are made from genuine tortoise shell. The latter includes guitar picks, combs, or jewelry made from genuine tortoise shell.
Satellite and Cable TV Descramblers	Plants and Seeds: Some plants that are considered "exotic" or "noxious" are prohibited from sale by federal, state, or local laws. (See **http://www.aphis.usda.gov/npb/statenw.html** for a state-by-state list.)
Drugs and Drug Paraphernalia	Postage Meters: These are available only from licensed manufacturers.
Firearms	Stocks and Other Securities: these are regulated by the U.S. Securities and Exchange Commission; leave any selling to a broker and don't try to sell it yourself. However, you can sell business inventory, information on how to start a business, or domain names. You *can* sell old or collectible stock certificates for business entities that no longer exist.
Fireworks	Mailing Lists or Personal Information. This includes not only the information itself but any software designed to send spam e-mail, too.

TABLE 16-1   Items Illegal to Sell on eBay

Each of the categories in Table 16-1 has specific dos and don'ts that are too detailed to list here, and that change occasionally. Go to the Questionable Items page (**http://pages.ebay.com/help/community/png-items.html**) and click on the link for the item you're considering to see if it falls into the banned or questionable category.

> **CAUTION**   *Many states have regulations that prohibit the shipping of alcohol either to or from the state by an individual. Check with your state's commerce commission or Department of Commerce to make sure.*

> **CAUTION**   *In addition to the items mentioned in Table 16-1, you cannot include links on your eBay listing to pages or Web sites that offer merchandise for sale that is not permitted on eBay.*

Stay Away from Questionable Items

eBay lists a type of sales item as "questionable" if you can sell it under certain narrowly defined circumstances. You'll find links to each item on the Questionable Items page (**http://pages.ebay.com/help/community/png-items.html**). If you want to be really safe and steer clear of trouble, avoid selling these items as well as the Prohibited Items mentioned in the preceding section. Some of the examples that I found personally surprising are listed here:

- **Artifacts**   Be especially careful if you describe a work of art or a craft item as being of Native American origin. You must be a member of a state or federally recognized Indian tribe yourself, according to the Indian Arts and Crafts act.

- **Autographed Items**   Autographs are frequently sold on eBay, but make sure the autograph you sell is genuine. You may want to contact one of the experts at **http://pages.ebay.com/help/community/auth-overview.html** to authenticate it.

- **Electronics Equipment**   Scanners or radios that can receive cellular transmissions cannot be sold on eBay.

- **Used Clothing**   Used clothing can be sold as long as it has been "thoroughly cleaned according to the manufacturer's instructions."

- **Weapons and Knives**   Many types of knives can be sold on eBay. However, other weapons such as blackjacks, brass knuckles, or even metal replica hand grenades are prohibited.

16

Get Notified of eBay Policy Changes

eBay's policies aren't written in stone. They change from time to time. If you sell a large quantity of items in a variety of categories, you need to know when the policies change. You have to change your user preferences to receive e-mail notifications of policy changes. Just follow these steps:

1. Go to the Change Notification Preferences page (**http://pages.ebay.com/ services/myebay/optin-login.html**).

2. Enter your User ID and password, and click Sign In.

3. When the eBay Change Your Preferences page appears, scroll down to the Legal and Other Emails section. Check the boxes next to User Agreement Changes and Privacy Policy Changes.

4. Click the Save My Changes button.

The User Agreement Changes option tells you of any changes to the list of prohibited or questionable items. The Privacy Policy Changes option lets you know of any changes in the way you handle customer information, or in the way your own information is handled by eBay.

Steer Clear of Shill Bidding

In February 2002, three individuals were arrested and charged with intentionally bidding on some highly desirable René Lalique glass that was being auctioned on eBay in an effort to inflate the final price. In shill bidding, individuals bid against one another with no intention of actually buying the item in question, but forcing serious buyers to bid higher and higher. The three in this case allegedly drove the bids up to more than $1.3 million. Such activity, known as *shill bidding*, is not only prohibited on eBay, but is a federal offense as well. The Federal Wire Fraud statute is a serious offense involving the use of interstate commerce to defraud. The three individuals were charged with wire fraud and could face five years in prison.

Shill bidding is one of the biggest threats to eBay's operation. Besides being illegal, it can destroy the trust that keeps online auctions running successfully. It might seem easy to set up shill bidding with a friend or relative, or even by setting up multiple User IDs, but the practice is so well-known that savvy bidders can spot it readily. Bidders who consistently bid and never win are suspicious, and a bidder's history can be easily checked to reveal such patterns. In addition, even though you might use multiple User IDs, if you use the same computer to place bids, that computer has a unique identifier called an *IP address* that it uses to connect to the Internet, and eBay can use the IP address to determine who is actually placing the bids. If you think you have been the victim of shill bidding yourself, go to **http://pages.ebay.com/help/confidence/programs-investigations.html**. Click the link Shill Bidding under Selling Offenses to access a form you can use to report the offense.

> CAUTION   *A related activity, shill feedback, occurs when a seller who has been conducting shill bidding wins his or her own auction. Before quickly relisting the item, the seller leaves positive feedback for him or herself in an effort to inflate feedback ratings. Such activities mislead buyers and erode the level of trust and community spirit that keeps eBay going.*

Lloyd's of London Insurance

Another eBay feature that helps makes transactions proceed smoothly is the fact that all buyers have their transactions covered by the Fraud Protection Program. The prestigious insurance company Lloyd's of London covers the high bidder/ purchaser for $200 of the final auction price, after a $25 deductible.

For sellers, the Fraud Protection doesn't do anything. It doesn't protect you from bounced checks or non-responsive buyers. It's just good to know the program exists, especially if a dispute occurs. Buyers, though, are only covered if they file a claim with their credit card company beforehand.

Where to Find It

- **eBay User Agreement**
  http://pages.ebay.com/help/community/png-user.html
  Information on what you can and can't do on eBay, either as a buyer or seller.

- **Login page for creating a pre-approved buyers list**
  http://cgi3.ebay.com/aw-cgi/eBayISAPI.dll?PreApproveBidders
  Enter your User ID and password, then click Sign In, to begin the process of creating a list of pre-approved buyers for one of your sales items.

- **ID Verify Accept Terms page**
  http://pages.ebay.com/services/buyandsell/idverify-terms.html
  Start the process of having your identity verified by a third party so you can have an ID Verify logo added to your User ID.

16

- **BBB Online**
  http://www.bbbonline.org
  Go here to obtain a BBB Online Reliability Seal.

- **SquareTrade**
  http://www.squaretrade.com
  Go here for dispute resolution or a SquareTrade Seal.

- **IDs for Secure E-Mail**
  http://www.verisign.com/products/class1/index.html
  Go here to obtain a Digital ID from VeriSign.

- **eBay Warranty Services**
  http://pages.ebay.com/help/warranty/seller_overview.html
  Information for eBay sellers on the Warranty Services program.

- **eBay Prohibited and Questionable Items**
  http://pages.ebay.com/help/community/png-items.html
  Lists of items that eBay has either prohibited or considers "questionable."

Chapter 17

Fulfill Your Accounting and Tax Requirements

How to…

- Create back-office financial functions for your eBay business
- Keep track of income and sales tax requirements
- Deduct your auction-related expenses
- Computerize your tax and accounting needs
- Locate professionals who can keep taxes from being taxing

As I write this, tax time is fast approaching. I'm dutifully gathering pay stubs in order to present them to my accountant. Chances are you're doing much the same thing. But what about the profit you realize from your sales on eBay—the income that isn't documented by W-2s or Form 1099s? The truth is simple: Income from your eBay business is subject to tax just like income from any other type of business activity. It doesn't matter whether eBay sales are your sole source of income or just a sideline. You have to report money you make from auctions just as you would any other income.

The good news is that because you have income from your eBay business, you can deduct the expenses associated with that business. That includes the camera you use to photograph the items you sell; the computer you use to prepare the sales; the fees you pay to eBay; and much more. It's all a matter of keeping appropriate financial records. It can actually be fun to keep track of where your eBay business is at financially and save a few bucks at tax time as well. I'm neither a tax expert nor an accountant; I am a self-employed individual who is used to paying business taxes and accounting for business expenses. This chapter is intended to give basic advice on the kinds of tax and accounting issues you need to know about; you should consult a tax professional or accountant to get specific advice that applies to your own situation.

What's Different About Being Self-Employed?

When I became a freelance writer, lots of things changed. Keeping track of money was one of the biggest changes—not only the source of the money, but how I make sure Uncle Sam gets his share. First of all, I have to pay taxes not once, but four times a year. I need to make an estimated tax payment based on the amount of taxes I think I'll have to pay at the end of the year.

I run a sole proprietorship (a legal type of business classification described in Chapter 18), so I have to report income and investments on Schedule C of Form 1040, Profit or Loss from Business. I need to document both my income and all my business-related expenses.

A sole proprietorship is relatively simple to run. Some eBay entrepreneurs, like Bob Kopczynski (who runs Maxwell Street Market, and is profiled in Chapter 4), have chosen to incorporate, and they have employees as well. Things get far more complicated in terms of tax and accounting when you run a corporation: You need to pay payroll tax, do withholding of payroll, issue W-2 forms, and much more. Bob has an accountant do the heavy lifting, though his wife Katy does day-to-day bookkeeping as well. There are, of course, benefits that go along with the extra work: You have limited liability in case one of your customers causes legal trouble; you can deduct some insurance costs; and because you have a team of employees, you can do more work and generate more income, too.

Doing my own bookkeeping and handling expenses and payments is more work than when I was a full-time office employee, but it's more satisfying, too. It's all part of running your own business. Whether you are a full-time eBayer or whether you make only a handful of sales a month, you can benefit by taking charge of your own bookkeeping and tax responsibilities.

> **TIP** *There are all kinds of formulas you can use to calculate your quarterly estimated tax payments, and all kinds of rules about what kinds of deductions you can take. I strongly recommend you hire an accountant to file your taxes for you. Mine continually comes up with new ways to lower the taxes I have to pay.*

Perform the Basic Accounting Practices

As eBay grows in popularity, the fact that many entrepreneurs like you are making good money by selling online is also becoming well known. In addition, eBay keeps records of all of your sales income. It's wise to establish some sort of regular record-keeping procedure, whether that procedure simply involves gathering all your receipts and stuffing them in an envelope, entering data in your hand-held device, or writing your mileage down when you're driving to the post office.

By doing business online, you have a big advantage: You can print out a list of your sales from eBay at tax time so you can add up exactly what you've sold. It's a little more work to keep records of your expenses, and the prospect of doing accounting and paying business taxes can seem intimidating. But it's not that hard, either. (If I can do it, anyone can, believe me.) It's a matter of keeping and storing receipts so you can add them up at tax time.

Is Big eBrother Watching?

Rumor has it that the Internal Revenue Service (IRS) is watching for eBay sellers who don't pay any taxes. In the current economic climate in which states are starved for income, it makes sense to pay attention to this. I've also seen postings on the eBay Café message board speculating that the IRS pays individuals to report on eBay users who don't pay their taxes. I haven't seen any hard proof that the eyes of the IRS are on eBay. If you're concerned about this, the best response is to simply pay your taxes.

The IRS makes it easy for you to learn about government regulations and taxes by providing information on a Web site designed for small businesses and self-employed people like you (**http://www.irs.ustreas.gov/businesses/small/index.html**).

TIP   *You don't have to take my word for all this. Consult the Internal Revenue Service's Publication 334, Tax Guide for Small Businesses http://www.irs.gov/pub/irs-pdf/p334.pdf.*

Cash-Basis versus Accrual-Basis Accounting

Do your eyes glaze over when you see the terms "*cash-basis*" and "*accrual-basis*"? They're just two different ways of describing when your business was paid. Chances are you'll simply use the cash-basis method, but it's good to know that the two options exist, if only so you can discuss them in an informed way with your accountant:

- **Cash-basis accounting**   You report income when you actually receive it and write off expenses when you pay them. This is the easy way to report income and expenses, and probably the way most new small businesses do it.

- **Accrual-basis accounting**   This method is more complicated than the cash-basis method, but if your online business maintains an inventory, you must use the accrual method. For instance, suppose your eBay business sells an inventory of surplus items. You report income when you actually receive the payment; you write down expenses *when services are rendered* (even though you may not have made the cash payment yet). For example, suppose 25 of your eBay sales are completed on June 31, and you ask your customers to get their payments to you by July 8. The payments don't all arrive, however, until July 15. You still record the income as having been received on July 8, when the payment was originally due. Accrual-basis accounting creates a more accurate picture of a business's financial situation. If a company is having cash flow problems and is extending payment on some of its bills, cash-basis accounting provides an unduly rosy financial picture, whereas the accrual-basis method would be more accurate.

Because eBay businesses aren't likely to have a steady inventory, chances are the cash-based method is the one to use.

NOTE *You probably assume that the accounting period you're going to use is the same as the calendar year: January 1 to December 31. When you're running a business, however, you don't have to stick to the calendar necessarily. In this case, the business picks a date other than December 31 to function as the end of the fiscal year. Many large organizations pick a date that coincides with the end of their business cycle. Some pick March 31 as the end, others June 30, and still others September 30. If you use the fiscal-year method of accounting, you must file your tax return three and a half months after the end of the fiscal year. If the fiscal year ends on June 30, for example, you must file by October 15.*

Practice Good Record-Keeping

It pays to be meticulous about keeping financial records. After all, the better your records, the more accurate your estimated tax payments will be, and the more deductions you'll be able to take. In the long run, keeping good records can actually save you money. Besides that, you won't have a realistic picture of how your business is doing—whether all your effort is worthwhile, in other words—unless you can accurately compare how much you're making to how much it costs to generate that income.

When you record how much you pay for supplies, how much you pay in fees to eBay, and how much you are paid by your bidders and buyers, you're doing the same thing Bob Cratchit did in the Dickens story "A Christmas Carol"—it's called bookkeeping. Even if you hire someone like Bob to do the work for you, it pays to have at least a passing familiarity with bookkeeping terms such as assets, liabilities, income, and expenses.

You might think of the financial side of your eBay business as consisting of different financial accounts. Every time a financial event occurs, an account's balance either decreases or increases. When someone purchases one of your auction items and you deposit the payment, your bank account increases and the money people

17

owe you decreases. The dual activity—one account goes up while another goes down—is known as *double-entry accounting*. This type of accounting makes use of standard types of business accounts:

- **Bank Account**   This is your income from sales—the good stuff.

- **Accounts Receivable**   This is the amount that people owe you and that you expect to receive at some point—those checks that are in the mail, and that money in your PayPal account that hasn't yet been transferred to the bank.

- **Asset Account**   This is the value of your business assets—your inventory, your equipment, the items you currently have up for sale.

- **Expense Account**   This is the amount you have allocated for expenses.

In double-entry accounting, any one business transaction affects two or more accounts, as illustrated in Table 17-1.

These somewhat dry concepts become more understandable if you take an online workshop such as the interactive presentation created by the Bank of America and provided on its online Resource Center (**http://www.va-interactive.com/ bankofamerica/resourcecenter/**). The workshop on cash flow, which discusses income, expenses, and accounts receivable, is shown below.

Event	Bank Account	Accounts Receivable	Asset Account	Expense Account
You make a sale	Increases	Decreases	No Change	No Change
You purchase supplies or equipment	Decreases	Increases	Increases	Increases
You buy inventory you plan to sell	Decreases	No change	Increases	No change
You incur a business-related expense	Decreases	No change	No change	Increases

TABLE 17-1   Double-Entry Accounting Example

TIP   *Since you're already familiar with computers, you might want to use an accounting program to record your records as described later in this chapter. You can also record expenses in a hand-held computing device if you have one. (The cost of purchasing such a device counts as a deductible business expense, of course.) Otherwise, one of the printed books that is specially designed for maintaining financial records can help. Go to your local office supply store and get a financial record book called a* journal, *which is set up with columns for income and expenses.*

Record Income

Brick-and-mortar businesses receive invoices for their income. As an eBay businessperson, you're likely to get income from any number of sources: personal checks, PayPal transfers, or direct deposits to your bank account from credit card companies. This is probably the most enjoyable thing you can record in your accounting software or booklet.

CAUTION   *I've seen estimates (which probably aren't very scientific) to the effect that as many as 60 percent of eBay sellers don't pay taxes on what they make from auction sales. If you have income that you didn't pay taxes on, the IRS will label it* unreported income, *and you will have to pay taxes and possibly fines and penalties on it.*

The best way to record your income is to be systematic about it: Just how should you record your revenue? For each item, write down a brief, informal statement. This is a personal record that you may make on a slip of paper or even on the back of a canceled check. Be sure to include the following information:

- The date of the transaction

- The type of payment (PayPal, credit card, or check)

- The amount you were paid

- The name of your high bidder or buyer

17

Don't Forget Your Business Assets

Every business has equipment of one sort or another that it uses to produce its goods or services. Such business equipment goes by the name assets in accounting jargon. As an eBay seller, you probably have assets such as:

- Your computer

- Your digital camera, scanner, or both

- Modems, hubs, cables, speakers, printers, and other computer-related equipment

- Packing materials: boxes, tape, packing peanuts, and the like

- Postage machines

You might have to *expense* (in other words, spread out) the original cost of the equipment that is expected to help you generate income over its useful life. Expensing the cost of an asset over the period of its "life span" is called *depreciation.* In order to depreciate an item, you estimate how many years you're going to use it and then divide the original cost by the number of years. The result is the amount that you report in any given year. For example, if you purchase a digital camera that costs $1,000, and you expect to use it in your business for five years, you expense $200 of the cost each year.

You need to keep records of your assets that include the following information:

- Name, model number, and description

- Purchase date

- Purchase price, including fees

- Date the item went into service

- Amount of time the item is put to personal (as opposed to business) use

File these records in a safe location along with your other tax-related-information.

Record Payments

If you scour flea markets and estate sales, you pay for the collectibles you sell on eBay. Such payments should be recorded for accounting purposes. In addition, like any online businessperson, you probably need to make regular payments to the company that gives you Internet access, and possibly Web page designers and computer technicians. If you hire employees to help you, the payment system becomes more involved.

Suppose you hire your cousin to handle shipping and packing and a neighbor to create auction listings. Your accountant is likely to bring up the question of how you pay such employees. You have two options: You can treat them either as full-time employees or as independent contractors. The IRS uses a stringent series of guidelines (see Publication 15A, **http://www.irs.gov/pub/irs-pdf/p15a.pdf**) to determine whether your helper is a contractor or a full-time employee. Hiring independent contractors rather than salaried workers is far simpler for you: You don't have to pay benefits to independent contractors, and you don't have to withhold federal and state taxes. Just be sure to get invoices from any independent contractor who works for you. If you have full-time employees whom you pay an hourly wage, things get more complicated, and you had best consult an accountant to help you set up the salary payments.

Business Expenses

When you spend the day at the flea market or at a government auction, do you chow down at the local burger joint? Be sure to get a receipt for that lunch, and file it away in your receipts envelope at the end of the day. Meals, gas, and postage are all business expenses—costs that you incur in order to produce revenue—and you can deduct them at tax time.

Pulling together evidence of expenses doesn't have to be a high-tech matter. If you have a tablet PC or hand-held device, great. Otherwise, get a big folder and use it to hold any receipts, canceled checks, or credit card statements. Be sure your records include basic information such as:

- Date the expense occurred

- Name of the person or company that received payment from you

- Type of expense incurred (equipment, utilities, supplies, and so on)

What About Sales Tax?

The question "Should I charge sales tax?" is one I hear all the time from people who conduct business online. There's no simple answer, because the question is continually being discussed by legislators and advocates of free commerce on the Internet. The question of whether sales tax should be assessed on out-of-state sales that occur online is continually being debated by legislators. The Internet Tax Freedom

Act, which is in effect at this writing, only calls for a freeze until October 2003 on new taxes related to Internet access and e-commerce. It does not mean that states cannot collect sales tax on Internet sales—only that they can't enact new tax requirements.

At this writing, you are required to add sales tax only to in-state transactions—unless, of course, you hang your hat in one of the five states that doesn't collect sales tax at all: Montana, Alaska, Delaware, New Hampshire, and Oregon. If you live in one of the states that does require you to collect sales tax, you need to collect only from your customers who live in the same state where you reside.

> TIP   *Most states require their merchants to charge sales tax not only on the purchase price but on shipping and handling charges as well. Check with your state to make sure. You'll find a list of links to state tax agencies at http://www.tannedfeet.com/state_tax_agencies.htm.*

Deduce Your Business Deductions

All of the work required to keep your books, collect taxes, and prepare your taxes pays off at the moment when you add up your deductions. You can reduce your tax payments substantially by taking all of the deductions for which you are eligible (check with your accountant to make sure which ones qualify as deductions). These include the computer equipment you use to prepare your auction sales, the spaces where you do your computer work and store your inventory, and the fees associated with going online and completing transactions.

Computer Equipment

It used to be that you had to depreciate computer equipment, but now you can deduct the cost all at once. Be sure to keep all of your receipts from the computer or electronics store or from the repair shop. If you buy digital cameras or computer-related components on eBay, be sure to print out the Web page that shows your high bid or Buy It Now price (or the e-mail from the seller that shows the total cost including shipping) so you have it for your records.

Your Home Office

If you work principally at home, you can deduct part of your mortgage and home-related expenses—specifically, the part that's related to your business. If you work out of a home office and your office is, for example, one room in a ten-room house, you can deduct one-tenth of your home-related expenses.

CAUTION *If you intend to deduct your home office, the space must be used exclusively for work purposes. You can't mix personal computing activities there. Ask your accountant to explain the requirements to you in more detail.*

Don't forget the miles you drive to the post office, to the estate sale or flea market where you buy things to sell, and other business-related driving. Postal fees definitely apply, as do the cost of subscribing to magazines like *eBay Life*.

TIP *Keep a notebook in your car so you can record your mileage as you make trips to the post office or shipping store.*

Internet Connections and Other Fees

Without some form of access to the Internet, you wouldn't have an eBay business at all. The monthly or yearly charges you pay for Internet access are deductible. So are these others:

- Part of your phone bill, if you use a dialup modem connection to get online

- Part of your cellular phone bill, if you use your cell phone to check your eBay transactions or talk to customers

- Web hosting charges, if you run an online business Web site

Find Accounting Help Online

If going to math class made you want to jump out the nearest window, maybe dealing personally with expenses, accounting periods, and income just isn't your thing. Luckily, there are plenty of reputable professionals you would be delighted to have you as a client. Even luckier, this not only counts as a business expense but can help you reduce your taxes as well. What's more, the time you save will enable you to give your undivided attention to running and promoting your online business.

On the other hand, you may be the ultimate do-it-yourselfer. Chances are, you won't have to enroll in a single business class. The following Web sites can give you the free instruction and advice that can make you into your own accountant before you can say, "one, two, three":

- **Accounting for everyone**   This site (**http://www.accountz.com**) includes online calculators and an Ask an Expert section. There's also a glossary full of accounting and bookkeeping terms.

17

■ **Entrepreneur's Help Page**   As it's name suggests, if you have your own business, this site is especially for you. It includes a Financial Records page (**http://www.tannedfeet.com/financial_records.htm**) that covers what you need to know about small business accounting.

■ **Accounting Over Easy**   The CPA who set up this Web site (**http://www.ezaccounting.com**) wants $19.95 from you if you want to examine it in detail. You can peek at a preview page, however, for free. His goal is to make it easy for beginning entrepreneurs to grasp the basics of accounting.

Where better to go to find accounting help than on eBay itself? Actually, you won't find accountants on eBay, but on its professional service partner, eLance. Just go to **http://elance.ebay.com**, and click **Taxes**. When I visited, a total of 141 tax preparers were listed (see Figure 17-1). You post your project and get these tax preparers to bid on your job. (See Chapter 13 for more information on how eLance works.)

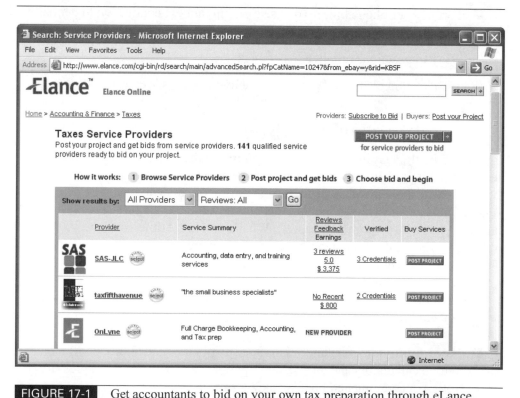

FIGURE 17-1   Get accountants to bid on your own tax preparation through eLance.

TIP   *The Tax and Accounting Sites Directory (**http://www.taxsites.com**) is a good starting point if you are looking for information on the Web related to tax requirements and links to accounting firms.*

Use Accounting Software

Whether you use a shoebox, filing cabinet, envelope, or a messy spot on your shelf, you've got to keep copies of all of your auction transactions. I can hear you saying, "But eBay keeps all the records for me on its site." There are two flaws in this argument. First, you can't depend on eBay to maintain your sales records for years at a time. Second, if you are audited, there's no guarantee the IRS will consider a Web page an adequate financial record. Be sure to print out receipts related to your sales, including postage, shipping, and insurance. Also track all of your eBay Final Value Fees and other fees you have to pay to get online and do business. Print out your eBay sales summary so you have a record on hand in case eBay servers go offline or the information is archived.

What, then, do you do with all of those facts and figures when you need to calculate your taxes? For many people, the best alternative is simply to push a few buttons, choose a few menu options, and let an accounting program do the heavy lifting. Accounting software can definitely make that part of your financial life easier.

A good software package can help save time when it comes to accounting and tax preparation for small businesses. All let you record income and expenses and prepare business reports. QuickBooks by Intuit is also highly recommended by many accountants and small business owners.

Pick the Package That's Best for You

Accounting programs are among the most highly competitive types of software on the market today. Each year, it seems, Microsoft, Intuit, and MYOB come out with new, souped-up editions of their software, each designed to have more features than the last. On top of that, most of the products come in several versions, each with a different set of features. Which program is right for you? Keep in mind that you're not simply trying to balance your checkbook, but you need to track accounts receivable and possibly employee salaries and payroll taxes. It's a good idea to pick the version of an accounting program that enables you to track business finances. Table 17-2 provides you with some features to compare.

The well-known packages described in this section have plenty of features and add-ons. Programs such as Microsoft Money and Quicken, for example, let you create customizable home pages that you can configure to provide up-to-the minute reports on your stock holdings. They also help you with financial planning.

17

Product	Web Site URL	Features
Quicken Premier Home & Business	http://www.quicken.com	Oriented toward home and personal finance needs. Gives you a place to track mileage and receivables. Includes a merchant account service so you can receive credit card payments.
QuickBooks Basic	http://www.quickbooks.com	Oriented toward small business needs. Helps you back up your data; gives you access to an online Help & Support Center. Lets you track your inventory.
Peachtree First Accounting	http://www.peachtree.com	Specifically designed for home users who are starting up a small business. Integrated to work with Microsoft Office products. Provides a variety of business services you can use online, such as payroll, tax filing, and bill payment.
Microsoft Money Deluxe & Business	http://www.microsoft.com/money/info	Ideal for users who do online banking. Enables you to track payroll, prepare taxes, and integrate database information with Microsoft Outlook.
MYOB AccountEdge	http://www.myob.com	AccountEdge is especially designed for Mac OS X users. Versions specific to the financial requirements of different countries are available, including the United States, United Kingdom, Australia, New Zealand, and Malaysia.

TABLE 17-2   Accounting Software Features

Since I find the prospect of doing my own accounting downright intimidating, I don't use accounting software myself. The only program that doesn't scare me half to death is a simple shareware product by OWL Software called OWL Simple Business Accounting (http://www.owlsoftware.com/sba.htm). It doesn't have a lot of automated gimmicks; it doesn't connect to a Web site automatically to get new features; it doesn't coordinate with your bank account online. All it does is provide you with a way to create accounts and enter income and expenses, and then generate reports that you can use to prepare your taxes.

Keep Your Books Online

In addition to purchasing and installing individual software programs, many of the commercial accounting programs have an online version. A site like QuickBooks Online Edition enables you to keep all of your books online. Although it costs $19.95 per month for this service, the advantage is that you don't have to download new versions of the software as they become available—and accounting programs are so highly competitive that new versions tend to appear virtually every year. You can try out the service for 30 days before you actually commit to buying it. Just follow these steps:

1. Connect to the QuickBooks Online Edition Web site (**http://quickbooks .intuit.com/qbcom/jhtml/skins/prod_ovw_online.jhtml**).

2. Click the TRY IT button.

3. The next page gives you the option to use fictional data provided by QuickBooks or enter your own financial data. For this example, click **Use Your Own Financial Data**.

4. If a security alert dialog box appears because you are moving to a secure Web page, click OK.

5. Check the button next to "I am new to QuickBooks Online Services." Fill out the form that asks for you to create a username and password. Then click **Start a Brand New Company**.

6. On the next page, fill out information about your business, then click **Next**.

7. On the next page, you see the question "Do you want help setting up your accounts?" Leave Yes selected, then answer the questions on the page to set up your accounts.

NOTE *Under May We Contact You?, if you do not want Intuit to send you promotional e-mail or call you on the phone, click* **contact you**. *When the pop-up window appears, check the options that describe the types of promotional communications you do not want (e-mail, phone, or mail). Then click OK.*

8. Check the box next to "I Accept." Click **Next**.

17

9. On the next page, click **Start Free Trial**.

10. On the next page, click **Proceed to QuickBooks Online Trial Edition**.

11. Click **Continue**.

12. If an alert dialog box appears asking if you want to download files, click Yes. You need the files to run QuickBooks Online Trial Edition. When the files have been downloaded, your home page on the QuickBooks Online Edition Web site appears (see Figure 17-2).

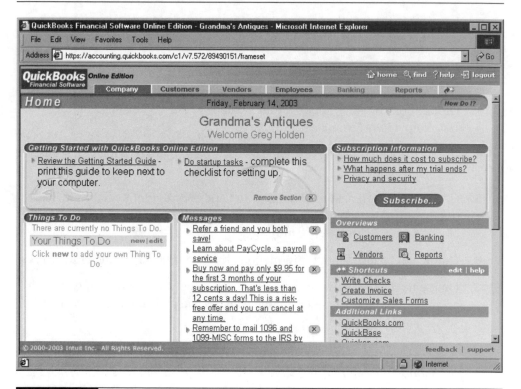

FIGURE 17-2 For a monthly fee, you can keep your accounting information online.

CAUTION   *QuickBooks Online Edition or any online accounting service works best if you have a broadband connection and are connected to the Internet all the time. You also need to realize that, when you use an online service to keep your financial records, you put a big level of trust in the Web site that you use. After all, they are holding your financial data on their Web site, not yours. Although such sites should and do protect your information, if a hacker manages to break in, your information could be compromised. In contrast, if you install and use accounting software on your computer, you control where it's located and how it's stored. It's also up to you to protect your files and make sure hackers can't break into your computer.*

Once you have an account established online, you can use the site to print tax forms, handle payroll records, or print invoices as shown in Figure 17-3.

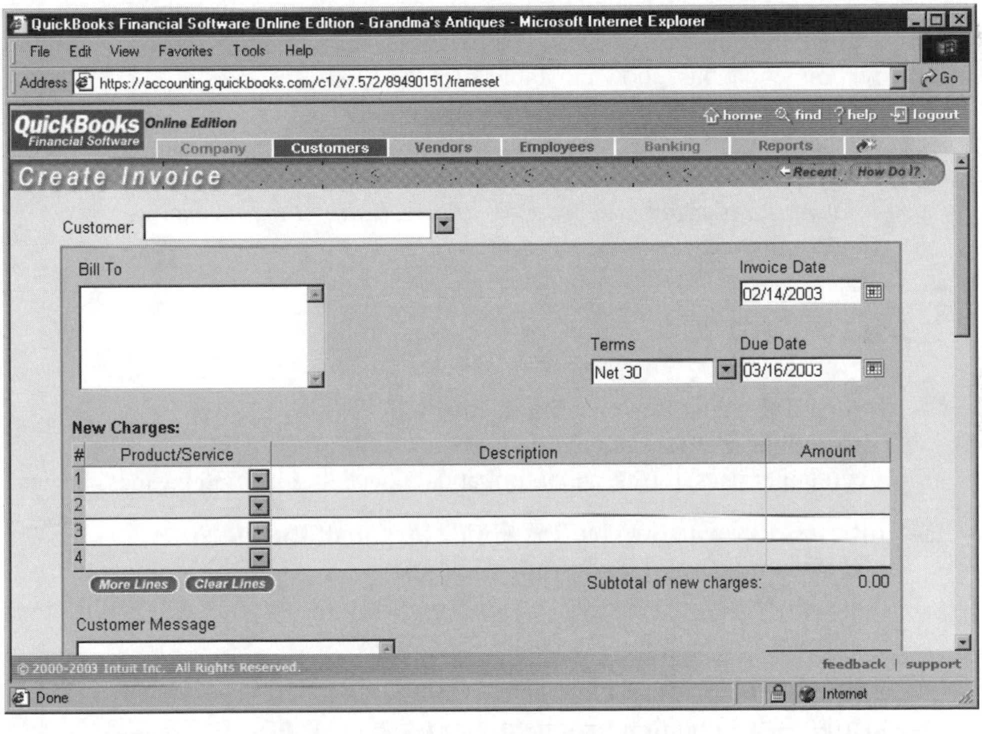

FIGURE 17-3   The QuickBooks Online site can provide you with tax forms and help with day-to-day accounting, too.

Type of Record	How Long to Keep It
Employment tax records (if you have employees)	4 years after tax is due or paid
Records relating to assets	Until the year in which you dispose of the property
You did not report income that you should have reported, and it amounts to more than 25 percent of your gross income	6 years
You filed a fraudulent tax return	No limit
You failed to file a tax return	No limit

TABLE 17-3   Guidelines for Keeping Business Records.

How Long Should You Keep Your Records?

The short answer to this question is: as long as you can. If you have the room to keep ten years' worth of tax records and receipts, do so to be on the safe side. However, the IRS, in its Publication 583, "Starting a Business and Keeping Records," has more specific recommendations, shown in Table 17-3.

TIP   *You'll find Publication 583 online at **http://www.irs.gov/pub/irs-pdf/p583.pdf**. In fact, you can view and print out a wide variety of tax forms and informational brochures from the IRS Web site at **http://www.irs.gov/ formspubs/index.html**.*

Where to Find It

- **Internal Revenue Service Small Bus/Self-Employed site**
  http://www.irs.ustreas.gov/businesses/small/index.html
  Tax requirements, forms, and information especially for small business owners.

- **Internal Revenue Service Tax Guide for Small Businesses**
  http://www.irs.gov/pub/irs-pdf/p334.pdf
  A complete publication you can view online or print out that explains how to file taxes when you have business income or expenses.

- **Entrepreneurs' Help Page list of state tax agencies**
  http://www.tannedfeet.com/state_tax_agencies.htm
  Links to state tax agency Web sites where you can look up sales tax requirements.

Part V

Keep Your eBay Business Running Smoothly

Chapter 18

Keep Your eBay Business Legal

How to...

- Avoid trouble by not copying what you don't own
- Protect your own trade name and copyright
- Decide on a legal form for your eBay business
- Pay your local licensing fees
- Observe your customers' privacy

Everyone on eBay has to play by the rules. If they didn't, auction chaos would result. Sales could end at any time; bidders could compete after the ending time; people might pay with peanuts rather than dollars. Just as you observe eBay's rules, you need to observe the rules set down by local and federal governments. If you don't keep your eBay business legal, chaos might not result on eBay, but a sort of chaos might hamper your ability to do business at all. You might get sued, you might get negative feedback, or you might be charged with breaking the law.

Chances are you're not a lawyer. You started out on eBay in the hope of making a few extra bucks, and you don't have experience in legal requirements for businesses. This chapter discusses ways to avoid legal trouble by following a few commonsense principles. You need to be aware of the laws that govern the type of business you operate, you need to avoid stepping on someone's trademarked or copyrighted material, you need to pay necessary fees, and you need to observe the privacy of those you meet on eBay. If you do these simple things, your business will run not only smoothly but profitably, and you'll be able to head off potential trouble before it occurs.

Copyright and Trademark Concerns

When you scan the pages and pages of auction listings on eBay, you're likely to see parts of auction descriptions that attract your attention. I've had sellers tell me, "I saw that graphic of a little doll, so I copied it and put it on my page," or, "I thought that description was really good, so I copied it and just pasted it onto my description."

Such copying might seem harmless, and it's certainly easy to do. In most cases, people don't complain if they see something that used to be on one of their Web pages now residing on someone else's page. If someone does complain, you should know that, technically, they have a right do so—a copyright, in fact. This section examines two legal pitfalls you need to avoid: copyright violations and trademark infringements.

eBay Sellers Can Be Sued

Can you be sued for attempting to sell products on eBay that were created by someone else who holds a copyright or trademark on those items? The answer is yes, depending on the copyright holder and depending on whether the items were copied illegally. Here are two examples of the sorts of legal morasses in which eBay sellers were embroiled in late 2002:

- December 2002   The Motion Picture Association of America sued nine people in eight states for infringing copyrights by allegedly selling illegal DVD copies of movies. One seller, who allegedly sold 414 copies of pirated movies, said he had purchased them from Asian-based sellers on eBay.

- December 2002   A group of Seattle-area knitters who sell yarn and knitting designs online hired a lawyer in order to fight back against legal representatives of Scottish knitting designer Alice Starmore. Starmore's representatives repeatedly had eBay sales canceled because they allegedly infringed on Starmore's copyright. Auctions were canceled that attempted to sell a tag from one of Starmore's skeins of yarn, and a seashell that was included with a shipment of Starmore yarns.

Don't Do a Copy-Wrong

Copyright is a legal term that describes the right of the creator of a creative work (or a person or entity to whom the creator has sold the copyright) to control how it is copied. If someone uses permission covered by copyright without asking the copyright owner, the copyright owner can sue and be compensated for any losses that have been suffered. The owner can even obtain a court order (called an *injunction*) that forces the infringing party to stop.

It often surprises people to learn that everything that is published on the Web, just like everything that can be considered intellectual property, is automatically covered by copyright law, whether it is accompanied by a formal copyright notice or not (such as the one at the bottom of an eBay auction listing and shown in Figure 18-1). So if you're in a hurry, you need to create 20 or 30 auction descriptions at a time, don't simply grab something from another auction listing and drop it on yours. At the same time, don't try to sell something like pirated software or entertainment material that, itself, represents an object that infringes someone's copyright.

18

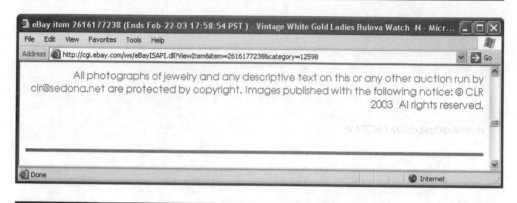

FIGURE 18-1   Images and text published on the Web are protected by copyright law.

If you do sell something that's in violation of copyright infringement, don't expect eBay to be legally liable. In a 2001 legal case, *Hendrickson v. eBay,* a federal judge in Los Angeles held that eBay was protected from secondary liability after a seller sold a pirated DVD at auction. In other words, if you sell something that's been pirated or that is copyrighted, *you're* liable.

TIP   *You can read about the copyright infringement case at **http://www .usatoday.com/tech/columnist/2001/09/13/sinrod.htm**.*

You can sell used books and records at auction as long as they are legitimate copies rather than pirated or bootlegged versions. But because they are copyrighted material, the way in which you sell those items can possibly get you in trouble. Here are some suggestions for avoiding copyright infringement trouble:

- Don't scan the trademarked logo on a book, record, or product and use it in your auction listing. (However, you can photograph an item, including its manufacturer's logo, and put that in your listing.)

- Don't copy the text or part of a record and include it in your auction listing, or in a link from your auction listing.

- Create your own description of the item, rather than copying promotional descriptions from the dust jacket (if it's a book) or the cover (if it's a record, CD, or DVD).

How to ... Determine Who Owns the Copyright

If you need to determine who owns the copyright on a printed work or other product, you only have to look at the copyright notice or the trademark. To check someone's trademark, you can go to the Trademark Electronic Search System (TESS) of the U.S. Patent and Trademark Office Web site (**http://www.uspto.gov/ main/trademarks.htm**), shown in Figure 18-2, and search for the legal owner of the trademark.

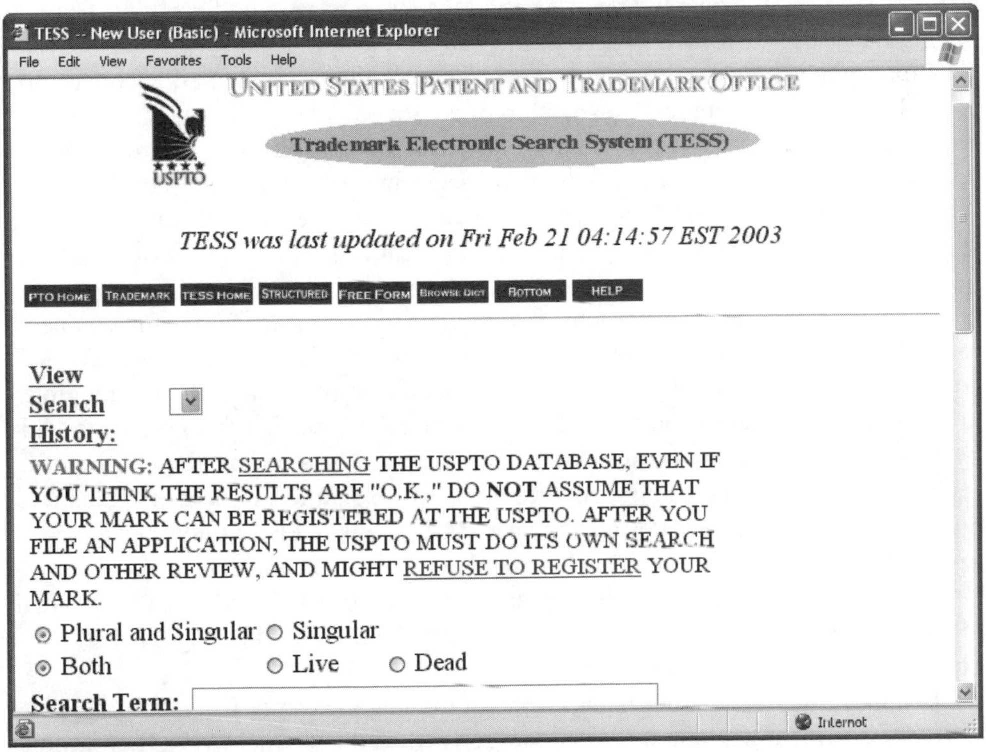

FIGURE 18-2   Search for a trademark holder on this government Web site

18

Make sure you describe where you got the property and why you have a right to sell it—in other words, how you came to own it. You might say you "bought it at a store, and I can provide the original receipt of purchase."

If you are accused of violating copyright, be sure to consult with an attorney before you respond.

Avoid Trademark Infringement

When you're in business, you are involved in *trade*. A business is known, whether on eBay or in the marketplace, by its *trade name*—for example, the name "eBay" itself. A trade name can also be *trademarked,* which means that the owner has taken the extra step of registering the trade name so it can't be used without permission. Commercial entities protect their trade names and trademarks, and frequently court battles erupt over who can legally use a name or something very close to it (such as the creators of the operating system Lindows, who were sued for trademark infringement by Microsoft, owners of the trade name Windows).

What, you ask, is the difference between copyright and trademark? Copyright is used to protect the creator's ownership of creative works such as writing, art, software, video, or cinema (but not names, titles, or short phrases). It provides the copyright owner a way to protest or seek damages in case someone copies the works without permission. A trademark is a way of controlling the use of distinctive words, symbols, slogans, or other things that serve to identify products or services in the marketplace.

What does all this mean for your fledgling auction concern? It means you need to be careful when you sell items that bear someone else's trade name or logo. A company can trademark any visual element that accompanies a particular tangible product or line of goods, and serves to identify and distinguish it from products sold by other sources. In other words, a trademark is not necessarily just for a business's trade name. In fact, you can trademark letters, words, names, phrases, slogans, numbers, colors, symbols, designs, or shapes. Just look at eBay's home page in Figure 18-3 and see how many trademarked symbols you can spot.

The lesson for you, the auction seller, is this: you can sell items that are related to a trademark holder, but you can't actually use the trademarked logo, name, or phrase in your auction description.

Because eBay cannot check every one of the items sold on its site for copyright or trademark infringement, it created the Verified Rights Owner (VeRO) program. VeRO enlists the help of eBay members themselves who report sales that infringe upon the copyright, trademark, or other rights of third parties. VeRO program participants and other rights owners can report infringing items, and have such items removed. You can become a member of the VeRO program yourself by

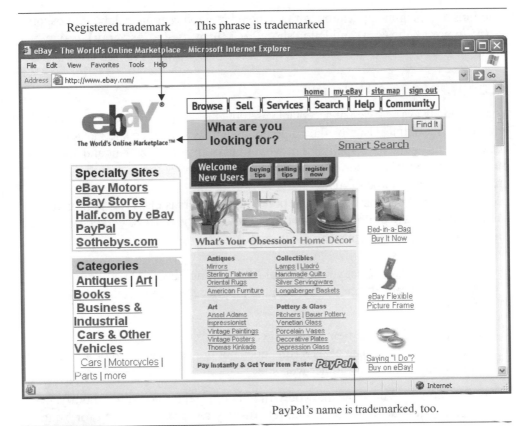

FIGURE 18-3 Be careful when you sell a trademarked item.

filling out the application for membership at **http://pages.ebay.com/help/community/ notice-infringe2.pdf**. You can view a list of VeRO members' About Me pages at **http://pages.ebay.com/help/community/vero-aboutme.html**. The members listed are companies and individuals who are concerned about protecting their trademarks and copyrighted items; you should be careful about trying to sell anything associated with anyone on the list.

Adding Digital Watermarks

You can protect your auction images and graphics through a process called *digital watermarking*. This process involves adding copyright or other information about the image's owner to the digital image file. The information added may or may not be visible. An application called Digimarc (**http://www.digimarc.com**), which functions as a plug-in application with the popular graphics tools Adobe Photoshop (**http://www.adobe.com**) and Paint Shop Pro 7 (**http://www.jasc.com**), is one of the most widely used watermarking tools.

Acceptable Use Policies

You should always be aware of acceptable use policies set up by agencies that control what goes out online. Usually, the company that hosts your Web site has a set of acceptable use guidelines spelling out what kind of material you can and can't publish. For example, America Online has its own policies for its members who create home pages through AOL.

In the case of auction listings, the policy that matters is eBay's User Agreement (**http://pages.ebay.com/help/community/png-user.html**). Have you actually read this agreement? Among other things, it says

- Section 6.2.(c): What you sell should not "infringe any third party's copyright, patent, trademark, trade secret or other proprietary rights or rights of publicity or privacy."

- Section 6.2.(i)(cc): Items you sell cannot be "concurrently listed for sale on a web site other than eBay's (this does not prevent linking to or advertising an eBay item from another web site)."

- Section 7: "You agree that you will not copy, reproduce, alter, modify, create derivative works, or publicly display any content (except for Your Information) from our website without the prior expressed written permission of eBay or the appropriate third party."

> TIP   *In addition, be sure to review the Listing Policies (**http://pages.ebay.com/help/community/png-list.html**) for more dos and don'ts of which you need to be aware when creating your auction descriptions.*

Protect Your Own Trade Name

To avoid getting sued for trademark infringement and having to change your trade name or even pay damages if you lose, you should conduct a trademark search before choosing a name for your business. A trademark search is an investigation whose goal is to discover any potential conflicts between your trade name and someone else's. Ideally, you do the search before you actually use your trade name or register for an official trademark.

NOTE

*You can determine whether someone has already trademarked the name you want to use. Just visit one of the Patent and Trademark Depository Libraries (which are listed at **http://www.uspto.gov/go/ptdl/ptdlib_1.html**). This approach can be time consuming, but the price is right (it doesn't cost anything). You can also pay a professional search firm to research a trademark for you. Professional search firms are listed in the Yellow Pages under Trademark Consultants or Information Brokers and typically charge between $25 and $50 per trademark searched.*

Just to make things a little more complicated, each state has its own set of laws establishing when and how trademarks can be protected in addition to federal trademark law. You can obtain trademark rights in the states in which your trademark is actually used, but you also need to file an application with the United States Patent and Trademark Office.

How to ... File an Application with the U.S. Patent and Trademark Office

Once you have made sure no one else is using the word, phrase, or graphic image you want to trademark, you can file an application with the Patent and Trademark Office online by following these steps:

1. Start up your browser and go to the Trademark Electronic Application System (TEAS) Home Page (**http://www.uspto.gov/teas/index.html**). The page contains instructions on how to either fill out your application online or print out the application form and mail it in to the Patent and Trademark Office.

2. Click **Apply for a NEW Mark** under PrinTEAS if you want to mail in your application, or under e-TEAS if you want to file online (as these steps assume).

3. A page with a list of application forms appears. Click **Trademark/ Servicemark Application, Principal Register**.

4. Fill out the Trademark/Service Mark Application Form Wizard page, read the Privacy Policy at the bottom of the page, and then click Next.

18

Fill out the Trademark/Service Mark Application form (see following illustration). Note that this form asks for the legal form of your business; the options are described in "Decide on a Legal Form for Your Business" later in this chapter. Be sure to include your credit card data (so that you can pay the $325 per application fee) and the electronic signature fields at the bottom of the application.

5. If you want to trademark an image of a symbol or logo, click the **Attach an Image** link. A new page appears that lets you specify the image.

6. Click **Validate Form**. If you filled out all the fields correctly, a Validation screen appears. If not, you return to the original form page so that you can correct it.

7. Print out the form for your records, and then click Submit.

If the process is successful, you see a confirmation screen and receive an e-mail acknowledgement of your submission.

Decide on a Legal Form for Your Business

You know that you run an eBay business. So do your customers. To describe your business to city and county agencies, however, you need to formally declare its legal form. The legal form of a business is a designation that is recognized by taxing and licensing agencies. You have a number of options to choose from, and the choice can affect the amount of taxes you pay and your liability in case of loss. The following sections describe the alternatives.

Should You Incorporate?

At least one of the eBay sellers I profile in this book (Bob Kopczynski, Chapter 4) decided to incorporate in order to reduce his liability in case of debt or other obligations. Forming a corporation isn't straightforward. You *can* file the necessary papers yourself, but do you really want to? You'll almost certainly want a lawyer to lead you through the process. Plus, you have to comply with the regulations made by federal and state agencies that oversee corporations.

Despite these downsides, you may want to consider incorporation for the following sorts of reasons:

- When you incorporate, you separate your business from the people who own and operate it. As a result, the company's managers (that's you) are shielded from liability in terms of debts and obligations.

- If you run a big-time auction operation and hire employees to help you get sales online and out the door, you can set up retirement and health insurance plans for those individuals (including yourself).

- It's easier to transfer ownership from one shareholder to another.

Once you decide to incorporate, you next have to pick one of two options: a C corporation or a subchapter S corporation. The latter is the most likely choice for small businesses, whether they are auction concerns or not.

Subchapter S Corporations

Liability protection is the big benefit of forming a subchapter S corporation. This form of incorporation enables start-up businesses that encounter losses early on to offset those losses against their personal income. Subchapter S is intended for

18

businesses with fewer than 75 shareholders. Another advantage: the income the S corporation gains is subject only to personal tax, not corporate tax.

Sounds great, doesn't it? Before you start looking for a lawyer to get you started, consider that in an S Corporation, like a C Corporation, you must pay an annual corporate tax, and the process of filing for S Corporation status can take weeks or even months. The prospect can be daunting for a lone entrepreneur who's just starting out and has only a few dozen sales a month. It's advisable to wait until you have enough income to hire an attorney and pay incorporation fees before you seriously consider incorporating, even as an S corporation.

C Corporations

Big-time businesses, rather than small auction sales operations, choose to become C corporations. I mention C corporations only in passing so you know what they are. Profits are taxed at the corporate level, and C corporations tend to be large and have lots of shareholders. In order to incorporate, all stockholders and shareholders must agree on the name of the company, the choice of the people who will manage it, and many other issues.

Limited Liability Corporations

The limited liability corporation (LLC) combines aspects of both S and C corporations. Limited liability corporations have a number of attractive options that make them good candidates for small businesses. These include

- Income and losses are shared by the individual investors, who are known as *members*.

- Members are subject to limited liability for debts and obligations of the LLC.

- LLCs receive favorable tax treatment.

The responsibilities of LLC members are spelled out in an operating agreement, an often complex document that you'll need a knowledgeable attorney to prepare.

Sole Proprietorship

When I started employing myself, I had to pay a $10 fee to register my business as a sole proprietorship. In return, I received a certificate that made me feel like I had "arrived."

In a *sole proprietorship,* you're the only boss. You make all the decisions and you get all the benefits. On the other hand, you take on all the problems that arise, too. This is the simplest and least expensive type of business because you can run it yourself. You don't need an accountant or lawyer to help you form the business (though it helps), and you certainly don't have to answer to partners or stockholders. To declare a sole proprietorship, you may have to file an application; check with your local county clerk.

Partnership

I don't have to tell you how much work it is buying antiques or other items, bringing them home, describing and photographing them, selling them at auction, and completing the transaction. It makes sense to share the work (and the benefit) with another person. You might want to draw up a formal partnership agreement that spells out how business decisions are made and how any disputes that arise should be settled.

In a partnership, all partners are held personally liable for losses. The partners share the risk and profit with each other. Ideally, your partners bring skills to the endeavor that complement your own contributions. One obvious advantage to a partnership is that you can discuss decisions and problems with your partner. The rate of taxes that each partner pays is based on his or her percentage of income from the partnership.

Licensing and Trade Restrictions

Even if you don't decide to turn your auction business into MyVeryOwnAuction, Inc., you'll probably have to process paperwork of one sort or another. Every online business has to pay any license fees to local agencies, and observe restrictions that limit what it can buy or sell.

Pay Your License Fees

Sure, you can set up shop in your basement and start hauling boxes of collectibles in and out. To be on the safe side, check with your city, county, or state licensing and zoning offices to make sure you aren't breaking a rule by doing so. Trade associations for your profession often have a wealth of information about local regulations as well. Also, check with your local chamber of commerce. If you fail to apply for a permit or license, you may have to pay a fine.

18

A small business—even a one-person operation that makes a few extra bucks each month on eBay—may need to conform to various local regulations, including

- **Taxes**   This shouldn't surprise you. Some cities tax small businesses as well as business assets such as office furniture and (uh-oh) computer equipment.

- **Zoning**   Your city or town government may have *zoning ordinances* that prevent you from conducting business in an area that is zoned for residential use, or they may charge you a fee to operate a business out of your home. This policy varies by community; be sure to check with your local zoning department.

- **Doing Business As**   If your business name is different from your own name, you may have to file a Doing Business As (DBA) certificate and publish a notice of the filing in the local newspaper. Check with your city or county clerk's office for more information.

Sales Permits

As you learned in Chapter 17, you need to collect, report, and pay sales tax on sales you make to individuals who live in the same state where you do business. In addition, you may need to obtain a sales permit for each place where you do business.

Reseller Certificates

Chances are you are not the original producer of the items you sell on eBay. Like so many other eBay sellers, you are reselling things that were made by many different manufacturers at widely varying times in the deep dark past. If that's the case, you may need to obtain a reseller certificate. Usually, you only need a reseller certificate if you sell large numbers of items to wholesale distributors—but check with your local agencies to make sure.

City Business Licenses

In addition, you may need to obtain one or more licenses to operate legally. If the business is located within an incorporated city limits, a license must be obtained from the city; if outside the city limits, then from the county. For more information contact the county or city office in your area.

Certificate of Occupancy

If you are planning on occupying a new or used building for your office space or to hold your auction inventory, for more information, contact the county or city office in your area.

Maintain Your Own and Your Buyers' Privacy

Any businesses with a Web presence need to address the issue of customer privacy. A Web-based business targeted to consumers may face more stringent requirements with regard to privacy issues and a higher level of scrutiny by federal agencies (such as the Federal Trade Commission) and state agencies. Furthermore, federal and state statutes limiting the collection and use of information from children, like the 1998 Children's Online Privacy Protection Act, may also come into play more for B2C oriented businesses than for B2B oriented businesses.

In other words, if you sell something to a child and you collect that child's personal information, you could technically be in violation of the Online Privacy Protection Act. If you sell things that kids might buy, you may want to tell people that they have to have their parents present, or remind them of the existing eBay requirement that they have to be more than 18 years of age.

Where to Find It

■ **Trademark Electronic Search System**
   http://www.uspto.gov/tmdb/index.html
   Go here to conduct a search for the legal owner of a trademark.

■ **eBay User Agreement**
   http://pages.ebay.com/help/community/png-user.html
   Here you'll find lots of restrictions about what you can and can't do on eBay, including infringing on someone else's copyright or trademark.

■ **eBay Listing Policies**
   http://pages.ebay.com/help/community/png-list.html
   This page lists requirements for creating auction descriptions that don't violate eBay rules.

■ **Trademark Electronic Application System (TEAS)**
   http://www.uspto.gov/teas/index.html
   This site has instructions on how to apply for your own trademark.

■ **VeRO Members' About Me pages**
   http://pages.ebay.com/help/community/vero-aboutme.html
   Links to About Me pages of individuals and organizations that watch for trademark and copyright infringement.

18

Chapter 19

What to Do in Case of Trouble

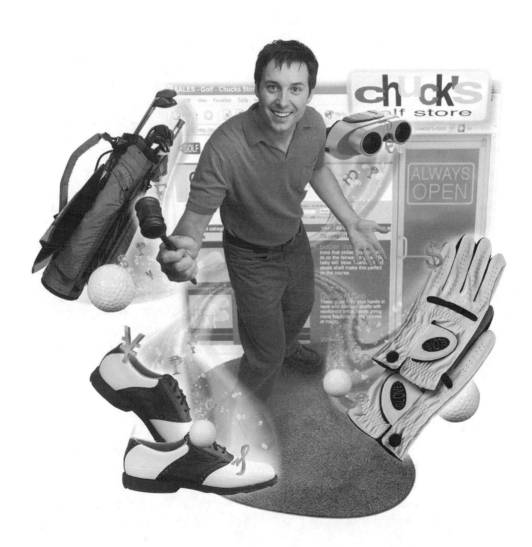

How to...

- Respond to non-paying bidders
- Avoid post-transaction confusion
- Handle complaints when the merchandise is received
- Head off potential trouble before the sale ends
- Try to resolve a dispute yourself
- Turn to third-party mediation when all else fails

The great fear of people who start using eBay is that something will go wrong with the sale. This, I think, is what makes people reluctant to start selling online: because you can't actually see the person you're dealing with, you have to trust that they'll follow through with their end of the bargain. If you buy something and send the payment, you're never sure the merchandise will actually arrive. If you sell something, you're never quite sure the high bidder will send the payment. Or the bidder might complain about something even after he or she does receive it.

Such problems do occur on eBay. I have heard reports (which seem to appear frequently in comments on eBay's message boards) that as many as 15 percent of eBay transactions turn out bad in some way. That might be true for some buyers and sellers, but I heard figures that were far less—ranging from one or three to five percent—from the sellers I interviewed. On the other hand, eBay claims that less than one percent of its transactions "go bad." It's hard to tell which figure is really accurate, but I believe that if you are a reputable seller and you function in a professional way, you'll find that disputes occur far less often than you think.

No matter how many problems you do encounter, you have plenty of safeguards and responses you can use to protect yourself and your customers, as described in this chapter.

If the Transaction Falls Through

Here's some free advice that applies to virtually all eBay transaction problems: Remain calm and businesslike at all times. You may not be a longtime businessperson, and you don't report to an employer, so it can be difficult not to get impatient. But remember that it is essential for you to remain in control of the transaction at all times. By getting mad, you sink down to the level of the bidder and lose control and credibility.

Another piece of advice that applies to problems in general: Leave feedback that is specific and brief and straightforward. Just state what happened ("Person never left payment") and don't be abusive or retaliatory. Also be sure to keep copies of all e-mails pertaining to the transaction until the payment has been received and feedback has been left. Such messages can provide essential evidence in case of a dispute.

Deadbeat Bidders/Buyers

The formal eBay-speak for individuals who don't follow through with a transaction and pay for what they have purchased is *Non-Paying Bidder*. But most eBay sellers call them deadbeat bidders (or worse). You'd think such bidders would read the message eBay sends before placing a bid, as shown below.

Here's what typically happens: At the end of the sale, eBay sends its automatic notices telling you that the sale has ended, and notifying the high bidder that he or she has won. You send an e-mail to the bidder with payment information. The buyer either does not respond or says he or she will pay, but never sends payment.

TIP   *You're not alone, so don't take it personally. Deadbeat bidders are a common problem on eBay, though they're not as widespread a problem as you might think. eBay has developed an FAQ to help you deal with deadbeat bidders at* **http://pages.ebay.com/help/basics/f-npb.html**.

19

Step 1: Don't Overreact

If you do not receive a response to your initial e-mail notification that the individual has won the merchandise (or any subsequent e-mail), don't immediately assume that your buyer is a deadbeat. The person may be having legitimate troubles with e-mail, which is by no means a trouble-free communications medium. The e-mail host may be flooded with other traffic, the individual's e-mail or Internet access account may be suspended for some reason, or the person may be sick or out of town. Try the following:

- Contact the person from another e-mail address, in case something is wrong with your mail server, not the buyer's.

- Request the buyer's contact information (address and phone number) from eBay (**http://cgi3.ebay.com/aw-cgi/eBayISAPI .dll?MemberSearchShow**). After entering the item number and User ID both buyer and seller will be e-mailed one another's contact information.

If you don't hear from someone within three days or more, go to Step 2.

Step 2: Send a Payment Reminder

A Payment Reminder is a e-mail form letter that you can customize and send to someone who hasn't responded to eBay's notice that they are the high bidder, or to e-mails from you telling the person where and how to send the payment. Payment Reminders are optional—since you have already presumably reminded the bidder about the need for payment, you can move on to the next step, which is a Non-Paying Bidder Alert. If you do send a Payment Reminder, eBay requires it to go out between 3 and 30 days after the end of the sale.

The 3 to 30 day rule is hardly a hard-and-fast rule, however. One longtime eBay seller, decoray, told me that when someone with a substantial amount of positive feedback purchases one of his items, he'll wait as long as one or two weeks before sending a "reminder" e-mail. If the purchaser is someone with little or no feedback, however, he sends an e-mail with a very different tone that requires the buyer to respond as soon as possible. You might send a reminder such as the following:

I'm happy that you are the high bidder on my item #XXXXXXXXXX. Now that the sale has ended, it's important that you acknowledge that you have received notification from eBay that you're the high bidder, and that you let me know that payment is on the way. Please do this as soon as possible. My payment requirements follow, etc.

TIP   *Find out more on eBay's Help page on Payment Reminders, at*
http://pages.ebay.com/help/sell/bidders_payment_reminder.html.

Step 3: Fill Out a Non-Paying Bidder Alert Form

If you have sent a Payment Reminder and still don't get a response (or if you've waited at least a week after the end of the sale and haven't received payment, and you don't want to send a Payment Reminder), the next step is to file a Non-Paying Bidder Alert Form with eBay.

eBay requires you to fill out the form shown in Figure 19-1 in order to receive a Final Value Fee credit for your item. When you submit the form, eBay notifies both you and the buyer that the buyer has been identified as a Non-Paying Bidder. eBay urges the bidder to complete the transaction, which takes that difficult task out of your hands. In other words, this is the buyer's last chance to pay up or the seller will request a refund.

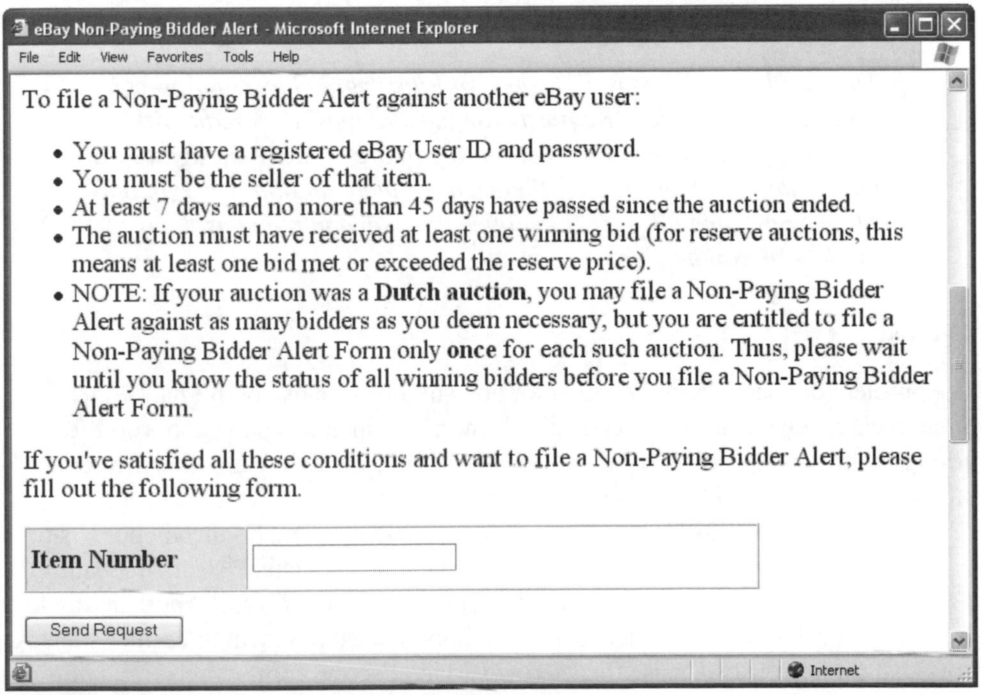

FIGURE 19-1   The Non-Paying Bidder Alert Form gives unresponsive buyers a last chance to work things out with you.

19

TIP

You can access the Non-Paying Bidder Alert Form at
http://cgi3.ebay.com/aw-cgi/eBayISAPI.dll?NPBComplaintForm.

Step 4: Request a Final Value Fee Credit

If you still haven't received payment within ten days of filing the Non-Paying Bidder
Alert Form, you can take the final step: requesting a Final Value Fee credit from eBay.
This not only gets you a refund of your fee within 48 hours, but it automatically
causes eBay to put a Non-Paying Bidder mark against the individual. Another two
such marks and the individual will be suspended from eBay.

If, after receiving your Final Value Fee credit, you work things out and receive
payment after all, you can remove the Non-Paying Bidder warning. (You can only
do this once, however, so make sure you have actually received payment before you
do this.)

If the bidder never pays, you have two options: you can make a Second Chance
Offer to someone on the original list of bidders for the item by filling out the form at
http://cgi3.ebay.com/aw-cgi/eBayISAPI.dll?PersonalOfferLogin. Alternatively,
you can relist the item.

TIP

*The Final Value Fee credit form is at **http://cgi3.ebay.com/aw-cgi/***
***eBayISAPI.dll?CreditRequest**. You must request the credit within*
60 days of the close of the auction. If you are unlucky enough to have
more than one Non-Paying Bidder in a Dutch auction, you can only
file a Non-Paying Bidder Alert once, but you can name as many
bidders as you need to.

Bounced Checks

The problem of checks being returned for non-sufficient funds doesn't happen terribly
often to eBay sellers, as far as I can tell. It's more common that someone won't follow
through with a sale at all. If someone does follow through, they are likely to send
payment promptly and have enough money in the bank to cover their check.

The simplest way to avoid running into a problem with a bounced check is to
simply hold delivery of your merchandise until the buyer's check clears the bank.
(Be sure to state in your auction Terms of Sale that you will do so.) Another way to
prevent the problem is to specify that you'll only request payment in cashier's check
or postal money order. Or use the escrow service Escrow.com, which waits until
checks clear before it notifies you that it's safe to send out merchandise to a buyer.

If you do have a check returned, deal with it in a courteous and businesslike
manner. After all, chances are the buyer made an honest mistake and will be

embarrassed that the problem occurred at all. Request that the buyer pay you in the form of a cashier's check or money order, and pay any fees the bank charges you for depositing a check that is returned. Be sure to hold on to the returned check in case you have a dispute and you need evidence. If you still don't receive payment, you can follow Steps 3 and 4 in the preceding section: file a Non-Paying Bidder Form with eBay, and then, if ten days go by without payment, file a Final Value Fee Credit Form.

Problems with the Seller (Yes, I Mean You)

This heading refers to you, the eBay seller: problems can occur at your end that either delay the sale or prevent it from finishing altogether. Sometimes, the problems occur unintentionally. For instance, you advertise that you will accept credit cards on your auction listings, but either your approval hasn't come through from the bank, or you have been approved, but you haven't set up your point-of-sale hardware or software. You have to tell seller that you need to wait for such approval and run the risk of unhappy buyers and negative feedback.

I've said this elsewhere, but you shouldn't plan to go on vacation or be out of town when your sale ends. If your buyers have to wait a week or more just for you to respond, they're going to begin to suspect that you're a deadbeat seller.

Don't Be a Deadbeat Seller

Sometimes (I shudder to say this) sellers don't follow through. For some reason, they decline to accept payment from the winning bidder or purchaser, or they never respond to the purchaser. This not only damages their reputation, but it detracts from the entire network of trust that keeps eBay going. If you're not going to follow through, don't sell at all.

CAUTION   *eBay may warn or suspend you if you don't follow through with a sale, and don't have a good reason for doing so. Read the notice at **http://pages.ebay.com/help/policies/non-selling-seller.html** to find out more.*

Make Sure You Tell All In Your Listings

It's hard to remember every single detail about a sale, especially when you are attempting to process dozens of sales at a time. That's why you should come up with a template for your sales that clearly lists your accepted payment methods and shipping options as well as any extra charges for credit card transactions or other things. Your auction template should include the standard information that buyers want to know, such as:

- Charges for using credit card systems

- Reminders that buyers should not send any payment until you have e-mailed them a message listing the amount required (the purchase price plus shipping or other charges)

- If you encourage buyers to obtain multiple auction items from you in order to save on combined postage, put in a reminder statement saying postage charged will be reduced, but not necessarily by a half (if two items are purchased), by one-third (if three items are involved), and so on. After all, the additional weight and additional packing required to ship multiple items may increase shipping charges. At the very least, you want to cover yourself if they do.

- A statement indicating when you expect the buyer to contact you and then send payment: "Buyers must contact me/us within three working days of the end of the auction, and payment must be received within __ days."

- If you have a policy of not accepting bids from sellers with no feedback or with a negative feedback rating, state that as well.

- If you don't want to ship overseas, state that in your auction terms.

- If, like many sellers, you wait for personal checks to clear before shipping out items.

- If you have a refund policy, such as "If you are unhappy with your purchase for any reason I will fully refund your purchase but only if the item(s) is returned in the original packaging and in the condition in which it was purchased."

All of these policies and statements are collectively called the *Terms of Sale*. By taking the time to create an accurate and comprehensive Terms of Sale, you decrease (though not eliminate) the number of questions you get from buyers, and you "cover yourself" in case someone complains.

Many of the options mentioned here, and some other useful specifications, are included in eBay seller decoray's Terms of Sale, shown in Figure 19-2.

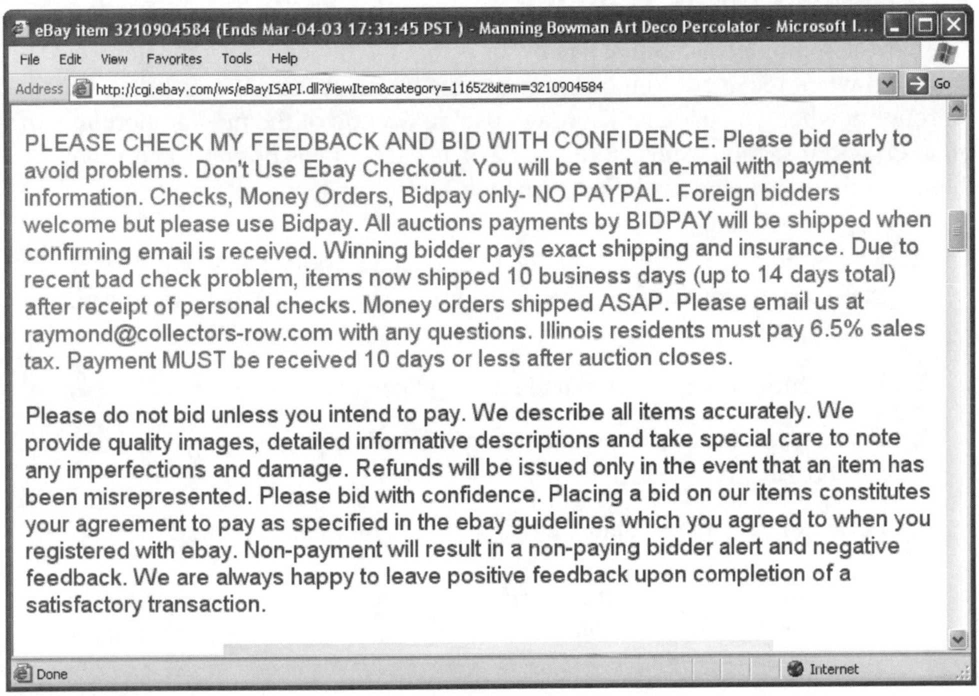

┌───┐
│ eBay item 3210904584 (Ends Mar-04-03 17:31:45 PST) - Manning Bowman Art Deco Percolator - Microsoft I... │
│ File   Edit   View   Favorites   Tools   Help   │
│ Address http://cgi.ebay.com/ws/eBayISAPI.dll?ViewItem&category=11652&item=3210904584   Go │
└───┘

PLEASE CHECK MY FEEDBACK AND BID WITH CONFIDENCE. Please bid early to avoid problems. Don't Use Ebay Checkout. You will be sent an e-mail with payment information. Checks, Money Orders, Bidpay only- NO PAYPAL. Foreign bidders welcome but please use Bidpay. All auctions payments by BIDPAY will be shipped when confirming email is received. Winning bidder pays exact shipping and insurance. Due to recent bad check problem, items now shipped 10 business days (up to 14 days total) after receipt of personal checks. Money orders shipped ASAP. Please email us at raymond@collectors-row.com with any questions. Illinois residents must pay 6.5% sales tax. Payment MUST be received 10 days or less after auction closes.

Please do not bid unless you intend to pay. We describe all items accurately. We provide quality images, detailed informative descriptions and take special care to note any imperfections and damage. Refunds will be issued only in the event that an item has been misrepresented. Please bid with confidence. Placing a bid on our items constitutes your agreement to pay as specified in the ebay guidelines which you agreed to when you registered with ebay. Non-payment will result in a non-paying bidder alert and negative feedback. We are always happy to leave positive feedback upon completion of a satisfactory transaction.

FIGURE 19-2   Spell out your Terms of Sale as clearly as possible in your auction listings to eliminate disputes after the auction closes.

NOTE   *In other chapters, I discuss problems that can crop up with eBay transactions. In Chapter 16, you learn how to make sure what you want to sell isn't illegal or questionable on eBay. In Chapter 17, you learn when you need to collect sales tax, and that you need to pay income tax on your eBay sales. In Chapter 18, you learn how not to infringe on someone's copyright or trademarks.*

If Problems Occur After You Ship

You might think that, after you receive payment and either ship the merchandise or it is picked up in person, your problems are over. Not necessarily. For one thing, the buyer can claim that the item was never received and lost in the mail unless you get some form of delivery confirmation from the U.S. Postal Service (or in the U.K., a Certificate of Posting).

19

The Buyer Claims Damage

One post-shipping problem that can occur is that the buyer claims the item was damaged when received. You can prevent this by inspecting the merchandise thoroughly when you pack it. Thorough packing is one of the most important parts of an eBay transaction. Make sure you pack as carefully as possible and follow these tips that were passed along to me by eBay seller decoray:

- Buy good boxes, either from the U.S. Postal Service (they will deliver the boxes to you in lots of 25 if you use Priority Mail) or from an office supply store.

- Use plenty of bubble wrap and packing "peanuts."

- If you have items that include multiple separate pieces, put pieces of cardboard between each piece.

- For extra valuable or delicate items, pack a box inside another box.

> NOTE
>
> *Shipping boxes from the U.S. Postal Service are free as long as they are used for Priority Mail shipments. If you use priority mail, you can also obtain free tape, labels, and envelopes. But it's a crime to use any of these shipping materials for any purpose other than Priority Mail.*

Leave a note with the item describing any damage that was present when it was purchased—for example, a sticky note with the words "This chip was described in the auction listing." You may also want to write down any serial numbers or identifying codes on the item itself so buyers can't claim it was damaged and return it while substituting another, similar item for the original.

You can obtain insurance for what you ship from the U.S. Postal Service or from private shippers. However, all the indications I've heard are that it's very difficult to get reimbursed if you make a claim. (It's up to you, the shipper, to make the claim, not the recipient.) All shippers stipulate that they won't pay claims if your packaging is judged by them to have been insufficient in some way.

> TIP
>
> *You can get confirmation of delivery from the U.S. Postal Service if you send a package using Delivery Confirmation, Signature Confirmation, Certified Mail, or Registered Mail. The options are explained at **http://www.usps.com/shipping/trackandconfirm.htm**.*

The Buyer Just Isn't Satisfied

Most people are happy with what they have purchased on eBay. The vast majority are overjoyed when they receive their package. Once in a while, however, someone just isn't satisfied. They claim that your merchandise isn't as big/clean/colorful as you said in your description. In one memorable posting I spotted on the eBay Motors message boards, someone who came in person to pick up the auto just purchased on eBay—and who had already submitted a deposit—expressed great dissatisfaction at the condition of the car, kicked the door in anger, and left in a huff.

That's an extreme example, of course, but if someone just isn't happy, you have two options. You can follow the letter of the law and state that the sale is final, and you don't have to accept the returned item because it wasn't damaged in transit. You'll probably receive negative feedback, however. Or, you can take the "big picture" view, and think of your business's long-term well being, and simply let the customer return the item and get a refund. You can resell it later on. Yes, you lose your Final Value Fee, and you have to go through the extra effort of reselling. But in the long run, you avoid a conflict, and you don't have a dispute, either.

If Problems Occur During the Sale

It's hard to pay attention to all of your sales all of the time, but try to check in once a day, or once every other day, to see who the high bidder is on each of your sales. Lots of things can happen while the sale is going on. The overwhelming majority of the time, bidding will progress smoothly. You may, in fact, never run into an instance of "interference" during an auction, but it's good to be aware of such incidents in case they do occur.

The fact that eBay buyers and sellers can all contact one another by e-mail means that some types of interference can arise before a sale ends. In theory, bidders are supposed to place their bids, perhaps pose some questions to you before the sale ends, and nothing more. In practice, eBay bidders can interfere with the sale by:

- Telling other bidders that the seller is not to be trusted because of past transgressions against the person making the complaint.

- Telling bidders that they can sell them the same object they're bidding on—at a lower price. They then direct bidders to one of their own sales or someone else's.

19

Beware eBay "Stalkers"

Like any public venue, eBay attracts a wide variety of people. The vast majority are well behaved and courteous, but a few are worthy of great caution. I spoke to one seller who actually encountered someone she describes as a "stalker," who repeatedly sent her e-mail messages long after a transaction was over, in a way that made her fear for her safety. She responded, courteously, that she couldn't become too friendly with all her customers because she was so busy.

The "stalker" began sending her more e-mail messages from a different e-mail address and, when she ignored his messages, he became abusive. Luckily, nothing happened, and that's possibly because she kept her cool and didn't confront the individual or get angry in a way that would only escalate his behavior. If anything like this happens to you, react calmly, and try to ignore the individual. If you fear for your safety, contact the eBay Investigations team at the URL given in this chapter. If someone harasses or abuses you by e-mail, contact your Internet Service Provider (ISP), as well as the offender's ISP. It's likely that individual is violating the ISPs terms of use and can have his or her e-mail account cancelled. You should also contact your local police department. Someone who threatens you in a way that makes you fear for your safety may well be prosecuted.

Both types of bidding interference are prohibited by eBay. If you detect such interference (or, hopefully, if one of your bidders tells you about it) report the incident to eBay's Investigations team (**http://pages.ebay.com/help/community/ investigates.html**).

How to Resolve a Dispute

What should you do if you and a buyer have a dispute that you just can't resolve through negotiation? First, realize that you aren't alone. As a first resort, turn to the eBay message boards and chat rooms if you are having trouble with a bidder and ask other sellers' advice. Sometimes, just hearing from others who have gone through similar troubles calms you down. One of the best resources available to you as an eBay seller is the dispute resolution service offered free of charge by SquareTrade (**http://www.squaretrade.com**). eBay's own Rules & Safety area (**http://pages.ebay.com/help/policies/topics.html**) simply directs you to SquareTrade for dispute resolution services.

Keep in mind the helpful advice that one eBay seller (who prefers to be anonymous) wanted me to pass along:

"For me, one of the most anxious parts of selling on eBay is the whole feedback system, and the potential that people will be ugly to you if something goes wrong. It seems to me that people can be more volatile or nasty by e-mail than they ever would face-to-face. If their claim or complaint seems legitimate, I offer them their money back. If I feel that they are lying or getting angry or might get abusive, I never answer their e-mail immediately. I always give myself a day to calm down before I respond. It's not worth it to get into an argument."

> **TIP**
>
> *If you do have to leave negative feedback for someone, just state the facts without being abusive. Just say, "Person never left payment" and leave it at that.*

Where to Find It

- **Find Members form**
  http://cgi3.ebay.com/aw-cgi/eBayISAPI.dll?MemberSearchShow
  A form you can fill out to obtain the contact information for individuals with whom you have had transactions.

- **Non-Paying Bidder Alert Form**
  http://cgi3.ebay.com/aw-cgi/eBayISAPI.dll?NPBComplaintForm
  A form you fill out if someone doesn't pay for a purchase; eBay sends the buyer a message encouraging the buyer to complete the transaction.

- **Final Value Fee credit form**
  http://cgi3.ebay.com/aw-cgi/eBayISAPI.dll?CreditRequest
  A form you can fill out if a Non-Paying Bidder refuses to pay after receiving an alert from eBay.

- **eBay Investigations Team**
  http://pages.ebay.com/help/community/investigates.html
  Descriptions of offenses eBay investigates and links to a form you can fill out to report trouble.

Appendix A · eBay Glossary

About Me   A page that you can create on eBay's Web site that provides some brief personal information about you, and collects your current sales on the same page as well.

as is   An item that you sell in its advertised condition and with no other warranty, either implied or stated.

bid increment   A predetermined amount by which bids are increased as they are placed. The increment varies depending on the current high bid.

bid retraction   The process of canceling a bid that has already been made. Retractions are only allowed in exceptional circumstances, such as the entry of the wrong bid amount, or if the description of the item changes "significantly." Such retractions are only allowed before the last 12 hours of a sale. See **http://pages.ebay.com/ help/buy/bid-retract.html** for more.

blocked bidder   Someone who has specifically been excluded from bidding on an item, usually because of problems with previous transactions.

bid shielding   A process in which two bidders conspire to defraud a seller out of a high bid. The high bidder retracts the bid at the last minute, so the partner's lower bid can win.

Buy It Now   A way to sell your item on eBay for a fixed price. Buy It Now auctions can be conducted in one or two ways. In a Fixed Price auction, you offer an item at a fixed Buy It Now price and the buyer purchases it immediately at that price. In an Online Auction, the buyer can buy the item at the Buy It Now price only before the first bid is placed; after a bid is placed the Buy It Now option disappears.

category gouging   A condition that occurs when one seller lists numerous similar items in one category, thus forcing their competition off of the main page and eliminating fair comparison for the buyers.

chargeback   A fee charged to a seller by a credit card company for accepting a credit card number for a purchase that turns out to be fraudulent.

Chat   Normally used as a shorthand term for Internet Relay Chat (IRC), a real-time communications method on the Internet. eBay regularly uses Chat to describe its Community Boards, which are really message boards.

checkout   A way of streamlining the end of a transaction in which the seller specifies how much to pay for shipping, insurance, and sales tax when the item is listed. The buyer then receives an e-mail at the end of the auction that automatically lists the total and where the item should be shipped.

consignment   The process of selling something for someone else. The seller who offers the merchandise and who conducts the sale usually collects a fee for his or her services.

cookie   A small bit of information that is placed on a visitor's computer by a Web site and that provides the site (such as eBay) with information when you revisit, so you don't have to log in again.

corporation   An organization established for the purpose of doing business.

counter   A utility that tracks the number of visits that have been made to a Web page.

Dutch auction   An auction format that enables a group of identical items to be sold to a group of bidders at once rather than in separate sales.

eBay Motors   An auction area on the eBay Web site where participants can buy and sell motor vehicles, including cars, boats, and planes.

eBay Stores   A feature that enables sellers to sell a group of items at a fixed price on a Web page they publish on eBay.

escrow   A way of completing transactions through the use of an intermediary. The buyer sends payment to the escrow company, the seller ships the item to the buyer, the buyer inspects and approves the item, and the escrow company releases funds to the seller.

feedback   A system of communication that enables eBay users who have been involved in transactions with other users to leave comments that describe their level of responsiveness, the quality of the transaction, or related (and sometimes unrelated) issues.

fink   Someone who turns out to be a fraudulent buyer or seller

Fixed Price format   A sales format in which eBay users can purchase an item for a fixed price specified by the seller; an alternative to an auction.

gallery   A eBay feature that enables sellers to post photos of their items that buyers can browse.

Half.com   An area of eBay where sellers can offer books, CDs, or other items at a discount.

hijacked account   An eBay account that has been taken over by someone who has stolen the owner's information.

HTF   Short for *hard to find,* a descriptor used frequently by participants in eBay's message board, or in auction listings.

HTML   Abbreviation for HyperText Markup Language, the set of instructions that is used to present text and images on Web pages (as well as eBay auction descriptions).

ID Verify   A program in which sellers or buyers have their personal information verified against consumer and business databases so others can trust that they are who they say they are.

A

keyword spamming   The practice of including brand names or other keywords that aren't related to the item being sold in an effort to get extra attention for the item.

live auction   An auction held in real time. eBay users can find out more at **http://pages.liveauctions.ebay.com/help/welcome/overview.html**.

MIB   An abbreviation for *mint in box* that occasionally appears in auction listings titles. The item in the box is in mint condition; the box may not be, however.

MIMB   An abbreviation for *mint in mint box.* The item in the box is in mint condition, and the box is, too.

My eBay   A starting page you can configure to include the items you have sold and the items you have obtained recently, or on which you have bid.

NIB   An abbreviation for *new in box;* see MIB.

Non-Paying Bidder   Someone who qualifies to obtain an item by being the high bidder, but then fails to complete the transaction by paying for the item.

NR   Abbreviation for *no reserve;* used to describe a sale for which a reserve amount has not been specified. The high bidder will win the item.

pink   Someone who works at eBay. When they post on message boards, their name is highlighted with a pink background. Whenever they post, you also see the eBay logo next to their name.

proxy bid   A bid that eBay places for you automatically based on the maximum amount you are willing to pay for an item. If someone outbids you, eBay automatically places proxy bids up to your maximum amount.

re-list   To put an item up for sale again after a sale has ended.

reserve price   An amount specified by a seller as the minimum price the seller is willing to accept in order to purchase it. The reserve price is kept secret until a bidder meets it. The seller is not obligated to sell an item if the reserve price has not been met.

Second Chance Offer   An eBay feature in which, if a winning bidder fails to buy an item or if the seller has a duplicate item for sale, the seller can offer the item to any one of the under-bidders.

shades   A sunglasses icon added to a User ID if the individual has changed that User ID within the last thirty days.

shill bidding   An illegal practice involving the use of family members or friends to drive up the bidding on an item. (Sometimes called "bid padding.")

Verified Rights Owner (VeRO) Program   A program in which owners of brand names, copyrights, or trademarks, or their authorized representatives, work to make sure that eBay sales do not infringe upon those intellectual property rights.

Index

NOTE: See Glossary for eBay terminology

INTERNATIONAL CONTACT INFORMATION

AUSTRALIA
McGraw-Hill Book Company Australia Pty. Ltd.
TEL +61-2-9900-1800
FAX +61-2-9878-8881
http://www.mcgraw-hill.com.au
books-it_sydney@mcgraw-hill.com

CANADA
McGraw-Hill Ryerson Ltd.
TEL +905-430-5000
FAX +905-430-5020
http://www.mcgraw-hill.ca

GREECE, MIDDLE EAST, & AFRICA
(Excluding South Africa)
McGraw-Hill Hellas
TEL +30-210-6560-990
TEL +30-210-6560-993
TEL +30-210-6560-994
FAX +30-210-6545-525

MEXICO (Also serving Latin America)
McGraw-Hill Interamericana Editores S.A. de C.V.
TEL +525-117-1583
FAX +525-117-1589
http://www.mcgraw-hill.com.mx
fernando_castellanos@mcgraw-hill.com

SINGAPORE (Serving Asia)
McGraw-Hill Book Company
TEL +65-6863-1580
FAX +65-6862-3354
http://www.mcgraw-hill.com.sg
mghasia@mcgraw-hill.com

SOUTH AFRICA
McGraw-Hill South Africa
TEL +27-11-622-7512
FAX +27-11-622-9045
robyn_swanepoel@mcgraw-hill.com

SPAIN
McGraw-Hill/Interamericana de España, S.A.U.
TEL +34-91-180-3000
FAX +34-91-372-8513
http://www.mcgraw-hill.es
professional@mcgraw-hill.es

UNITED KINGDOM, NORTHERN,
EASTERN, & CENTRAL EUROPE
McGraw-Hill Education Europe
TEL +44-1-628-502500
FAX +44-1-628-770224
http://www.mcgraw-hill.co.uk
computing_europe@mcgraw-hill.com

ALL OTHER INQUIRIES Contact:
McGraw-Hill/Osborne
TEL +1-510-420-7700
FAX +1-510-420-7703
http://www.osborne.com
omg_international@mcgraw-hill.com